MOTORCYCLE

MOTORCYCLE

THE DEFINITIVE VISUAL HISTORY

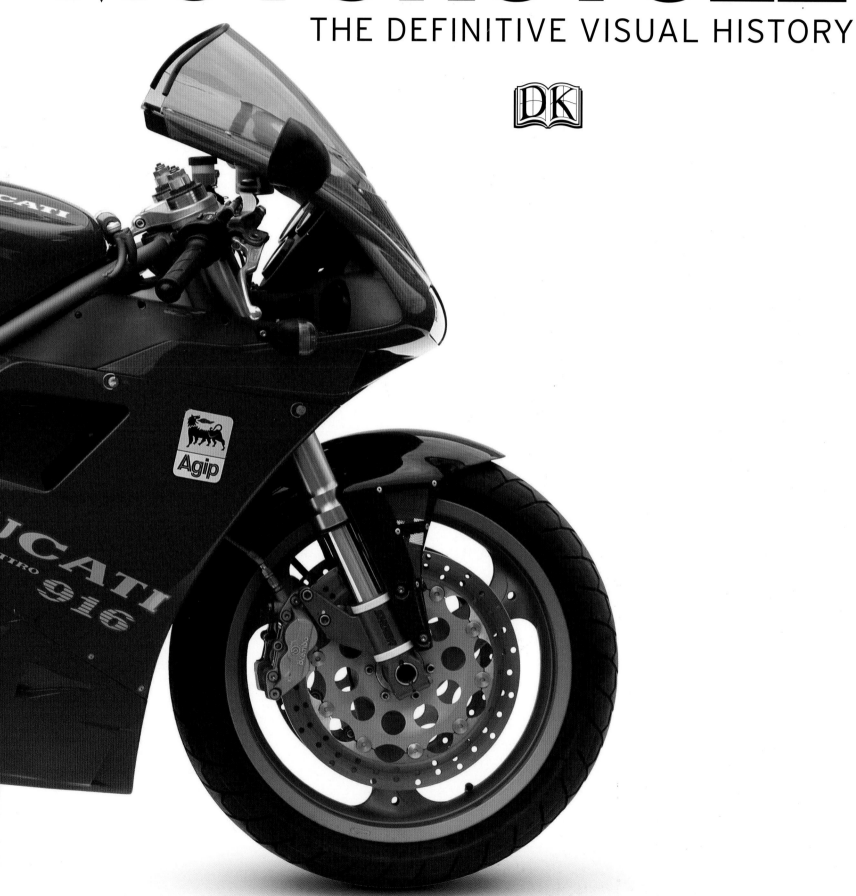

DK

LONDON, NEW YORK, MELBOURNE, MUNICH, AND DELHI

DORLING KINDERSLEY
Senior Project Editor Jemima Dunne
Senior Art Editor Helen Spencer
Editors David Summers, Alison Sturgeon, Sam Atkinson, Victoria Wiggins
US Editor Christine Heilman
Designers Amy Orsborne, Paul Drislane, Philip Fitzgerald, Richard Horsford, Steve Woosnam-Savage
Photographers Gary Ombler, James Mann, Simon K. Fielder, Deepak Aggarwal
Picture Research Nic Dean
DK Picture Library Claire Bowers, Emma Shepherd, Laura Evans
Jacket Designer Steve Woosnam-Savage
Database David Roberts, Peter Cook
Production Editors Tony Phipps, Ben Marcus
Production Controller Linda Dare
Managing Editor Esther Ripley
Managing Art Editor Karen Self
Publisher Laura Buller
Art Director Phil Ormerod
Associate Publishing Director Liz Wheeler
Publishing Director Jonathan Metcalf

DK INDIA
Senior Editor Monica Saigal
Senior Art Editor Sudakshina Basu
Editors Suparna Sengupta, Sreshtha Bhattacharya
Assistant Editor Gaurav Joshi
Art Editors Shriya Parameswaran, Pallavi Narain, Nico Alba
Assistant Art Editors Jomin Johny, Neha Sharma, Niyati Gosain, Nidhi Mehra
Production Manager Pankaj Sharma
DTP Manager Balwant Singh
DTP Designers Nand Kishor Acharya, Dheeraj Arora, Mohammad Usman, Vishal Bhatia, Jaypal Singh Chauhan
Deputy Managing Editor Pakshalika Jayaprakash Sinha
Managing Art Editor Arunesh Talapatra

Editor-in-chief Mick Duckworth
Contributors Phil Hunt, Malcolm McKay, Hugo Wilson, James Robinson
US Consultant Mark Mederski

First American Edition, 2012
Published in the United States by
DK Publishing
375 Hudson Street
New York, New York 10014

12 13 14 15 16   10 9 8 7 6 5 4 3 2 1
001—182744—Apr/2012

Copyright © 2012 Dorling Kindersley Limited
All rights reserved

Published in Great Britain by Dorling Kindersley Limited.

A catalog record for this book is available from the Library of Congress.

ISBN 978-0-7566-9052-6

DK books are available at special discounts when purchased in bulk for sales promotions, premiums, fund-raising, or educational use. For details, contact: DK Publishing Special Markets, 375 Hudson Street, New York, New York 10014 or SpecialSales@dk.com.

Printed and bound in China by Leo Paper Products

Discover more at
www.dk.com

Contents

BEFORE 1920

Gottlieb Daimler's gas-powered engine on a bicycle set fire to the seat on its maiden voyage, but it heralded the birth of the motorcycle. The new century saw rapid progress in design, durability, and performance.

THE 1920s

After World War I there were bikes for the masses and sports machines capable of covering ground faster than any other vehicle. Mighty V-twins were built for speed or for hauling the family in a sidecar.

THE 1930s

Through the Great Depression, the emphasis switched from speed to economy, but machines became more sophisticated in appearance and performance. Racing continued to test out new technology.

THE 1940s

While the world was at war, motorcyle development was put on hold with military bikes from BSA, Triumph, and DKW becoming workhorses throughout the conflict. After the war, everyone needed a motorcycle.

THE 1950s

With cars still a luxury, simple two-strokes were the obvious choice, although powerful twin cylinders were aimed at the prosperous US market. The scooter was on the rise, the ubiquitous Honda Super Cub was launched, and the Japanese made their first Grand Prix appearance.

THE 1960S

The rise of the car hit the motorcyle industry hard, but new niche markets included scooters for Mods and powerful bikes for Café Racers. Beautifully engineered Japanese machines with six gears and push-button starting began to infiltrate European and US markets.

THE 1970S

Classic marques like Norton and Royal Enfield went to the wall, unable to compete with the superbike offerings from Japanese manufacturers. Motocross bikes were launched for the young and trailbikes for US adventurers.

THE 1980s

Although the motorcycle industry had little to celebrate in the economic boom, bikes were refined and updated with water-cooled engines, electronic ignition, improved aerodynamics, and better handling and braking power. Interest in classic bikes also influenced the design of new machines. Bikes became more specialized, from race replicas and fully equipped tourers to rugged off-roaders.

THE 1990s

A period of sales growth saw an increased demarcation of product classes, and a revival of several defunct marques, the most successful being Triumph in the UK. Stylish and economic scooters also gained a new generation of fans faced with rising fuel costs and traffic congestion.

FROM 2000

Motorbike riders in the new millenium are rewarded with remarkable sophistication: antilock brakes, power reduction at the flick of a switch, exotically styled lightweight frames, luxury, and comfort. There is even an effective electric motorcycle available.

THE ENGINE

Engines: A single engine size has been given in cubic centimeters (cc) for each catalog entry. Engine sizes can be converted to cubic inches (cu in) by multiplying the cubic centimeters (cc) figure by 0.061.

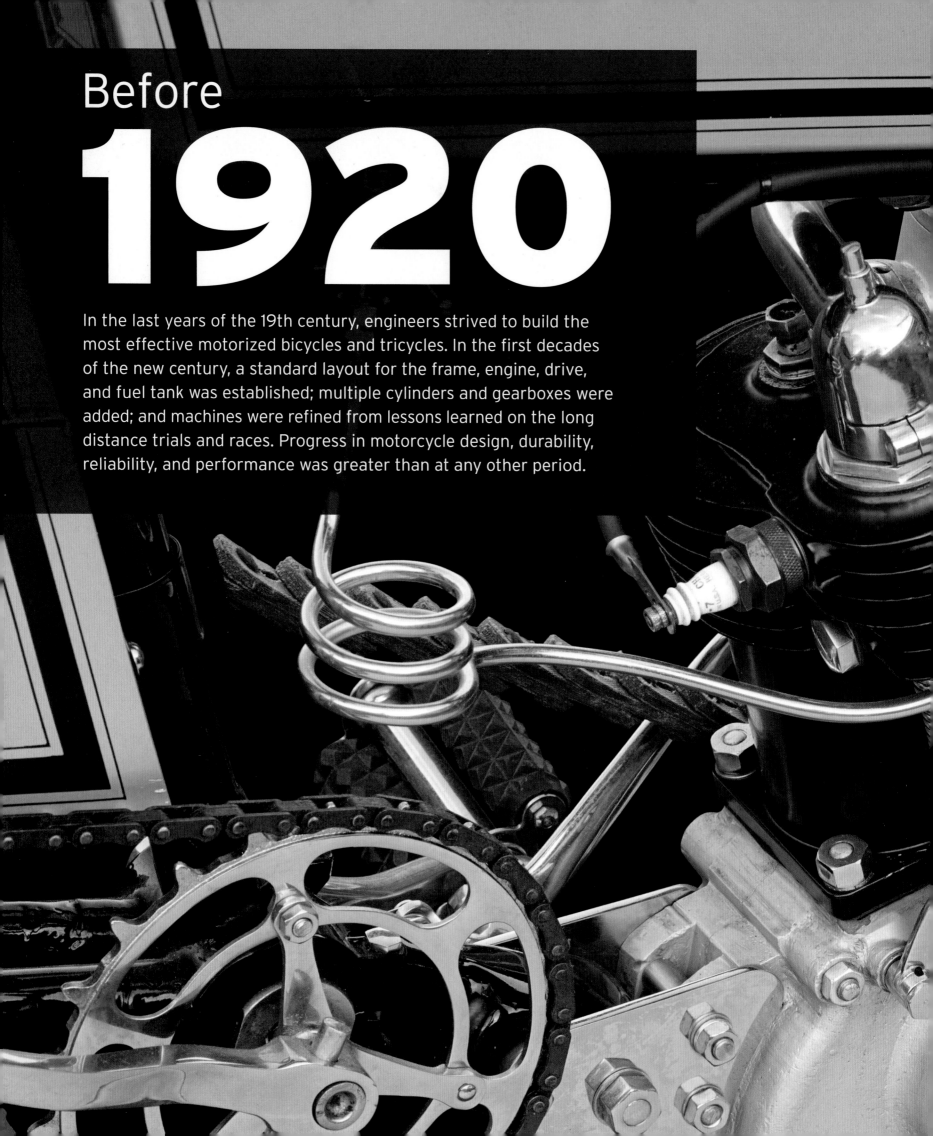

Before
1920

In the last years of the 19th century, engineers strived to build the most effective motorized bicycles and tricycles. In the first decades of the new century, a standard layout for the frame, engine, drive, and fuel tank was established; multiple cylinders and gearboxes were added; and machines were refined from lessons learned on the long distance trials and races. Progress in motorcycle design, durability, reliability, and performance was greater than at any other period.

Early Pioneers

Bicycles had reached an advanced stage of development by the 1880s, most of them closely resembling machines we still ride today. As soon as a small internal combustion engine was invented, it was a logical step to attach it to a bicycle, creating the first motorcycle. Almost all early development took place in Europe, and the brilliance of some designs— and the impracticality of others—was breathtaking.

▽ **Daimler Reitwagen 1885**

Origin Germany

Engine 264cc, single-cylinder

Top speed 7 mph (11 km/h)

Gottlieb Daimler and Wilhelm Maybach were inspired pioneers, designing a high-revving (600 rpm), benzine-fueled engine that they added to this "riding car" in 1885.

△ **Hildebrand & Wolfmüller Motorrad 1894**

Origin Germany

Engine 1,489cc, inline twin

Top speed 28 mph (45 km/h)

The world's first production motorcycle used the rear wheel as its flywheel/crankshaft with a direct drive from the two connecting rods, and the rear mudguard to carry water.

◁ **Gaillardet Gaillardette 1899**

Origin France

Engine 800cc, single-cylinder

Top speed 27 mph (43 km/h)

Frédéric Gaillardet was involved with several pioneering French tricycles. His engine design was a side-valve with easily changeable valves, mounted behind the rear axle.

▽ **Perks Birch Motorwheel 1900**

Origin UK

Engine 222cc, single-cylinder

Top speed 22 mph (35 km/h)

This brilliant design by Edwin Perks and Frank Birch incorporated an engine, fuel tank, carburetor, and magneto within a two-sided, cast-alloy wheel.

◁ **Singer 200 1901**

Origin UK

Engine 208cc, single-cylinder

Top speed 28 mph (45 km/h)

Singer purchased the rights to build the Perks Birch Motorwheel in 1901 and installed it in both the rear of bicycles and the front of tricycles until 1904.

▷ **Werner 1901**

Origin France

Engine 262cc, single-cylinder

Top speed 40 mph (64 km/h)

Franco-Russian pioneers Michel and Eugène Werner patented this influential motorcycle layout in 1902, with the engine incorporated into the bottom of the frame.

◁ **Ormonde 1901**

Origin UK

Engine 220cc, single-cylinder

Top speed 28 mph (45 km/h)

Ormonde used Belgian Kelecom engines in this well-designed motor bicycle layout, which was to become an ancestor of the Velocette marque.

▷ **Cyklon 1901**

Origin Germany

Engine 300cc, single-cylinder

Top speed 22 mph (35 km/h)

Cyklon used the French Werner engine, mounted on the front forks and driving the front wheel by a belt, placing the rider rather close to noise and fumes.

◁ **H. Collier & Sons Silent Matchless 1902**

Origin UK

Engine 160cc, single-cylinder

Top speed 25 mph (40 km/h)

London bicycle-maker Henry Collier & Sons built its first motorcycle in 1899. They started production for bikes such as this one in 1901, using engines from MMC.

▷ **Bayliss Thomas Excelsior 1902**

Origin UK

Engine 160cc, single-cylinder

Top speed 25 mph (40 km/h)

Generally considered the first British motorcycle, the Excelsior was made in Coventry from 1896 with Minerva, De Dion, MMC, or Werner engines slung under a bicycle-type frame.

◁ **Triumph Minerva 2½ hp 1902**

Origin UK

Engine 239cc, single-cylinder

Top speed 30 mph (48 km/h)

Siegfried Bettmann's Triumph bicycle company had built this, its first motorcycle, by 1902, using a Belgian Minerva engine, which itself originated from a Swiss design.

▷ **MMC 1903**

Origin UK

Engine 216cc, single-cylinder

Top speed 30 mph (48 km/h)

Entrepreneur Harry Lawson's Motor Manufacturing Company of Coventry built this motorcycle powered by a close copy of the French-made De Dion engine.

◁ **Coventry-Eagle Motorized Bicycle 1903**

Origin UK

Engine 216cc, single-cylinder

Top speed 26 mph (42 km/h)

This Victorian bicycle-maker built motorcycles from 1898. This model had an engine from MMC hung from the downtube, with a belt drive and a trailer to carry a passenger.

Early Indian model
photographed in 1910

Great Marques
The Indian Story

One of America's finest motorcycling pioneers, Indian rapidly built a reputation for quality and performance second to none. Although the company survived the Depression, strong competition in the postwar years brought production to a halt in 1953. However, a recent takeover promises to revitalize a marque that has never lost its iconic status.

GEORGE M. HENDEE originally set up the Hendee Manufacturing Company in Springfield, Massachusetts, to make pedal cycles. In 1901 he joined forces with technically minded Carl Oscar Hedstrom to build Indian motorcycles, first sold to the public in the following year.

Indian badge
(introduced 1930)

Admired for their durability, early single-cylinder machines sold well, and the company enjoyed many successes in early American racing and endurance events, which hastened technical development. Factory riders included Canadian-born Jake de Rosier, winner of countless races on board tracks and dirt ovals; Charles B. Franklin, who covered 300 miles (483 km) in 300 minutes in 1912; and Erwin "Cannonball" Baker, who rode across North America in 11 days, 12 hours, and 10 minutes in 1914.

However, finishing first, second, and third in the grueling Isle of Man Senior TT race of 1911 showed that Indian had arrived as a world-leading manufacturer.

In 1907 Indian developed a V-twin with the engine layout that became synonymous with American motorcycling. The 42-degree V angle became an Indian trademark, as did front suspension by a leaf spring with trailing fork links, adopted in 1913. On the 61 cu in (1,000cc) Powerplus twin of 1915, side valves replaced the previous inlet-over-exhaust layout to create a quieter, cleaner engine. More than 40,000 twins were supplied to the US military during World War I.

In the early 1920s the 45 cu in (750cc) Scout, the 61 cu in (1,000cc) Chief, and the 74 cu in (1,200cc) Big Chief were launched. Designed by Charles Franklin, they were noted for their strong performance, comfort, and reliability. Their popularity made Indian the world's largest motorcycle maker, producing 250,000 a year.

Having bought the failing Ace company, Indian launched a version of the factory's four-cylinder bike, the Indian Ace, in 1927. Engineers then added two extra crankshaft bearings and strengthened the frame to create the first 77 cu in (1,265cc) Four, launched in 1928.

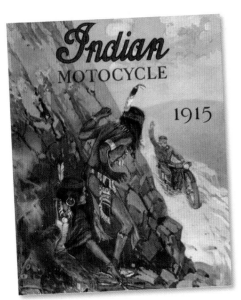

Sales brochure
As seen on this 1915 sales brochure, American Indians featured heavily in early publicity for Indian motorcycles, stressing an image of ruggedness and adventure.

"You can't **wear out** an Indian Scout."

1920s ADVERTISING SLOGAN

Indian's achievements arguably peaked in 1928 with the 101 Scout, a sturdy and well-balanced machine still favored for wall-of-death shows. However, affordable cars like the Ford Model T were beginning to erode America's motorcycle industry, and despite Indian's expertise and attempts to diversify, it took heavy losses. Fortunately, the industrial giant DuPont stepped in to buy Indian

Indian in Australia
Photographed in Australia in 1921, a uniformed driver and sidecar passenger pose on a hard-worked Indian V-twin combination with covered-in wheels.

Single 1¾ HP

V-twin Roadster

Chief

Velo 500

1901 The Indian company is founded; a prototype and two production units are successfully built and tested.
1902 The first Indian motorcycles featuring innovative belt-drives and streamlined styling go on sale.
1903 Indian co-founder and chief engineer Oscar Hedstrom sets a motorcycle speed record of 56 mph (90 km/h).
1904 Indian wins the Gold Medal for Mechanical Excellence at the 1904 St. Louis Exposition.

1907 Indian releases the first American production V-twin after several years of development and testing; the New York Police Department selects Indians for the first motorcycle police unit.
1909 The Indian "loop frame" positions the fuel tank on the front horizontal frame member for the first time.
1911 Indian takes a 1-2-3 finish at the Isle of Man Senior TT race.
1914 Indian sells the world's first motorcycle with electric lights and starter.

1920 The 45 cu in (750cc) Scout is released.
1922 Launch of the 61 cu in (1,000cc) Chief.
1928 The first all-Indian Four goes on sale.
1929 Indian is bought by DuPont.
1937 Indian rider Ed Kretz wins the inaugural Daytona 200 race.
1945 Ralph B. Rogers takes control of the company from DuPont.
1947 Indian releases a new range of vertical twin motorcycles.
1948 Floyd Emde takes Indian's last Daytona 200 win.

1949 The Brockhouse-owned Indian Sales Corp. is formed.
1953 Production ends at the Springfield plant.
1955 Royal Enfield motorcycles start to be badged as Indians for the US market.
1960 British Associated Motor Cycles group acquires Indian Sales Corp.
1968 Floyd Clymer markets Indian-badged European machines.
1999 The IMC starts production in California.
2004 New owner Stellican sets up a factory.
2011 Indian is acquired by Polaris Industries.

Fleet of Indians
The Los Angeles Motor Corporation displays a new fleet of Indian motorcycles in 1922. The police used theirs to enable them to enforce relatively new speed restrictions.

shortly before the 1929 Wall Street Crash and invested heavily in motorcycle production.

The design of the Four continued to be refined, although changing from an inlet-over-exhaust valve layout to an exhaust-over-inlet layout in 1936 proved to be an error. Indian reverted to the previous format after two seasons, but sales had been lost.

In 1940, W. Briggs Weaver, a former DuPont Motors designer, applied his talents at Indian to create the streamlined range of motorbikes with full-skirted fenders that are now icons of Americana. In the same year the Chief's and the Four's frames were equipped with plunger-type rear suspension. When the US joined World War II, Indian made the innovative 841 V-twin with transverse cylinders and shaft drive for military use.

Entrepreneur Ralph B. Rogers took over the company in 1945 with financing from the Atlas Corporation.

An all-new range of Weaver-designed overhead-valve (ohv) singles and vertical twins was launched, eclipsing production of the V-twins. They were marketed without proper development, damaging the company's reputation. Even the revival in 1951 of the revered Chief V-twin, with an enlarged 80 cu in (1,300cc) engine, failed to improve the company's fortunes.

Rogers accepted the blame and resigned. Financiers split the company into a manufacturing operation and the Indian Sales Corporation (ISC). The latter was owned by the British Brockhouse Engineering, maker of the Indian Papoose mini-scooter, which imported British motorcycles badged as Indians. In 1960 another British company, Associated Motor Cycles (AMC), acquired ISC.

The end of production in Springfield, in 1953, began a 20-year period when machines manufactured outside the United States were marketed as

Indian motorcycles. In 1968, after AMC's demise, automotive publisher and Indian aficionado Floyd Clymer attempted a revival. His V-twin with European cycle parts was unsuccessful, but Indian-badged singles and vertical twins built by Italjet in Italy with British Velocette and Royal Enfield engines were sold. The venture ended when Clymer died in 1970.

Despite everything, the marque's iconic status endured, attracting operators seeking to make a profit from branded merchandise. In the 1990s there were rival claims to the trademark and more than one announcement that big twins would be produced again. Following a court decision, in 1999 the California-based Indian Motorcycle Company set up production using bought-in V-twin engines, but they suffered from technical problems and the venture proved unprofitable.

Five years later, British private equity companies acquired the rights to the trademark and set up Indian Motorcycle Limited (IML). A North Carolina factory made V-twins with proprietary engines from 2009 until 2011, when IML was sold to Polaris Industries of Minneapolis.

As the established manufacturer of Victory motorcycles, alongside all-terrain vehicles and snowmobiles, Polaris has the resources to put the revered Indian marque firmly back on its feet after 50 turbulent years.

Three-wheelers

Pedal tricycles were as well developed as bicycles in the late 19th century, so these too attracted the attention of inventors; after all, it was easier to handle a tricycle with a heavy engine attached than a bicycle. Driving twin back wheels was not so easy, however, so some soon reversed the layout and went on to add a forward-mounted seat to carry a passenger or two.

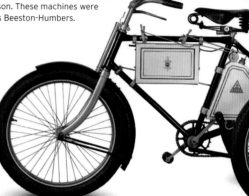

△ Humber Tricycle 1894

Origin UK

Engine 400cc, single-cylinder

Top speed 30 mph (48 km/h)

Cycle-maker Humber built these De Dion tricycles under license for motoring entrepreneur (later convicted fraudster) Harry Lawson. These machines were also sold as Beeston-Humbers.

△ Dennis Speed King Tricycle 1898

Origin UK

Engine 250cc single-cylinder

Top speed 30 mph (48 km/h)

Dennis of Guildford, Surrey, began with bicycles and moved on to trucks, along the way making this sports bicycle with a British De Dion-type engine at the rear.

▷ Ariel Tricycle 1898

Origin UK

Engine 239cc, single-cylinder

Top speed 24 mph (39 km/h)

Ariel of Birmingham had been making bicycles for 28 years when it began building this popular tricycle using a De Dion engine, mounted behind the rear axle.

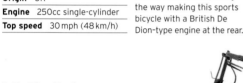

▷ De Dion-Bouton 1¼ CV Tricycle 1900

Origin France

Engine 185cc, single-cylinder

Top speed 23 mph (37 km/h)

Marquis Jules-Albert de Dion designed the first high-revving engine, hitting 3,500 rpm in trials and normally running at 2,000 rpm. It was ideal for motorizing this tricycle.

△ Century 3½ hp Forecar 1902

Origin UK

Engine 510cc, single-cylinder

Top speed 35 mph (56 km/h)

With steering by a long lever and hand controls for the throttle, brake, and fuel mixture, this bike's driver was kept very busy. Its engine was De Dion, Aster, or MMC.

△ Garrard Forecar 1904

Origin UK

Engine 500cc, single-cylinder

Top speed 35 mph (56 km/h)

Charles Garrard began by importing French Clément engines and installing them on bicycles, before making this practical forecar with a three-speed gearbox and shaft drive.

△ Raleigh Raleighette Tandem Tricar 1904

Origin UK

Engine 3½ hp, single-cylinder

Top speed 37 mph (60 km/h)

Cycle-maker Raleigh made its first motorcycle in 1899 and this first forecar four years later, using a 3½ hp water-cooled engine and two-speed gearing.

△ **National Forecar 1904**

Origin	UK
Engine	9 hp, twin cylinder
Top speed	50 mph (80 km/h)

With a water-cooled, two-cylinder engine, this bike was one of the most sophisticated of its type, but was soon made obsolete by vehicles with better weather protection.

△ **Quadrant Forecar 1904**

Origin	UK
Engine	6 hp, 2 x single-cylinder
Top speed	40 mph (64 km/h)

In this tricycle, Quadrant adopted an unusual approach to meet varying power needs by putting two engines side by side, the second brought into use when loads demanded it.

◁ **Riley 4½ hp Forecar 1904**

Origin	UK
Engine	517cc, single-cylinder
Top speed	38 mph (61 km/h)

Riley continually updated its forecars. This version has the optional two-speed gearbox; its saddle and handlebars would soon be replaced as the model became more carlike.

◁ **Rex Rexette 5 hp 1905**

Origin	UK
Engine	632cc, single-cylinder
Top speed	45 mph (72 km/h)

Known as the "king of little cars," the Rexette had a proper seat for the driver, a fully enclosed water-cooled engine, two-speed gearbox, and for 1905 even a steering wheel.

◁ **Auto-Carrier Deluxe Tri-car 1910**

Origin	UK
Engine	636cc, single-cylinder
Top speed	47 mph (76 km/h)

John Weller's delivery trikes, forerunners of the AC car, were commercially successful and built for many years. The engine, which is under the seat, is fan-cooled.

△ **Clyno Military Combo Sidecar 1914**

Origin	UK
Engine	744cc, V-twin
Top speed	50 mph (80 km/h)

Fitted with a Stevens AJS engine, several hundred of these bikes were made for WWI use; the machine gun was set up on a tripod before firing.

Birth of an Industry

Hundreds of entrepreneurs jumped on the motorcycle-building bandwagon at the turn of the 20th century, seeing its huge growth potential. Some were motivated by cash, others by the chance to have a hand in the rapid development of new technology. All forms of suspension arrangements and early types of variable gearing were tried as engines became more refined and speed potential grew.

◁ Laurin Klement Slavia 1½ hp Model B 1903

Origin Bohemia (Czech Republic)

Engine 184cc, single-cylinder

Top speed 25 mph (40 km/h)

Founded in 1895 to build bicycles in the Austro-Hungarian Empire, the company that became Skoda built motorcycles from 1899 with an underslung De Dion-type engine.

▷ Allright 2¾ hp 1903

Origin Germany

Engine 300cc, single-cylinder

Top speed 40 mph (64 km/h)

Allright started making motorcycles around 1901. This model had a Belgian FN engine and front and rear contracting-band brakes; it was also sold as the Vindec Special.

◁ Indian Single 1¾ hp 1904

Origin USA

Engine 213cc, single-cylinder

Top speed 25 mph (40 km/h)

George Hendee and Carl Hedström produced this, their first chain-driven motorcycle, in 1901. In 1903 Hedström set the world motorcycle speed record at 56 mph (90 km/h).

▷ Advance 2¾ hp 1904

Origin UK

Engine 360cc, single-cylinder

Top speed 40 mph (64 km/h)

Advance's bikes had advanced engines, which used a mechanical exhaust valve and automatic flap inlet valve. Far more engines were sold than complete motorcycles.

△ **Rex 3 hp 1904**

Origin	UK
Engine	372cc, single-cylinder
Top speed	30 mph (48 km/h)

Calling itself the "King of British Motors," Rex had over 50 machines on display at the 1904 Cycle Show, including this one, with all components built in-house.

△ **BAT 2¹/₂ hp 1904**

Origin	UK
Engine	327cc, single-cylinder
Top speed	35 mph (56 km/h)

Samuel R. Batson mounted De Dion and then MMC engines in this simple cycle frame with probably the first rear suspension and healthy performance.

▷ **Rex 500 SV 1907**

Origin	UK
Engine	500cc, single-cylinder
Top speed	47 mph (76 km/h)

Harold and Billy Williams steered Rex to lead the British bike market, with this patented engine cradle, spring fork, sprung saddle, mechanical exhaust valve, and more.

△ **Matchless 2¹/₂ hp 1905**

Origin	UK
Engine	327cc, single-cylinder
Top speed	30 mph (48 km/h)

Matchless added leading-link front suspension to their machines in 1905, using a range of MMC, De Dion, or JAP engines, of which this MMC was the smallest.

▷ **NSU 3 hp 1906**

Origin	Germany
Engine	402cc, single-cylinder
Top speed	35 mph (56 km/h)

Originally a knitting-machine-maker, NSU is named after the town of Neckarsulm. These simple and lightly built bikes benefited from innovations learned from racing.

△ **Lincoln Elk 3 hp 1908**

Origin	UK
Engine	402cc, single-cylinder
Top speed	40 mph (64 km/h)

James Kirby began making Lincoln Elk motorcycles in Lincoln in 1902 with 2¹/₄ hp engines, later expanding the range to include 3 hp and 3¹/₂ hp variants.

△ **Douglas Model D 1910**

Origin	UK
Engine	339cc, flat-twin
Top speed	45 mph (72 km/h)

From its first motorbike in 1907, Douglas built a flat-twin engine that was popular with other makers; by 1909 a two-speed gearbox was optional (though not installed here).

Seattle Motorcycle Club, 1911
The earliest American motorcycle clubs formed soon after the machines became available. The clubs were social groups, with organized events such as picnics, hill climbs, and track races, but also great sources of information and support.

Birth of an Industry (cont.)

Many manufacturers began making their own engines, rather than buying them in or producing them under license. As the first decades of the 20th century progressed, design stabilized around the crossbar-mounted fuel tank with the engine mounted vertically below it, and an optional gearbox behind. Foot pedals disappeared as engines became more powerful and other ways to start them were devised.

◁ Triumph 3¹⁄₂hp Roadster 1908

Origin UK

Engine 474cc, single-cylinder

Top speed 48 mph (77 km/h)

The affordable two-stoke lightweight, nicknamed the "Baby Triumph," had a two-speed gearbox and dispensed with pedals. Uprated after WWI, it sold until 1925.

◁ Humber 3¹⁄₂hp Touring 1910

Origin UK

Engine 500cc, single-cylinder

Top speed 57 mph (92 km/h)

Humber returned to motorcycle production in 1909 with this conventional machine featuring sprung front forks and an optional two-speed rear axle.

△ Triumph 2¹⁄₄hp Junior "Baby" 1913

Origin UK

Engine 225cc, single-cylinder

Top speed 35 mph (56 km/h)

Launched just before WWI, Triumph's affordable machine had a two-speed gearbox and dispensed with pedals; it could be started on its stand.

▽ Rudge Multi 1914

Origin UK

Engine 499cc, single-cylinder

Top speed 65 mph (105 km/h)

A year after launching its first motorcycle, Rudge produced the Multigear, using variable groove-depth pulleys to give 21 wide-ranging forward speeds.

△ Rudge 3¹⁄₂hp 1911

Origin UK

Engine 499cc, single-cylinder

Top speed 50 mph (80 km/h)

Long-established bicycle-maker Rudge Whitworth started selling Werner motorcycles in 1909, then in 1911 produced this inlet-over-exhaust 3¹⁄₂ hp machine.

△ Rover 500 TT 1913

Origin UK

Engine 500cc, single-cylinder

Top speed 63 mph (101 km/h)

Rover built over 10,000 motorcycles from 1902 to 1924, introducing a new 3¹⁄₂ hp in 1910, from which this shorter TT model was derived. It won the 1913 Isle of Man TT team prize.

▷ Motosacoche 2¹⁄₂hp 1913

Origin Switzerland

Engine 293cc, single-cylinder

Top speed 30 mph (48 km/h)

From 1900 Henri and Armand Dufaux sold an "engine in a bag" (motosacoche) to attach to a bicycle such as this one; later, their MAG engines were used around the world.

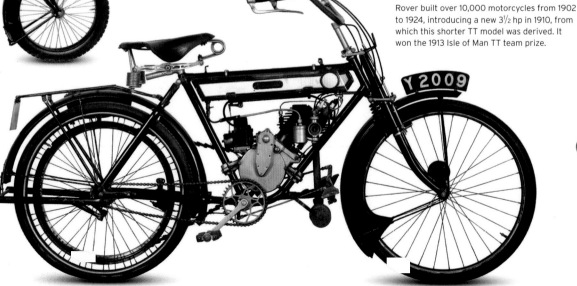

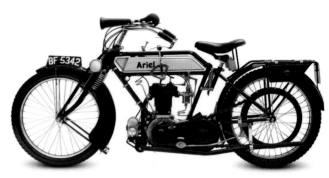

△ TD Cross TDC 3½hp 1914

Origin	UK
Engine	300cc, single-cylinder
Top speed	35 mph (56 km/h)

Bicycle component-maker TD Cross & Sons built engines for numerous brands, and from 1914 to 1915 made complete machines using its own make or Precision engines.

△ Ariel 3½hp Roadster 1914

Origin	UK
Engine	499cc, single-cylinder
Top speed	60 mph (97 km/h)

In 1911 Ariel began building the White & Poppe engines for its own use and offered an optional three-speed gearbox (as here) on this quality low-built bike.

△ Sun 2½hp 1914

Origin	UK
Engine	269cc, single-cylinder
Top speed	40 mph (64 km/h)

Sun made bicycle parts in Birmingham from 1885 and its own motorcycles from 1911. In 1919 this two-stroke Villiers engine was offered, also available with two-speed gears.

△ BSA 4½hp 1914

Origin	UK
Engine	556cc, single-cylinder
Top speed	62 mph (100 km/h)

Long-established armaments-maker BSA made motorcycle components, then complete 3½hp bikes from 1910, moving up to this powerful model as WWI broke out.

▽ Sunbeam Single 1914

Origin	UK
Engine	500cc, single-cylinder
Top speed	55 mph (89 km/h)

Sunbeam made high-quality bicycles, then cars, then motorcycles, starting with this 3½hp single-cylinder in 1914 and quickly adding a twin to the range.

△ Yale 6½hp Model 37 1914

Origin	USA
Engine	1,000cc, V-twin
Top speed	72 mph (115 km/h)

The Consolidated Manufacturing Co. added one of the first V-twins to its established 500cc singles in 1910. The bike was given a racier frame in 1913.

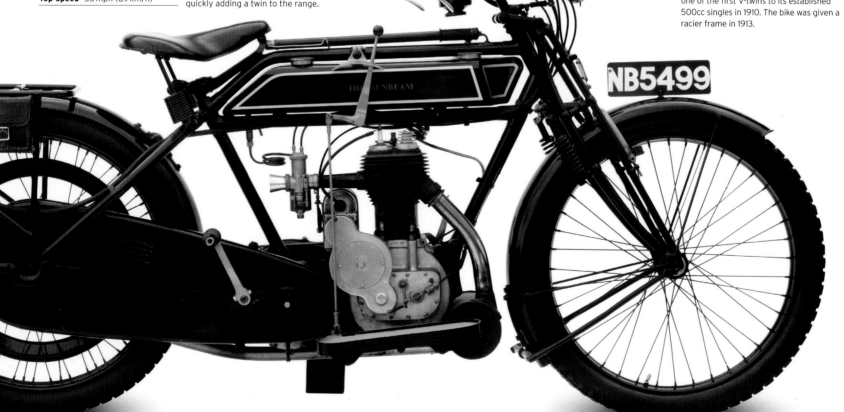

An Enfield Model J from the 1930s

Great Marques
The Royal Enfield Story

The first Royal Enfield motorcycle was made in 1901, and production continues today. The story began in the Industrial Revolution in Great Britain and was later taken up on the Indian subcontinent. Along the way, the company has produced one of the most iconic models in the history of the motorbike in the form of the evergreen Bullet.

IN THE MID-19TH CENTURY, in the town of Redditch in the industrial heartland of England, George Townsend & Co. manufactured machine parts, including needles for sewing machines. The company expanded into bicycle production, and after founder Townsend's departure in 1890, Albert Eadie and Robert Smith took over. Contracts to make rifle parts for the Royal Small Arms Factory in Enfield, Middlesex, led to their becoming the Enfield Manufacturing Company in 1892, with the "Royal" prefix added the following year.

The marque's first motorized transportation was created in 1899 in the form of a 1½ hp engine that powered a vehicle available in three- or four-wheeled variants. Royal Enfield's first motorcycle was unveiled in 1909: a 2¼ hp V-twin model that would continue in a larger-capacity variant until the outbreak of World War I in 1914.

Royal Enfield badge
(introduced 1955)

Now established as a maker of solid, reliable motorcycles—reflected in the company's slogan "Made like a gun…"—Royal Enfield was tasked with providing the British Army with machines for the war effort. Its range of models included stretcher carriers and machine-gun-armed bikes. During this period, Royal Enfield started to develop its first powerplants, having previously added engines from other companies to its frames. Innovations included a prototype featuring the world's first three-cylinder, two-stroke unit.

The postwar period saw the marque develop a range of new models and engines. A 976cc twin engine in 1918 was followed in 1924 by Royal Enfield's debut four-stroke, single-cylinder model, which featured a JAP powerplant. By this time, the marque was capitalizing on the popularity of sidecars, producing its own examples; and a program of expansion through the decade meant that by 1930 the company's strong lineup included smaller 225cc side-valve motorcycles as well as big-twins.

In 1931 Royal Enfield unveiled what would become its most celebrated model: the Bullet, a single-cylinder machine that came into its own at the end of the decade with the introduction

Youth appeal
In the late 1950s Enfield diversified into lower-capacity road models such as the 250cc Crusader, designed to appeal to young motorcyclists.

of a 350cc variant that was the basis for the marque's postwar models. Its innovations included telescopic front forks and an advanced rear-suspension setup that featured the early use of a swingarm. However, before the machine could be embraced by the public, World War II intervened. As well as producing practical machines such as the Flying Flea, which could be parachuted down in a cage with

airborne troops, Royal Enfield was redirected to manufacture specialty items for the war effort.

In the postwar surge in the economy, Royal Enfield took up where it left off by introducing telescopic front shock absorbers and swingarm rear on the J2 model in 1947. In 1949 a 500cc twin was released in response to the successful Speed Twin by rival Triumph. In 1949

Model 182 Sports

Model K

Trials Bullet

350 Bullet Machismo

1892 The Enfield Manufacturing Company is formed; "Royal" is added to the name the following year.
1899 The first motorized models from the company include three-wheeled vehicles.
1909 The 2 ¼hp V-twin model is unveiled; it uses an externally-made powerplant.
1914 Enfield first installs its own engine into a V-twin model.
1924 The debut four-stroke single, featuring a 350cc JAP unit, is released.

1931 A new single-cylinder model is launched; it is labeled the Bullet from 1932.
1936 Enfield JF is released, incorporating a four-valve, single-cylinder unit.
1939 Bullet 350 debuts, forming the basis for postwar models.
1947 Telescopic forks appear on the new J2.
1948 The 500 twin model is unveiled; it remains in the lineup for a decade.
1956 Enfield India Ltd. is set up as an offshoot of the parent company, making complete bikes under license.

1960 Enfields are now sold under their own name in the US.
1962 The company is bought by the E & HP Smith Group.
1965 Release of the 750cc Interceptor twin, aimed at the US market.
1967 The Aerco Jig & Tool Co. buys the Royal Enfield name; Enfield Precision Engineers is set up.
1971 The last British-made bikes are manufactured. Enfield India is now an independent business.

1973 The Crusader model is introduced, aimed at younger Indian motorcyclists.
1984 Enfield India begins exporting models back to the UK.
1990 Taurus Diesel becomes the world's first diesel-powered motorcycle.
1994 Enfield India is bought by the Eicher Group, and the company adopts the original British name of Royal Enfield Motors Ltd.
2004 The Bullet Electra International model is launched in the UK.

Royal Enfield was commissioned to supply Bullet models to the Indian Army, and six years later Enfield India Ltd. was established. The 350cc Bullet was originally sent over in separate parts for assembly in India, but ultimately the entire model would be constructed there.

Back in Britain, the 1950s was a fruitful decade. Enfield expanded its range to cover everything from 125cc singles to scramblers, up to the 750cc

Meteor twin. In the US, Enfield models were sold via the Indian marque, but when the American manufacturer was bought out in 1960, the bikes were then sold under the Royal Enfield name.

When the company was acquired by the E & HP Smith engineering group in 1962, a rather stolid image was shaken off by 250cc sports machines aimed at young riders and even a 250cc GP5 road racer. But they were not enough to outshine the Japanese imports, and by 1967 a 750cc Interceptor was the only model.

The Redditch plant closed and a new company, Enfield Precision Engineers, was formed in 1967, but all production ended in 1971.

Work and play
In addition to being used for day-to-day law enforcement duties, Royal Enfields are at the heart of the Indian police force's display team.

At the same time, Enfield India became completely independent and grew stronger. The Bullet continued to be made, essentially to a 1954 specification but with minor improvements and some adaptation to the local environment.

Throughout the 1970s and 1980s, the Enfield India marque expanded its range of models. The 175cc Crusader two-stroke was aimed at the younger market, while new

was being exported by 1990 and a novel but sluggish 325cc diesel motorcycle, the Taurus, was produced from 1993 to 2002.

Although the company's fortunes dipped during the mid-1990s, they were revived by a buyout by the Eicher Group, an Indian conglomerate, in 1996, and in 2004 the company fully secured its rights to the full Royal Enfield name.

Now producing a small range of motorbikes from its Chennai headquarters, including a selection of Bullet variants and a Classic 500 model that combines postwar styling

Military use
Women from the Auxiliary Territorial Service ride 350cc four-stroke Enfield motorcycles. During World War II the company also supplied the military with a 126cc two-stroke.

"Made like a gun, goes like a bullet."

THE ROYAL ENFIELD MOTTO

lightweights in the 1980s included the Silver Plus step-through, with a semiautomatic gearchange designed to appeal to female motorcyclists. So successful was the Indian company at this time that it even began exporting its models back to the UK and Europe.

Over the next two decades the marque broadened its operations. A 500cc version of the iconic Bullet

with 21st-century features such as fuel injection, Royal Enfield has become an international success story. This originally British company has flourished under its Indian offshoot through the simple approach of pairing traditional designs with reliable, no-nonsense engines. It is a wonderful example of the empire striking back.

Multiple Cylinders

Engineers saw multiple-cylinder engines as a way of increasing power output, especially for sidecar pulling, and achieving greater flexibility along with smoother running. The V-twin seemed the ideal solution, compact and a perfect fit in a normal frame, but others tried flat-twins in various layouts, or even inline four-cylinder engines mounted carlike, fore-and-aft in the frame.

▷ **Minerva 4½hp V-twin 1906**

Origin Belgium

Engine 577cc, V-twin

Top speed 50 mph (80 km/h)

Sylvain de Jong's Minerva built high-quality V-twin (as here) and single-cylinder machines until 1909, but then turned production over to luxury cars.

△ **Norton 5hp V-twin 1906**

Origin UK

Engine 700cc, V-twin

Top speed 80 mph (129 km/h)

Starting up in 1902, James Norton was soon installing Peugot engines. His rider Rem Fowler won the twins class of the first Isle of Man TT in 1907 on a machine like this one.

△ **FN Four 1911**

Origin Belgium

Engine 498cc, in-line four

Top speed 45 mph (72 km/h)

This revolutionary luxury four-cylinder motorbike with shaft drive started with a 362cc capacity in 1905 and grew to 748cc in 1914, continuing after WWI.

▽ **Wilkinson TMC 1912**

Origin UK

Engine 848cc, in-line four

Top speed 75 mph (120 km/h)

Built by the Wilkinson Sword company from 1911 to 1916, this top-of-the-line motorcycle featured shaft drive and full suspension, with a car-type water-cooled engine.

△ **Zenith 8/10hp Gradua 1913**

Origin	UK
Engine	986cc, V-twin
Top speed	85mph (137 km/h)

Freddy Barnes devised the Gradua gear, combining a variable pulley with sliding the rear wheel fore and aft. It was briefly banned as an unfair advantage in competitions.

▽ **BAT Combination 1913**

Origin	UK
Engine	770cc, V-twin
Top speed	45mph (72 km/h)

In 1905 T. H. Tessier took over BAT, which went on to build a good reputation for its sturdy and comfortable V-twins that were ideal for sidecar combinations.

◁ **NUT 3½hp Sports 1914**

Origin	UK
Engine	497cc, V-twin
Top speed	65mph (105 km/h)

Founded in Newcastle upon Tyne in 1912 by Hugh Mason and Jock Hall, the NUT factory made well-engineered and fast V-twins. Mason won the 1913 Junior TT on this one.

◁ **Royal Enfield 3hp V-twin 1914**

Origin	UK
Engine	425cc, V-twin
Top speed	60mph (97 km/h)

After concentrating for a few years on cars, Royal Enfield returned to building motorcycles in 1909. By 1913 its inlet-over-exhaust twin was enjoying race track success.

▷ **AJS Model D 1915**

Origin	UK
Engine	749cc, V-twin
Top speed	65mph (105 km/h)

The Stevens family was building engines very early in the century and started AJS motorcycles in 1909. This big V-twin of 1913 was popular for combinations.

△ **Douglas 2¾hp Lady's Model 1915**

Origin	UK
Engine	345cc, flat-twin
Top speed	45mph (72 km/h)

Douglas was among the first to introduce a specific model for ladies. This bike's lower frame and guards made riding in a long skirt possible, and had controls.

▷ **Wooler 2¾hp Flat-twin 1919**

Origin	UK
Engine	345cc, flat-twin
Top speed	55mph (89 km/h)

Boasting variable speed gearing and full suspension, the advanced Wooler, painted yellow and nicknamed the "Flying Banana," competed in the 1919 Isle of Man TT, but without success.

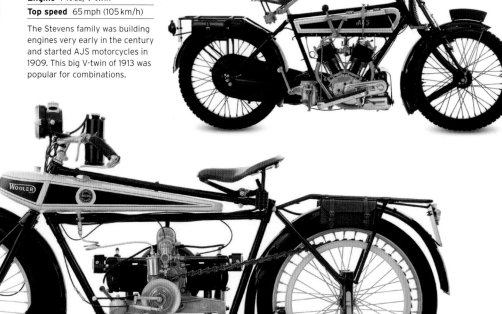

FN Four

Unveiled in 1905, the fabulous FN Four was one of the first genuinely efficient four-cylinder motorcycles on the market, sporting a shaft drive and a dedicated motorcycle frame. The original 362cc engine was increased to the near-500cc capacity of this 1911 model before a final 748cc version emerged in 1914. By this stage, FN had shown that four-cylinder bikes could be just as practical and smooth-riding as singles and twins.

THE SOUTH BELGIUM-BASED FN (Fabrique Nationale d'Armes de Guerre) was an early pioneer of single-cylinder motorcycles at the start of the 20th century. By 1905 the manufacturer was breaking new ground with the development of its first four-cylinder bike. The company hired Paul Kelecom, an acclaimed engineer who had been producing highly regarded engines under his own name, as well as for other manufacturers. Kelecom used his technical know-how to construct an innovative four-cylinder motorcycle for FN,

a bike that would set the standard for other early machines with the same engine configuration. The model was progressive in other ways, too, with an integrated frame, magneto ignition, and lubrication system. As the Four developed, there were further refinements: rear drum brakes from 1909; an optional two-speed gearbox from 1911; and a kick-starter from 1913. The following year saw the debut of the 700, which was produced until the early 1920s, and was the last of this classic motorcycle's line.

FRONT VIEW

REAR VIEW

Rifles to bikes
As its full name suggests, Fabrique Nationale d'Armes de Guerre (FN) originally manufactured munitions. By 1900 the company had diversified into motorcycle production, and the resulting logo—combining a rifle with cycle pedals—reflected both areas of expertise.

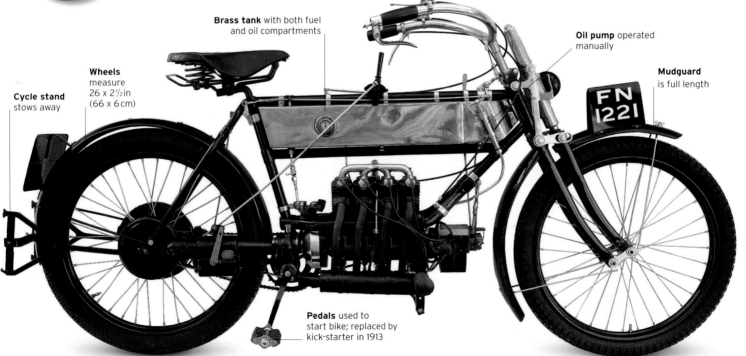

Brass tank with both fuel and oil compartments

Oil pump operated manually

Mudguard is full length

Wheels measure 26 x 2½in (66 x 6cm)

Cycle stand stows away

Pedals used to start bike; replaced by kick-starter in 1913

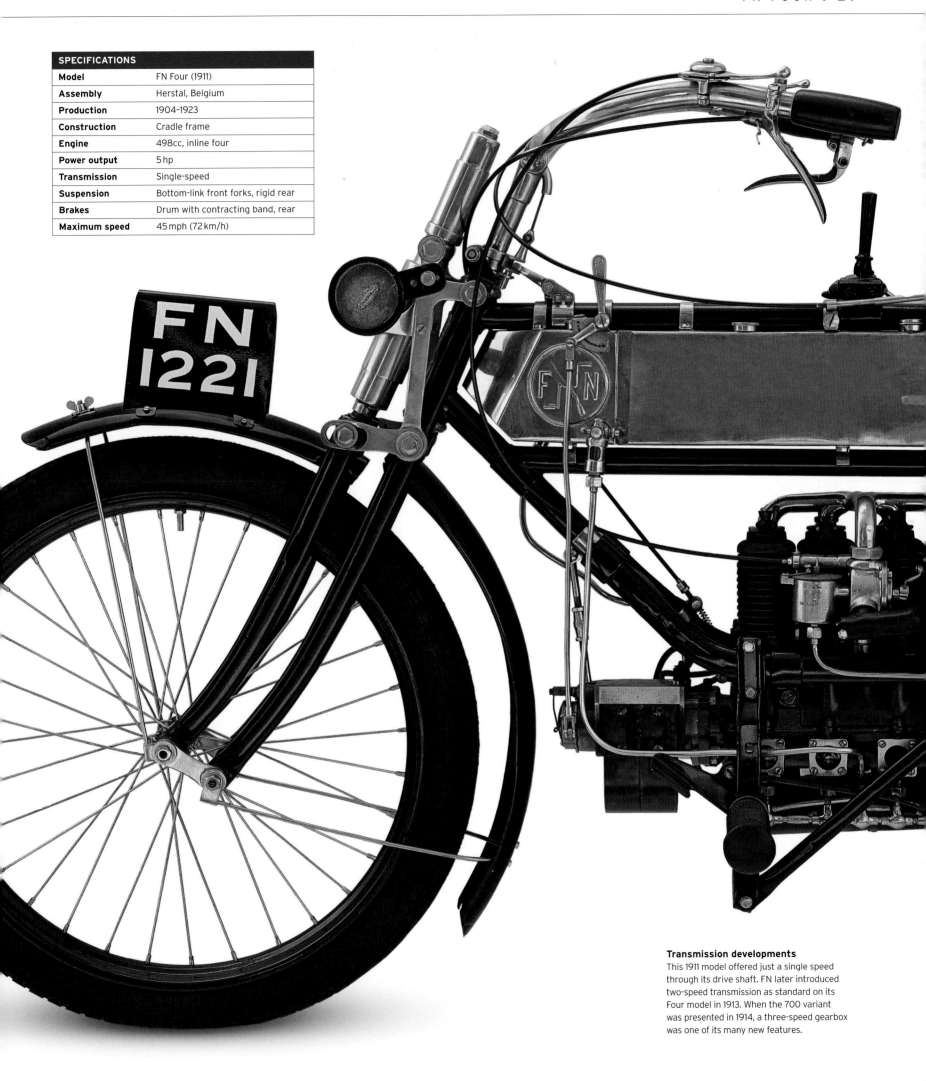

SPECIFICATIONS	
Model	FN Four (1911)
Assembly	Herstal, Belgium
Production	1904-1923
Construction	Cradle frame
Engine	498cc, inline four
Power output	5 hp
Transmission	Single-speed
Suspension	Bottom-link front forks, rigid rear
Brakes	Drum with contracting band, rear
Maximum speed	45 mph (72 km/h)

Transmission developments
This 1911 model offered just a single speed
through its drive shaft. FN later introduced
two-speed transmission as standard on its
Four model in 1913. When the 700 variant
was presented in 1914, a three-speed gearbox
was one of its many new features.

THE BIKE

Style and substance went hand in hand on the FN Four. As well as looking good, the leading link front forks helped provide a smooth riding experience, while the brass tank under the cross tube was split into fuel and oil sections. Useful features included viewing windows inside the crankcase—which made it possible to check the oil level—and auxiliary lubrication provided by a manual pump on the oil tank.

1. FN badge with rifle and pedals 2. Carburetor air lever on handlebar 3. Oil metering device 4. Fuel gauge 5. Enclosed fork springs 6. Leather saddle 7. Fuel tap 8. Pivoting-link forks 9. Final drive casing 10. Hand-operated oil pump 11. Chain for pedaling 12. Back sprocket and rear brake

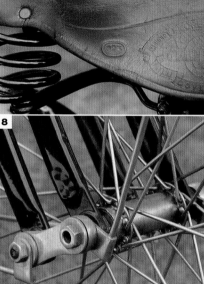

ENGINE

The FN's four-cylinder engine was enlarged a number of times over its lifetime. The engine was redesigned for 1910 and remained unchanged for the 1911 model shown. The engine size increased to 498cc, the carburetor position was moved, and a new oiling system was introduced. The final 750cc version of the Four replaced automatic inlet valves with a mechanically operated side-valve configuration. This produced a model with sufficient power to be employed as a sidecar motorcycle, and was also used by German forces in World War I.

13. Left-side view of engine 14. Exhaust header pipes 15. Spark plug 16. Single carburetor and float chamber with priming plunger 17. Ignition distributor 18. Oil levels

America's Golden Age

The early 20th century saw motorcycle development grow rapidly in the US, and while some bought in technology from Europe, most American makers chose to forge ahead with their own various solutions. Roads between cities were entirely unpaved, so effective suspension was a vital development, as was rugged construction, ease of access for tire repairs, and forms of gearing to cope with hilly terrain.

△ Pierce Four 1910

Origin USA

Engine 699cc, in-line four

Top speed 60 mph (97 km/h)

Best-known for its cars, Pierce-Arrow began with bicycles and built the first Pierce Four motorcycle in 1909. It was innovative but expensive and bankrupted the company by 1914.

◁ Emblem 4 hp 1910

Origin USA

Engine 531cc, single-cylinder

Top speed 48 mph (77 km/h)

Emblem's V-twins and singles had their own engines in loop frames; the smallest variety was installed in this model. The company, whose slogan was "Class, Power, Speed, and Satisfaction," faded after WWI.

△ Pope Model L 7/8 hp 1911

Origin USA

Engine 998cc, V-twin

Top speed 65 mph (105 km/h)

A unique rear suspension, overhead valves, and a three-speed gearbox were advanced features of the Pope Model L, which cost as much as a Ford Model T.

△ Henderson 7 hp Four 1912

Origin USA

Engine 934cc, in-line four

Top speed 60 mph (97 km/h)

Built from 1912 to 1931, Hendersons became popular with police forces, as they were faster than anything else on the roads; one was ridden around the world between 1912 and 1913.

△ Harley-Davidson Model X8 1912

Origin USA

Engine 494cc, single-cylinder

Top speed 35 mph (56 km/h)

The original single-cylinder Harley-Davidson of 1903 had been refined into this model by 1912. The company's products of this period were known as "Silent Gray Fellows."

◁ Harley-Davidson 11 hp 1915

Origin USA

Engine 989cc, V-twin

Top speed 60 mph (97 km/h)

With mechanical lubrication, interconnected clutch, three-speed gear-change, and an optional electrical kit, this rugged machine coped well with unpaved roads.

△ Indian V-Twin Roadster 1912

Origin USA

Engine 633cc, V-twin

Top speed 55 mph (89 km/h)

In addition to the touring V-twins, Indian offered these race-derived roadster models with twist-grip controls and lightweight construction—ideal for amateur competition.

▷ Indian 4 hp Single 1913

Origin USA

Engine 500cc, single-cylinder

Top speed 40 mph (64 km/h)

Indian built 32,000 bikes in 1913, 90 percent of them twins, but also produced this single, which benefited from advanced swingarm rear suspension.

▷ Sears Deluxe "Big Five" 1914

Origin USA

Engine 575cc, single-cylinder

Top speed 50 mph (80 km/h)

The Sears Roebuck catalog sold a range of motorcycles from 1912 to 1916, with trailing-link front suspension and engines made by Spake, as on this "magneto model."

△ Indian Two-Sixty Standard Model 1914

Origin USA

Engine 988cc, V-twin

Top speed 55 mph (89 km/h)

This one-liter luxury twin was the first motorcycle with electric lighting included as standard. Some versions were made with an electric starter as well.

◁ Smith Motor Wheel 1915

Origin UK

Engine 150cc, single-cylinder

Top speed 27 mph (43 km/h)

In 1914, A. O. Smith Corporation of Milwaukee acquired US rights to the British Wall Motorwheel, which clipped onto any bicycle to provide instant power assistance.

△ Cleveland 2½hp 1919

Origin USA

Engine 179cc, single-cylinder

Top speed 38 mph (61 km/h)

With its small two-stroke engine turned transversely to the normal layout, this low-slung Cleveland was distinctive and, being inexpensive, sold rather well.

Racing Machines/Scooters

Organized racing burgeoned in the 1900s. Europe had city-to-city road races, while US sports favored closed dirt tracks and wooden board Motordromes. In Britain, roads were closed for the Isle of Man Tourist Trophy (TT) races and the banked Brooklands circuit opened in 1907. At the other end of the scale, the first motor scooters were being aimed at the general public.

▽ **NLG Peugeot 1907**

Origin	UK
Engine	944cc, V-twin
Top speed	76 mph (122 km/h)

Custom-built by North London Garages with a highly tuned Peugeot engine, the NLG won the first motorcycle race at Brooklands in 1908, averaging 63 mph (101 km/h).

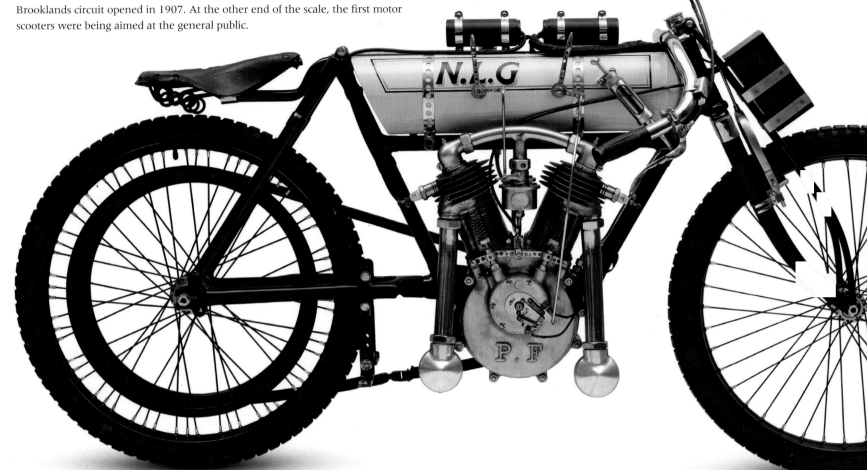

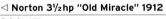

◁ **Norton 3½ hp "Old Miracle" 1912**

Origin	UK
Engine	490cc, side-valve single
Top speed	82 mph (132 km/h)

A 1912 speed record holder, this legendary single was ridden by tuner D. R. O'Donovan at 71.54 mph (115.13 km/h) for 5 miles (8 km) in 1913 and bettered 82 mph in 1915.

△ **Indian Track Racer 1912**

Origin	USA
Engine	999cc, ohv V-twin
Top speed	90 mph (145 km/h)

This advanced four-valves per cylinder twin won on US board tracks. In the UK, Charles B. Franklin covered 300 miles (483 km) in less than 300 minutes on one.

△ **Corah 6 hp 1912**

Origin	UK
Engine	746cc, ohv V-twin
Top speed	not known

The short-lived Corah company fielded this single-speed racing machine with an overhead-valve engine made by JAP, Britain's most advanced commercial engine-maker.

△ NSU 350TT 1912

Origin Germany

Engine 349cc, V-twin

Top speed not known

NSU's 350 V-twin achieved fourth and seventh place finishes at the 1913 Isle of Man Junior TT, despite the machine's lack of suspension or gears.

▽ Scott Two-speed TT 1913

Origin UK

Engine 486cc, two-stroke twin

Top speed 70 mph (113 km/h)

The unorthodox two-speed Scott two-stroke was the fastest machine in the Isle of Man TT in 1912 and 1913, winning two Senior races.

◁ Flying Merkel 471 1914

Origin USA

Engine 985cc, V-twin

Top speed 70 mph (113 km/h)

Notable for its monoshock rear suspension, the Flying Merkel V-twin was prominent in US racing during the marque's short life from 1909 to 1915.

▽ Harley-Davidson 11KR Roadster Racer 1915

Origin USA

Engine 988cc, V-twin

Top speed 76 mph (122 km/h)

Successful in speed events in both the US and Europe, Harley-Davidson sold this model as the basis for a competitive privateer racer.

▽ Autoped Autoped 1915

Origin USA

Engine 155cc, side-valve single-cylinder

Top speed 20 mph (32 km/h)

Ridden standing up, the novel Autoped with a front-mounted engine was started and stopped by moving the handlebar column, seen here folded down for portability.

▽ Reynolds Runabout 1919

Origin UK

Engine 269cc, two-stroke single

Top speed not known

The maker of this "stretch" scooter took customers' comfort seriously. The seat was mounted on a combination of coil and leaf springs.

△ Stafford Mobile Pup 1919

Origin UK

Engine 142cc, ohv single-cylinder

Top speed not known

The flimsy-looking Pup had a four-stroke engine driving the front wheel. It was made in Coventry by T. G. John, who later produced Alvis cars.

Scott Two-speed

One of the first examples of original British motorcycle design, the Scott Two-speed laid the foundations for the marque's success. Introduced in the first decade of the 1900s, the pioneering model incorporated several innovative features that made it stand out from the crowd. The racing versions won the Isle of Man Senior TT in both 1912 and 1913, giving the Scott profile a boost. The standard Two-speed continued in production until the end of the 1920s.

ALFRED SCOTT'S PIONEERING approach produced the first genuinely modern-looking motorcycle that had been fully thought through. Its original design included a twin-cylinder two-stroke engine with outstanding hill-climbing ability. Fast cornering was another attribute, aided by the effective front suspension and a low center of gravity achieved by the open, triangular frame. The two-speed mechanism, operated by a rocking pedal, switched drive between differentially-geared primary chains. As well as being technically advanced, Scotts were light and speedy. Racing versions, such as the model shown here, won the Isle of Man TT in 1912 and 1913, the first two-stroke machines to take the title. Though later Scott models—the "Squirrels"—would win wide acclaim from the 1920s, Scott's success was forged here in this fast, lightweight twin that was undeniably far ahead of its time.

FRONT VIEW

REAR VIEW

Engineering genius
The Yorkshire-based engineer Alfred Scott first put his name to a motorcycle in 1901, when he developed a twin-cylinder, two-stroke engine to power a bicycle. Seven years later, the Scott Engineering Company was set up.

Race number of competition model (winner of 1913 Isle of Man TT)

Fuel tank mounted low with large cap for fast pit work

Radiator to provide water cooling for the engine

Fork springs are fully enclosed

Front brake with bicycle-type blocks

Kick-starter was a Scott invention

Water jacket to cool cylinder and cylinder head

Unusual profile

The open frame and low-slung fuel tank made the Scott look different from most motorcycles of the time, and the water-cooled engine was of unique design. The straight handlebars were a feature of the racing version, while road models had curved designs better suited to a traditional cycling position. Other special racing features included a rotary inlet and transfer valve behind the cylinders and twin-plug ignition. Oil for the positive lubrication system was carried in the upper frame of the motorcycle.

SPECIFICATIONS	
Model	Scott Two-speed TT (1913)
Assembly	Shipley, England
Production	Not known
Construction	Triangulated frame
Engine	486cc, two-stroke twin
Power output	6 hp (estimated)
Transmission	Two-speed
Suspension	Slider front forks, rigid rear
Brakes	Blocks, front and rear
Maximum speed	70 mph (113 km/h) estimated

THE BIKE

Scotts of the period brimmed with original ideas. Mounting the fuel tank on the seat support tube kept weight low, and the slider-type front forks predated the telescopic forks that would be commonplace several decades later. The two-speed mechanism operated by a heel-and-toe pedal incorporated a clutch mechanism that allowed drive to switch between two primary chains, which gave different gear ratios. Scott was the first motorcycle maker to use a kick-starter, and when it was operated by racer Eric Myers at the start of the 1909 TT, the crowd cheered.

1. Scott trademark 2. Engine oil control 3. Cellulose handgrip 4. Water filler 5. Oil syringe 6. Fork sliders 7. Two-speed control 8. Saddle maker's badge 9. Front brake blocks 10. Oil filler cap 11. Magneto 12. Magneto sprocket 13. Rear sprocket

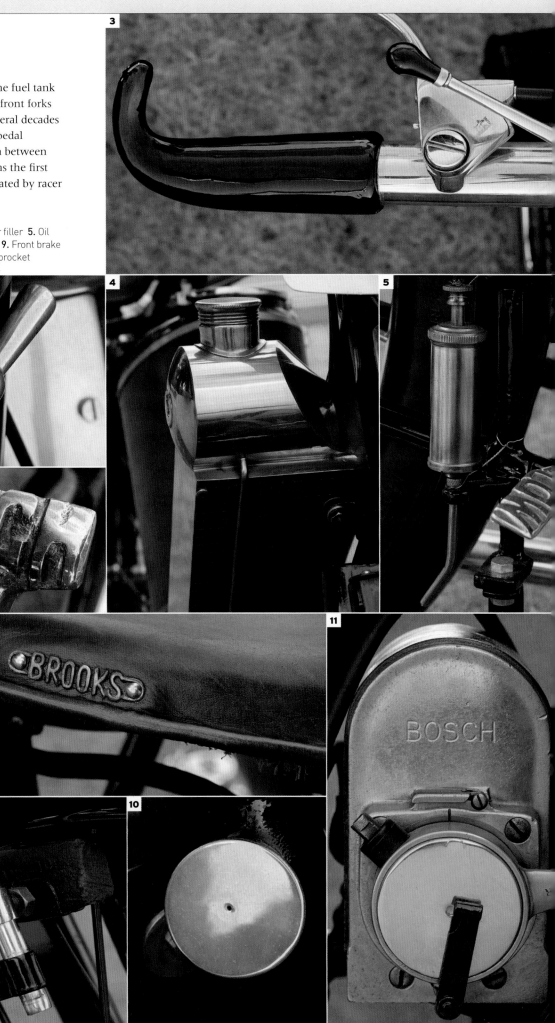

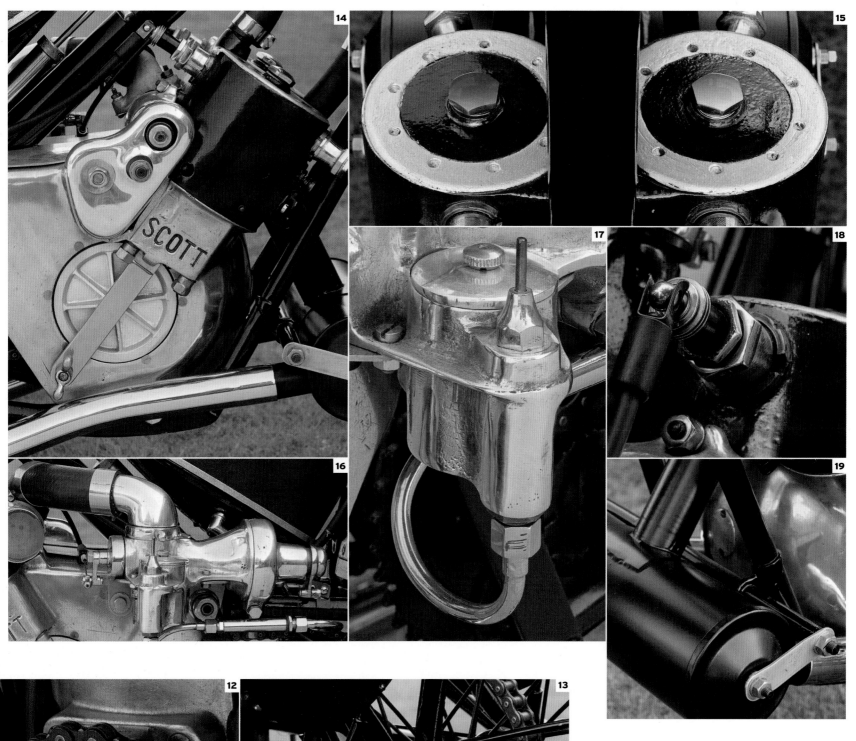

THE ENGINE

Scott's two-stroke, twin-cylinder engine was unique: like a 19th-century stationary engine, it had a central flywheel with an overhung crank on each side, each one contained in its own low-volume crankcase. On this racing engine a rotating valve controlled inlet and transfer timings for optimum power and torque. There was no water pump; the coolant was circulated through the one-piece cylinder and head by a thermosiphon effect.

14. Cylinder water jacket **15.** Rotary valve housing
16. Carburetor **17.** Fuel float bowl primer on carburetor
18. Rear spark plugs **19.** Muffler box

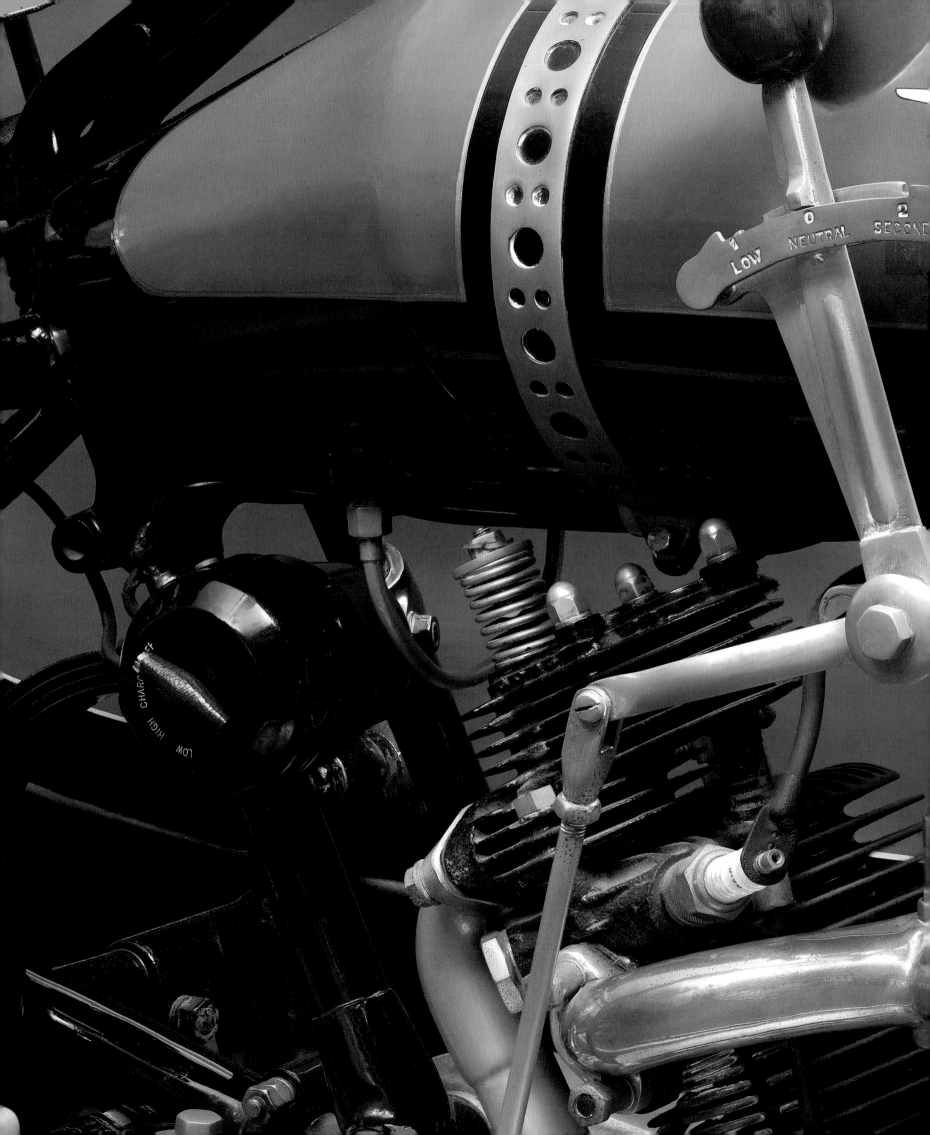

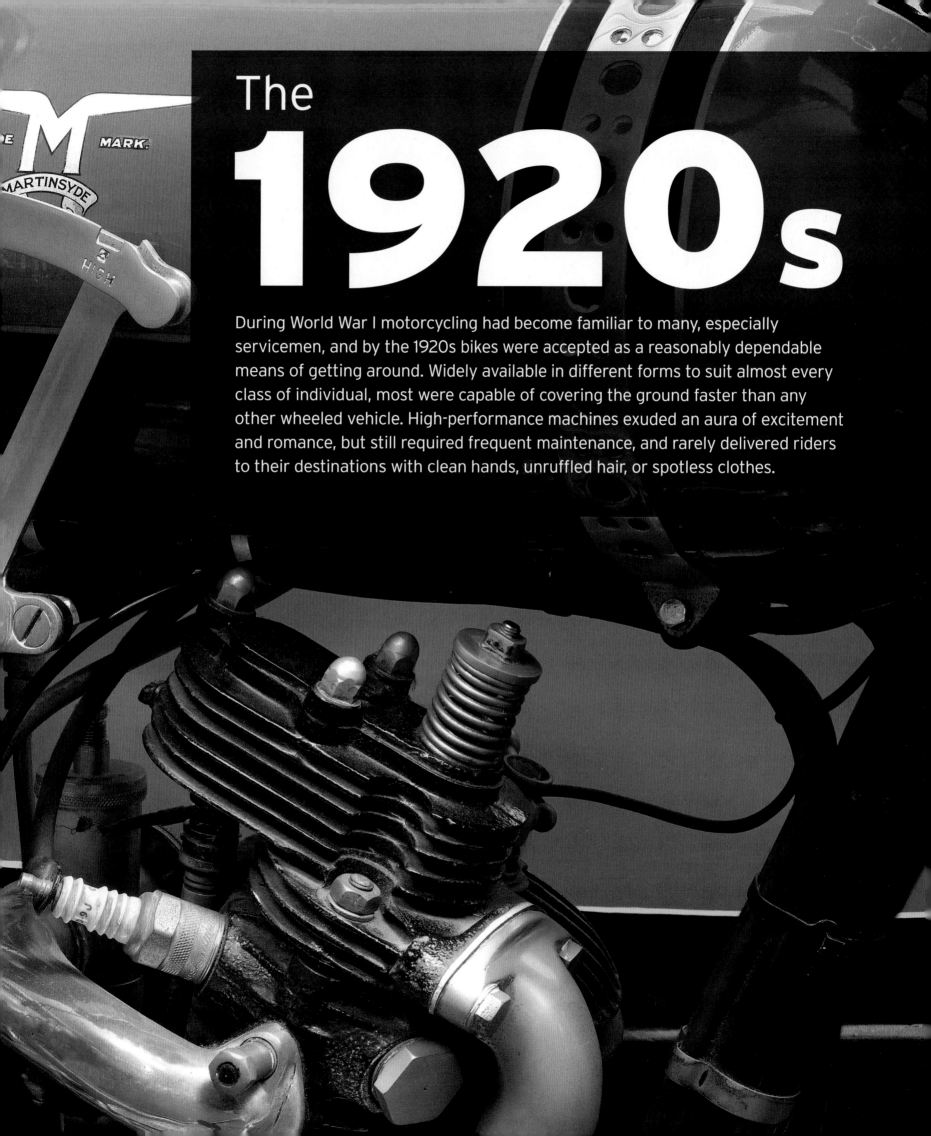

The 1920s

During World War I motorcycling had become familiar to many, especially servicemen, and by the 1920s bikes were accepted as a reasonably dependable means of getting around. Widely available in different forms to suit almost every class of individual, most were capable of covering the ground faster than any other wheeled vehicle. High-performance machines exuded an aura of excitement and romance, but still required frequent maintenance, and rarely delivered riders to their destinations with clean hands, unruffled hair, or spotless clothes.

Two-wheelers for the Masses

Building the cheapest forms of motorized transportation, a first step up from a bicycle, exercised the minds of numerous inventors in the 1920s, each finding their own best way to achieve it. Four-stroke engines were mostly side-valve for simplicity, while two-stroke engines with their rugged simplicity offered more power for your money. Small-wheeled scooters were still around, but in dwindling numbers.

◁ ABC Skootamota 1920
Origin UK
Engine 123cc, single-cylinder
Top speed 15 mph (24 km/h)

The All British Cycle company's scooter was designed by Granville Bradshaw. With a rear-mounted four-stroke engine, it predated products that came decades later.

▷ DKW Hilfsmotor 1920
Origin Germany
Engine 118cc, single-cylinder
Top speed 25 mph (40 km/h)

DKW's bicycle auxiliary engine proved very popular, being easily attachable to any lady's or gent's bicycle. Some 30,000 were sold in four years of production.

△ Triumph Knirps 2½ hp 1920
Origin Germany
Engine 276cc, single-cylinder
Top speed 52 mph (84 km/h)

Originally an offshoot of the English Triumph company, the Nuremberg factory made typewriters as well as motorcycles. This popular two-stroke was called the Knirps, meaning "tot."

◁ DKW Lomos 1922
Origin Germany
Engine 143cc, single-cylinder
Top speed 37 mph (60 km/h)

After the crude Golem scooter of 1921, DKW brought out the much neater Lomos with 143cc and later 170cc power. However, it failed to catch on—just 2,500 were sold.

△ Triumph Model W 1927
Origin UK
Engine 277cc, single-cylinder
Top speed 48 mph (77 km/h)

New for 1927, this lightweight, inexpensive Triumph had a side-valve engine and just fitted within a 220 lb (98 kg) UK taxation limit, making it attractively cheap to run.

▷ Velocette D2 1921
Origin UK
Engine 220cc, single-cylinder
Top speed 48 mph (77 km/h)

Successor to the Veloce, this Velocette two-stroke boasted throttle-controlled lubrication. Although not cheap, it was practical, and variants were sold until 1946.

◁ Ardie 3PS 1922
Origin Germany
Engine 304cc, single-cylinder
Top speed 52 mph (84 km/h)

Ardie's early motorcycles were equipped with two-stroke engines of the company's own manufacture. Modern styling and high equipment levels made them popular.

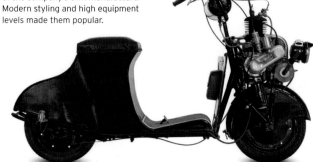

△ Autoglider Model D 1921
Origin UK
Engine 269cc, single-cylinder
Top speed 45 mph (72 km/h)

Charles Townsend's 1919 platform machine could carry one or two people standing; a seat was added to later models, along with storage space and efficient mudguards.

◁ **Motobécane MB1 Ecclesiastique 1923**

Origin France

Engine 175cc, single-cylinder

Top speed 42 mph (68 km/h)

Charles Benoit and Abel Bardin produced their first motorcycle in 1923. This ladies' and clergy model with a lowered top tube became very successful.

△ **Royal Enfield 225L 1924**

Origin UK

Engine 225cc, single-cylinder

Top speed 40 mph (64 km/h)

This is the ladies' version of Royal Enfield's successful little two-stroke runabout with two speeds. It was also available with a top-tube-mounted fuel tank.

▷ **Levis Model K 1925**

Origin UK

Engine 247cc, single-cylinder

Top speed 58 mph (93 km/h)

Built by Butterfields of Birmingham, this was one of the leading British two-strokes. It won many races, including the first 250cc Lightweight class at the Isle of Man TT in 1922.

▽ **BSA Model B 1925**

Origin UK

Engine 249cc, single-cylinder

Top speed 45 mph (72 km/h)

Known as the "Round Tank," this cheap and successful model was chosen by the British Post Office for its telegram service. A front brake was deemed unnecessary.

SV~6573

◁ **Puch 220 1926**

Origin Austria

Engine 223cc, single-cylinder

Top speed 47 mph (76 km/h)

A bicycle manufacturer from 1889, Puch made cars and motorcycles from about 1900. This distinctive double-piston two-stroke machine joined the range in 1923.

◁ **Terrot FT 1927**

Origin France

Engine 247cc, single-cylinder

Top speed 53 mph (85 km/h)

This affordable touring two-stroke bike with two or three gears came from a well-established French factory that had been making motorcycles since 1902.

▽ **Indian Prince 1928**

Origin USA

Engine 350cc, single-cylinder

Top speed 55 mph (89 km/h)

This second attempt by Indian at a lightweight "starter" motorcycle did not catch on, even when modified from side valves to overhead valves in 1926; its sales ended in 1928.

Brough Superior SS100

Often referred to as *the* vintage superbike, the SS100 was guaranteed to be capable of 100 mph (160 km/h), making it the machine of choice for affluent, speed-hungry enthusiasts. One famous fan was T. E. Lawrence (Lawrence of Arabia), who owned four SS100s in succession. When the machine was launched in late 1924, creator George Brough touted it as the "Rolls-Royce of Motorcycles." It is a testament to the Brough Superior's superb build quality and performance that the car-maker never challenged his claim.

GEORGE BROUGH was 29 when he left the established motorcycle company run by his father, William Brough, to set up on his own in 1919. George would take a different approach from his father's: rather than building his engines from scratch, George picked the best available components and assembled his machines from these. Propulsion for early Brough Superiors was provided by the smooth "90 bore" side-valve JAP V-twin engine, as well as the Swiss-built MAG V-twin

engines. The acclaimed SS80 of 1922, powered by a V-twin JAP, topped the range until 1924, when the SS100 was introduced. Powered by the overhead-valve, record-breaking 1,000cc JAP V-twin, this machine enjoyed a high profile among wealthy sporting riders. Later SS100s incorporated Matchless V-twin engines. Ironically, the last Brough Superiors, produced until 1940, were built on Vernon Road in Nottingham—in William Brough's old factory.

A superior brand
George Brough's choice of name may have rankled his father and former employer, William Brough, implying as it did that the original Brough bikes, still being built by the older man's company, were inferior machines.

FRONT VIEW

REAR VIEW

Hard pannier featured on the SS100 Alpine Grand Sports model

Saddle is sprung to absorb road bumps

Oil tank has extra fuel capacity gained by attaching tank to rear frame downtube

Hand-change gear lever is mounted on front fuel tank support

Lever on side of electric headlight allows it to be dipped manually

Front forks of Harley-Davidson origin, modified and branded "Castle"

Rear brake is an 8-inch (20-cm) drum

Full cradle frame with single front downtube and box section head lug

A rare sight
Often regarded as the ultimate classic
motorcycle, the SS100 is rarely seen
today. Less than 400 of all variants
were manufactured from 1924 to 1939,
and a minority of those were in Alpine
Grand Sport trim, as seen here. All the
surviving Brough Superiors are now
highly prized by collectors.

SPECIFICATIONS	
Model	SS100 (1927)
Assembly	Nottingham, England
Production	Approximately 400
Construction	Rigid cradle frame
Engine	998cc, V-twin
Power output	45 hp
Transmission	Three-speed
Suspension	Castle front forks, rigid rear
Brakes	Drum brake, front and rear
Maximum speed	102 mph (164 km/h)

THE BIKE

Glamour and performance sold the Brough Superior. A champion rider himself, George Brough built machines to match his high standards, the cradle frame and Harley-Davidson-type front forks combining to give a very stable ride. The JAP engine was bought in, as were the Sturmey Archer three-speed gearbox and the Enfield hubs with drum brakes. Other features included luggage boxes equipped with inner carry cases.

1. Model logo **2.** Choke lever **3.** Fuel filler cap **4.** Friction damper with star motif **5.** Speedometer **6.** Hand-change for the gears **7.** Knee grips on either side of fuel tank **8.** Oil level sight glass **9.** Klaxon horn **10.** Gearchange linkage **11.** Fuel tap **12.** Speedo drive (in rear wheel) **13.** Front brake **14.** Front exhaust outlet with unusual tiered metal design **15.** Rear exhaust outlet **16.** Gearbox **17.** Alpine Grand Sports badge

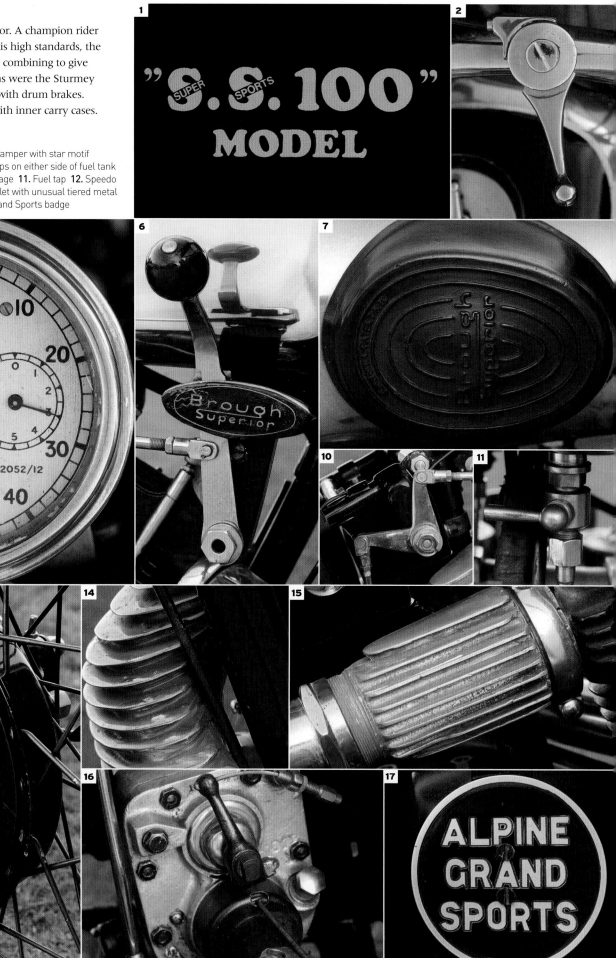

THE ENGINE

The SS100 had JAP's overhead valve engine, which from 1927 had its ignition magneto and lighting dynamo sited alongside the crankcase and bevel drive. The single, slide-type carburetor with twin float chambers supplied both cylinders. The Alpine Grand Sports had around 45 hp, which increased to 50 hp using high-compression pistons.

18. Right side of engine **19.** Left side of engine showing magneto, dynamo, and oil pump **20.** Carburetor float bowl **21.** Oil tap **22.** Oil pump **23.** Valve rocker **24.** Combined magneto and dynamo

The Mighty V-twins

For the 1920s rider, a V-twin represented the ultimate in performance and power. The shape of the engine fitted neatly in a motorcycle frame with no bulk at the sides and no need to make the wheelbase uncomfortably long; even a 1,000cc V-twin could be reasonably compact. Some were built for speed, others for low-down power, hauling a heavy sidecar with the whole family on board.

△ **Martinsyde 680 Combination 1921**
Origin UK
Engine 677cc, V-twin
Top speed 58 mph (93 km/h)

Aircraft-builders Martinsyde switched to motorcycles in 1919, using single and V-twin engine designs by Howard Newman, as in this bike. Fire destroyed the factory in 1922.

△ **Excelsior 20R 1920**
Origin USA
Engine 1,000cc, V-twin
Top speed 100 mph (160 km/h)

Excelsior launched its V-twin in 1911, adding a chain drive and sprung fork in 1913, three-speeds in 1915, and 1,200cc in 1921; it was the first 100 mph (160 km/h) production bike.

▷ **BSA Model A 1922**
Origin UK
Engine 770cc, V-twin
Top speed 55 mph (89 km/h)

Britain's biggest motorcycle-maker produced its first V-twin immediately after WWI, with an enclosed chain drive and a three-speed gearbox.

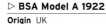

△ **James Model 12 1925**
Origin UK
Engine 495cc, V-twin
Top speed 53 mph (85 km/h)

Bicycle-maker turned motorcycle-builder, James made V-twins from 1913 until 1925. The Model 12 has a Burman three-speed gearbox. There was also a larger-capacity model.

◁ **Husqvarna T180 1926**
Origin Sweden
Engine 550cc, V-twin
Top speed 60 mph (97 km/h)

Husqvarna made bicycles in the 19th century and motorcycles from 1903. This V-twin was the first to use its own engine and was modeled on US V-twins of the time.

▽ **Burney V-twin 1926**
Origin UK
Engine 680cc, V-twin
Top speed 70 mph (113 km/h)

Edward Alexander Burney designed the original Blackburne engine, and later made bikes in his own name. This stylish, sporty machine boasted a JAP engine and twistgrip controls.

▷ **Coventry-Eagle Flying 8 1925**
Origin UK
Engine 980cc, V-twin
Top speed 100 mph (160 km/h)

Hand-built and very expensive, the overhead-valve Flying 8 was one of the few worthy rivals to a Brough Superior; it was long and low, with power and brakes to match.

▷ **Brough Superior SS100 1927**

Origin UK

Engine 998cc, V-twin

Top speed 102 mph (164 km/h)

George Brough built the most collectible of British motorcycles, of which the SS100 is leader of the pack. Its JAP engine could power racing versions to 130 mph (209 km/h).

△ **New Imperial Model 8 1927**

Origin UK

Engine 680cc, V-twin

Top speed 60 mph (97 km/h)

Sold principally as a sidecar combination, with coupe, tradesman's, and tandem options, New Imperial's JAP-engined V-twin was a workhorse.

△ **Harley-Davidson Model JD 1925**

Origin USA

Engine 1,213cc, V-twin

Top speed 75 mph (120 km/h)

Harley launched its 74-cu-in (1,213cc) V-twins in 1922, and in 1925 updated its styling with a long, low, teardrop-tank. On the JD, it still offered only one color—olive drab.

△ **Royal Enfield Model 182 Sports 1928**

Origin UK

Engine 976cc, V-twin

Top speed 78 mph (126 km/h)

Royal Enfield produced V-twins from 1912, using both its own and proprietary engines. The saddle tank was added in 1928. Both brakes were operated by foot pedal.

△ **Indian 101 Scout 1928**

Origin USA

Engine 745cc, V-twin

Top speed 70 mph (113 km/h)

Longer and lower than before, this front-braked Scout had a light, well-designed frame. Noted for its handling, it was popular for racing, hill climbing, and stunt riding.

△ **BSA Cycle Cab 1928**

Origin UK

Engine 996cc, V-twin

Top speed 50 mph (80 km/h)

BSA built around 100 sidecar taxi units from 1920 to 1925, based on the Model E/G and known as "Cycle Cabs." This big V-twin was ideal for sidecar-hauling.

Indian Scout

"Legendary" is how the Indian Motorcycle Company likes to describe its machines. Founders George Hendee and Oscar Hedstrom had set out to lead the US market, and the Scout, unveiled in 1920, heralded a decade of domination by Indian bikes as they went on to take every speed and distance record in America. The revolutionary Scout initially had a 40 cu in (606cc) engine, increased to 45½ cu in (745cc) in 1927 to challenge the growing popularity of Excelsior's rival Super X machine.

INDIAN WAS A COMPANY on the move in the early years of the 20th century, before the outbreak of WWI. Sales had soared since the birth of the company in 1901 and by the 1920s Indian was engaged in a fierce battle with Harley-Davidson for the spot of America's top motorcycle manufacturer. The Scout, designed by Irish-born Charles Bayly Franklin, was at the sharp end of Indian's drive for sales. First introduced in 1920, the bike was an instant hit. The Scout was given a thorough revamp for the 1928 season in the form of the acclaimed 101 series, with a new frame, raked-out forks, and a lower saddle height. The 101 proved especially popular with stunt riders owing to its low center of gravity and excellent handling, making it ideal for performing feats like the "wall of death." Despite the success of the 101 model, it was discontinued in 1932. During the 1930s, Scouts became progressively heavier and handling deteriorated, although the 1934 Sport Scout redressed the problem somewhat. A favorite of the US Army, Scouts were employed extensively in World War II. The manufacture of Scouts ceased completely in 1949.

FRONT VIEW

REAR VIEW

All-American
The name Indian was chosen by the manufacturers to suggest a truly all-American product. "Scout" conjured up a certain toughness and eagerness to explore new horizons, appealing to riders who identified closely with the pioneering spirit of America.

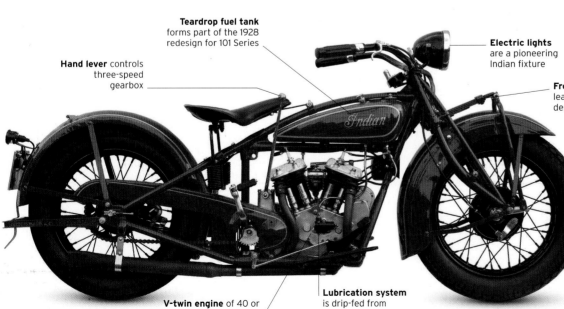

Teardrop fuel tank forms part of the 1928 redesign for 101 Series

Hand lever controls three-speed gearbox

Electric lights are a pioneering Indian fixture

Front forks are of a leaf-sprung, trailing-link design, peculiar to Indian

V-twin engine of 40 or 45½ cu in (606 or 745cc)

Lubrication system is drip-fed from pump on crankcase

Indian Scout

If one motorcycle had to be picked to represent America's two-wheeled history, it would be the Scout; if one variant of the Scout had to be selected, it would be the 101. Performance, reliability, agility, durability, the Scout 101 had it all—the quintessential all-American motorcycle.

SPECIFICATIONS			
Model	Indian 101 Scout (1928)	**Power output**	18 hp
Assembly	Springfield, MA	**Transmission**	Three-speed
Production	17,430	**Suspension**	Leaf-sprung, trailing-link front forks; rigid rear
Construction	Rigid cradle frame	**Brakes**	Single-leading drum, front and rear
Engine	45½ cu in (745cc) V-twin	**Maximum speed**	70 mph (113 km/h)

THE BIKE

The Scout 101 capitalized on what had gone before, and improved it. Wheelbase increased from 54½ in (138 cm) to 57⅛ in (145 cm), while the saddle was lowered too (to just 26¼ in/66.75 cm). Riders thought that the handling and stability of the Scout was near-perfect and considered the 101 Series to be the best Indian ever built. Some went further, claiming the 101 to be one of the best motorcycles ever made. It was certainly the model that sustained Indian during the Great Depression. Over three times the number of the larger 750cc model were produced than of the 600cc version.

1. Indian Scout tank script **2.** Indian badge **3.** Headlight **4.** Leaf spring on front wheel **5.** Right handlebar with ignition **6.** Fuel and oil filler caps **7.** Trailing-link forks **8.** Patent list on steering head **9.** Ammeter and light switch on dashboard panel **10.** Klaxon horn **11.** Oil tap **12.** Kick-starter **13.** Saddle spring **14.** Mudguard detail

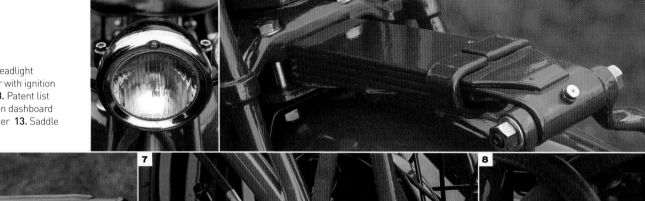

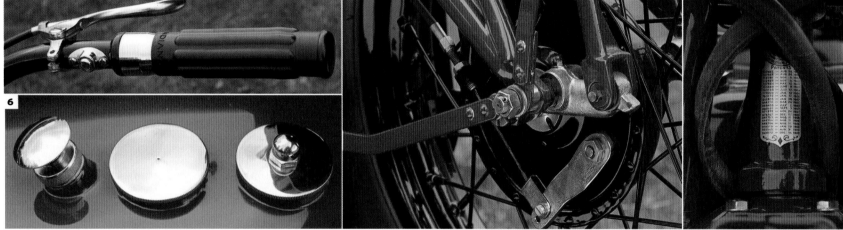

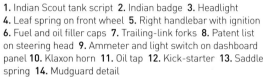

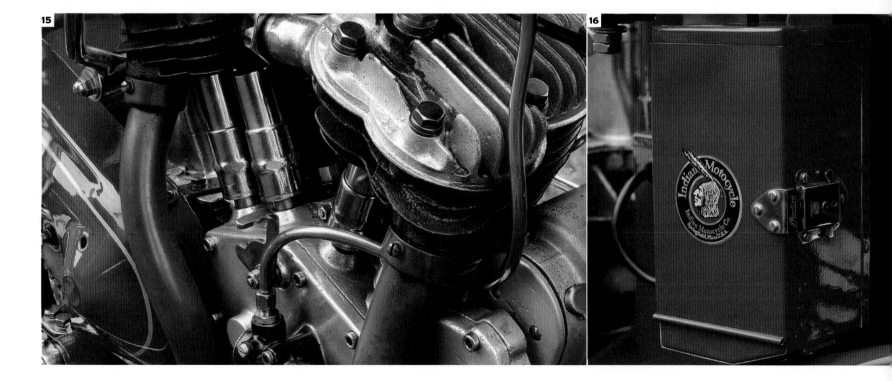

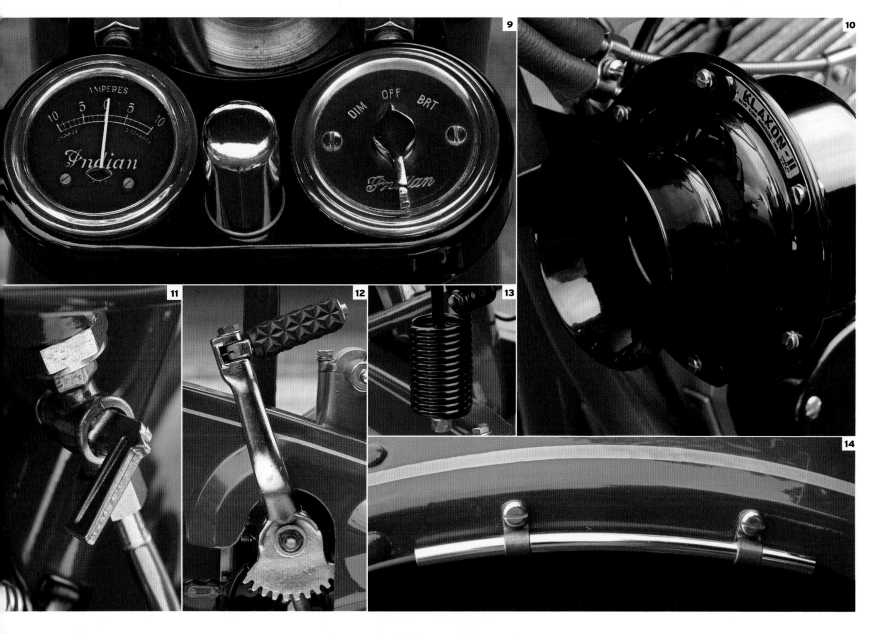

THE ENGINE

The rugged engine had two gear-driven camshafts, and the train of gears that drove them also powered the ignition magneto, which was sited ahead of the front cylinder. The oil pump was mounted on the outside of the gear casing. The three-speed gearbox was bolted onto the rear of the crankcase, with the primary drive by quiet and reliable helical gears.

15. 750cc engine 16. Battery box 17. Side view of engine showing V-twin cylinders 18. Magneto and dynamo 19. Choke lever on carburetor 20. Fuel tap 21. External oil pump 22. Fuel priming cup

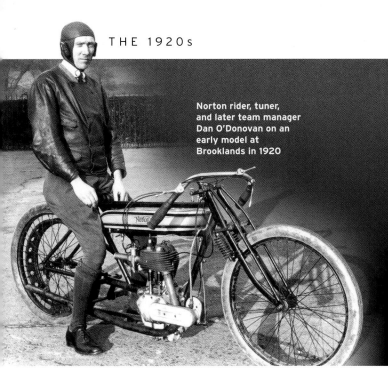

Norton rider, tuner, and later team manager Dan O'Donovan on an early model at Brooklands in 1920

Great Marques
The Norton Story

Great motorcycles and business brains do not always go hand in hand. Few stories illustrate the point more acutely than the mixed fortunes of Norton. But the marque that was responsible for such classics as the Dominator and the Commando has shown in recent years that it is a brand that will not die.

ONE OF THE GREAT names of British motorcycling, Norton has teetered on the brink of oblivion so many times that its successes are always in danger of being overshadowed by its failures. But the fact that Norton has been revived so often indicates just how much the marque means to many motorcycle enthusiasts.

Norton Logo
(introduced 1914)

James Lansdowne Norton was only in his late twenties when, in 1898, he founded the Norton Manufacturing Company in Birmingham and began to build motorcycles. The company did not, however, emerge fully formed. For the first decade or so, engines from overseas powered motorcycles like the Engerette of 1902.

Much of the reason for Norton's assured place in British motorcycling history has been its association with the Isle of Man TT races. The connection began with a victory when the event was first staged in 1907. This was followed by many more successes over the next six decades. In 1908 a Norton bike with an actual Norton engine made its debut, but the year 1913 brought another less welcome first: bankruptcy. The marque had to be bailed out, after which it traded under the name Norton Motors Ltd.

Milestone engine
Photographed in 1940, this road machine was powered by Norton's milestone overhead camshaft engine of 1928.

Just before James Norton's death in 1925, there were further TT wins, but it was the CS1 bike of 1927 that ushered in a golden period. Specializing in an overhead camshaft, these single-cylinder bikes proved popular with the public and a successful policy for the racetrack. Norton could hardly have been more dominant in the Senior TT. Eight races from 1931 to 1938 brought seven victories (with the same number in the Junior 350cc race).

World War II interrupted the TT, but from 1947 it was business as usual, with the Norton sweeping the board in the 500cc class for eight consecutive years. Advertisements lauded the achievement with the strapline "Unapproachable Norton."

For dealers, a major expansion to the Norton range was the twin-cylinder Model 7 Dominator of 1949.

Arguably, many of the important features of the bikes—most particularly the engine—were failing to move with the times, but this was not true of the frame, especially on production machines after 1951. Irish design genius Rex McCandless, who worked with brother Cromie, had told Gilbert Smith, head of Norton, in 1949: "You are not 'Unapproachable' and you are not the world's best roadholder. I have a bicycle which is miles better." He backed these strong words with a featherbed frame that was used on the 500cc Manx racing machines in 1950 and sailed through every test. It was a revolution in handling.

3½HP

500T

Dominator 88

F1 Sport

1898	James Lansdowne Norton founds the company in Birmingham.
1907	Harry Rembrandt "Rem" Fowler wins the twin-cylinder class at the first Isle of Man TT on a Norton with a Peugeot engine.
1908	Norton's own engines replace French and Swiss powerplants.
1913	R. T. Shelley & Co. rescue Norton from bankruptcy.
1922	The Model 18 production bike hits over 89 mph (143 km/h) on the track.

1924	Alec Bennett wins the Isle of Man Senior TT on a Norton, while George H. Tucker takes the Sidecar title.
1925	James Norton dies at the age of 56.
1927	The Walter Moore-designed overhead camshaft single engine has its racing debut.
1931	A decade of success starts with 350cc and 500cc TT wins for Tim Hunt with a redesigned overhead camshaft engine.
1937	Norton supplies over 100,000 of Britain's military motorbikes.

1949	Successful Triumph Speed Twin has a rival in Norton's Dominator Model 7.
1950	Manx Nortons become the world's best-handling racing bikes, using the featherbed frame
1952	Production bikes incorporate the featherbed frame, resulting in the Norton Dominator 88.
1954	Ray Amm gives Norton its eighth straight victory in the Isle of Man Senior TT.
1962	Norton relocates to southeast London.

1967	The 750cc Commando, with vibration-reducing isolastic system, is viewed as the world's first production superbike.
1975	Commando Interstate MkIII is one of just two Norton machines still produced.
1992	Norton receives a welcome boost when Steve Hislop wins the classic Senior TT.
2008	New owner Stuart Garner announces plans to revive the marque.
2010	The twin-cylinder Commando 961 is unveiled and small-scale production begins at the new UK factory.

Pride of Britain
An advertisement for the Norton Dominator De Luxe, which was exhibited at the 1952 Earl's Court Exhibition and promoted as "a superb example of British craftsmanship."

Such was the frame's popularity that Norton became a victim of its own success, unable to keep up with demand, and in 1953, within two years of the featherbed's appearance on production models, Norton was sold into the stable of Associated Motor Cycles (AMC).

The steady erosion of Norton's position in the postwar years reflected the decline of the whole British motorcycle industry. From the end of the 1950s, triumphs on the track were offset by blunders in the boardroom. Inefficient and outmoded equipment and practices, policies stuck in the past, and poor industrial relations led influential designer Bert Hopwood to say of Norton's management: "Never for one moment did they seem to grasp that these particular things were

motorcycles and that we were supposed to be earning a living making them."

In the face of these difficulties, it was a wonder that the marque continued to produce motorcycles of quality; yet in the early 1960s the 650SS Dominator debuted with a new "slimline" featherbed frame. This proved in tests to be superior even to the Triumph Bonneville. Financial calamity, however, always seemed

> ## "It's a **race-bred** bike with loads and **loads** of **torque**. It sure is a **handful**."
> STEVE MCQUEEN ON THE NORTON METISSE, 1966

close at hand. Production was moved from Birmingham to London in 1962, then AMC collapsed in 1966, resurfacing as Norton-Villiers.

Competition from Japanese imports was strong. Norton responded in forceful terms with the Commando range, taking big bikes into a new era. The smooth-riding Commando of 1968 was arguably the best British bike of the time and its 750cc engine took Peter Williams to a popular 1973 TT

Senior TT win
Steve Hislop rides his 180 mph (290 km/h) rotary-engined Norton to the marque's first Isle of Man TT victory for 19 years.

win on the innovative Norton Monocoque racer. Nevertheless, glorious one-offs could not stem the seemingly unstoppable flow of imports.

The marque lurched from crisis to crisis. The merger that created Norton Villiers Triumph in 1973 was followed by constant uncertainty over government subsidies. The final model in the Commando range was the Interstate MkIII 850ES of 1975; by the end of the decade, Norton was no longer a major player in Britain.

A Rotary power unit developed in the 1970s was adopted for a partially successful 1980s relaunch under new management. But, although Steve

Hislop took an epic Senior TT win on a Norton Rotary racer in 1992, it proved to be another false dawn. Grassroots enthusiasm was always present, but the funding and organization to translate this into something more meaningful was harder to come by.

Much later, a savior seemed to arrive in the form of an American, Kenny Dreer. Initially restoring classic Commando models, Dreer was on the cusp of launching the new-design 961 Commando when funds ran out in 2006. The baton was then seized by British entrepreneur Stuart Garner, who oversaw the creation of several 961 variants including Special Edition and Cafe Racer models.

Norton's future now looked more promising. With the company located at Donington Park racing circuit, only around 37 miles (60 km) separated the new Norton base from where its story began. On reviewing the new model, the *Daily Telegraph* declared: "Welcome back, Norton."

Sporting Rides

In Europe, single-cylinder machines were seen as the best sporting mounts. For optimum performance, engineers looked to combustion chamber shape, overhead valves, then overhead camshafts, and even four valves per cylinder. Engine sizes stayed small, partly for nimble handling but also because they were built to racing limits (250, 350, or 500cc). In the US, there were no such limitations.

▷ **Duzmo Sports 1920**

Origin UK

Engine 496cc, single-cylinder

Top speed 85 mph (137 km/h)

Racing enthusiasts John Wallace and Bert le Vack created the Duzmo but struggled to finance its manufacture. Its engine was built by Advance of Northampton, England.

◁ **Blackburne 4 hp 1923**

Origin UK

Engine 500cc, single-cylinder

Top speed 65 mph (105 km/h)

The first Blackburne was introduced in 1913 and updated with three gears and an all-chain drive by 1919. This model, equipped with a large outside flywheel, was smooth-running.

△ **Rudge Multi 1921**

Origin UK

Engine 499cc, single-cylinder

Top speed 65 mph (105 km/h)

While most other makers adopted gearboxes, the Rudge company of Coventry stuck with its variable belt system until it introduced chain drive with a three-speed gearbox on this machine in 1921.

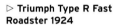

▷ **Triumph Type R Fast Roadster 1924**

Origin UK

Engine 499cc, single-cylinder

Top speed 84 mph (135 km/h)

Harry Ricardo designed this bike, with a four-valve head, which, aided by dry sump lubrication and a light aluminum crankcase, finished second in the 1922 Isle of Man TT.

△ **AJS E6 Big Port 1924**

Origin UK

Engine 349cc, single-cylinder

Top speed 75 mph (121 km/h)

These powerful machines from a 1914 design were steadily improved with overhead-valves in hemispherical combustion chambers to remain competitive in Isle of Man TT racing.

△ **Monet et Goyon Tourisme 1924**

Origin France

Engine 269cc, single-cylinder

Top speed 50 mph (80 km/h)

Joseph Monet and Adrien Goyon made tricycles for disabled servicemen, then motorcycles with Villiers engines such as this one, setting world speed records with a tuned ZS model.

American Fours

In the US, bigger was better, and manufacturers faced fewer restrictions on engine size for racers. Engines grew and they built inline four-cylinder engines bigger than those used to power small sports cars in Europe. These were shoehorned into motorcycle frames to give relaxed, long-legged performance over long and mostly straight American roads. There was "no substitute for cubes."

△ **ACE EXP-4 1923**

Origin USA

Engine 1,229cc, inline four

Top speed 130 mph (209 km/h)

Founded by William G. Henderson in 1920, Ace set out to prove its bikes were the world's fastest, setting a world speed record of 129.61 mph (208.59 km/h) with this bike in 1923.

▷ **Henderson KJ Streamline 1929**

Origin USA

Engine 1,301cc, inline four

Top speed 102 mph (164 km/h)

Improved cooling, leading-link forks, an inlet over exhaust layout, and a five-bearing crank made this the ultimate Henderson; even the 1929 Wall Street Crash could not kill it.

△ NSU 18PS Sport 1924

Origin Germany

Engine 1,000cc, V-twin

Top speed 76 mph (122 km/h)

NSU introduced a V-twin in 1905, enlarged it to nearly 1,000cc in 1909, and set a US coast-to-coast speed record with it in 1910. It continued to develop in the 1920s, as seen in the model shown.

△ Spiegler 350 1924

Origin Germany

Engine 348cc, single-cylinder

Top speed 56 mph (90 km/h)

A beam-type frame, with sheet metal covering, gave this Spiegler a distinctive look. The company made side-valve as well as overhead models from 1923 to 1932.

▷ Velocette Model K 1925

Origin UK

Engine 348cc, single-cylinder

Top speed 75 mph (121 km/h)

Percy Goodman designed an overhead-camshaft engine for the 1925 Velocette; it was good enough to win its first Junior TT by a 10-minute margin.

△ Cleveland Tornado 1929

Origin USA

Engine 1,000cc, inline four

Top speed 102 mph (164 km/h)

A most unfortunately timed launch, Cleveland's guaranteed 100 mph (160 km/h) Tornado arrived weeks before the Wall Street Crash. Very few were completed before the model was dropped.

△ Indian 402 1930

Origin USA

Engine 1,265cc, inline four

Top speed 95 mph (153 km/h)

Indian purchased Ace in 1927 and developed the 402 with a sturdier twin-downtube frame and five-bearing crankshaft—it made a great police pursuit machine.

Sporting Rides (cont.)

By the close of the 1920s, many makers were abandoning flat, box-shaped fuel tanks in favor of the more shapely and streamlined saddle tanks, so called because of the way they fitted over the bike frame. Tubular frames with rigid rear ends were the norm, but there were bold attempts to break away from the "engine-in-a-bicycle" format.

△ **Schüttoff F350 RS 1926**

Origin Germany

Engine 348cc, single-cylinder

Top speed 70 mph (113 km/h)

Arthur Schüttoff made four-strokes and two-strokes from 1923. This four-valve 350 enjoyed racing success, but the company was absorbed by DKW in 1931.

◁ **Zündapp EM250 1927**

Origin Germany

Engine 249cc, single-cylinder

Top speed 60 mph (97 km/h)

Zündapp's 1921 "motorcycle for every man" was replaced in 1925 by this improved 250 two-stroke, with a reinforced frame and fork web. It became a best-seller.

▷ **Francis-Barnett Super Sport 1927**

Origin UK

Engine 172cc, single-cylinder

Top speed 60 mph (97 km/h)

The F-B's bolted-up frame could be dismantled and packed in a golf bag. The Super Sport's little Villiers engine boasted numerous speed records.

▷ **Norton Model 18 1927**

Origin UK

Engine 490cc, single-cylinder

Top speed 78 mph (126 km/h)

This is a road version of Norton's first overhead-valve single, winner of both the Sidecar and Senior TT races in 1924 and holder of the world 1km record at 89.22 mph (143.59 km/h). Road Model 18s were made until 1954.

△ **Ardie 500 1927**

Origin Germany

Engine 490cc, single-cylinder

Top speed 56 mph (90 km/h)

After the death of founder Arno Dietrich, the Bendit family took over and built conventional and powerful machines like this model with British JAP engines and Hurth gearboxes.

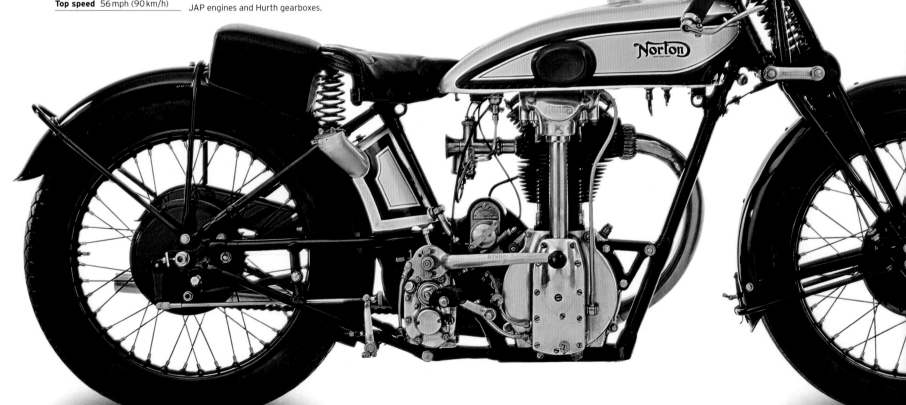

△ Ariel Model E 1928

Origin UK

Engine 499cc, single-cylinder

Top speed 73 mph (117 km/h)

Ariel recruited Val Page to update its engines in 1925, and the new rakish-looking Ariels dramatically improved sales. Between 1927 and 1928, sales were 10 times higher than in 1925.

◁ Moto Guzzi Tipo Sport 1928

Origin Italy

Engine 498cc, single-cylinder

Top speed 76 mph (122 km/h)

Founded in 1921, the sporting Italian factory favored a near-horizontal cylinder to keep weight low. Overhead-camshaft factory racers like this one were race winners.

△ Mars A20 Sport 1928

Origin Germany

Engine 956cc, flat-twin

Top speed 88 mph (142 km/h)

Bicycle-maker Mars started adding engines in 1903. In 1920 Claus Franzenburger designed this legendary "White Mars," with a pressed/welded frame and Maybach engine.

△ Dot J343 1928

Origin UK

Engine 350cc, single-cylinder

Top speed 72 mph (115 km/h)

Manchester-based Dot courted racing success in its early years; by the late 1920s it used an overhead-valve JAP engine. But the company struggled for sales.

△ Harley-Davidson Model B 1928

Origin USA

Engine 350cc, single-cylinder

Top speed 53 mph (85 km/h)

Like Harley's other single-cylinder bikes—both side- and overhead-valve—this Model B was every inch a scaled-down V-twin. These bikes were introduced in 1926 to rival Indian's range of smaller machines.

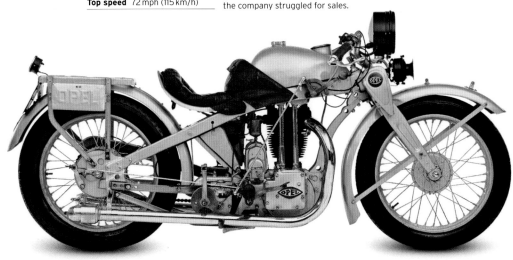

◁ Sunbeam Model 9 1929

Origin UK

Engine 493cc, single-cylinder

Top speed 82 mph (132 km/h)

Sunbeam's high-quality range included the overhead valve long-stroke Model 9 for sports riding. It had a fully enclosed chain and this one has a picnic basket.

△ Opel Motoclub 1929

Origin Germany

Engine 496cc, single-cylinder

Top speed 74 mph (119 km/h)

Alongside bicycles, sewing machines, and cars, Opel also made motorcycles from 1901 to 1930. Its finest bike was this overhead-valve sporting machine, with a novel pressed-steel frame.

◁ Norton CS1 1928

Origin UK

Engine 488cc, single-cylinder

Top speed 85 mph (137 km/h)

The CS1 (Competition Senior) had Norton's landmark overhead-camshaft engine, winner of the 1927 Senior TT, which would soon be eclipsed by a redesigned engine.

◁ Norton 16H 1929

Origin UK

Engine 490cc, single-cylinder

Top speed 68 mph (109 km/h)

The side-valve 16H was descended from Norton's earlier side-valve racer, which set many world speed records. First used in 1916, the model code survived until 1954.

TT winner Stanley
Woods on a Moto Guzzi
in the 1930s

Great Marques
The Moto Guzzi Story

With an illustrious racing pedigree and a constant emphasis
on ingenuity, Moto Guzzi has been making high-quality
motorcycles since the end of World War I. Its Grand Tourer
and performance models have earned the marque a reputation
for producing some of the finest bikes in the world.

THE SEEDS OF AN IDEA for an all-new motorcycle company were sown by three friends serving in the Italian Air Corps during World War I. However, before Carlo Guzzi, Giorgio Parodi, and Giovanni Ravelli could turn their engineering talents to bikes, tragedy struck: Ravelli was killed in an air crash just days after the end of the war.

Undeterred, the following year Guzzi and Parodi built their first prototype in a workshop in Mandello del Lario in northern Italy, where the

Carlo Guzzi
(1889-1964)

Recognizing the value racing could have in promoting the new company, Carlo Guzzi entered two bikes in the Milan–Naples race of 1921. Although they finished down the field, the potential of the Moto Guzzi bikes was realized a few weeks later when Gino Finzi won the illustrious Targa Florio event for them. That the marque could take such prestigious racing laurels in its first year heralded a golden era of competition success that would see Moto Guzzi secure more than 3,000 Grand Prix wins by 1957.

"Guzzi **gadabouts** have all the fun!"

1960S ADVERTISEMENT FOR MOTO GUZZI SCRAMBLER

factory remains. Known as the GP after the two founders' initials, the 500cc single featured elements of aircraft-engine technology and could reach 62 mph (100 km/h). Key to Carlo Guzzi's philosophy was that every component should be thoroughly considered and that the bike should be fun to ride. It was an ethos that would underpin the company.

The project really took shape when Parodi's father, Emanuele Vittorio, provided backing for the enterprise. By the time the first production model, the Normale, was ready, in 1921, the Società Anonima Moto Guzzi company had been formed.

The fledgling company expanded and new premises allowed annual production to shoot up from 17 bikes in 1921 to 1,200 in 1925. Innovation was always at the core of Moto Guzzi. Attached to the Normale's frame was a center stand—which would soon become standard on most motorcycles—and in 1928 a swingarm rear suspension was introduced on its Guzzi GT.

Wind-tunnel pioneers
In 1950 Moto Guzzi became the first motorcycle manufacturer to build a dedicated wind tunnel in which to develop its machines. This resulted in models with blistering performance.

Dondolino

V8

Le Mans MkI

Daytona 1000

1919 Friends Carlo Guzzi and Giorgio Parodi
build the first prototype, a 500cc single.
1921 Società Anonima Moto Guzzi
is established, releasing its debut
Normale model; Gino Finzi wins the
Targa Florio on a Moto Guzzi.
1924 Guido Mentasti wins the European
Championship on a 4V model.
1928 The Guzzi GT becomes the first Grand
Tourer motorcycle on the market.
1935 Stanley Woods wins both the 250cc
and 500cc TT races on a Moto Guzzi.

1936 The Airone 250 debuts, featuring a
pedal-operated four-speed transmission.
1946 Introduction of the 65 Guzzino, a frugal
two-stroke that will be developed into
the Cardellino and produced into the
early 1960s.
1950 Moto Guzzi becomes the first
manufacturer to build a dedicated wind
tunnel to test its motorcycles.
1955 Debut of Moto Guzzi's fabulous
500cc water-cooled V8 Grand Prix
racing engine.

1965 A 700cc 90-degree V-twin engine is
debuted; it will become the core
configuration for larger models.
1967 A V7 model is unveiled, which in an
enlarged special version will break
several speeds records at Monza in
1969; SEIMM takes over the company.
1971 The California V-twin tourer enters the
US market; it is still in production.
1973 De Tomaso Industries buys Moto Guzzi.
1975 The Guzzi 254, featuring a four-
cylinder engine, is released.

1976 The 850 Le Mans is unveiled: a fast
superbike that will be made until 1993.
1977 The V35 is released, featuring a V-twin
unit on a smaller (350cc) engine.
2000 Moto Guzzi is taken over by fellow
Italian motorcycle maker Aprilia.
2004 The Moto Piaggio Group buys the
Aprilia-Moto-Guzzi concern, forming
Europe's largest motorcycle
manufacturer.
2008 The Guzzi Stelvio adventure-touring
bike is released to great acclaim.

By the mid-1930s Moto Guzzi was Italy's principal motorcycle manufacturer. A new 120-degree V-twin engine had been developed that could power the 500 cc twin to speeds in excess of 125 mph (200 km/h), while other key models included the P125 and P150, plus racing bikes such as the Condor, Albatross, and Dondolino. Notable competition wins included victory at the 1935 Isle of Man TT, the first non-English marque to achieve the feat for 24 years. The decade was rounded off with the release of the ultra-successful Airone 250 model, which would be produced until 1957.

A brief pause during World War II did nothing to halt Moto Guzzi's innovative streak. The marque met the Italian demand for lightweight, inexpensive models with offerings such as its debut twin-cylinder bike, the Guzzino 65, and in the 1950 Galletto, the world's first large-wheeled scooter. In 1955 Moto Guzzi's celebrated designer Giulio Cesara Carcano devised a landmark racing machine, the Guzzi Otto Cilindri. It was the first eight-cylinder machine seen in Grand Prix racing, capable of 177 mph (285 km/h). However, before the V8's potential was realized, commercial realities forced Guzzi to withdraw from racing at the end of 1957.

V-twin power
One of the seminal motorcycles in Moto Guzzi's history, the V7 featured the marque's first 90-degree V-twin engine.

The 1950s and early 1960s saw a dip in fortunes for Moto Guzzi, as cheap cars threatened the motorcycle market. After Carlo Guzzi's death in 1964, Giorgio Parodi's brother Enrico took over. Three years later Moto Guzzi was bought by SEIMM, and the new owner's decision to produce low-cost models was reflected in the release of mopeds such as the Trotter.

However, large-capacity bikes were not overlooked. The 1967 V7 featured the company's first transverse V-twin engine with shaft final drive, developed out of a military vehicle contract. The larger-capacity V7 Special was designed for the North American market, and served as the basis for US models, including the California.

In 1973 De Tomaso Industries bought Moto Guzzi. The new owners diversified the company's model range, and new four-cylinder bikes and small-capacity tourers were unveiled. Important high-performance models that boosted exports including the striking 850cc Le Mans of 1977 and the 1992 Daytona 1000, with an overhead camshaft engine developed in the US by John Wittner.

During the 1990s Moto Guzzi went back to producing the classically styled models for which it was renowned. However, the company went through a transitional period as profits slumped during the early part of the decade. Several changes in ownership culminated in Aprilia's taking control of the Moto Guzzi marque in 2000. Moto Guzzi was again under new ownership four years later when the Piaggio Group bought the company to create Europe's largest motorcycle manufacturer. Since then, new models have been released that reflect the company's sporting (Griso 1100) and touring (Norge 1200) heritage, as well as updated versions of iconic models such as the V7 Classic of 2008.

With 90 years of uninterrupted motorcycle production under its belt, Moto Guzzi continues to personify the spirit and passion of Italy more than any other motorcycle marque.

Expanding company
In the first decade of the 21st century, Moto Guzzi's output steadily increased, and it is now part of Europe's largest motorcycle manufacturing group.

Survival of the Fittest

Flexible power and easy handling were the most important requirements for the average 1920s motorcyclist, who simply wanted a comfortable and economical means of transportation for work and play. While some machines were built more cheaply and turned out in quantity, other marques fell by the wayside as they could neither afford to update their technology nor cut their prices.

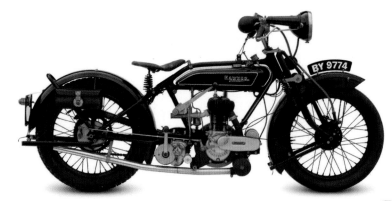

◁ Clyno 2¼hp 1920
Origin UK
Engine 269cc, single-cylinder
Top speed 45 mph (72 km/h)

Frank and Ailwyn Smith made motorcycles from 1910, having taken over the Stevens engine factory, but moved entirely to car-making in 1923.

△ Hawker Model C 1922
Origin UK
Engine 348cc, single-cylinder
Top speed 52 mph (84 km/h)

To occupy their aircraft mechanics in the lull after WWI, Harry Hawker and Tom Sopwith built motorcycles from 1920 to 1924, this one with a Blackburne side-valve engine.

△ Sun Vitesse 1923
Origin UK
Engine 269cc, single-cylinder
Top speed 56 mph (90 km/h)

Sun took over production of the advanced, VTS two-stroke engine with rotary-valve induction and made this sportster. The company made no bikes from 1932 to 1948.

△ Seal Four-seater 1924
Origin UK
Engine 980cc, V-twin
Top speed 50 mph (80 km/h)

This extraordinary Seal three-wheeler allows the driver to sit in the sidecar with the passengers, steering by remote linkage. This model was discontinued after 1924.

◁ Ivy Three 1924
Origin UK
Engine 346cc, single-cylinder
Top speed 55 mph (89 km/h)

Ivy's two-stroke tourer has the latest type of drum front brake, footboards, and leg shields. A 350cc Ivy won a Brooklands 500-mile (805-km) race averaging 52 mph (84 km/h).

▷ **Quadrant 4¹/₂hp 1924**

Origin UK

Engine 624cc, single-cylinder

Top speed 57 mph (92 km/h)

Quadrant's robust side-valve single has its inlet valve behind the cylinder, but these unexciting machines began to look dated by the mid-1920s.

◁ **Triumph Model P 1925**

Origin UK

Engine 493cc, single-cylinder

Top speed 65 mph (105 km/h)

Britain's cheapest 500 ever, this was Triumph's first mass-produced motorcycle; 1,000 were turned out every week. Early quality problems were addressed by 1926.

△ **Henley Blackburne Tourer 1925**

Origin UK

Engine 545cc, single-cylinder

Top speed 57 mph (92 km/h)

Henley made motorcycles in Birmingham from 1920, soon settling on a range of side-valve Blackburne engines. This largest one was also sold with a sidecar.

▷ **Sunbeam 3¹/₂hp Model 5 Solo 1925**

Origin UK

Engine 499cc, single-cylinder

Top speed 80 mph (129 km/h)

The Model 5, with its low-revving, long-stroke, side-valve engine, was built to go long distances. Sunbeam's 1922 Senior TT win was the last by a side-valver.

△ **BSA S28 1928**

Origin UK

Engine 493cc, single-cylinder

Top speed 60 mph (97 km/h)

Harold Briggs joined BSA from Daimler in the 1920s to design new engines, including this flexible side-valve 500 that was ideal for touring and combinations.

◁ **Wanderer K500 1928**

Origin Germany

Engine 499cc, single-cylinder

Top speed 59 mph (95 km/h)

This is a sophisticated shaft-drive machine with leaf spring forks. Wanderer, which had built motorcycles since 1902, stopped production in 1929 and then sold this design to Jawa.

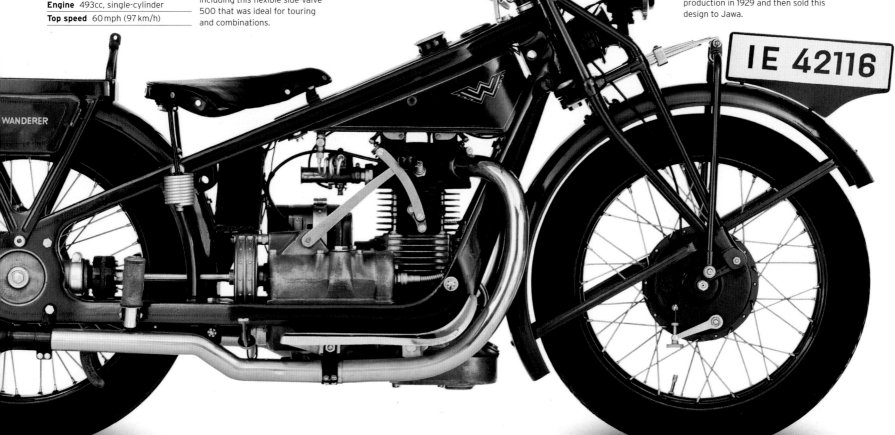

La Jumella ("The Twin"), 1922
Captured at the Champ-de-Mars, Paris, this unusual motorcycle is possibly an extended version of an early Ner-a-Car model. Similar in concept to a forecar, but with just two wheels, it may have been used as a commercial taxi.

Out of the Mainstream

Innovative engineers experimented with many new ideas for two-wheeled transportation in the 1920s, some brilliantly practical, others technological dead ends. Air, water, and oil were used as coolants, horizontally opposed cylinders were laid transversely across the frame, and radical ideas were tried in attempts to boost power from two-stroke engines. Chassis technology was slower to change, although there were some bold attempts to break the mold.

◁ **Humber 4¹/₂hp 1921**
Origin UK
Engine 601cc, flat-twin
Top speed 60 mph (97 km/h)

After a most unusual flat-three in 1913, Humber made flat-twins from 1915, including this quality "Silent Humber" with a three-speed gearbox and chain transmission.

△ **ABC 400 1921**
Origin UK
Engine 398cc, flat-twin
Top speed 70 mph (113 km/h)

Innovative designer Granville Bradshaw's ABC pioneered the transverse flat-twin engine and rear frame springing. It was built by Sopwith Aviation.

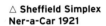

△ **Sheffield Simplex Ner-a-Car 1921**
Origin UK
Engine 285cc, single-cylinder
Top speed 35 mph (56 km/h)

Designed by American Carl Neracher and built in both the US and the UK, this was a very stable bike with constantly variable transmission, a low build, and hub-center steering.

△ **OK Bradshaw 1922**
Origin UK
Engine 349cc, single-cylinder
Top speed 60 mph (97 km/h)

Fred Dawes and Ernie Humphries made motorcycles from 1911. The Bradshaw engine relied on oil cooling for its cylinder barrel, but was known as the "oil boiler."

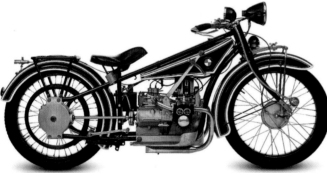

△ **BMW R32 1923**
Origin Germany
Engine 486cc, flat-twin
Top speed 59 mph (95 km/h)

The first motorcycle from BMW had the now-traditional flat-twin layout with wet sump lubrication and aluminum alloy cylinders and heads, plus a shaft drive.

△ **DOT Bradshaw 1923**
Origin UK
Engine 349cc cc, single-cylinder
Top speed 60mph (97 km/h)

Harry Reed of Manchester built successful sporting bikes; this one had an oil-cooled Bradshaw engine, internal expanding brakes, three gears, and a chain drive.

△ **Smart Celle du Salon 1923**
Origin France
Engine 150cc, single-cylinder
Top speed 50 mph (80 km/h)

This simple two-stroke model, with a two-speed gearbox and enclosed primary drive, was the product of a short-lived marque that only lasted from 1923 to 1927.

△ Dunelt Model K 1925

Origin	UK
Engine	249cc, single-cylinder
Top speed	65 mph (105 km/h)

Reliable Dunelt Model K engines used double-diameter pistons to boost cylinder filling from the crankcase. An earlier 500cc version was replaced by this 250cc single.

▽ Scott Super Squirrel 1927

Origin	UK
Engine	498cc, inline twin
Top speed	80 mph (129 km/h)

Alfred Scott's innovative two-stroke engine design lasted well after his death in 1923. The popular three-speed Super Squirrel sports bike was sold in 500cc, as here, or in 600cc form.

△ Böhmerland Three-seater 1927

Origin	Czech Republic
Engine	603cc, single-cylinder
Top speed	70 mph (113 km/h)

This extraordinary bike has cast-alloy wheels, rear-mounted fuel tanks, and a very long tubular frame with tension spring front forks. The engine has open valve gear.

◁ Windhoff 750-4 1928

Origin	Germany
Engine	748cc, inline four
Top speed	74 mph (119 km/h)

An unorthodox machine with an oil-cooled, overhead-camshaft, inline four-cylinder engine. A subframe attached to the power unit carried the shaft-driven rear wheel.

▷ DKW ZSW 500 1929

Origin	Germany
Engine	494cc, inline twin
Top speed	62 mph (100 km/h)

DKW was the world's largest motorcycle-maker at the time, so it could afford to experiment with unconventional machines like this water-cooled, two-stroke twin.

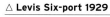

△ Levis Six-port 1929

Origin	UK
Engine	247cc, single-cylinder
Top speed	66 mph (106 km/h)

Levis won an Isle of Man TT with its sporty two-strokes, and this was their fastest. The Six-port had extra cylinder joints that cooled the piston with incoming unburned fuel.

Track Contenders

Many motorcycle-makers subscribed to the view that racing improved the breed, and there was plenty of evidence to support that contention. Overhead camshafts and four-valve cylinder heads became more common on racing machines in the 1920s, while minimizing weight led to the construction of clean, simple, and effective frames, and the use of lightweight alloys for engine and transmission casings.

△ Norton Model 9 1920

Origin UK

Engine 490cc, single-cylinder

Top speed 70 mph (113 km/h)

The Model 9's side-valve engine dated back to James Lansdowne Norton's first engine of 1908. It was flexible and powerful but outdated, with no clutch or gears.

△ Harley-Davidson Eight-valve Racer 1920

Origin USA

Engine 1,000cc, V-twin

Top speed 120 mph (193 km/h)

Also known as the Model 12 racer, this bike was built in very small numbers up to 1928. It was a highly specialized machine with four valve heads, no exhaust pipes, just one speed, and no brakes.

▷ Indian Model H 1920

Origin USA

Engine 1,000cc, V-twin

Top speed 120 mph (193 km/h)

Indian's powerful V-twins were top contenders in board track racing from the start. This machine uses a side-valve engine based on the Powerplus model.

△ Harley-Davidson Model 28S Board Racer 1926

Origin USA

Engine 345cc, single-cylinder

Top speed 85 mph (137 km/h)

Called "peashooters" because of the noise they made, Harley's ultra-light 216-lb (98-kg) board racers with overhead-valve engines cleaned up on the flat tracks in the 1930s.

◁ Megola 1921 1923

Origin Germany

Engine 640cc, rotary five-cylinder

Top speed 88 mph (142 km/h)

A Monosoupape aero engine driving the front wheel (and rotating with it) was the method of propulsion for the Megola. The bike won a German Championship race in 1924.

◁ **OEC Claude Temple 1923**

Origin UK

Engine 996cc, V-twin

Top speed 121mph (195 km/h)

Lincoln motorcycle-maker OEC built frames for Brooklands champion Claude Temple, who equipped this bike with a British Anzani aero engine to set world speed records from 1923 to 1926.

△ **Sunbeam Sprinter 1923**

Origin UK

Engine 499cc, single-cylinder

Top speed 95mph (153 km/h)

After WWI and throughout the 1920s, stripped-down Sunbeams like the Sprinter were hugely successful in sprints and racing, winning all over Europe.

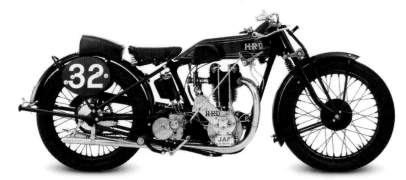

△ **HRD HD90 1924**

Origin UK

Engine 488cc, single-cylinder

Top speed 100mph (160 km/h)

One of his early motorcycles, Howard Raymond Davies (HRD) built bikes from 1924 to 1928 to race in the Isle of Man TT and for road use. He won the TT on his own machine in 1925.

▽ **Indian Scout Hillclimber 1927**

Origin USA

Engine 740cc, V-twin

Top speed 75mph (120 km/h)

With a low build, small front wheel, negligible brakes, and a big rear cog, this Indian was built for hill climbing—a sport developed to encourage sales of smaller bikes.

◁ **Scott TT Super Squirrel 1927**

Origin UK

Engine 498cc, inline twin

Top speed 95mph (153 km/h)

The water-cooled Scotts won the Isle of Man Senior TT race before WWI. The bikes were competitive in the 1920s too, but did not win. This Super Squirrel is British rider Harry Langman's 1927 TT bike.

▷ **Moto Guzzi SS 1928**

Origin Italy

Engine 247cc, single-cylinder

Top speed 78mph (126 km/h)

After WWI, the aircraft mechanic Carlo Guzzi designed an overhead-camshaft, horizontal engine that continued to be manufactured for the next for 45 years; in a rigid, light frame, it gave a low centre of gravity.

▷ **Chater-Lea Special "Copperknob" 1929**

Origin UK

Engine 348cc, single-cylinder

Top speed 110mph (177 km/h)

Ben Joe Bickell built Copperknob with a damaged Chater-Lea frame and an overhead-camshaft Chater-Lea engine, then won races at Brooklands.

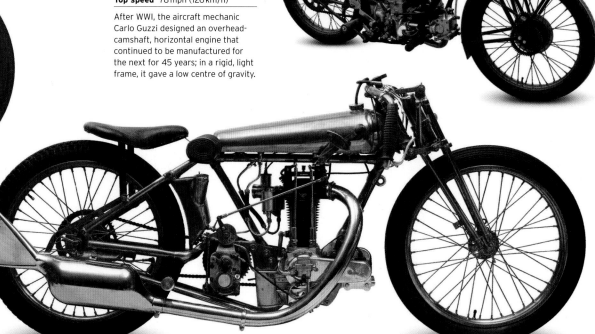

The
1930s

The Great Depression that followed the 1929 collapse of the New York Stock Exchange changed the emphasis of motorcycle production from speed to economy. Some manufacturers came through the crisis as buyers looked for the best-priced transportation, but many were unable to compete and disappeared. In the later 1930s international markets opened up, spreading innovative ideas around the world. European racing saw a flowering of engine technology; by contrast, US racing moved toward special editions only available to a few.

New Sophistication

Having established an effective formula for making a motorcycle in the previous decade, the focus in the 1930s was on refining and improving. Manufacturers sought to produce prestige machines, with improvements in performance, comfort, reliability, and cleanliness. Following the fashion of the time by featuring colorful paint finishes and bright chromium plating, these were the most stylish and comfortable machines yet produced. However, they reached the market during the severe recession that followed the 1929 New York stock market crash.

△ AJS S3 1931

Origin UK

Engine 498cc, side-valve V-twin

Top speed 65 mph (105 km/h)

The transversely mounted engine was unusual, but the S3 offered no big advantage over simpler machines and was soon dropped from the AJS range.

△ Ascot-Pullin Utility De Luxe 1930

Origin UK

Engine 496cc, ohv single-cylinder

Top speed 80 mph (129 km/h)

The novel pressed-steel bodywork of this machine housed a horizontally mounted engine with an integral gearbox. It was well engineered, but did not sell.

△ Ariel 4F Square Four 1931

Origin UK

Engine 498cc, ohc square four

Top speed 85 mph (137 km/h)

Four cylinders in a square layout made the 4F impressively fast, smooth, and compact compared to other machines; but it was complex.

◁ Ariel SG 1931

Origin UK

Engine 499cc, ohv single-cylinder

Top speed 80 mph (129 km/h)

Sloping cylinders were briefly popular with some manufacturers in the 1930s. Ariel offered them alongside their usual vertical-engined models.

◁ Matchless Model A Silver Arrow 1930

Origin UK

Engine 394cc, side-valve V-twin

Top speed 55 mph (89 km/h)

The Silver Arrow combined the luxury of rear suspension with the low performance of a 400cc side-valve engine; it was not a big seller.

△ Matchless Silver Hawk 1933

Origin UK

Engine 592cc, ohc V-four

Top speed 80 mph (129 km/h)

Built in response to the Ariel 4F Square Four, the equally sophisticated Matchless had a far shorter life span and was discontinued in 1935.

△ Scott Model 3S Triple 1938

Origin UK

Engine 986cc, two-stroke three-cylinder

Top speed 100 mph (160 km/h)

The 1938 version of the Scott triple was innovative and stylish. The outbreak of WWII halted production; only eight were ever built.

△ BMW R12 1935

Origin Germany

Engine 745cc, side-valve flat-twin

Top speed 68 mph (109 km/h)

The R12 was the first production bike with hydraulically damped telescopic forks; its advanced specification also included a four-speed gearbox.

△ BMW R66 1938

Origin Germany

Engine 597cc, ohv flat-twin

Top speed 90 mph (145 km/h)

With a plunger rear suspension, telescopic forks, shaft drive, and a four-speed gearbox, the R66 was among the best-equipped bikes in the world.

△ Indian Four 1939

Origin USA

Engine 1,265cc, inline four

Top speed 90 mph (145 km/h)

The smooth power of the four-cylinder engine was ideal for these high-performance, long-distance machines that topped the Indian range in the 1930s.

▽ Brough Superior Dream 1939

Origin UK

Engine 998cc, opposed four-cylinder

Top speed not known

The Dream never made it to production; only prototypes of this extraordinary shaft drive flat-four were built before Brough stopped making motorcycles.

△ Gnome et Rhône Type X 1939

Origin France

Engine 724cc, ohv flat-twin

Top speed 90 mph (145 km/h)

This was one of the most imposing French-built machines of the 1930s and was ideal for use with a sidecar.

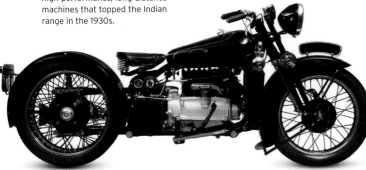

△ Brough Superior Austin Four 1932

Origin UK

Engine 800cc, side-valve inline four

Top speed 80 mph (129 km/h)

With a water-cooled car engine and an electric starter, this shaft-driven luxury machine with twin rear wheels was intended mainly for sidecar use.

Ariel 4F Square Four

Created by legendary motorcycle designer Edward Turner, the Ariel 4F Square Four was a revelation when it was unveiled in 1930. It had the proportions of a single-cylinder bike, yet boasted a powerful, compact four-cylinder engine. The model originally featured a 498cc unit, but larger-capacity engines of up to 995cc were later offered. During the Square Four's 28-year life span, the bike gained a reputation as a fine touring and sidecar machine.

A BOLD DECISION by Ariel's chief, Jack Sangster, led to Ariel's production of the Square Four, when it could easily have been made by another marque. Edward Turner had been touting his innovative design for an overhead camshaft four-cylinder engine to various motorcycle manufacturers before Sangster saw its potential and hired the designer to develop a machine using this configuration. Presented at the 1930 Olympia Motorcycle Show, the Square Four was an immediate hit, with crowds impressed by the creative box-shape arrangement of the engine's four cylinders (the configuration which gave rise to its name, as well as its nickname— the "Squariel"). In 1932, the engine was enlarged to 601cc and for 1937 it was redesigned as a 995cc unit with pushrod valve gear. Into the 1940s, the bike was advertised with slogans such as "Sets the pace and the standard," alongside impressive performance times such as 0–60mph (100km/h) in 8½ seconds. By the time the Square Four had ceased production at the end of the 1950s, it had earned its place as one of the most appealing British machines of the era.

FRONT VIEW

REAR VIEW

Cycle roots
The Ariel name was first seen on bicycles in the late 19th century. The Ariel Cycle Company began developing motorized versions of its bicycles in the first few years of the 20th century.

Spring for girder
front forks

Instrument console
on fuel tank

Lever for hand-
operated gears

Muffler for twin-pipe
exhaust system

Sprung saddle
attaches directly
to frame

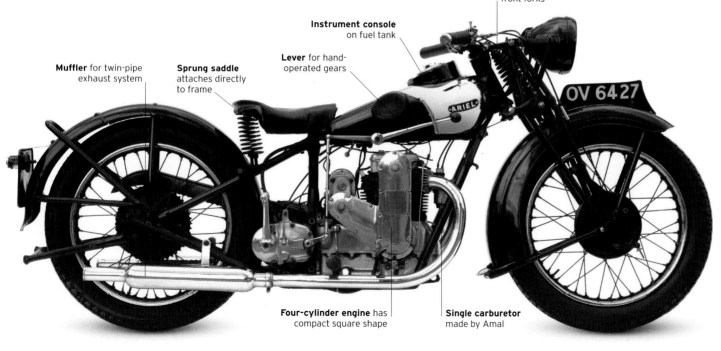

Four-cylinder engine has
compact square shape

Single carburetor
made by Amal

Early features

The 4F Square Four's Burman-made gearbox was originally operated by a lever located next to the fuel tank. The twin-girder front forks, as seen here, were replaced in 1946 by hydraulically damped telescopic forks.

SPECIFICATIONS			
Model	Ariel 4F Square Four (1931)	**Power output**	24 hp at 6,000 rpm
Assembly	Birmingham, England	**Transmission**	Four-speed
Production	15,641 (all models)	**Suspension**	Girder front forks
Construction	Steel frame	**Brakes**	Drums, front and rear
Engine	498cc, ohc square-four	**Maximum speed**	85 mph (137 km/h)

THE BIKE

The 4F Square Four was not really about brisk performance, the bike aimed to achieve exceptional smoothness and flexibility. These qualities were combined with reliability in the more sedate post-1936 overhead-valve models. The 1,000cc version was considered the ultimate civilized touring machine and ideal for pulling sidecars. The ride-on postwar version was improved by telescopic front forks and the option of plunger rear suspension, while the MkII, manufactured from 1953, was the first version capable of hitting 100mph (160km/h).

1. Ariel badge **2.** Choke lever on handlebar **3.** Lights switch
4. Six-volt headlight **5.** Comfortable saddle **6.** Four-speed hand-change gearbox **7.** Fuel cap and dashboard panel **8.** Drive sprocket
9. Front suspension damper **10.** Horn **11.** Rear brake pedal
12. Kick-starter **13.** Muffler

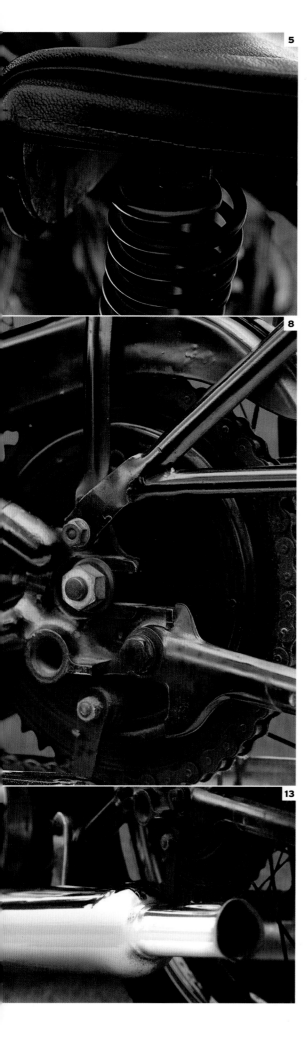

THE ENGINE

Turner's original four-cylinder engine was created by using two parallel twin units within a single crankcase. Engine capacity increased to a final 995cc unit on the 1937 4G model, with an ohv configuration. Later key changes included replacing the MkI's iron cylinder head and barrel with lighter, alloy components from 1949, and a redesigned head on the MkII in 1953.

14. Compact engine unit **15.** Ignition magneto under six-volt dynamo **16.** Camshaft chain casing **17.** Main and reserve fuel taps **18.** Ignition distributor **19.** Air intake

Speed Club

By the start of the 1930s, racing influence, led by the high-mileage Isle of Man TT races, had advanced development of sporting motorcycles. Ever-higher top speeds saw some 500cc machines approaching the 100 mph (161 km/h) mark. Engines were revving harder, while stronger frames and much-improved forks helped handling. Throughout the decade, British motorcycles led the way in technology.

▷ **Chater-Lea Super Sports 1930**

Origin UK

Engine 350cc, single-cylinder

Top speed 95 mph (153 km/h)

This model's engine had an unusual face-cam system for its valve operation. A tuned example raised the 350cc flying kilometer record to 102.99 mph (165.74 km/h).

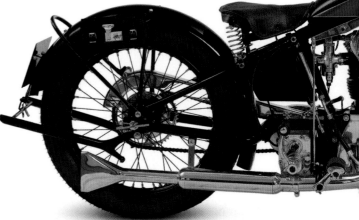

◁ **Scott TT Replica 1930**

Origin UK

Engine 498cc, single-cylinder

Top speed 88 mph (142 km/h)

Alfred Scott's fastest twin was based on a pre-WWI design. It was no longer competitive in TT racing but it was still in demand for fast road riding.

▷ **Sunbeam Model 90 1930**

Origin UK

Engine 493cc, single-cylinder

Top speed 91 mph (146 km/h)

Despite being fundamentally a 1920s design, the Model 90 was still competitive with the best of the Nortons in 1930, aided by a four-speed gearbox and saddle tank.

△ **Norton ES2 Model 18 1934**

Origin UK

Engine 490cc, single-cylinder

Top speed 82 mph (132 km/h)

Norton finally enclosed its valve gear in 1938, making it much quieter and cleaner; the ES2 also had a full cradle frame and, optionally, a plunger rear suspension.

▽ **Norton International Model 30 1936**

Origin UK

Engine 490cc, single-cylinder

Top speed 95 mph (153 km/h)

The most handsome sporting motorcycle of its time, Model 30 was also available with an all-aluminum engine and race-style oil tank for wealthy riders who wanted a race-winning machine.

▷ Standard Rex Sport 1935

Origin Germany

Engine 491cc, single-cylinder

Top speed 80 mph (129 km/h)

Standard Rexs were built from 1925. This sporting Rex had an overhead-camshaft engine with an inclined cylinder and front forks made under license from Brough Superior.

▷ Excelsior Manxman 1936

Origin UK

Engine 250cc, single-cylinder

Top speed 80 mph (129 km/h)

The prototype twin-cam, four-valve Manxman won the Lightweight TT in 1933, but the production bike had two valves until 1936, when this four-valve was launched.

◁ Harley-Davidson EL61 1936

Origin USA

Engine 989cc, V-twin

Top speed 70 mph (113 km/h)

Harley added overhead valves to its V-twin in 1936. This became known as the "Knucklehead" engine and was used in a new, more modern frame: the classic Harley.

△ Rudge Ulster 1937

Origin UK

Engine 499cc, single-cylinder

Top speed 92 mph (148 km/h)

A speedy machine named after Rudge's first four-valver win at the 1928 Ulster Grand Prix. The troubled company was bought by the Gramophone Company in 1936.

▷ Brough Superior SS80 1937

Origin UK

Engine 982cc, V-twin

Top speed 85 mph (137 km/h)

Introduced in the early 1920s, the SS80 was guaranteed to reach 80 mph (129 km/h). In 1935 the original JAP engine was replaced with the Associated Motor Cycles (AMC) engine seen on this model.

▷ Ariel Red Hunter 1937

Origin UK

Engine 497cc, single-cylinder

Top speed 84 mph (135 km/h)

Val Page conceived the Red Hunter series in 1932, with 250, 350, and 500cc engines. Robust, reliable, and powerful, these bikes sold well right up to 1959.

Speed Club (cont.)

By the 1930s the motorcycle market had become relatively sophisticated, with a variety of buyers seeking different styles of bikes. For many, performance was a major factor and the manufacturers responded by offering sporting versions of their basic models, or by creating special high-performance machines with highly tuned engines that were, in some cases, directly related to racing models. And obviously it was important to advertise the bike's potential by making sure that it looked good too.

△ **Indian Sport Scout 1936**

Origin USA

Engine 737cc, side-valve V-twin

Top speed 85 mph (137 km/h)

The Scout formed the basis for many racing machines; owners removed the headlight and other extras, tuned the engine, and took to the track.

◁ **AJS R10 1936**

Origin UK

Engine 495cc, ohc single-cylinder

Top speed 90 mph (145 km/h)

Matchless took over AJS and continued production. The super-sporting R10 boasted a race-proven engine with chain drive to the overhead camshaft.

▷ **BMW R51 RS 1938**

Origin Germany

Engine 7,494cc, flat-twin

Top speed 95 mph (153 km/h)

Developed from BMWs landmark R5 overhead-valve twin engine, the R51 featured plunger rear suspension. This is an RS in racing trim.

△ **Royal Enfield JF 1936**

Origin UK

Engine 499cc, ohv single-cylinder

Top speed 85 km/h (137 km/h)

The JF was one of the few machines built in the 1930s with a four-valve cylinder head. Enfield also tried three-valve heads before reverting to two.

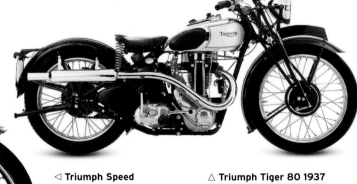

◁ **Triumph Speed Twin 1937**

Origin UK

Engine 498cc, ohv parallel-twin

Top speed 94 mph (151 km/h)

The Speed Twin, with its parallel twin-cylinder engine, set the pattern for British motorcycles for the next 40 years. It was compact, stylish, and fast.

△ **Triumph Tiger 80 1937**

Origin UK

Engine 349cc, single-cylinder

Top speed 78 mph (126 km/h)

When Edward Turner was appointed to head Triumph, he revamped this 350 with a chrome tank, polished cases, high exhaust, new paint, and a racy new name.

◁ **Vincent HRD Rapide Series A 1938**

Origin UK

Engine 998cc, ohv V-twin

Top speed 110 mph (177 km/h)

By doubling up their single-cylinder engine, Vincent created a superfast V-twin. A wartime design would create the most iconic Vincent twin.

◁ **Vincent HRD Comet 1938**

Origin UK

Engine 498cc, single-cylinder

Top speed 92 mph (148 km/h)

Philip Vincent, who bought HRD in 1928, adopted a high-camshaft engine designed by Australian Phil Irving from 1935. The engine powered racers as well as this Comet.

▽ **Crocker 1938 1938**

Origin USA

Engine 1,000cc, ohv V-twin

Top speed 110 mph (177 km/h)

Only made from 1936 to 1942, Crocker V-twins were fast, of high quality, and very expensive. This is the later type with vertical overhead valves.

△ **BSA Empire Star 1936**

Origin UK

Engine 496cc, ohv single-cylinder

Top speed 80 mph (129 km/h)

BSA shed its stolid image with the dashing Star series of sports singles. Forerunner to BSA's famous Gold Star, the Empire Star was redesigned in 1937.

▽ **BSA M24 Gold Star 500 1938**

Origin UK

Engine 496cc, ohv single-cylinder

Top speed 95 mph (153 km/h)

This all-alloy-engined bike is named after the badge awarded for lapping Brooklands at 100 mph (160 km/h), which a tuned BSA single did in 1937.

◁ **Matchless G80 1939**

Origin UK

Engine 498cc, ohv single-cylinder

Top speed 85 mph (137 km/h)

The chrome tank and high-level exhaust of the London-built G80 made it a good-looking machine; it delivered good performance too.

Sunbeam Model 9, c. 1930
A handsome motorcyclist riding a Sunbeam clearly impresses a group of sunbathing beauties in this 1930s ad. The Sunbeam's distinctive black tank with gold-leaf pinstriping was a match for its excellent build quality.

Reliable Transportation

There was still plenty of variety in "everyday" European bikes of the 1930s as manufacturers either traded on their innovations of the previous decade or picked the best of what others had invented and added their own twist. Components were widely shared across Europe, but individual marques still retained a great deal of character and, for the most part, were easily recognizable.

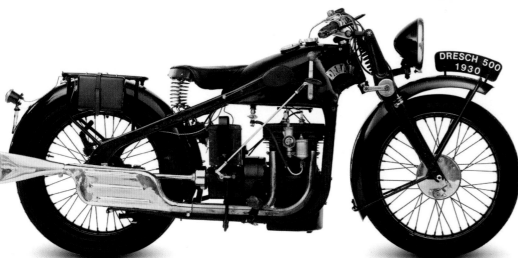

◁ **Stylson Blackburne 1930**

Origin France

Engine 350cc, single-cylinder

Top speed 60 mph (97 km/h)

This French marque—produced from 1919 to 1940—hoped to be seen as the two-wheeled Bugatti. Their high-quality machines boasted strong sporting results, mostly using British-made engines.

△ **Cotton Blackburne 250 1930**

Origin UK

Engine 249cc, single-cylinder

Top speed 63 mph (101 km/h)

Lawyer Bill Cotton designed a superb triangulated frame in 1918 that went on to win the Isle of Man TT races in 1923 and 1926. Cotton bought in both Blackburne and JAP engines.

△ **Dresch 5CV 1930**

Origin France

Engine 499cc, inline twin

Top speed 65 mph (105 km/h)

Henri Dresch built motorcycles from 1923 to 1939, selling up to 10,000 a year. The 500, popular with the Paris police, had a monobloc engine and shaft drive.

△ **OD TS 50 1931**

Origin Germany

Engine 498cc, single-cylinder

Top speed 70 mph (113 km/h)

Willi Ostner of Dresden made high-quality motorcycles from 1927 to 1936, using MAG engines from Motosacoche and scoring much success in competition.

△ **BMW R2 1931**

Origin Germany

Engine 198cc, single-cylinder

Top speed 59 mph (95 km/h)

BMW's bread-and-butter machine had a shaft drive, Bosch electrics, and a carlike, three-speed gearbox. In Germany, sub-200cc bikes did not need to be licensed until 1938.

◁ **Victoria KR 50 S 1931**

Origin Germany

Engine 495cc, single-cylinder

Top speed 74 mph (119 km/h)

Bicycle-maker Victoria built motorcycles in Nürnberg from 1901. From 1928, British-made Sturmey Archer engines were used, with overhead-valves on the "S" model.

▷ Wimmer GG35 1932

Origin Germany

Engine 344cc, single-cylinder

Top speed 60 mph (97 km/h)

Wimmer motorcycles were built in Germany from 1921 until WWII, the company's mainstay being a series of well-engineered 350 singles.

△ Motosacoche Jubilée 424 1932

Origin Switzerland

Engine 498cc, single-cylinder

Top speed 69 mph (111 km/h)

Launched to celebrate the marque's silver jubilee, this durable machine was powered by a low-maintenance side-valve engine with a car-type battery and coil ignition. Many components were British.

△ Triumph Model 6/1 1934

Origin UK

Engine 649cc, inline twin

Top speed 76 mph (122 km/h)

Designer Valentine Page's flagship Triumph was primarily intended to haul sidecars. Its vertical twin engine layout was later to be widely adopted.

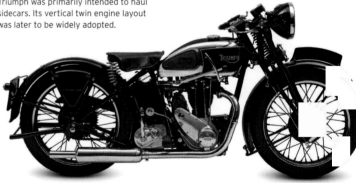

△ Triumph Model 2/1 1936

Origin UK

Engine 250cc, single-cylinder

Top speed 60 mph (97 km/h)

Page designed a range of solid and dependable Triumph singles for 1933. They were cosmetically revamped by Edward Turner for the company's 1937 relaunch.

◁ Tornax Universal 1934

Origin Germany

Engine 592cc, single-cylinder

Top speed 75 mph (120 km/h)

Tornax built bikes from 1926, mostly with British JAP engines. In 1934 the National Socialist government banned foreign components, so they used a Columbus engine.

△ Douglas Endeavour 1936

Origin UK

Engine 494cc, flat-twin

Top speed 60 mph (97 km/h)

Douglas had always built flat-twins, but mounted them in line with the frame; this was its first transverse model with a shaft drive. Though a good buy, it failed to sell.

Reliable Transportation (cont.)

As the 1930s progressed, motorcycles gradually became more sophisticated: rear suspension for comfort; overhead-valve gearing for efficient combustion and improved power and fuel economy; and styling influences, such as curvy "saddle" tanks for fuel, placed astride the top frame-tube. The big, lazy V-twins were reserved for heavy-duty sidecar hauling machines that still represented a bargain compared to buying a small family car.

▷ Peugeot P108 1932

Origin France

Engine 248cc, single-cylinder

Top speed 47 mph (76 km/h)

Peugeot focused on well-equipped machines like this one, with a small unit-construction engine and gearbox, and soon dominated the French motorcycle industry.

◁ Harley-Davidson RL 1935

Origin USA

Engine 737cc, V-twin

Top speed 70 mph (113 km/h)

Harley's second model with the smaller Flathead V-twin helped the marque weather the Great Depression, offering great Harley style with lower costs.

△ Nimbus MkII 1934

Origin Denmark

Engine 746cc, inline four

Top speed 75 mph (120 km/h)

Denmark's only serious motorcycle-builder operated from 1934 to 1939, building 12,715 units of this powerful machine with a car-type engine and an optional sidecar.

▷ AJS Model 2 Combination 1936

Origin UK

Engine 982cc, V-twin

Top speed 64 mph (103 km/h)

Matchless took over AJS in 1931. The new Model 2 (or Matchless X) was a side-valve slogger for hauling luxury sidecars, which provided cheaper family transportation than an Austin 7.

◁ BSA G14 Combination 1937

Origin UK

Engine 996cc, V-twin

Top speed 65 mph (105 km/h)

BSA made V-twins from 1919, and this side-valve slogger continued relatively unchanged through the 1930s; it was ideal for use with a sidecar for family transportation.

▷ Bianchi ES250/1 Sport 1937

Origin Italy

Engine 248cc, single-cylinder

Top speed 67 mph (108 km/h)

One of Italy's earliest bike-makers, Bianchi built competitive racers from the 1920s, and this road bike shows the benefits, including its overhead-valve twin-port engine.

▷ New Imperial Model 76 1937

Origin UK

Engine 496cc, single-cylinder

Top speed 82 mph (132 km/h)

New Imperial pioneered unit construction of the engine and gearbox, as well as rear springing, across its range; at the top of the line was this very fine twin-port 500.

△ OK-Supreme 350 1937

Origin UK

Engine 348cc, single-cylinder

Top speed 75 mph (120 km/h)

Birmingham-based maker OK was scaling down its road-bike production to concentrate on speedway machines when this JAP-engined machine was produced.

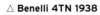

△ Benelli 4TN 1938

Origin Italy

Engine 500cc, single-cylinder

Top speed 90 mph (145 km/h)

Founded by six brothers in 1911, Benelli had great racing success with its overhead-camshaft bikes, from which this fine road machine was developed.

△ OEC Commander 1938

Origin UK

Engine 498cc, single-cylinder

Top speed 82 mph (132 km/h)

John Osborn's ingenious duplex steering had benefits but probably put off buyers, unlike his excellent 2-in (5-cm) travel rear springing on this fine touring machine.

△ Coventry Eagle 250 1938

Origin UK

Engine 247cc, single-cylinder

Top speed 57 mph (92 km/h)

A novel, pressed-steel frame, two-stroke Villiers engine, and a low line characterized the 1930s Coventry Eagle range, but it failed to attract significant sales.

◁ Matchless Model X Sports Tourist 1938

Origin UK

Engine 990cc, V-twin

Top speed 80 mph (129 km/h)

Effectively identical to the AJS Model 2, the Model X was revamped in 1937 in a shorter frame as a luxury sporting machine, using the same engine as the Brough SS80.

▷ Royal Enfield Model K 1939

Origin UK

Engine 1,140cc, V-twin

Top speed 85 mph (137 km/h)

Effortless power was on tap for the Model K owner: from a huge side-valve V-twin, equally at home hauling a heavy sidecar or, with hand-clutch conversion, for riding solo.

An early BMW R32 at an historic bike rally

Great Marques
The BMW Story

It was easy to admire the early, sturdy BMW motorcycles, yet rather harder to love them. But as bikes with a real personality began to emerge—such as the R90S—the aesthetics became as appealing to the public as performance. Together they made an irresistible combination.

THE ORIGINS OF BMW stretch back to the merger of two Bavarian aviation companies during World War I. Karl Rapp's business, based near Munich, made aircraft engines, while Gustav Otto's factory specialized in small aircraft. By 1917 Rapp and Otto had left their companies; the businesses subsequently merged under the name BMW (Bayerische Motoren Werke). After the war, when German companies were forbidden to produce aircraft and aircraft engines, BMW's focus shifted to motorcycles.

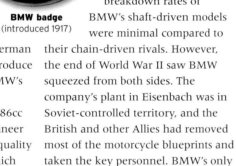

BMW badge
(introduced 1917)

BMW's first motorbike, the 486cc R32 of 1923, developed by engineer Max Friz, was admired for the quality and rock-solid reliability for which the marque would later be known, and its flat-twin boxer engine established the template for decades to come. However, rider Ernst Henne's record-breaking exploits were high-profile reminders that BMWs were more than simply trustworthy. In 1936 the R5 was developed; it was a cheaper bike than its predecessors, while also being stronger and lighter. Next came the R12, a world leader with its hydraulically dampened front forks.

The marque's famed reliability served BMW well in wartime. In desert zones, the breakdown rates of BMW's shaft-driven models were minimal compared to their chain-driven rivals. However, the end of World War II saw BMW squeezed from both sides. The company's plant in Eisenbach was in Soviet-controlled territory, and the British and other Allies had removed most of the motorcycle blueprints and taken the key personnel. BMW's only option was to start again. Their first result was the 1949 R24 single, and demand was so strong that the factory struggled to keep up with orders.

Much of the motorcycle's appeal in the postwar years was based on affordability, but the 1950s was a time of growing prosperity. Car-owning aspirations made it a tough decade for all motorcycle manufacturers. Major

Fast reputation
By the 1930s BMW could lay claim to making some of the fastest motorcycles in the world, something the company was eager to promote in advertising.

financial investment was a show of faith that gave the marque some confidence that a difficult economic period could be navigated. This was coupled with the development in 1955 of the R69S, a bike that really turned heads as it passed them at a maximum speed of around 110 mph (177 km/h). An all-time favorite for many BMW fans, the R69S pointed the way for the modern sport tourer.

Although the R69S was produced for a decade, the background picture was not rosy. The pessimistic predictions for the industry in the 1950s continued into the 1960s. By 1969 only 1 in 20 of BMW's vehicle sales was a motorcycle. With car production taking priority, the bike operation was moved from Munich to a suburb of Berlin. If that was taken as a sign that the motorcycle had been sidelined, a convincing counter argument was the /5 Series with an all-new boxer engine that revived the marque. The R50/5, R60/5, and 75/5 laid the foundations for a reappraisal of BMW, culminating in the /6 Series of 1973, which took the company to a new level.

It was around this time that words such as "efficient" and "capable," which had been used consistently about BMWs, began to be replaced by "exciting," "classy," and even "sexy." Shaking off the conservative shackles,

the R90S combined power and speed with an arresting appearance. Even the all-conquering Japanese manufacturers were forced to sit up and take notice. With that precedent in place, the R100RS of 1976 became

Speed kings
In 1955 Wilhelm Noll set a new motorcycle speed record of 174 mph (282 km/h) on a specially made 500cc BMW motorcycle. The marque had been breaking speed records on advanced machines since Ernst Henne's feats in the late 1920s.

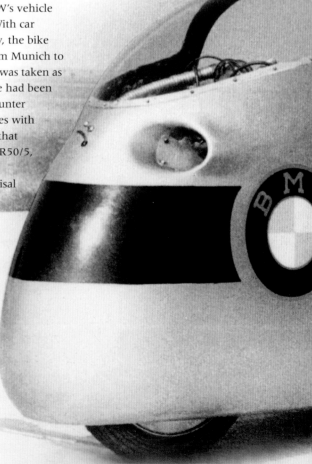

R32

R69

K1200S

G650GS

1923 Five years before BMW produces its first car, the R32 makes it debut.
1926 On an R37, Rudolph Schleicher wins the International Six Day Trials (ISDT).
1929 Riding a BMW, Ernst Henne sets a new world record of 134 mph (215 km/h).
1939 George Meier leads a BMW one-two in the Isle of Man Senior TT; during World War II, the R75 proves itself in the campaigns of North Africa.
1954 Wilhelm Noll and Fritz Cron win the World Sidecar championship.

1959 Riding a BMW, John Penton smashes the New York to Los Angeles record (previously held by a Harley-Davidson) by the huge margin of 24 hours.
1969 Production of BMW motorcycles moves to Spandau in the west of Berlin; the /5 series starts a concerted relaunch of the marque.
1973 Available in dashing orange, the R90S promises a bright future for BMW; the number of BMW motorcycles produced tops 500,000.

1974 Klaus Enders wins the last of his six World Sidecar crowns; it is the 19th title win for BMW in 21 years.
1980 The R80GS—for Geländ/Strasse or "off-road"—is unveiled and becomes a best-seller.
1981 France's Hubert Auriol wins the Dakar Rally; he repeats the feat two years later, before Belgian Gaston Rahier triumphs in 1984.
1991 On March 18, a K75RT is the millionth BMW motorcycle to be produced.

1993 The F650ST is the first BMW motorcycle to be chain-driven.
1995 The last of the traditional boxer engines is produced. Later, 2004's R1200GS features an all-new boxer.
1999 Riding the F650RR, France's Richard Sainct wins the Dakar Rally; he also wins the following year.
2000 The motorcycle division is renamed BMW Motorrad.
2011 The marque debuts its first six-cylinder models, the K1600GT and K1600GTL.

the world's first fully-faired mass production bike. Confirming that reliability still underpinned everything BMW did, the marque ground out three victories in the Dakar Rally, in 1981, 1983, and 1984. The first of these was on a R80GS, and a year later a road version, the R80RT, capitalized on the success. The marque was now more innovative, adding K-Series machines with three- and four-cylinder inline engines to the range. BMW led the way with an antilock braking system (ABS) and, on the K100LT tourer, an electronically adjustable windshield.

Arguably, the high-performing K1 superbike of 1989 overstepped the mark. Its aerodynamically adept

Operations center
BMW's high-tech manufacturing plant in Berlin is home to the company's motorcycle manufacturing operations. Almost 100,000 bikes were produced in 2010.

design and digital electronics system were not embraced in the way the marque anticipated. The red-and-yellow decorations that led to its nickname "ketchup 'n' mustard" did not help.

However, one breakthrough that was welcomed was the Telelever arrangement for the front suspension of 1993's R1100GS, with a spring-supporting extra swingarm assisting when the brakes were hit hard.

In 1999 and 2000 there were successive victories for the F650RR in the Dakar Rally. This event and motorcycle featured in Charley

The F800S and F800ST were both impressive additions to their class divisions in 2006, and even though the K1200S suffered some technical problems on its release, the machine offered formidable power.

"It's difficult to create scenarios where the big GS doesn't excel," wrote author Peter Gantriis of the R1200GS, which cemented the marque's reputation in the adventure-touring class. In just over three years, between 2004 and 2007, BMW set a

"My **first reaction** to the BMW was that it's **the only bike** for this trip."

EWAN MCGREGOR, TV SERIES *LONG WAY ROUND*

Boorman's *Race to Dakar* (2006), a TV series documenting his intrepid trip from Lisbon to Dakar. For the 2004 series *Long Way Round*, in which he was accompanied by movie star Ewan McGregor, each rode the R1150GS Adventure, and in 2007's *Long Way Down*, the R1200GS Adventure.

company record by producing 100,000 of the RG1200GS and R1200GS Adventure.

While BMW motorbikes have always been characterized by solid dependability, the marque has now added color and a splash of panache, giving riders the best of all worlds.

Economy Travel

By the 1930s, buyers had come to realize that economy travel did not have to mean puttering along on a noisy, gutless machine that barely outstripped a bicycle. Economical motorcycling now went hand in hand with a 100–250cc engine, 40–50 mph (64–80 km/h) cruising speeds, and increasing sophistication. While some makers added enclosing panelwork to attract a new group of riders, others relied on up-to-the-minute engineering and chic styling to sell their machines.

△ Peugeot P108 1930

Origin France

Engine 249cc, single cylinder

Top speed 50 mph (80 km/h)

Peugeot's mainstay throughout the 1930s was this well-made (and progressively updated) four-stroke, side-valve-engined machine with a three-speed gearbox.

◁ Velocette GTP 1930

Origin UK

Engine 249cc, single-cylinder

Top speed 57 mph (92 km/h)

This high-quality piston-port two-stroke single was notable for throttle-controlled positive lubrication and coil ignition. TP stood for twin ports, feeding two exhaust pipes.

△ DKW Luxus 200 1931

Origin Germany

Engine 198cc, single-cylinder

Top speed 44 mph (71 km/h)

Known as the "Blood Blister" (*Blutblase*) because of its red tank, this sporty two-stroke helped DKW become the world's biggest-selling bike-maker at the time.

▷ BSA H31 Sloper 1930

Origin UK

Engine 557cc, single-cylinder

Top speed 65 mph (105 km/h)

Launched in 1927 with an overhead-valve engine mounted at an angle to allow a lower top tube and seat, the Sloper later acquired a side-valve option, seen here.

△ **Francis-Barnett Cruiser 1933**

Origin UK

Engine 249cc, single-cylinder

Top speed 45mph (72 km/h)

Aimed at non-enthusiast buyers looking for a more convenient alternative to the bus, the Cruiser's pressed-steel bodywork offered good weather protection.

△ **Panther 250 Red Panther 1932**

Origin UK

Engine 249cc, single-cylinder

Top speed 58mph (93 km/h)

Unlike bigger Panther singles, the 250 had a frame downtube as well as a sloping cylinder. It was the UK's cheapest machine in this class.

▷ **DKW RT125 1938**

Origin Germany

Engine 123cc, single-cylinder

Top speed 50mph (80 km/h)

With DKW's pioneering Schnurle loop scavenging, two-stroke engine, the RT125 was the most copied motorcycle postwar. Similar models were produced in the UK, Russia, the US, and Japan.

△ **Royal Enfield Bullet 250 1936**

Origin UK

Engine 346cc, single-cylinder

Top speed 70mph (113 km/h)

The Bullet model was born in the 1930s, but the unit's general appearance would remain remarkably similar for decades. This single-cylinder's engine oil was stored in the crankcase.

▷ **Terrot Tourisme 1938**

Origin France

Engine 346cc, single-cylinder

Top speed 60mph (97 km/h)

Terrot made bicycles in Dijon from 1890 and motorcycles from 1902, winning French 250, 350, and 500cc Championships in 1932. This is a touring side-valve model.

△ **Phänomen Bob 100 1938**

Origin Germany

Engine 98cc, single-cylinder

Top speed 32mph (51km/h)

A utility lightweight with large wheels, a two-stroke engine, and two-speed gearbox. Pedals were needed for starting and to help the engine when climbing steep hills.

▽ **Cushman Auto-Glide Model 1 1938**

Origin USA

Engine 202cc, single-cylinder

Top speed 32mph (51km/h)

Having built engines since 1913, Cushman produced their first scooter in 1936. During WWII the model was adapted to be dropped with parachute troops.

◁ **BSA C11 1939**

Origin UK

Engine 249cc, single-cylinder

Top speed 66mph (106 km/h)

A neat overhead-valve lightweight built for durability rather than speed, the C11 would return after World War II with the addition of telescopic front forks.

Hot Competition

Despite worldwide recession in the 1930s, racing continued to keep engineers and designers occupied with finding new ways to outdo their competitors. In road racing, overhead camshafts were becoming essential for four-stroke engines, and two-stroke engine development advanced rapidly, especially in Germany. Superchargers boosted speed, as did rear suspension on bumpier tracks. Fast circuits like Brooklands in the UK and Monza in Italy were regularly lapped at 100 mph (161 km/h).

△ Harley-Davidson DAH 45 Hillclimber 1930

Origin USA

Engine 718cc, V-twin

Top speed 95 mph (153 km/h)

Specially built for extreme off-road hill-climbs popular in the US, this National Championship winner has a tiny fuel tank, low gearing, rear tire chains, and no front brake.

△ Velocette KTT 1930

Origin UK

Engine 348cc, single-cylinder

Top speed 105 mph (169 km/h)

Conceived in the 1920s, the KTT with a bevel-driven overhead camshaft and the first positive-stop foot gearchange was the top 1930s privateer racer in the 350 class.

◁ Raleigh 500 TT 1931

Origin UK

Engine 496cc, single-cylinder

Top speed 112 mph (180 km/h)

Raleigh employed Brooklands tuning wizard Dr. O'Donovan to get the most from its TT racers; a 7th in the 1931 TT ridden by Arthur Tyler was their best result.

△ AJS R7 1930

Origin UK

Engine 350cc, single-cylinder

Top speed 110 mph (177 km/h)

To get more out of its 350, AJS devised a chain drive to an overhead camshaft, setting many records and winning races in the 1930s once it had been perfected.

▷ Rudge Four-valve 1931

Origin UK

Engine 499cc, single-cylinder

Top speed 110 mph (177 km/h)

Four-valve pushrod singles of 250, 350, and 500cc gained Rudge four Isle of Man TT wins in the early 1930s. Replicas like this one were sold to private collectors.

▽ AJS V4 1939

Origin UK

Engine 494cc, V4

Top speed 135 mph (217 km/h)

Supercharged and water-cooled (it had overheated in air-cooled form), the bulky V4 set a 100 mph (161 km/h) lap at the Ulster Grand Prix. Development was halted by the start of WWII.

△ Excelsior Mechanical Marvel 1933

Origin UK

Engine 246cc, single-cylinder

Top speed 100 mph (161 km/h)

Winner of the 1933 Isle of Man Lightweight TT, this machine earned its nickname from its complex Blackburne engine, which had four radial valves and two carburetors.

▷ **New Imperial TT 500 1937**

Origin UK

Engine 500cc, V-twin

Top speed 120 mph (193 km/h)

In 1934 Ginger Woods averaged 102.2 mph (164.5 km/h) for an hour at Brooklands on a TT 500. The model excelled on faster tracks but did not do well in the Isle of Man.

△ **Husqvarna TT 500 1935**

Origin Sweden

Engine 500cc, V-twin

Top speed 120 mph (193 km/h)

Designer Folke Mannerstedt improved the 500 racer with light alloys to keep the weight low. Stanley Woods nearly won the 1934 TT but ran out of gas on the last lap.

△ **NSU Kompressor 1939**

Origin Germany

Engine 500cc, inline twin

Top speed 211 mph (340 km/h)

The Kompressor was unable to show its potential as superchargers were banned after WWII. An NSU engine of this type set a 210 mph (338 km/h) record in 1955.

△ **Norton International 1938**

Origin UK

Engine 500cc, single-cylinder

Top speed 125 mph (201 km/h)

Norton was the top racing marque of the 1930s. The overhead camshaft International custom racer, based on works machinery, had plunger rear suspension from 1938.

▽ **DKW SS250 1939**

Origin Germany

Engine 250cc, single-cylinder

Top speed 115 mph (185 km/h)

DKW's bold winning ideas included twin pistons with a single combustion chamber and a third piston used purely to supercharge mixture. The exhaust noise was deafening.

△ **BMW R51 Kompressor 1939**

Origin Germany

Engine 494cc, flat-twin

Top speed 174 mph (280 km/h)

In 1937 Ernst Henne set a world speed record that lasted 14 years on an overhead-cam supercharged BMW. This model won many races, including the 1939 Senior TT.

The
1940s

World War II brought most new motorcycle development to an abrupt halt, as the main demand was for simple, reliable, rugged, and easily repaired dispatch machines and light gun transport. But when the war ended, there was a demand for bikes from demobilized servicemen. Manufacturers hastily reintroduced old models, but some of the best designs of 1939 could now thrive: DKW's 125cc two-stroke design spread across the world, handed out in "war reparations." Soon, motorcycles were twice as numerous as they had been before the war.

On Military Service

Most military motorcycles were used for communication—carrying messages, especially when other means were not available. The machines needed to be rugged, reliable, and capable of crossing rough terrain, and, because they were entrusted to inexperienced riders, simple to ride. Manufacturers produced no-frills machines, usually based on existing models, and equipped them with accessories deemed necessary for military use. These included racks, special lighting equipment, sump guards, and, in some cases, gun holsters.

△ **Velocette MAC-MDD 1940**

Origin UK

Engine 349cc, ohv single-cylinder

Top speed 75 mph (120 km/h)

Originally militarized for a canceled French Army contract, the MAC-MDD was subsequently replaced by the more specialized MAP used by the Royal Air Force.

△ **Triumph 3TW 1940**

Origin UK

Engine 349cc, ohv parallel-twin

Top speed 60 mph (97 km/h)

The only batch of this unusually light and lively army motorcycle was destroyed, along with the Triumph factory, when Coventry, England, was bombed in 1941.

▽ **Ariel W/NG 1940**

Origin UK

Engine 347cc, ohv single-cylinder

Top speed 65 mph (105 km/h)

This overhead-valve model was based on a relatively sporty prewar roadster. Nearly 50,000 were supplied, and many stayed in civilian use after the war.

△ **Triumph 3HW 1944**

Origin UK

Engine 343cc, ohv single-cylinder

Top speed 65 mph (105 km/h)

Based on the prewar civilian Tiger 80, over 30,000 were produced during the war, after Triumph resumed business at their new Meriden factory.

◁ **Zündapp KS750 1940**

Origin Germany

Engine 751cc, ohv flat-twin

Top speed 60 mph (97 km/h)

Designed to carry three soldiers and arms over rough ground, the KS750 had eight forward gears and two reverse gears, plus a driven sidecar wheel.

◁ **Matchless G3/L 1941**

Origin UK

Engine 347cc, ohv single-cylinder

Top speed 70 mph (113 km/h)

The significant improvement of the G3/L over the previous model, and over other British military bikes, was its hydraulically damped telescopic forks.

▷ **Matchless G3/L
North Africa Version c. 1941**

Engine 347cc, ohv single-cylinder

Top speed 70 mph (113 km/h)

Destined for service in the African desert, this machine was painted appropriately. Chrome was absent and a rubber shortage meant using canvas handlebar grips.

△ **BMW R12 1940**

Origin Germany

Engine 745cc, side-valve flat-twin

Top speed 50 mph (80 km/h)

Launched in 1936, the first year for BMW's telescopic front forks, the R12 side-valver was built exclusively for military use from 1938 to 1942.

△ **BMW R75 1941**

Origin Germany

Engine 745cc, ohv flat-twin

Top speed 60 mph (97 km/h)

Built to the same brief as the Zündapp KS750, the R75 was made with a high- and low-ratio gearbox with reverse gears and a driven sidecar wheel.

△ **BMW R35 1946**

Origin Germany

Engine 342cc, ohv single-cylinder

Top speed 70 mph (113 km/h)

This prewar BMW design was built at the BMW factory in Eisenacher, which was located in Communist East Germany after the war.

◁ **Norton Big Four 1940**

Origin UK

Engine 633cc, side-valve single-cylinder

Top speed 50 mph (80 km/h)

A personnel, ammunition, and gun carrier, Norton's sidecar outfit could keep going over rough terrain as both the rear wheel and sidecar wheel were driven.

△ **Norton 16H 1942**

Origin UK

Engine 490cc, side-valve single-cylinder

Top speed 55 mph (89 km/h)

The long-running 16H was adapted to military specification in WWII, when Norton supplied 100,000 machines to the Allied forces.

Canadian dispatch riders, 1943
Fast and reliable motorbikes were essential for delivering urgent messages between military units. A wing of dispatch riders from the Canadian Army is briefed by a senior officer before going on duty during World War II.

On Military Service (cont.)

Along with the basic military motorcycle, machines for specific roles were also produced in the 1940s. These included lightweight bikes that could be stored easily on boats and aircraft, and in some cases dropped by parachute to provide instant mobility to advancing troops. Some sidecar outfits were developed to carry heavy guns too, and sometimes equipped with a driven sidecar wheel to allow them to be used in battlefield terrain. However, these were made obsolete by the arrival of the Jeep.

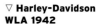

△ Harley-Davidson U Navy 1940

Origin USA

Engine 1,213cc, side-valve V-twin

Top speed 75 mph (120 km/h)

The U range had larger capacity and higher specification than Harley's W models; only limited numbers were made and supplied during the war.

◁ Harley-Davidson XA 1942

Origin USA

Engine 738cc, side-valve flat-twin

Top speed 65 mph (105 km/h)

A batch of 1,000 of these BMW-inspired, shaft-drive flat-twins was made, but the arrival of the Jeep meant no more were produced.

▽ Harley-Davidson WLA 1942

Origin USA

Engine 738cc, side-valve V-twin

Top speed 65 mph (105 km/h)

To convert the civilian WL model to military specification, Harley added a bash plate under the engine, modified the mudguards, and added a gun holster.

▷ Harley-Davidson WLC 1942

Origin USA

Engine 739cc, side-valve V-twin

Top speed 65 mph (105 km/h)

Harley supplied over 80,000 bikes to Allied forces. The WLC supplied to the Canadian military differed only in detail from the original WLA.

△ **Indian 741 1942**

Origin	USA
Engine	500cc, V-twin
Top speed	53 mph (85 km/h)

Based on the civilian Thirty-fifty, the 741 was a sturdy, reliable war machine used mostly by couriers and scouts, and supplied to several Allied ground forces.

△ **Indian 841 1941**

Origin	USA
Engine	737cc, side-valve V-twin
Top speed	65 mph (105 km/h)

Developed especially for the US military, this shaft-drive machine was unlike any previous Indian model, but it never reached mass production.

△ **Welbike with carry pack 1942**

Origin	UK
Engine	98cc, two-stroke single
Top speed	40 mph (64 km/h)

With no suspension and only one brake, the Welbike was simple, light, and portable. Intended for parachute drops, many were used for airfield transportation.

△ **BSA M20 1942**

Origin	UK
Engine	496cc, side-valve single-cylinder
Top speed	55 mph (89 km/h)

The simple and rugged BSA M20 was the most common bike used by British forces in WWII. Well over 100,000 were produced.

△ **NSU Kettenkrad HK101 1944**

Origin	Germany
Engine	1,488cc, ohv inline four
Top speed	43 mph (69 km/h)

Stretching the definition of a motorcycle, this handlebar-steered tractor transported soldiers and other loads over rough terrain. It was widely used in the 1941 Russian campaign.

◁ **Royal Enfield Flying Flea WD/RE125 1948**

Origin	UK
Engine	126cc, two-stroke single
Top speed	40 mph (64 km/h)

This lightweight, copied from a German DKW design, was developed for dropping by parachute or for airborne delivery to the front line in troop gliders.

Harley-Davidson WLC

Harley-Davidson's military WL motorcycles were some of the finest workhorses of World War II. Although most were used by US Forces in WLA form, a large number of these 45-cubic-inch V-twins were issued to the Canadian military and, like this model, were designated WLCs. Rugged, practical, and utterly dependable, the WLC was a fine example of how the simplicity of Harley's side-valve power plant made it perfectly suited to the rigors of warfare.

THREE YEARS after Harley-Davidson unveiled its W-series 750cc twins in 1937, the Milwaukee-based marque was forced to turn its attention to manufacturing motorcycles for the war effort. The straightforward nature of the side-valve engines at the heart of the W-series made them an obvious choice for military use, and by the end of the conflict more than 80,000 had been deployed by the Allies. The WLC model was produced for the Canadian forces between 1941 and 1944, Harley-Davidson stepping up to the mark when British manufacturers Norton and BSA were struggling to meet the huge demand for wartime machines

from Britain and Canada. Among the bike's military specifications were olive-drab paint for camouflage, blackout lighting, and extended forks for greater ground clearance over rough terrain, while some examples also sported a rifle holster on the front forks. The Canadian variant differed in several respects, including an alternative throttle-lever position, an auxiliary clutch hand lever, and wheels that were interchangeable. By 1945, the WLA and WLC Harley bikes had been recognized as extremely successful combat motorcycles, and in the postwar era many continued to be used by civilians.

FRONT VIEW   **REAR VIEW**

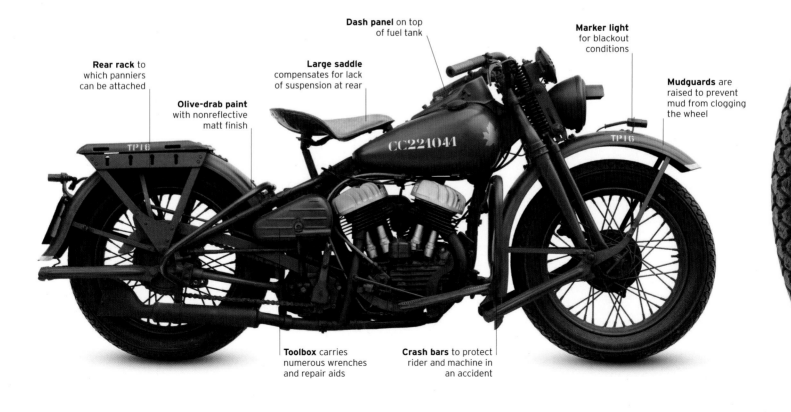

Dash panel on top of fuel tank

Marker light for blackout conditions

Rear rack to which panniers can be attached

Large saddle compensates for lack of suspension at rear

Olive-drab paint with nonreflective matt finish

Mudguards are raised to prevent mud from clogging the wheel

Toolbox carries numerous wrenches and repair aids

Crash bars to protect rider and machine in an accident

Light approach
Canadian Army WLC riders were equipped with a "blackout kit" that contained shrouds for the front and rear lights that directed light downward during blackout conditions. To compensate for this, small marker lights were positioned on the front and rear mudguards.

SPECIFICATIONS			
Model	Harley-Davidson WLC (1942)	Power output	23 hp
Assembly	Milwaukee, WI	Transmission	Three-speed
Production	More than 80,000	Suspension	Leading-link front forks, rigid rear
Construction	Tubular cradle frame	Brakes	Drums, front and rear
Engine	45 cu in (739cc) side-valve V-twin	Maximum speed	65 mph (105 km/h)

CC221044

THE BIKE

The military WLs were based on the W Series "Baby Flathead" twins already in production. Special equipment included a revision to Harley-Davidson's traditional leading-link forks to allow increased ground clearance, as well as footboards and protective crash bars. The WLC saw action in several theaters of war from 1941 to 1945, including the Normandy landings and many other major conflict zones across Europe.

1. Identification number **2.** Horn **3.** Fork spring **4.** Speedometer **5.** Gear change **6.** Headlight mask revealing only a small rectangle of light **7.** Front marker light **8.** Front fork-ride adjuster knob **9.** Fuel filler **10.** Rear sprocket **11.** Data plate attached to top of tank **12.** Kick-starter **13.** Canadian emblem displayed on either side of tank **14.** Clutch control **15.** Rear lights

WLC MODEL CAUTION
USE H-D. SPARK PLUGS   DO NOT EXCEED 65 M.P.H.
LUBRICATION :-
ENGINE AND { ABOVE + 32° F DND #395
TRANSMISSION { BELOW + 32° F DND #365
            { BELOW + 10° F DND #345
PUBLICATIONS APPLYING TO THIS VEHICLE :-
PARTS LIST HD-WLC-04 MAINTENANCE MANUAL M/C-HD-
HARLEY-DAVIDSON MOTOR CO.   MILWAUKEE, WIS.

THE ENGINE

Key to the success of Harley's side-valve (or "Flathead") V-twin was the absence of any moving parts in its cylinder head, which simplified maintenance in battlefield conditions. The bike's reliability was further enhanced by an upgraded lubrication system and an oil-bath air filter to keep out dust, grit, and sand.

16. Air intake hose **17.** Rugged side-valve engine
18. Ignition timing unit **19.** Carburetor floatbowl
20. Inlet manifold

Innovation and Evolution

The ravages of a war that had affected virtually every nation and every person in the world meant that postwar, many motorcycle manufacturers resorted to reviving prewar designs. However, some factories had been working on innovations, and there were useful technical spinoffs from the accelerated development of vehicles and aircraft during wartime, including better alloys and synthetic materials.

◁ **Indian 440 1940**
Origin USA
Engine 1,265cc, inline four
Top speed 90 mph (145 km/h)

Indian's ranges for 1940 and 1941 appeared before the US entered the war. It added skirted mudguards and plunger rear suspension before dropping the four in 1942.

△ **Harley-Davidson FL74 1941**
Origin USA
Engine 1,208cc, V-twin
Top speed 100 mph (160 km/h)

The "Knucklehead" engine, so called because of the knobby appearance of the rocker covers, was enlarged to 1,208cc, raising its top speed to 100 mph (160 km/h).

△ **Harley-Davidson WLD Sport Solo 1941**
Origin USA
Engine 740cc, V-twin
Top speed 75 mph (120 km/h)

A sports version of Harley's long-running 750cc side-valver, with high-compression cylinder heads. The WLDR racer and WL military bikes were other variants.

△ **Triumph Speed Twin 1946**
Origin UK
Engine 498cc, inline twin
Top speed 85 mph (137 km/h)

Edward Turner's good-looking and powerful 1937 parallel-twin masterpiece continued to be just as influential after the war, when it boasted telescopic front forks.

◁ **AJS Model 16M 1946**
Origin UK
Engine 347cc, single-cylinder
Top speed 72 mph (115 km/h)

Little updating was done to the 1939 AJS after the war—apart from adding telescopic forks. Yet it remained in demand, with a waiting list of up to 12 months through the 1940s.

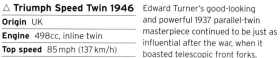

△ **Sertum VT-4 250 1947**
Origin Italy
Engine 250cc, single-cylinder
Top speed 65 mph (105 km/h)

This Milan engine-maker built motorcycles from 1931 to 1951, launching its 250 with full suspension in 1937. It did well in competition and was made again after the war.

△ **EMC 350S MkI 1947**

Origin	UK
Engine	346cc, single-cylinder
Top speed	72 mph (115 km/h)

After WWII, Joseph Ehrlich built split-single two-strokes. Based on a Puch design from his native Austria, they sold slowly. Ehrlich later had some racing success.

△ **Indian Chief 1947**

Origin	USA
Engine	1,200cc, V-twin
Top speed	85 mph (137 km/h)

The Chief was launched in 1922, gaining skirts and full suspension in 1940. Handsome and comfortable, it was rather heavy but could reach 100 mph (160 km/h) if tuned.

△ **BSA A7 1949**

Origin	UK
Engine	495cc, inline twin
Top speed	87 mph (140 km/h)

The new twin to rival Triumph's 500 was launched in 1946 and had optional rear suspension from 1949, when the Star Twin sports version arrived.

△ **Royal Enfield J2 1948**

Origin	UK
Engine	499cc, single-cylinder
Top speed	76 mph (122 km/h)

Based on 1930s practice, the J2 now had telescopic front forks. The prewar Bullet name was applied to a sportier 500 single from 1953.

△ **Norton 500T 1949**

Origin	UK
Engine	490cc, single-cylinder
Top speed	80 mph (129 km/h)

An early custom-built trials bike, the rigid framed 500T had an all-alloy version of Norton's ES2 engine, a slim fuel tank, a raised muffler, and a rubber saddle.

◁ **FN Modèle XIII 1948**

Origin	Belgium
Engine	444cc, single-cylinder
Top speed	77 mph (124 km/h)

Unusual trailing-link front forks distinguish early postwar machines of the Belgian marque. Rubber was used for the rear suspension and the front forks from 1949.

△ **MV Agusta 125 Tourismo 1949**

Origin	Italy
Engine	123cc, single-cylinder
Top speed	50 mph (80 km/h)

Count Domenico Agusta added motorcycle manufacture to the output of his family's aircraft factory. This model with swingarm rear suspension was a major advance.

Innovation and Evolution (cont.)

By the latter part of the decade, manufacturers had hit their stride and some genuinely fresh designs were appearing, as well as revived versions of 1930s machines. Among the new departures were completely redesigned twins from Vincent-HRD and Harley-Davidson with advances in both engine and chassis design, innovative Sunbeams that clearly showed BMW influence, and a clutch of ill-starred, new-look Indians.

△ **Norton International 1948**

Origin	UK
Engine	490cc, single-cylinder
Top speed	90 mph (145 km/h)

Returning in road trim only, the sporty, overhead-camshaft "Inter" now had Norton's Roadholder front forks. It was available in 350cc and 500cc form.

◁ **Indian 149 Arrow 1949**

Origin	USA
Engine	213cc, single-cylinder
Top speed	55 mph (89 km/h)

Ralph Rogers took control of Indian in 1945, introducing European-style machines, this being the single-cylinder version. However, they lacked quality and performance.

▽ **Indian Super Scout 249 1949**

Origin	USA
Engine	426cc, inline twin
Top speed	75 mph (120 km/h)

Parallel twin versions of Indian's new range were also let down by underdevelopment and poor build quality. After 52 years, Indian ceased production in 1953.

△ **NSU Fox 1949**

Origin	Germany
Engine	98cc, single-cylinder
Top speed	50 mph (80 km/h)

NSU's first postwar design was offered with either a two-stroke engine or the four-stroke unit seen here. Neat and sophisticated, the Fox had monoshock rear suspension.

▽ **Triumph TR5 Trophy 1949**

Origin	UK
Engine	498cc, inline twin
Top speed	80 mph (129 km/h)

Named after Triumph's successes in the International Six-Day Trials, the Trophy was a light, maneuverable machine that was suitable for both commuting and trials competition.

△ **Harley-Davidson FL Hydra Glide 1949**

Origin	USA
Engine	1,208cc, V-twin
Top speed	95 mph (153 km/h)

Harley's all-new, overhead-valve FL engine for 1948 was nicknamed the "Panhead." The following year, "Hydra Glide" oil-damped, telescopic front forks were another significant addition to FL models.

△ **Norton ES2 1949**

Origin UK

Engine 490cc, single-cylinder

Top speed 82 mph (132 km/h)

Norton's established, long-stroke singles kept soldiering on. This one, the ES2 top model, now featured plunger rear suspension and Roadholder telescopic front forks.

△ **Norton Model 7 Dominator 1949**

Origin UK

Engine 497cc, inline twin

Top speed 88 mph (142 km/h)

Norton's robust response to the Triumph parallel-twin was launched in 1949. The engine design, with splayed exhaust ports, would be used until the 1970s.

◁ **Vincent Black Shadow 1949**

Origin UK

Engine 998cc, V-twin

Top speed 122 mph (196 km/h)

Easily the world's fastest production motorcycle, this mighty machine had a black-enameled V-twin engine, "frameless" construction, and a large 150 mph (241 km/h) speedometer.

◁ **Sunbeam S8 1949**

Origin UK

Engine 487cc, inline twin

Top speed 83 mph (134 km/h)

The twin now had a leaner look, with conventional wheels. Although this bike was faster and markedly more reliable than the S7, it is less sought after by today's collectors.

▷ **Sunbeam Model S7 De Luxe 1949**

Origin UK

Engine 487cc, inline twin

Top speed 78 mph (126 km/h)

After buying Sunbeam, BSA made this overhead-camshaft twin, with shaft drive and balloon tires, as a luxury tourer. It was smooth and quiet, but not fast.

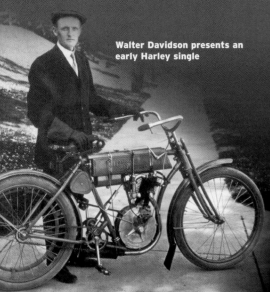

Walter Davidson presents an early Harley single

Great Marques
The Harley-Davidson Story

One of the greatest of all American companies, Harley-Davidson came into being more than a century ago from the efforts of four entrepreneurial individuals. They founded what would go on to become a pioneering, forward-thinking motorcyle brand that has become a symbol of both the American Dream and the freedom of the open road.

AT THE START OF the 20th century, motorcycle manufacture in the US was in its infancy. Several bicycle makers were attempting to attach engines to bike frames, but just a handful of companies were trying to develop motorized transportation

William A. Davidson, Walter Davidson, Arthur Davidson, and William S. Harley

from the ground up. It was against this backdrop that, in 1903, William S. Harley and Arthur Davidson began assembling their first motorcycle in a shed outside the Davidson family home in Milwaukee, Wisconsin. They were joined soon after by Arthur's brothers, Walter and William A., whose innovative approach would distinguish the company's later years.

A 1920s poster
Advertising campaigns and the development of a nationwide dealership network boosted Harley-Davidson's growth in the early years.

Officially set up in 1907, the Harley-Davidson Motor Company expanded rapidly. Just three examples of the original 24.74 cu in (405cc) single-cylinder motorcycle were produced in 1903, but by 1910 more than 3,000 bikes were rolling off the production line, in the company's new premises. Early innovations included the sprung fork and chain drive, but it was the V-twin engine that would play a key role in the direction of the company. In full production from 1911, this cylinder configuration has been at the heart of Harley's model range ever since. By the time the US entered World War I in 1917, Harley-Davidson had a reputation for making robust, dependable machines, and the company was contracted to provide more than 20,000 bikes for the war effort. Competition laurels had also been secured by the official works racing team, which took honors at dirt and board tracks across the US.

By the 1920s the company was exporting machines in both Europe and Japan and sought to expand these markets. The establishment of an extensive dealership network across North America enabled Harley-Davidson to supersede Indian as the biggest motorcycle manufacturer in the US by the middle of the decade. In 1929 a new configuration was added to the marque's inlet-over-exhaust and single-cylinder engines when

a side-valve V-twin debuted on the D Series. The side valve was so reliable that it was used on some models well into the early 1970s. In 1936 Harley-Davidson unveiled their landmark 61EL "Knucklehead", so called for the fistlike appearance of the engine's rocker covers.

World War II provided further opportunities for Harley-Davidson, with the supply of over 70,000

Wild Angels
Peter Fonda (second from right) pictured on a Harley-Davidson custom Panhead in the 1966 movie *The Wild Angels*.

WLA military bikes to the Allies. When civilian motorcycle production resumed in 1945, the marque was given the rights to manufacture the 125cc two-stroke bikes originally made by German company DKW. In 1948 the "Knucklehead" engine was replaced by the Panhead engine,

MODEL JD

FL HYDRA GLIDE

74FLHB ELECTRA GLIDE

VRSCA V-ROD

1903 The first Harley-Davidson, a single-cylinder model, is produced in a wooden shed in Milwaukee.
1907 Harley-Davidson Motor Company is formed.
1914 The first year of the official Harley-Davidson racing team, which soon achieves racetrack success.
1920 Harley-Davidson becomes the world's largest motorcycle manufacturer.
1929 The classic 45 cu in V-twin powerplant, or Flathead, debuts on the Model D.

1936 The Knucklehead engine is introduced.
1937 Joe Petrali sets the world land speed record on a Harley-Davidson, clocking 136 mph (219 km/h).
1941 Harley builds tens of thousands of WLA bikes for the war effort.
1948 The Panhead engine is unveiled.
1949 The Hydra-Glide model features the marque's first hydraulic front forks.
1952 The Model K prefigures the 1957 Sportster, one of the world's longest-running bike models.

1960 Harley-Davidson buys a share of Italian Aermacchi company.
1969 AMF buys a controlling stake in Harley-Davidson.
1970 The XR750 model is unveiled. A later, refined version of this dominates dirt-track racing in the US through to the 21st century.
1981 The management buys the company back from AMF, inspiring their slogan "The Eagle Soars Alone."
1983 Harley Owners' Group (HOG) is set up.

1984 The successful Evolution engine is introduced, contributing to a turnaround in the company's fortunes.
1999 The Twin Cam 88 engine replaces the Evolution powerplant.
2001 The VRSC V-Rod model is unveiled, featuring Harley's first fuel-injected engine with liquid cooling.
2009 Harley-Davidson announces that it will be extending operations into the Indian subcontinent, one of the world's largest motorcycle markets.

which had additional rocker covers. While 1949 saw the introduction of the hydraulically damped telescopic forks used in the production of the Hydra-Glide model. Harley-Davidson's large-capacity bikes were supplemented during the 1950s by smaller-capacity V-twins produced in

response to a stylish breed of British motorcycles from Triumph and BSA that were lighter and faster than anything the US marque had to offer. Notable was the XL Sportster from 1957, which remains one of the longest-running Harley motorcycles still in production.

The 1970s saw the arrival of the XR750 dirt-track racer, which would become the most successful US racing bike. During this decade Harley-Davidson also acknowledged the postwar trend for customizing its bikes, popularized by the Harley choppers featured in the 1969 movie

included the 1990 Fat Boy with its distinctive disc wheels, and in 1999 the new Twin Cam 88 V-twin engine. The company also released a range of models that played on Harley's heritage, combining retro styling with the latest technology. This appealed to a new breed of motorcycle buyer who wanted a stylish American motorcycle but not the typical "biker" image.

Into the new millennium, Harley-Davidson presented exciting new products such as the futuristic V-Rod in 2001 and powerful sports bikes under the Buell name. In 2003 the marque celebrated its centennial with a series of events culminating in a rally in Milwaukee attended by over 100,000 owners. With inroads now made into the lucrative Chinese and Indian markets, Harley-Davidson has—through prudent management and a belief in innovation—emerged as an ultra-successful global brand.

> "Let's **chase sunsets** whether gas is 6 bucks or 6 red cents... Let's **ride** to parties like **rock stars.**"
> HARLEY-DAVIDSON SLOGAN, 2008

In 1960 Harley-Davidson bought a stake in the Italian Aermacchi company. Its single-cylinder bikes were rebadged as Harleys and perfectly suited the new demand for economical runabouts. However, Japanese manufacturers had since emerged offering cheaper, more advanced motorcycles, prompting Harley to introduce the electric starter in 1965 and create the iconic Electra Glide.

Nevertheless, foreign imports began affecting the company's fortunes. Even after a stock-market flotation in 1965, Harley-Davidson continued to struggle, and in 1969 AMF (American Metal Foundries) bought a majority share in the company. AMF's ownership would last until 1981, during which time Harley's image continued to suffer as it experienced quality and reliability issues.

Easy Rider. Pairing a big-twin engine with Sportster styling, the FX Super Glide from 1971 was the first of Harley's factory-built custom models.

The 1980s dawned with the company in a depressed state. The much-needed change came with a 1981 management buyout of AMF that resulted in more efficient production methods, better quality-control, and the decision to promote Harley-Davidson as an American company that was proud of its heritage. In 1984 Harley-Davidson unveiled the Evolution big-twin engine that signified the company was back on track. Powerful, efficient, and—most importantly—reliable, this engine was especially suited to machines such as the Super Glide, a model that cemented Harley's reputation as the maker of America's finest tourers. Further innovations

The V-Rod's fuel injection system
Introduced in 2001, the Revolution engine was a liquid-cooled, fuel-injected V-twin used on the marque's VRSC models.

Economy Transportation

The austerity of wartime and its aftermath meant that inexpensive two-wheelers were in demand to provide mobility rather than to satisfy a sporting or recreational need. During this postwar period, new lineages were established that would prove very successful in the ensuing years, notably Honda in Japan and the Italian Lambretta scooter.

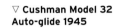

◁ Indian Junior Scout 1940

Origin USA

Engine 500cc, V-twin

Top speed 60 mph (97 km/h)

Launched in 1932, the Junior Scout used a 500 V-twin in the lightweight Prince frame. In 1940 it was dressed with skirts that were added to all Indian models.

◁ Whizzer Model F 1943

Origin USA

Engine 138cc, single-cylinder

Top speed 35 mph (56 km/h)

Whizzer began selling its engines for bicycles in 1939. The belt-drive Model F, launched during WWII "for defense workers only," went on general sale in 1945.

▽ Cushman Model 32 Auto-glide 1945

Origin USA

Engine 318cc, single-cylinder

Top speed 44 mph (71 km/h)

The Ammon family launched their first Auto-glide in 1937 and soon found a ready market for parachute-drop war machines, as well as this fully enclosed civilian version.

△ Cyc-Auto Model J 1947

Origin UK

Engine 98cc, single-cylinder

Top speed 30 mph (48 km/h)

Responding to a 1931 UK tax concession for sub-100cc motorcycles, this machine started an autocycle craze in Britain; later versions were made up to 1958.

◁ Triumph 3T De Luxe 1949

Origin UK

Engine 349cc, inline twin

Top speed 68 mph (109 km/h)

Originally planned for 1940, this slower, less glamorous, version of Triumph's overhead valve vertical-twin came out in 1946 with telescopic front forks.

△ Imme R100 1948

Origin Germany

Engine 99cc, single-cylinder

Top speed 50 mph (80 km/h)

Named after Immenstadt, where it was made, this elegant design features a compact power unit that pivots with the rear suspension, and a single-side front fork.

▷ Lambretta Model B 1948

Origin Italy

Engine 123cc, single-cylinder

Top speed 44 mph (71 km/h)

Innocenti built nearly 10,000 Lambretta Model As before launching the Model B in November 1948. Sales really took off: 35,014 were sold by January 1950.

△ **Ducati Cucciolo 1949**

Origin	Italy
Engine	48cc, single-cylinder
Top speed	40mph (64km/h)

Lawyer Aldo Farinelli and engineer Aldo Leoni invented the Cucciolo clip-on engine during WWI. Postwar, it brought Ducati into the bike market, with 200,000 sold by 1952.

△ **BSA Bantam D1 1949**

Origin	UK
Engine	123cc, single-cylinder
Top speed	53mph (85km/h)

War reparations brought BSA the blueprints for a prewar, two-stroke DKW. They adapted it to create a little workhorse with a three-speed gearbox and telescopic forks.

◁ **Salsbury Model 85 "Super Scooter" 1949**

Origin	USA
Engine	320cc, single-cylinder
Top speed	60mph (97km/h)

E. Foster Salsbury built his first scooter in 1936 and perfected it for the huge Model 85, with automatic transmission, foot brake and throttle, and a super-stylish body.

▽ **Brockhouse Corgi 1949**

Origin	UK
Engine	98cc, single-cylinder
Top speed	30mph (48km/h)

Brockhouse director John Dolphin founded Corgi Motorcycles in 1946 to make a civilian version of his wartime folding Welbike. A total of 27,050 were made up to 1956.

△ **Honda Model D Dream 1949**

Origin	Japan
Engine	98cc, single-cylinder
Top speed	40mph (64km/h)

Soichiro Honda began adding military-surplus engines to bicycles in 1946. His first real motorcycle, the Dream, had a two-stroke engine and two gears.

△ **VéloSoleX 45 1949**

Origin	France
Engine	45cc, single-cylinder
Top speed	21mph (34km/h)

Conceived during WWII and still in production 65 years later, this simple, motorized bicycle has sold millions. The engine drives the front tire via a friction roller.

Racing Resumes

When racing began again after World War II, the machines used were largely based on prewar designs. In some instances, the very same bikes had been quietly hidden away for the duration of the conflict, to reemerge when the fighting was over. The banning of supercharging allowed single-cylinder racers to be competitive in Grand Prix, and it took some time for multi-cylinder engine designs to come to the fore.

◁ **Indian Sports Scout 1940**

Origin USA

Engine 745cc, side-valve V-twin

Top speed 105 mph (169 km/h)

A race winner and record-breaker in the prewar US, the Sport Scout was still competitive in the late 1940s. There were no brakes on this oval track racer.

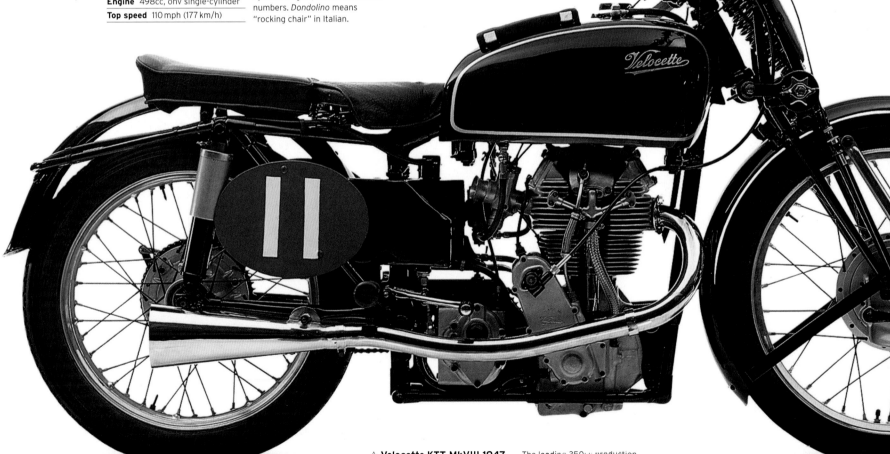

△ **Harley-Davidson WR 1941**

Origin USA

Engine 738cc, side-valve V-twin

Top speed 110 mph (177 km/h)

A match for Indian and competitive into the 1950s, the WR with aluminum cylinder heads was ready-stripped for racing. This example is in dirt-track trim.

△ **Moto Guzzi Dondolino 1946**

Origin Italy

Engine 498cc, ohv single-cylinder

Top speed 110 mph (177 km/h)

This production racing machine, using Guzzi's traditional horizontal-cylinder engine, was built in small numbers. *Dondolino* means "rocking chair" in Italian.

△ **Velocette KTT MkVIII 1947**

Origin UK

Engine 348cc, ohc single-cylinder

Top speed 115 mph (185 km/h)

The leading 350cc production racer, with extensive cylinder finning and swingarm rear suspension, the MkVIII was first issued to selected riders in 1949.

△ **Indian 648 Scout 1948**

Origin	USA
Engine	737cc, side-valve V-twin
Top speed	110 mph (177 km/h)

Indian's ultimate side-valve racer was known as the Big Base. Just 50 were built; one of them won the Daytona 200 in 1948, ridden by US biking champion Floyd Emde.

△ **Benelli 250 GP 1949**

Origin	Italy
Engine	249cc, dohc single-cylinder
Top speed	112 mph (180 km/h)

Benelli's 250 single won the 1939 Isle of Man Lightweight TT. Still competitive in 1950, it won both the TT and the 250cc World Championship.

▽ **Triumph Grand Prix 1949**

Origin	UK
Engine	499cc, ohv parallel-twin
Top speed	120 mph (193 km/h)

Ernie Lyons won the 1946 Manx Grand Prix on a production-based bike with an all-alloy engine. Triumph went on to sell a batch of racers that were based on it.

△ **Norton 30M Manx 1949**

Origin	UK
Engine	499cc, ohc single-cylinder
Top speed	100 mph (160 km/h)

For privateers competing in 500cc TT and Grand Prix road racing, the 30M was the machine of choice. The 1930s plunger frame saw its final year in this model.

△ **AJS 7R 1949**

Origin	UK
Engine	348cc, sohc single-cylinder
Top speed	100 mph (160 km/h)

Recognized by its gold-painted casing housing the chain drive to the overhead camshaft, the AJS 7R had a long and successful racing career.

△ **Gilera Saturno San Remo 1949**

Origin	Italy
Engine	499cc, ohv single-cylinder
Top speed	115 mph (185 km/h)

Although Gilera was best known for its four-cylinder Grand Prix racers, the single-cylinder San Remo models were successful in lesser events.

◁ **Excelsior JAP Speedway 1949**

Origin	UK
Engine	497cc, ohv single-cylinder
Top speed	not known

Excelsior produced specialized Speedway frames at a time when the sport drew huge crowds in the UK, and JAP's potent, methanol-burning engine was dominant.

Norton Manx

For fans of British road-racing motorcycles, the Norton Manx conjures up misty-eyed nostalgia. Made in small numbers for privateer racers from 1947, the big single was modeled on Norton's world championship–winning Grand Prix machines and became a mainstay of racing grids, with many wins in the Manx Grand Prix and four Daytona 200 victories. Constantly developed, the Manx engine acquired the factory racer's double overhead camshafts from 1949. The Manx was Great Britain's preeminent postwar racing model.

NORTON'S ASSOCIATION with the Isle of Man Tourist Trophy goes back to the competition's earliest days, when Rem Fowler won the inaugural (twin-cylinder) race in 1907 on a Norton. The marque went on to dominate the Senior and Junior TTs with its overhead-camshaft singles during the 1930s. Race replicas to "Manx Grand Prix specification" were cataloged and when Norton released a new customer racer after the war, it was called the Manx. In 30M (500cc) and 40M (350cc) forms, the Manx originally had a frame with plunger rear suspension, unkindly nicknamed the "garden gate." From 1951, the Manx featured Norton's superb Featherbed frame, used on the bike ridden by the legendary Geoff Duke to win that year's 350cc and 500cc World Championships. The Manx continued to be produced after Norton withdrew from top-class racing in 1954, and was raced for several years after production of the model ceased in 1962. Replicas of this highly revered model now compete in classic races at its spiritual home, the Isle of Man.

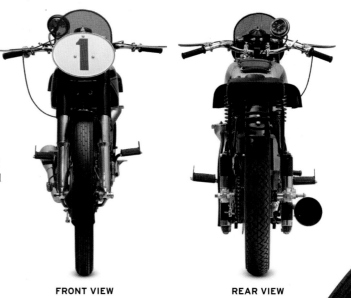

FRONT VIEW   **REAR VIEW**

Born to compete
The Norton logo first appeared on bikes around 1915. The design was supposedly created by the Norton family and has since undergone various subtle adaptations.

Mudguard pad behind saddle for rider to adopt racing crouch

Fuel tank has a capacity of around 4¾ gallons (21.5 liters)

Smiths tachometer is rubber-mounted and reads to 8,000 rpm

Tiny flyscreen offers only token protection for rider

Front fork is hydraulically damped "Roadholder"

Front brake drum measures 8 in (20cm) in diameter

Rear wheel has plunger suspension system

Exhaust pipe is straight through (no muffler), featuring "megaphone" styling

SPECIFICATIONS

Model	Norton 30M Manx (1949)
Assembly	Birmingham, England
Production	1,900
Construction	Steel cradle frame
Engine	499cc, ohc single-cylinder
Power output	52 hp at 7,200 rpm
Transmission	Four-speed
Suspension	Telescopic front forks, plunger rear
Brakes	Drums, front and rear
Maximum speed	100 mph (160 km/h)

Famous forks

Front suspension on the Manx was courtesy of Norton's patented "Roadholder" telescopic forks, which used oil for their hydraulic damping. Advertisements of the time promoted the bike as "the world's best roadholder."

THE BIKE

Aside from the tuned power plant, the Manx featured additional competition components that set it apart from other bikes in the Norton range. These included a close-ratio gearbox, racing magneto, and a quick-release fuel filler cap. From 1951, the Featherbed double-cradle frame with swingarm rear suspension gave the Manx a competitive advantage, providing superior handling on the most challenging courses.

1. Tank script **2.** Air lever **3.** Chain oiler **4.** Oil quick-filler
5. Tachometer **6.** Steering damper knob **7.** Saddle spring
8. Fuel filler **9.** Ventilated front brake **10.** Rear axle fixing
11. Hairpin valve springs **12.** Rear brake pedal

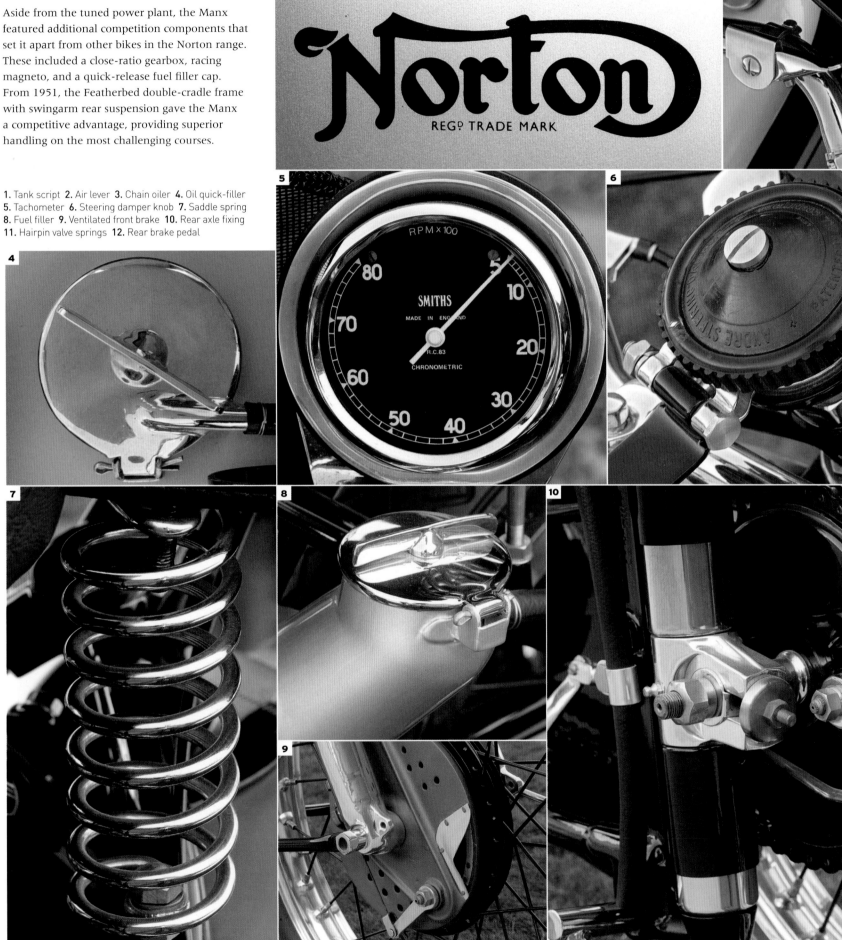

THE ENGINE

With the generously finned head and barrel constructed from aluminum alloy and a crankcase of super-light magnesium alloy, the overhead-camshaft engine was built for the demands of Grand Prix. Later Manxes with twin camshafts and a shorter piston stroke could hit 140 mph (225 km/h) on high gearing.

13. Open primary chain **14.** Side view of the engine **15.** Magneto
16. Carburetor floatbowl **17.** Intake bellmouth **18.** Four-speed gearbox

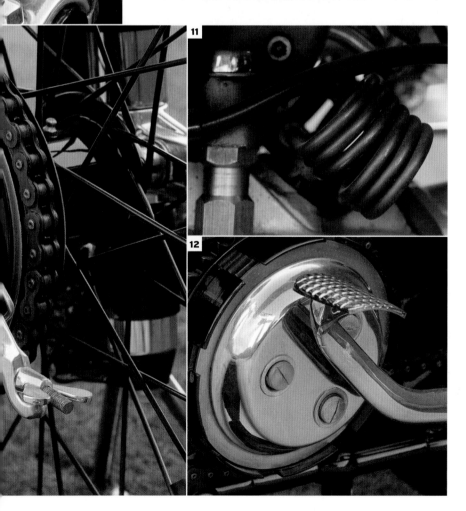

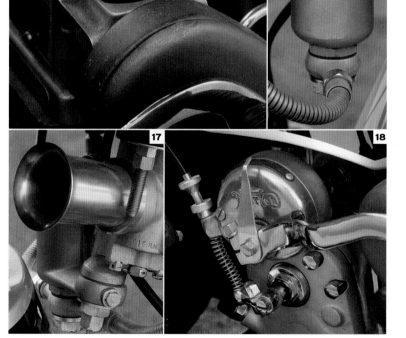

The 1950s

The decade began with the British motorcycle industry at the fore, thanks to an aggressive export policy that would support it for years to come. In most of Europe, motorcycles served as everyday transportation, and as cars were still too expensive for many, simple, cheap, economical two-strokes were the obvious choice. The Italian scooter and French moped spread throughout the world, selling in millions. Prosperity in the US saw the shrinking home industry battling for sales against a mounting tide of European imports.

Scooters

Few could afford a car in the immediate postwar years, but not all were prepared to get dirty and soaked on a conventional motorcycle. The scooter was the answer, crude at first but increasingly sophisticated as the decade progressed—with storage compartments, up to four gears, and even electric starting. Soon the scooter became more of a style statement than merely a form of transportation.

△ **Indian Papoose 1954**
Origin UK/USA
Engine 98cc, single-cylinder
Top speed 30 mph (48 km/h)

UK company Brockhouse made the Corgi, a civilian version of the wartime folding Welbike scooter. The scooter was sold in the US with Indian badging.

△ **Peugeot S157 1956**
Origin France
Engine 147cc, single-cylinder
Top speed 55 mph (89 km/h)

With incentives from the French government, Peugeot designed this scooter on car lines—it was heavy and had two storage bins and comprehensive equipment.

▷ **Heinkel Tourist 1956**
Origin Germany
Engine 174cc, single-cylinder
Top speed 57 mph (92 km/h)

The "Rolls-Royce" of the scooter world, this model was better equipped, quieter, cleaner, and easier to ride than its competitors, but commensurately expensive. Over 100,000 were sold.

▽ **Vespa 125 1957**
Origin Italy
Engine 125cc, single-cylinder
Top speed 43 mph (69 km/h)

Piaggio's little "Wasp" had pressed-steel unitary construction, exceptionally clean lines, and, from 1948, full suspension and a large engine that was still economical.

△ **Capri 70cc 1956**
Origin Italy
Engine 69cc, single-cylinder
Top speed 40 mph (64 km/h)

Bicycle-maker Agrati joined the scooter race relatively late in the 1950s, commissioning somewhat smaller engines from Garelli to power this slender and attractive scooter.

Working Scooters

The ultra-compact scooter power unit, integral with its small rear wheel, was ideal for propelling a small inner city delivery vehicle, so the scooter with a box at the front was born. Swapping it around to drive twin rear wheels and make a "van" offered yet more versions, which soon powered a range of vehicles ideal for a variety of jobs. For novices learning to ride, Lambretta even made a Schoolmaster model with dual controls.

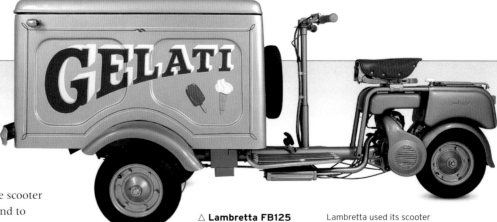

△ **Lambretta FB125 Ice-cream Truck 1950**
Origin Italy
Engine 125cc, single-cylinder
Top speed 28 mph (45 km/h)

Lambretta used its scooter running gear to power light delivery vehicles, adding a big box on the front that could carry up to 440 lb (200 kg) on twin steered and braked wheels.

△ Dürkopp Diana 1957

Origin Germany

Engine 194cc, single-cylinder

Top speed 50 mph (80 km/h)

One of the oldest motorcycle manufacturers, Dürkopp launched its scooter in 1953. It was a luxurious machine with a four-speed gearbox and (later) an electric starter.

▷ Lambretta LD 150 1957

Origin Italy

Engine 148cc, single-cylinder

Top speed 50 mph (80 km/h)

Designed by aeronautical engineers and launched in 1947, like the Vespa, the Lambretta sold in huge numbers. The LD was a refined and powerful version, with optional electric starter.

△ Zündapp Bella R201 1957

Origin Germany

Engine 197cc, single-cylinder

Top speed 60 mph (97 km/h)

Large and heavy with 12 in (30 cm) cast-alloy wheels, the Bella soon grew from 150cc to 200cc and an electric starter was offered from 1955. Over 130,000 were sold up to 1964.

△ Simplex Automatic Scooter 1958

Origin USA

Engine 150cc, single-cylinder

Top speed 50 mph (80 km/h)

A centrifugal clutch and variable transmission added appeal to the Simplex Automatic, but its simple lines never resulted in high sales and the company closed in 1960.

△ Cushman Highlander 1958

Origin USA

Engine 318cc, single-cylinder

Top speed 50 mph (80 km/h)

Cushman's first civilian scooter to have its simple, side-valve engine exposed, the Highlander paved the way for the more motorcycle-like Eagle (right).

△ Cushman Eagle 1958

Origin USA

Engine 318cc, single-cylinder

Top speed 52 mph (84 km/h)

Cushman made engines in Nebraska from 1901 and began putting them in simple scooter frames in the 1930s. This motorcycle-like Eagle was sold for 16 years.

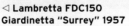

◁ Lambretta FDC150 Giardinetta "Surrey" 1957

Origin Italy

Engine 148cc, single-cylinder

Top speed 37 mph (60 km/h)

Lambretta light commercials changed to a rear-mounted load compartment in 1952 and a 150cc engine in 1955. In 1957 the FDC150 gained a roof and reverse gear.

▷ Lambretta LI 150 1957

Origin Italy

Engine 148cc, single-cylinder

Top speed 53 mph (85 km/h)

The all-new LI brought more storage, a modern design, a new engine, and four gears, but was heavy and slow. This Schoolmaster model has a clutch and brake for the instructor.

Lambretta LD 150

The Lambretta LD was a stylish runabout that epitomized Italian manufacturer Ferdinando Innocenti's initial inspiration for a motor scooter. The fully enclosed model was technically superior to the earlier Lambrettas, combining the simplicity and reliability that people came to expect from the Innocenti stable with extra power and flair. First entering the market as a 125cc model late in 1951, a 150cc version (featured here) was presented in 1954, which successfully combined classy design with low running costs.

INNOCENTI'S 1950 ADVERTISING CAMPAIGN encouraged long-distance scooter journeys with the slogan "More than 100,000 kilometers on a Lambretta," setting the tone for the decade. Scooter clubs, rallies, and newsletters created an exciting atmosphere of youthful freedom, and longer trips were now possible on scooters with increased power and reliability. The Lambretta LD 150, with its single-cylinder, two-stroke engine generating 6 bhp and a top speed of 50 mph (80 km/h), helped to demonstrate that scooters could be used for more adventurous outings, as well as for short hops. Comfort for the driver and passenger was increased by the addition of a hydraulic damper to the torsion bar in the new rear suspension, while a forced-air cooling system using a fan positioned on the flywheel prevented the engine from overheating, even on long journeys. The Lambretta LD was the first of Innocenti's models to be manufactured outside Italy. A great commercial success, it had a production run lasting more than six years. The end of its construction also signaled the end of the company's shaft-driven vehicles.

FRONT VIEW

REAR VIEW

Made in Milan
Production of the first Lambretta scooters began in 1947 at the Innocenti factory in Milan. The name Lambretta derives from the Lambro, a small river near the manufacturing works.

Spare wheel mounted with fuel/oil container and carrier

Handle for passenger

Steel panels enclose engine and transmission

Storage compartment also serves as base for speedometer and clock

Leg shields protect against wind, rain, and dirt

Pressed-steel wheels are interchangeable and equipped with low-inflation-pressure tires

Muffler box is a pressed steel chamber with outlet to rear

Luxury features

An array of chic options and aftermarket accessories embellish this Lambretta LD 150 MkIII. Most obvious are the front windshield, a rear carrier with spare wheel and extra fuel tank, heel plates, and footboard extensions.

SPECIFICATIONS	
Model	Lambretta LD 150 MkIII (1957)
Assembly	Milan, Italy
Production	110,186
Construction	High-tensile steel tube frame
Engine	148cc, single-cylinder
Power output	6 hp at 4,600 rpm
Transmission	Three-speed
Suspension	Trailing-arm front, torsion bar/hydraulic damper rear
Brakes	Drums, front and rear
Maximum speed	50 mph (80 km/h)

THE BIKE

Advertised as "the ideal personal transport machine", the Lambretta LD 150 boasted a winning combination of balance, comfort, and simplicity. Its controls were easy to master, allowing those who had never driven a motorized vehicle before to quickly acquire confidence on the road. The high-tensile steel tube frame ensured rigidity and minimized vibration, the interchangeable wheels were easily removed, and changing gear with the handlebar twistgrip was a breeze. Novices found it approachable, while experienced drivers relished its reliability and extra power.

1. Maker's badge **2.** Key locks steering **3.** Lights switch **4.** Handlebar gear change **5.** Clock **6.** Rear brake pedal **7.** Horn **8.** Spare fuel and oil **9.** Filler for petrol/oil mix **10.** Footboard **11.** Panel release **12.** Air outlet **13.** Chromed guard accessory **14.** Kick-starter **15.** Air intake **16.** Front wheel **17.** Rear lamp and indicators **18.** Exhaust outlet

ENGINE

The single-cylinder, two-stroke engine and transmission of the Lambretta LD 150 were completely enclosed, leading distributors to advertise that "no protective clothing is necessary" to ride the bike— a campaign aimed at stylish dressers and women riders. The fan-cooled engine had a flywheel ignition magneto, an inclined cast-iron cylinder with an alloy cylinder head, a high-tensile steel connecting rod, built-up crankshaft, multi-plate clutch, and three-speed gearbox with constant mesh gears. Designed to keep the peace in urban areas, noise was diminished by attaching an expansion chamber to the exhaust pipe and adding an air cleaner to prevent dust from entering the carburetor.

19. Casing removed to show engine **20.** Ignition coil **21.** Intake manifold
22. Exhaust downpipe **23.** Fan intake

Sports Twins

The 1950s saw a huge growth in the market for purely recreational sports motorcycles, especially in the prosperous US. Harley-Davidson, the only US marque still in volume production, offered big engines, while British factories combined high performance with nimble handling. Germany went for more refinement and exclusivity. By the end of the decade, sports twins that could exceed 100 mph (160 km/h) were plentiful.

◁ **Triumph 6T Thunderbird 1950**

Origin UK

Engine 649cc, inline two

Top speed 98 mph (158 km/h)

In response to US demands for more power from the Speed Twin, Triumph enlarged the engine and achieved a sales breakthrough. Native American mythology inspired its name.

◁ **Royal Enfield 500 Twin 1951**

Origin UK

Engine 496cc, inline twin

Top speed 78 mph (126 km/h)

Enfield used its excellent Bullet frame for the 500 Twin, giving it swingarm suspension and coil ignition. However, it was one of the less popular British twins.

△ **Triumph TR5 Trophy 1956**

Origin UK

Engine 498cc, straight-two

Top speed 93 mph (150 km/h)

Tuning kits were available for Triumph's Trophy and Tiger 100 models' revvy all-alloy 500cc engine. Triumphs had swingarm frames from 1954.

△ **Triumph T120 Bonneville 1959**

Origin UK

Engine 649cc, inline twin

Top speed 115 mph (185 km/h)

Twin carburetors and a stronger crankshaft for Triumph's 650cc twin created the Bonneville, a fast model that would stay in production for decades.

△ **Matchless G9 1951**

Origin UK

Engine 498cc, inline two

Top speed 85 mph (137 km/h)

Well-finished and built for comfort with Teledraulic forks and a swingarm frame, the smallest Matchless twin was sold alongside the similar AJS version until 1961.

▽ **Matchless G11 CSR 1958**

Origin UK

Engine 593cc, inline twin

Top speed 105 mph (169 km/h)

Matchless steadily increased the size and power output of its big twins; the tuned CSR was the first production bike to record over 100 mph (160 km/h) in one hour in 1958.

◁ **Harley-Davidson Model K 1952**

Origin USA

Engine 743cc, V-twin

Top speed 85 mph (137 km/h)

This smaller-engined Harley was intended to rival the lighter, better-handling British bikes that were storming the US market, but it needed further tuning to achieve that.

◁ **BSA A7 1952**

Origin UK

Engine 495cc, inline two

Top speed 87 mph (140 km/h)

A redesign for 1951 improved the A7, which was available in both standard and sports versions. This is one of three A7s to complete a 5,000-mile (8,050-km) reliability test in 1952.

▽ **Harley-Davidson XL Sportster 1957**

Origin USA

Engine 883cc, V-twin

Top speed 100 mph (161 km/h)

Harleys came to life with the overhead-valve "Ironhead" XL engine in the K-series frame. Good enough to rival British competitors, it continued to be listed until 1972.

△ **BSA Super Rocket 1957**

Origin UK

Engine 646cc, inline two

Top speed 105 mph (169 km/h)

With a high compression head and Amal TT carburetor, and a duplex swingarm frame, BSA's flagship twin was a strong rival for the Norton and Triumph competition.

◁ **Douglas 90 Plus 1953**

Origin UK

Engine 348cc, flat-twin

Top speed 100 mph (160 km/h)

Equipped with a huge front brake and highly tuned engine, just 250 of the rapid 90 Plus were made over four years, while Douglas underwent reorganization due to poor sales.

▷ **Horex Imperator 1955**

Origin Germany

Engine 392cc, inline two

Top speed 90 mph (145 km/h)

This bike had an overhead camshaft unit construction engine and drive chain enclosure. Production ended in 1960, but Horex is being revived with a V6 design.

▽ **BMW R69 1959**

Origin Germany

Engine 594cc, flat-twin

Top speed 100 mph (160 km/h)

This flat-twin with shaft drive was the last word in speed, comfort, silence, and reliability. Front suspension was by Earle's patent leading-link fork.

△ **Norton Dominator 88 1959**

Origin UK

Engine 497cc, inline two

Top speed 90 mph (145 km/h)

The twin-cylinder Dominator contenders were available in 500cc 88 and 600cc 99 versions. Both had Norton's own sturdy four-speed gearbox and the Featherbed frame.

Lively Lightweights

Machines of 250cc and under were popular in Europe. Their benefits included low taxation, economy, easy handling, and suitability for commuting. Lightweights were also ideal for young novice riders, so manufacturers offered sports versions, often with two-stroke engines offering a favorable power-to-weight ratio. The end of the decade saw early Japanese arrivals, a foretaste of the future.

◁ Indian 250 Warrior 1951

Origin USA

Engine 500cc, inline twin

Top speed 85 mph (137 km/h)

Indian struggled after the war: the vertical twin Warrior was a brave try but was poorly developed and no match for cheaper and more reliable imports from Europe.

△ Excelsior Talisman Sports 1952

Origin UK

Engine 244cc, inline twin

Top speed 65 mph (105 km/h)

This long-established company outshone UK rivals with this zesty twin-carburetor two-stroke twin, although it had basic undamped suspension and weak electrics.

△ MV Agusta 175CSS Supersport 1953

Origin Italy

Engine 172cc, single-cylinder

Top speed 62 mph (100 km/h)

A shapely fuel tank earned MV's overhead-camshaft sport bike the nickname Disco Volante ("Flying Saucer"). The leading link front forks are a British Earles design.

△ Moto Morini Turismo 2T 1953

Origin Italy

Engine 123cc, single-cylinder

Top speed 55 mph (89 km/h)

Alfonso Morini judged the postwar market well, introducing this lively two-stroke bike with three-speed gearbox just after the war, even winning races with one.

◁ Victoria V35 Bergmeister 1953

Origin Germany

Engine 345cc, V-twin

Top speed 80 mph (129 km/h)

This sophisticated shaft-drive, four-stroke motorcycle was a perfect midrange machine for the German market, though a delayed release hampered sales.

△ Triumph Tiger Cub 1954

Origin UK

Engine 199cc, single-cylinder

Top speed 68 mph (109 km/h)

A neat and effective four-stroke single with a reasonable top speed for its time, the Tiger Cub was considered rather noisy—a bike for young riders with pretensions.

△ Adler MB200 1954

Origin Germany

Engine 195cc, inline two

Top speed 65 mph (105 km/h)

The beautifully engineered Adler two-strokes featured clockspring front suspension and other ingenious details. Production dried up as Adler turned to making typewriters.

◁ NSU Supermax 1957

Origin Germany

Engine 247cc, single-cylinder

Top speed 78 mph (126 km/h)

NSU steadily improved its 250 singles throughout the decade, adopting a monocoque pressed-steel frame in 1953. By 1955 it was the world's biggest motorcycle builder.

△ FB Mondial 175 Turismo Veloce 1956

Origin Italy

Engine 181cc, single-cylinder

Top speed 65 mph (105 km/h)

Founded by Count Giuseppe Boselli in 1948, FB was soon making small top-quality motorcycles such as this one, as well as winning world championships with its racers.

△ Ambassador Super S 1958

Origin UK

Engine 249cc, inline twin

Top speed 70 mph (113 km/h)

Heavy mudguarding was added to this conventional lightweight bike with a Villiers engine in 1958. Ambassador was founded after World War II by racing driver Kaye Don.

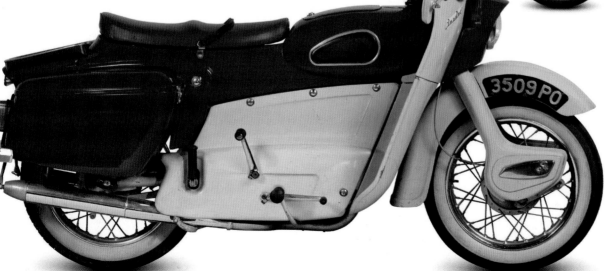

3509 PO

△ Yamaha YD2 1959

Origin Japan

Engine 247cc, inline twin

Top speed 68 mph (109 km/h)

The first Yamaha sold in Europe (from 1960), the YD2 had a super-reliable two-stroke twin engine based on the Adler design, but with oil injection, and very chunky styling.

◁ Ariel Leader 1959

Origin UK

Engine 249cc, in-line twin

Top speed 70 mph (113 km/h)

A brave attempt to build a motorcycle that would keep its rider as clean as on a scooter, the Ariel Leader was a good but expensive effort with a new Adler-like two-stroke engine.

Soichiro Honda at the Asama Kazan race in 1955

Great Marques
The Honda Story

For the past 50 years the Honda Motor Company has been the world's largest motorcycle manufacturer. However, the Japanese company's birth in the mid-1940s was a very low-key affair, which belied its multi-billion-dollar future. That dream outcome was down to the initiative, determination, and vision of one man—Soichiro Honda.

POST–WORLD WAR II Japan was a nation stricken by overcrowded mass transit and fuel restrictions. It was against this backdrop that self-taught engineer Soichiro Honda came up with an idea that would eventually allow his company to bring motorcycles to the masses.

Honda acquired 500 war-surplus two-stroke electric motors designed for portable electric generators used in military radios, and adapted them for attaching to push-bikes. The makeshift motorbikes were so successful that when they sold out, Honda designed and built his own 50cc unit. The Honda Motor

Honda Benly poster
A 1950s poster advertises the first-generation Honda Benly. Appearing with a four-stroke engine and a new frame with a pressed steel backbone, the Benly had a shaky start but eventually became a highly popular model.

Company was formed in 1948, and the next year the first Honda motorcycle to feature a Honda-designed motor and frame was produced. The two-stroke 98cc machine was called the Model D, with the D standing for "Dream"—a name that would regularly be used over the next few decades.

Eager to expand its range, in 1951 Honda introduced its first four-stroke motorcycle, the Dream E. The following year saw the debut of a 50cc motorized bicycle sporting a title that would be adopted by Honda for its small-capacity models through to the present day—the Cub.

As a racing fan, the company's founder was soon developing models that could be pushed to their limits

"It was a **devastating win** for the Orient."

THE *ISLE OF MAN EXAMINER*, ON HONDA'S 1961 TT VICTORY

on the racetrack. Soichiro Honda took inspiration from the European bikes he witnessed at the Isle of Man TT races in the mid-1950s. The marque was first represented at the famed race series in 1959, when several 125cc machines secured Honda the manufacturers' title in the ultra-lightweight class. Two years later, the company announced its arrival on the world racing scene when British rider Mike Hailwood became 250cc World Champion.

Honda badge
(introduced 1988)

The 1960s saw Honda flourish as it capitalized on its competition success and expanded overseas. A foothold was established in the US through the establishment of a dedicated sales division in Los Angeles. Despite a slow start, the marque grew at a phenomenal rate, and by the end of 1962 Honda was selling 40,000 bikes a year in the US market.

Key to this expansion was the creation of a dealership network and a promotional drive that focused on the fun aspect of its different-looking new "clean" motorcycles—principally the 50cc Super Cub model. An example was a 1962 advertising campaign that ran with the slogan, "You meet the nicest people on a Honda." For consumers used to the traditional oil-stained image of the motorcycling world, this was a breath of fresh air.

By the end of the 1960s, Honda's model development program had produced a wide variety of bikes, ranging from small mopeds to large road bikes. Arguably the most important of its bikes was the CB750, which set new standards for what could be achieved on a production model in terms of equipment levels and performance capabilities.

Over the following two decades Honda further broadened its lineup, with classic offerings such as the

company's inaugural long-distance tourer, the 1974 Goldwing, and the successful 250cc Elsinore motocross model. In 1979, the Elsinore rolled off the production line at a new plant in Ohio, making Honda the first Japanese manufacturer to build bikes in the US.

Grand Prix racing continued to prove fruitful for Honda. Freddie Spencer's 1983 and 1985 wins in the 500cc World Championship were highlights among several achievements in this and other race series. Key road models such as the VF750F and a new

Model D

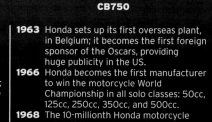

CB750

Goldwing GL1500 SE

CBR1000RR Fireblade

1948 The Honda Motor Company is formed.
1949 The 98cc Model D becomes the company's first motorcycle.
1951 Honda's first four-stroke bike, the Dream E, makes its debut.
1958 The Super Cub 50cc model is released; in this and later variants it will become the world's best-selling vehicle, with 60 million built by 2008.
1959 The company makes its first appearance at the Isle of Man TT races.
1961 Honda wins the 125cc and 250cc TTs.

1963 Honda sets up its first overseas plant, in Belgium; it becomes the first foreign sponsor of the Oscars, providing huge publicity in the US.
1966 Honda becomes the first manufacturer to win the motorcycle World Championship in all solo classes: 50cc, 125cc, 250cc, 350cc, and 500cc.
1968 The 10-millionth Honda motorcycle rolls off the production line.
1969 The CB750 makes its debut as Honda's first four-cylinder model.

1974 Honda enters the touring market with the Goldwing, a model that finds favor with North American buyers.
1978 The NR500 model is introduced; developed for grand prix racing, it has 32 valves and oval pistons.
1982 French rider Cyril Neveu wins the motorcycle class of the Paris−Dakar Rally on a Honda XR500R.
1986 Motorcycle production starts in Spain.
1991 The founder of Honda, Soichiro Honda, dies at age 84.

1996 Honda's CBR1100 Blackbird becomes the fastest production motorcycle on the planet, at 177 mph (285 km/h).
2001 The marque records its 500th motorcycle grand prix victory.
2007 Spanish rider Toni Bou wins the Trials World Championship on a Spanish-built Montessa-Honda.
2008 Honda builds its 200-millionth bike.
2010 The cutting-edge VFR1200F, featuring a push-button gear-change system, is unveiled.

US-made Goldwing tourer featuring a huge six-cylinder, 1,520cc engine ensured that Honda remained one of the world's leading manufacturers.

In 1991 the company mourned the passing of its founder, Soichiro Honda. Nevertheless, the expansion plans continued with initiatives to make inroads into the Chinese market and the introduction of class-leading products that included the RC45 superbike and the CBR900RR Fireblade, which redefined the sports bike through its exceptional power-to-weight ratio. Notable milestones were reached when the 20-millionth Super Cub model was manufactured, in 1992, and an impressive total of 100 million bikes had been produced by Honda by 1997.

The new millennium brought with it an exciting new racing V-twin, the SP-1, which secured the World Superbike Championship in its debut year of 2000, while Valentino Rossi took MotoGP titles in

Honda engine
This cutaway illustration of a Honda 750cc K2 motorcycle engine shows its gearbox (bottom left) and clutch (bottom right). The four-cylinder, four-stroke engine is a single overhead camshaft type.

2002 and 2003. A continued dedication to overseas markets led to the opening of new plants in China and the expansion of operations in other parts of the world. With a raft of innovations, such as the world's first motorcycle airbag and investment in fuel-cell technology, the pioneering spirit of Soichiro Honda remains very much alive within the company.

MotoGP testing
Italian MotoGP rider Max Biaggi takes a curve on his Repsol-Honda motorbike during the official test session at Catalunya's racetrack, near Barcelona, Spain, in 2005.

Tourers

In the 1950s, mature riders who were unconcerned by racer performance had a wide selection of comfortable, powerful, and practical machines to choose from. Built to provide smooth, quiet cruising, these bikes were used for weekend recreation as well as daily transportation. Machines of 500cc or more were often used to pull a sidecar for a partner or child.

▷ **Watsonian JAP Combo 1950**

Origin UK

Engine 996cc, V-twin

Top speed 80 mph (129 km/h)

Ron Watson built Watsonian sidecars, and had this prototype motorcycle with a sturdy JAP engine made to haul them; but JAP declined production, so this was the only example ever built.

△ **Royal Enfield 500 Twin 1951**

Origin UK

Engine 496cc, inline twin

Top speed 78 mph (126 km/h)

Built for comfort with excellent suspension for its time, the Enfield twin was a great touring bike that continued in production for 10 years.

▽ **Royal Enfield Constellation Airflow 1959**

Origin UK

Engine 692cc, inline twin

Top speed 100 mph (160 km/h)

At 700cc the Constellation was the biggest parallel-twin in the market. This innovative "Airflow" version had an aerodynamic molded fairing as well as a touring screen.

△ **Ariel KH Hunter 1954**

Origin UK

Engine 498cc, inline twin

Top speed 80 mph (129 km/h)

Ariel's first parallel-twin engine was launched in 1948 and their updated KH Hunter with swingarm suspension and an alloy cylinder head followed in 1954.

△ **BSA A10 Golden Flash 1953**

Origin UK

Engine 646cc, inline twin

Top speed 95 mph (153 km/h)

BSA followed rivals by enlarging its 500 to a 650 in 1950, targeting the US market. Flexible and strong, the Golden Flash was well able to haul a sidecar if required.

▽ **Ariel Square Four MkII 1955**

Origin UK

Engine 995cc, Square Four

Top speed 100 mph (161 km/h)

This Ariel features the improved and final 1954 to 1959 version of the 1,000cc Square Four. The flexible engine pulled from 10 mph to 100 mph (16 km/h to 160 km/h) in top gear.

△ **Hoffmann Gouverneur 1954**

Origin Germany

Engine 248cc, flat-twin

Top speed 70 mph (113 km/h)

Established in 1948, Hoffmann developed its own flat-twin, four-stroke engine for the Gouverneur, but it had problems with overheating. The company folded in 1954.

△ **Harley-Davidson FL Panhead 1955**

Origin USA

Engine 1,200cc, V-twin

Top speed 95 mph (153 km/h)

Harley-Davidson's overhead-valve "Panhead" V-twin was introduced in 1948 and used until 1965. This FL tourer is in US police trim, carrying special equipment.

△ **Douglas Dragonfly 1955**

Origin UK

Engine 348cc, flat-twin

Top speed 70 mph (113 km/h)

This last Douglas motorcycle to be made had a BMW-like flat-twin engine layout and shaft drive. It was smooth and comfortable but lacked power.

▷ **Vincent D Black Prince 1956**

Origin UK

Engine 998cc, V-twin

Top speed 120 mph (193 km/h)

Last of the legendary Vincent V-twin motorcycles, the Black Prince boasted fully enveloping fiberglass bodywork. However, sales were poor and production ended after 1955.

△ **IFA BK350 1956**

Origin Germany

Engine 343cc, flat-twin

Top speed 68 mph (109 km/h)

East German IFA's flat-twin, two-stroke had a low center of gravity combined with a shaft drive and full suspension, which made this a comfortable touring machine.

△ **BMW R50 Combo 1957**

Origin Germany

Engine 494cc, flat-twin

Top speed 72 mph (115 km/h)

The torque and flexibility of the R50's flat-twin made it a natural choice for pulling a sidecar. Germany's Steib unit, shown here, matches the BMW's superior quality.

△ **Triumph Twenty-one 3TA 1958**

Origin UK

Engine 349cc, inline twin

Top speed 80 mph (129 km/h)

Perhaps with an eye on the success of scooters, Triumph introduced this middleweight bike with a rear enclosure that was nicknamed the "bathtub." It had relatively small 17-in (43-cm) wheels.

Flyweights

For the vast majority of people at the beginning of the 1950s, the only personal transportation option was the bicycle. Many leapt at the option to motorize it for a relatively small outlay: adding a motorized rear wheel cost around $70. As the decade progressed, manufacturers—led by Italy and Japan—offered ever more integrated packages, and the moped was born.

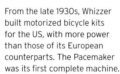

△ Triumph BDG 125 1950

Origin Germany

Engine 123cc, split-single-cylinder

Top speed 56 mph (90 km/h)

Made by Triumph Werke Nürnburg (TWN), this ultra-lightweight featured a split single two-stroke engine with two pistons and one combustion chamber, as pioneered by DKW.

△ Cyclemaster 1951

Origin UK

Engine 32cc, single-cylinder

Top speed 23 mph (37 km/h)

This prewar German DKW design was built by EMI and sold as Cyclemaster in the UK from 1950; popular and easy to add to any bicycle, it grew from 26cc to 32cc in 1951.

△ Trojan Mini-Motor 1951

Origin UK

Engine 50cc, single-cylinder

Top speed 20 mph (32 km/h)

Designed in Italy in 1946 and made under license in the UK by Trojan, the engine powered a bicycle via a roller on the rear tire.

▽ Whizzer Pacemaker 1951

Origin USA

Engine 199cc, single-cylinder

Top speed 35 mph (56 km/h)

From the late 1930s, Whizzer built motorized bicycle kits for the US, with more power than those of its European counterparts. The Pacemaker was its first complete machine.

◁ BSA Winged Wheel 1952

Origin UK

Engine 35cc, single-cylinder

Top speed 23 mph (37 km/h)

Attachable to any standard cycle frame (though BSA did make some frames of their own, with front suspension), the bicycle motor was soon superseded by the moped.

△ Honda Cub 1952

Origin Japan

Engine 49cc, single-cylinder

Top speed 22 mph (35 km/h)

Honda's first products were bicycle motors providing basic powered transport in postwar Japan. The company made 6,500 Cub kits per month in the early 1950s.

△ **NSU Quickly N 1954**

Origin	Germany
Engine	49cc, single-cylinder
Top speed	28mph (45km/h)

Over half a million Quicklys were built from 1953 to 1963. It was one of the best mopeds, with a pressed-steel backbone frame and forks, two gears, and a front suspension.

△ **Honda 50 Super Cub 1958**

Origin	Japan
Engine	49cc, single-cylinder
Top speed	30mph (48km/h)

This brilliant design propelled Honda to success—the rider-friendly Cub four-stroke with an automatic clutch and plastic leg-shields was a massive seller in Southeast Asia.

△ **Moto Guzzi Galletto 200 1958**

Origin	Italy
Engine	192cc, single-cylinder
Top speed	55mph (89km/h)

The Galletto ("rooster") four-stroke scooter made from 1950 to 1958 had motorcycle-like stability, thanks to large wheels. A spare was mounted across the leg-shields.

△ **New Hudson Autocycle 1957**

Origin	UK
Engine	98cc, single-cylinder
Top speed	32mph (51km/h)

BSA acquired New Hudson during WWII and reintroduced the inexpensive Autocycle, updating it through the 1950s. A forerunner of the later mopeds, it survived until 1958.

△ **Kreidler Florett K53M 1959**

Origin	Germany
Engine	49cc, single-cylinder
Top speed	35mph (56km/h)

Kreidler began making small bikes in 1951 and by 1959 had captured a third of the German motorcycle market with its powerful and well-built, full-suspension mopeds.

◁ **Motom Super Sport 1958**

Origin	Italy
Engine	48cc, single-cylinder
Top speed	50mph (80km/h)

Motom put a small yet powerful two-stroke engine in a pressed-steel frame with integral fuel tank to create one of the earliest sports mopeds.

A Vespa is ridden through Rome in the late 1940s

Great Marques
The Vespa Story

Although it was born out of a need to provide a means of cheap travel in the impoverished postwar years, the Vespa became a style icon for the free-spirited, carefree, and fashion-conscious around the world. The scooter whose name means "wasp" in Italian created a buzz that none of its rivals could equal.

AFTER WORLD WAR II, with Italy financially crippled and physically in disarray, Enrico Piaggio needed to find a new purpose for his factory in the Tuscan town of Pontedera. The company he had inherited with his brother had produced boats, railroad cars, and, most notably, aircraft. Now they had to satisfy a consumer need for cut-price goods. Extensive bomb damage had left the country's roads pockmarked with craters, so Piaggio saw a gap in the market for a form of transportation that would be able to negotiate the pitted road surfaces swiftly and safely. The new motorcycle was to be maneuverable,

Enrico Piaggio (1905–1965)

streamlined, and a good buy. But these considerations were not to be at the expense of style.

Piaggio did not like the first prototype, called the MP5, so he turned to Corradino D'Ascanio, an aeronautical engineer. His initial standpoint was his dislike of motorcycles; seeing them as cumbersome and ugly, D'Ascanio steered well clear of traditional templates. In his design, he was "trying to build the machine as simply as possible."

Scooters had been made before, but not like this. The concealed engine was mounted above the rear wheel and the gear lever was incorporated into the handlebar. Influenced by his aeronautical background, D'Ascanio shaped the body from sheet metal. There was no drive chain because the rear wheel was powered from the transmission. Helped by the front splash guard, this made dirt-free riding a possibility. The famous step-though feature left the center area of the bike free, which increased its appeal to women. The fact that the front and rear were linked by this slim middle section led Piaggio to compare the machine to a wasp, immediately renaming the MP6 prototype "Vespa."

However, acceptance was by no means immediate. In early 1946 journalists and the public alike were

intrigued but confused by the Vespa 98. Sales of the first 50 models were sluggish. With a top speed of 37 mph (60 km/h), it was slow to fire the imagination. But its combination of being relatively inexpensive (payment could be made in installments) and very stylish soon turned its fortunes round.

Sense of freedom
By the mid-1960s Vespa had established a strong identity as a manufacturer of stylish and fun scooters that were attractive to the youth market.

As early as 1947 a black-market trade to avoid waiting lists had built up. Between 1947 and 1950 Vespa sales rose dramatically—from 2,500 to 60,000. The money-can't-buy publicity from Vespas' many movie appearances helped

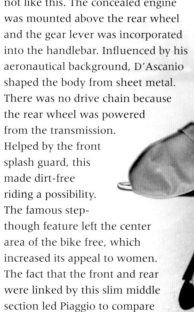

Scooters for all
As this advertisement from the early 1960s highlights, Vespa was keen to promote the idea that its scooters were an object of desire for women as well as men.

125

VBB Sportique

ET3

LX 50

1946 On April 23 a patent is submitted for what would become the Vespa.
1948 The Vespa 125 is the first model to come with rear suspension.
1950 The Vespa 125 Corsa takes first and second at the Bologna Grand Prix.
1951 The Vespa Torpedo sets a record for the flying kilometer, covering the distance in just over 21 seconds at an average speed of 106.3 mph (171.1 km/h).
1952 Worldwide membership of the Vespa Club reaches 50,000.

1953 The brand is given a huge boost through exposure in the hit movie *Roman Holiday.*
1954 The release of the Vespa 150 is a landmark for Piaggio and for scooters in general.
1956 The millionth Vespa is sold, just a decade after the first model appeared.
1962 Surrealist artist Salvador Dalí customizes a Vespa belonging to two students in his own inimitable way.
1965 Enrico Piaggio dies.

1970 Regulations in France require the Vespa 50 to have pedals; the feature makes the model highly collectible.
1972 A first for Vespa: a 200 cc model, with electronic ignition to boot.
1977 The Vespa P125 X features a reworked front suspension and redesigned handlebars.
1985 The PX series is given a sporty makeover with the T5 Pole Position, which also has a revised rear end and a small windshield at the front.

1991 The Vespa 50 Special Revival is released.
1996 The ET4 is equipped with a four-stroke engine; with the Vespa celebrating its half-century, total estimated sales now stand at 15 million.
2001 The ET2 and ET4 signal the reintroduction of the Vespa to North America after a gap of 20 years.
2003 The Granturismo (GTS) 125 and 200 come with 12-inch wheels.
2008 Piaggio releases the Vespa GTS 300 Super, the most powerful Vespa ever.

"It looks like a **wasp**!"

ENRICO PIAGGIO, ON SEEING THE VESPA PROTOTYPE

transform the brand into an international phenomenon. Defined by Gregory Peck and Audrey Hepburn zipping through the streets of the Eternal City in the 1953 movie *Roman Holiday*, the Vespa became cinematic shorthand for cool. When ridden by a movie character, it conveyed youth and liberation. As Hollywood stars rode them both on and off screen, sales skyrocketed,

and markets opened up across Europe and farther afield, from South America to East Asia.

Although one-off models such as 1950's Montlhéry and the following year's Torpedo both set world speed records, power was never really the point of the single-cylinder, two-stroke Vespa. However, Enrico Piaggio took the step of discontinuing the 98cc models at the close of 1947; the focus was now on 125cc machines. In turn, these were followed in the mid-1950s by the Vespa

Cult exposure
Quadrophenia, the 1979 movie about British mods and rockers, reflected how the Vespa had become an emblem of the mod subculture in the 1960s.

150—the model regarded as perhaps the most striking production scooter ever. The GS version even broke the 60 mph (97 km/h) barrier.

The markets certainly responded, as seen in the early 1960s when the Vespa 50 proved irresistibly seductive to cost-conscious young riders. As the last Vespa designed by D'Ascanio, it marked the end of an era.

With total sales of the model having reached 3 million, it was a fitting way to bow out. However, that did not signal the end of Vespa innovation. For a time in the 1960s more Vespas were sold in the UK than in any other country. The swinging 60s would have been missing one of its major icons without this scooter. Into the 1970s the marque released the Vespa 200 Rally, which offered riders increased speed and electronic ignition.

In an era when the full-throated motorbikes coming out of Japan were presenting formidable challenges,

Vespa countered with a more aggressive body design allied to greater engine performance figures. The T5 Pole Position of 1985 was a feisty and sporty addition, while in 1996 the traditionally two-stroke Vespa engine became a four-stroke operation with the ET4 125.

There was a damaging two-decade absence from the North American market from the early 1980s, but encouraging inroads first made by the ET series were followed by the GTS and LX. An updated and improved 2011 version of the PX, originally released three decades earlier, still maintained the importance of the Vespa tradition. As the British *Independent* newspaper stated in its review: "What you are getting is the classic scooter experience." As well as the marque's reestablishment of a US presence, financial concerns closer to home were taken care of by Roberto Colaninno, who assumed presidency of the Piaggio Group.

With a firm direction for the 21st century, Vespa remains beloved and, what is more, relevant, with urban parking an increasing problem and the Vespa's low running costs making more sense than ever. Not that enjoyment has been diminished in any way. Listen to Vespa owners and certain words crop up repeatedly: fun, lifestyle, and liberation. For this timeless scooter, trends are temporary, but class is permanent.

Useful Lightweights

Those who could afford a "real" motorcycle in the 1950s expected something that was a definite cut above the basic bicycle-based transportation of the past. Manufacturers responded with ever more comfort and sophistication, wrapped around small, mostly two-stroke engines of neater appearance. Unit construction arrived for engine and gearbox, full suspension became commonplace, and even electric gear selection was tried.

▷ James Comet 1950

Origin UK

Engine 98cc, single-cylinder

Top speed 40 mph (64 km/h)

James's postwar bikes were two-stroke, Villiers-powered until AMC took over in 1951, substituting its own engines on all bikes except the Comet, which was made up to 1964.

△ NSU 251 OSL 1951

Origin Germany

Engine 242cc, single-cylinder

Top speed 65 mph (105 km/h)

Descended from a 1933 design used by wartime dispatch riders, the lively, overhead-valve single would be superseded in 1953 by the more modern NSU Max.

▷ Excelsior Skutabyk 1954

Origin UK

Engine 98cc, single-cylinder

Top speed 38 mph (61 km/h)

Looking like a half-hearted attempt to cash in on the scooter boom, this 100cc motorcycle, clad with leg shields and ungainly steel enclosures, did not sell.

△ Harley-Davidson S-125 "Hummer" 1952

Origin USA

Engine 123cc, single-cylinder

Top speed 53 mph (85 km/h)

Harley-Davidson acquired the 125cc DKW two-stroke engine design as part of war reparations, and used it in this novice bike, known as the Hummer from 1955.

▽ Express Radex 200 1954

Origin Germany

Engine 197cc, single-cylinder

Top speed 67 mph (108 km/h)

This handy runabout was powered by a JLO engine. Along with a number of other German marques, Express was absorbed into the Zweirad Union motorcycle combine in 1957.

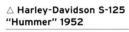

◁ **Victoria KR21 Swing 1956**

Origin Germany

Engine 199cc, single-cylinder

Top speed 59 mph (95 km/h)

The technically advanced Swing's engine and transmission pivoted inside the frame, moving with the rear suspension. Electric gear changing was added from 1956.

▷ **MZ RT 125 1956**

Origin East Germany

Engine 123cc, single-cylinder

Top speed 50 mph (80 km/h)

The original 1939 DKW 125 continued in production after WWII in the original factory in East Germany, where it became known as an MZ. This model was built up to 1965.

△ **DKW RT 175 VS 1957**

Origin Germany

Engine 174cc, single-cylinder

Top speed 65 mph (105 km/h)

The company that made two-stroke motorcycles popular continued to build them after WWII. Upgraded front and rear suspension was added to the VS model in 1956.

◁ **BMW R26 1957**

Origin Germany

Engine 247cc, single-cylinder

Top speed 80 mph (129 km/h)

BMW's luxury single was steadily updated from its introduction in 1948. By 1956 it had an enclosed driveshaft, swingarm rear suspension, and Earles forks.

△ **Simplex Servi-cycle 1957**

Origin USA

Engine 125cc, single-cylinder

Top speed 40 mph (64 km/h)

Simplex improved its original 1935 direct-drive single with an automatic clutch and variable transmission. The two-stroke engine's rotary valve helped it return 100 mpg (35 km/l).

△ **Velocette LE MkII 1958**

Origin UK

Engine 192cc, flat-twin

Top speed 52 mph (84 km/h)

Conceived as transportation for everyman, the LE had a silent, water-cooled engine, with a hand-starter in a sheet-steel frame. A large number were used as police patrol bikes.

▷ **BSA C15 1958**

Origin UK

Engine 249cc, single-cylinder

Top speed 68 mph (109 km/h)

The C15's unit-construction engine was a cousin of the Triumph Tiger Cub. Stolid rather than exciting, it was extremely popular with learner motorcyclists in Britain.

Singles

The four-stroke single was the ideal machine for postwar Europe. It was economical and robust and suitable for touring, commuting, and, with minor modifications, for racing, scrambles, or trials competition. In the 1950s most machines were based on successful prewar designs, but were gradually restyled and upgraded, with the addition of an improved suspension as the decade progressed. However, the arrival of faster and more luxurious twin-cylinder machines gradually overshadowed them.

◁ **BSA Gold Star 1950**

Origin UK

Engine 349cc, ohv single-cylinder

Top speed 90 mph (145 km/h)

A tuned version of the standard BSA single, the Gold Star was a versatile, amateur competition bike or a road-going hot rod for tearaways.

▽ **Gilera Saturno 1951**

Origin Italy

Engine 498cc, ohv single-cylinder

Top speed 85 mph (137 km/h)

The Saturno was a high-quality machine with the engine and gearbox in a unitary construction, and equipped with a unique rear-suspension system.

◁ **Vincent Comet 1952**

Origin UK

Engine 499cc, ohv single-cylinder

Top speed 90 mph (145 km/h)

Vincent's single-cylinder models were as well engineered as the company's big twins, but lacked the impressive performance of the bigger machines.

▷ **Moto Guzzi Falcone 1952**

Origin Italy

Engine 498cc, ohv single-cylinder

Top speed 84 mph (135 km/h)

The horizontal single-cylinder engine with an exposed flywheel used on the Falcone had been a feature on Guzzis since the first model in 1921.

△ **Norton 30M International 1953**

Origin UK

Engine 490cc, ohc single-cylinder

Top speed 95 mph (153 km/h)

The final version of the International, now with the Featherbed frame, won the 1953 Isle of Man Senior Clubman's TT. It sold until 1957.

◁ **BSA B31 1956**

Origin	UK
Engine	348cc, ohv single-cylinder
Top speed	70 mph (113 km/h)

BSA added a spring frame to its worthy ohv single in 1954; it made the bike more comfortable but increased weight and dulled performance.

▽ **Horex Regina 1955**

Origin	Germany
Engine	342cc, ohv single-cylinder
Top speed	75 mph (120 km/h)

The Regina was a popular machine in postwar Germany, featuring an enclosed final drive chain and a plunger rear suspension.

△ **Ariel NH 350 Red Hunter 1955**

Origin	UK
Engine	346cc, ohv single-cylinder
Top speed	70 mph (113 km/h)

Based on an engine introduced in 1925, the NH 350 evolved from a rigid-framed sportster to a trusty trouper over a long production run.

△ **Ariel HS Mk3 1957**

Origin	UK
Engine	499cc, ohv single-cylinder
Top speed	85 mph (137 km/h)

A scrambler version of Ariel's 500 single, the HS had an alloy cylinder and other upgrades, but was still eclipsed by the BSA Gold Star.

◁ **Matchless G3LS 1955**

Origin	UK
Engine	348cc, ohv single-cylinder
Top speed	70 mph (113 km/h)

The Matchless 350 was given a spring frame in 1949, and the distinctive shape of the suspension units gave it its "jam pot" nickname.

▽ **Velocette MAC 1958**

Origin	UK
Engine	349cc, ohv single-cylinder
Top speed	80 mph (129 km/h)

Velocette did not rush to embrace change. The long-running MAC model got a sprung frame in 1953, but there were few other changes before production ended in 1960.

△ **Velocette Venom 1959**

Origin	Italy
Engine	499cc, ohv single-cylinder
Top speed	100 mph (160 km/h)

The sporting version of the Velocette single had a mix of engineering quality and eccentricity that encouraged owners with similar values.

Vespa lineup, *c.* 1955
Following its starring role in the Hollywood movie *Roman Holiday*, the Vespa scooter became synonymous with style. As Vespas were increasingly popular with women, they figured prominently in Vespa advertisements.

Trials and Scramblers

Scrambles are races over a rough course, while in trials the rider and bike must complete a series of short, challenging tests over obstacles. Originally, converted road machines were used for both disciplines, but in the 1950s specialized models were developed. At first trials and scrambler bikes looked similar—with knobby tires, wide handlebars, and good ground clearance—but as each sport's challenges increased, the appearance of the bikes began to differ.

△ Matchless G3L Trials 1953

Origin UK

Engine 347cc, single-cylinder

Top speed 75 mph (120 km/h)

A prewar design given swingarm rear suspension and an alloy head by 1951, the four-stroke G3L was a popular trials machine with club riders.

△ Matchless G80CS 1957

Origin UK

Engine 498cc, single-cylinder

Top speed 90 mph (145 km/h)

The CS (Competition Suspension) G80 was a powerful and effective scrambler. A stronger short-stroke engine with an alloy cylinder barrel was introduced from 1956.

△ Royal Enfield Trials Bullet 1950

Origin UK

Engine 346cc, single-cylinder

Top speed 70 mph (113 km/h)

After winning numerous events including the 1953 International Six Days Trial with modified Bullets, Royal Enfield introduced this specially built trials model.

◁ Greeves 20T 1955

Origin UK

Engine 197cc, single-cylinder

Top speed 65 mph (105 km/h)

From their first year of production, Greeves' sturdy but light two-strokes with a rubber front suspension and cast-alloy downtube proved ideal for trials and scrambling.

△ AJS 16MC Trials 1956

Origin UK

Engine 348cc, single-cylinder

Top speed 70 mph (113 km/h)

A top trials marque, successful in one-day observed events as well as Scottish Six Days Trials, AJS introduced rear suspension on its consumer model for 1956.

◁ Matchless G11 CSR 1958

Origin UK

Engine 593cc, inline twin

Top speed 105 mph (169 km/h)

The CSR was a new model for 1958, combining the CS's sweet-handling scrambler frame with a high-compression twin-cylinder engine to make a potent road bike.

◁ **Triumph Tiger Cub Scrambler 1957**

Origin UK

Engine 199cc, single-cylinder

Top speed 65 mph (105 km/h)

The lightweight Tiger Cub proved a useful off-road machine, with Roy Peplow beating large-capacity opposition to win the Scottish Six Days Trial on a Cub in 1959.

▽ **Norton Nomad 600 1958**

Origin UK

Engine 597cc, inline twin

Top speed 95 mph (153 km/h)

Built for the US market, the Nomad packed a tuned-up Dominator engine into a sturdy frame designed for off-roading, although it was a heavy machine. Around 350 were sold.

△ **Triumph Trophy TR6 1958**

Origin UK

Engine 650cc, inline twin

Top speed 90 mph (145 km/h)

The Trophy model name celebrated Triumph's international Six Days Trial success. The high-pipe machine was originally produced as a 500; the 650 was made from 1956.

△ **Ariel HT500 1957**

Origin UK

Engine 497cc, single-cylinder

Top speed 85 mph (137 km/h)

With an all-alloy, four-stroke engine and light, compact construction, the HT5 was a potent and effective trials machine developed from the Red Hunter road bike.

△ **BSA B34 Clipper 1957**

Origin UK

Engine 499cc, single-cylinder

Top speed 90 mph (145 km/h)

Made only for export, the alloy-engined Clipper was closely related to the Gold Star and featured a central oil tank, a lightweight trials saddle, and a wide ratio gearing.

◁ **BSA DBD34 Catalina Gold Star Scrambler 1959**

Origin UK

Engine 499cc, single-cylinder

Top speed 90 mph (145 km/h)

The ultimate scrambler derivative of the all-conquering Gold Star was named in honor of Chuck Minert's 1956 win in the US Catalina Scrambling Grand Prix.

Racers

In 1950 the Senior TT race at the Isle of Man was won by a Norton at 92 mph (148 km/h); 10 years later it was won by an MV Agusta at 102 mph (164 km/h). Technological development was fierce as teams improved not only the power output of engines, but suspension, braking, and fairings to improve aerodynamics too. Perhaps the most significant event of the decade was the 1959 TT with the first appearance of a Japanese team at a Grand Prix.

▷ DKW 350 3-cylinder 1950

Origin Germany

Engine 349cc, three-cylinder two-stroke

Top speed 130 mph (209 km/h)

DKW's three-cylinder two-stroke achieved limited success, but it pointed the way ahead. By the mid-1970s, two-strokes dominated Grand Prix racing.

△ NSU Rennmax 1953

Origin Germany

Engine 248cc, dohc parallel-twin

Top speed 130 mph (209 km/h)

NSU's Grand Prix career was short and successful. The Rennmax was raced in 250cc Grand Prix for two seasons, winning the championship both times.

▽ Rotrax Jap Speedway 1950

Origin UK

Engine 490cc, ohv single-cylinder

Top speed 60 mph (97 km/h)

Typical speedway bikes in the 1950s used methanol-fueled JAP engines in specially made frames. The Rotrax JAP was among the leading machines.

◁ AJS E95 1954

Origin UK

Engine 496cc, dohc parallel-twin

Top speed 115 mph (185 km/h)

Les Graham was the first postwar 500cc World Champion (1949) riding an E90 AJS, from which the E95, with distinctive pannier tanks, was developed.

▷ MV Agusta 350 1953

Origin Italy

Engine 349cc, dohc inline four

Top speed 130 mph (209 km/h)

MV created a 350 racer in 1953 by reducing the capacity of their 500. By the end of the decade it was a World Championship winner.

▽ NSU Sportmax 1954

Origin Germany

Engine 247cc, ohc single-cylinder

Top speed 125 mph (201 km/h)

A production racer based on the NSU Max road bike, the Sportmax was very successful, winning several Grands Prix and the 1955 World Championship.

△ BMW Rennsport 1954

Origin Germany

Engine 494cc, ohc flat-twin

Top speed 130 mph (209 km/h)

The flat-twin engine and shaft drive were not ideal for a solo racing machine, but Rennsport engines were incredibly successful as sidecar power units.

△ Gilera Four 1954

Origin Italy

Engine 493cc, dohc inline four

Top speed 140 mph (225 km/h)

Gilera had raced a supercharged four before WWII and built a new non-supercharged Four for postwar competition. It won four World Championships.

▽ Matchless G45 1957

Origin UK

Engine 498cc, ohv parallel-twin

Top speed 120 mph (193 km/h)

The G45 was an attempt to make a competitive 500 class racer using the chassis from a 350, and the modified engine from the G9 road bike.

▽ FB Mondial 250 1957

Origin Italy

Engine 249cc, dohc single-cylinder

Top speed 135 mph (217 km/h)

Winner of the 1957 250cc World Championship, ridden by Cecil Sandford, the Mondial revved to over 10,000 rpm. Full streamlining was banned the following year.

▽ Moto Guzzi V8 1957

Origin Italy

Engine 499cc, dohc V8

Top speed 178 mph (286 km/h)

One of the most extraordinary racers ever built, the Guzzi was a masterpiece of miniaturization that could rev to 13,000 rpm and produced around 80 hp.

◁ Matchless G50 1959

Origin UK

Engine 496cc, ohc single-cylinder

Top speed 138 mph (222 km/h)

This production racer for privateers was based on the 350cc AJS 7R. The G50 engine was successfully used in other chassis throughout the 1960s.

△ Honda RC160 1959

Origin Japan

Engine 249cc, dohc inline four

Top speed 125 mph (201 km/h)

Honda's first four-cylinder bike was built to race in Japan, but it paved the way for the successful World Championship machines of the 1960s.

△ Honda RC142 1959

Origin Japan

Engine 124cc, dohc twin-cylinder

Top speed 105 mph (169 km/h)

Honda's first foray into Grand Prix racing was on this machine at the 1959 Isle of Man TT when they won the manufacturer's prize in the 125cc race.

The 1960s

The availability of low-priced cars hit the European motorcycle industry hard; development stagnated in the big British and US factories, and some small marques disappeared. However, the rapidly growing Japanese industry had set its sights on world markets, especially the US, where recreational motorcycling was booming. Competitively priced and well-engineered, their products appealed to the entry-level riders and fostered brand loyalties to be exploited in the future. Scooters and mopeds continued to attract riders, especially in warmer climates.

Roadburners

As cars became affordable and the world more prosperous in the 1960s, the motorcycle's role changed from essential transportation to leisure and fun. American baby boomers wanted fast and stylish machinery, while Britain was in the grip of the speed-obsessed Café Racer craze. The arrival of Honda's sensational CB750 in 1969 signaled the end of the dominance of British marques.

◁ **BSA Gold Star DBD34 1960**

Origin UK

Engine 499cc, single-cylinder

Top speed 110 mph (177 km/h)

Winner of 11 Clubman's TTs, the Gold Star single was a raw and aggressive, street-legal racer with its big Amal carburetor and alloy engine. Its passing in 1963 was mourned by many.

▷ **Matchless G15 CSR 1965**

Origin UK

Engine 745cc, inline two

Top speed 115 mph (185 km/h)

The ultimate sporting Matchless, with a twin carburetor Norton Atlas engine, swept-back exhausts, slim alloy mudguards, and dropped handlebars, was built up to 1968.

▷ **BSA A65L Spitfire MkII 1966**

Origin UK

Engine 654cc, inline two

Top speed 110 mph (177 km/h)

The super-sports version of BSA's biggest twin featured Amal GP track carburetors and a fiberglass fuel tank. A top speed of 120 mph (193 km/h) was claimed.

◁ **BSA Rocket 3 A75 1970**

Origin UK

Engine 740cc, inline three

Top speed 125 mph (200 km/h)

With its Triumph-derived aluminum triple engine, three Amal carburetors, and great handling, the showroom sales of Rocket 3 did not reflect its success on the track.

△ **Indian Velocette 1969**

Origin USA

Engine 499cc, single-cylinder

Top speed 107 mph (172 km/h)

Floyd Clymer briefly revived the Indian brand in 1969. His 500cc machine sported a single-cylinder British Velocette engine and an Italian frame. Just 200 were built.

▷ **Royal Enfield Interceptor Series 1 1965**

Origin UK

Engine 736cc, inline two

Top speed 115 mph (185 km/h)

The first British 750cc twin—from one of the oldest makers—the beefy Interceptor was made in Series 1 form in 1962, and in final Series 2 guise from 1969 to 1970.

▷ **Velocette Thruxton Venom 1967**

Origin UK

Engine 499cc, single-cylinder

Top speed 105 mph (169 km/h)

Velocette, another old British marque soon to be wiped away by Japanese innovation, built this powerful bike to win production races. It won an Isle of Man TT in 1967.

Grand Tourers

Affluent riders preferred sophisticated high-status machines that were built for traveling at high speed over long distances, rather than mere street-cruising or blasting from one café to the next. Top choices included the stately 74-cu-in (1.2-liter) Harley Electra Glide V-twin, the exclusive and charismatic MV Agusta Four, and Germany's colossal and costly high-velocity autobahn cruiser, the Münch Mammoth.

△ **Harley-Davidson FLHB Electra Glide 1965**

Origin USA

Engine 1,208cc, V-twin

Top speed 80 mph (129 km/h)

The last of the legendary "Panhead"-engined Harleys was the first to boast electric starting. Its large high-output battery is situated on the right side of the frame. In 1966 Harley-Davidson introduced the revised "shovelhead" engine, produced until 1984.

◁ **Norton Atlas
750SS 1962**

Origin UK

Engine 745cc, inline two

Top speed 119 mph (192 km/h)

Built for export, principally to the US, the Atlas suffered from vibration that was characteristic of a large two-cylinder engine. Yet it offered great performance and high-speed cruising.

△ **Triumph Bonneville T120R 1966**

Origin UK

Engine 649cc, inline twin

Top speed 110 mph (177 km/h)

Continuously improved, the Bonneville was reaching the peak of its form, and was in great demand worldwide. Versions produced from 1966 to 1970 are considered to be the best.

◁ **Norton Commando
Fastback 1969**

Origin UK

Engine 745cc, inline two

Top speed 120 mph (193 km/h)

With an ingenious new frame isolating the rider from the engine's inherent vibrations, the Commando was a great success despite its now aged engine design.

△ **Triumph Trident T150 1969**

Origin UK

Engine 740cc, inline three

Top speed 125 mph (200 km/h)

Triumph chose three cylinders for its 750cc flagship, to avoid twin-cylinder vibration. Although fast, Trident could not match the superior specification of the Honda CB750.

△ **Honda CB750 1969**

Origin Japan

Engine 736cc, inline four

Top speed 125 mph (200 km/h)

On this pioneering machine, Honda popularized the transverse inline, overhead-cam, four-cylinder layout, together with the front disc brake, for the ultimate sports bike.

△ **MV Agusta 600 1968**

Origin Italy

Engine 592cc, inline four

Top speed 106 mph (170 km/h)

The first roadster four from the top 500cc Grand Prix marque MV, the Agusta featured twin camshafts and disc front brakes. It had shaft final drive.

◁ **Münch Mammoth
4TTS 1967**

Origin Germany

Engine 1,177cc, inline four

Top speed 130 mph (209 km/h)

Friedl Münch built a gargantuan motorcycle with an NSU car engine (tuned to 88 bhp in TTS form) and many innovative details, such as the steel V-spoke rear wheel.

Triumph Bonneville

Marketed as "The Ultimate in Power," the Bonneville T120 was a landmark model from the golden era of British motorcycles. Unveiled in late 1958, the "Bonnie" featured an iconic 649cc vertical-twin engine that made it the envy of rival manufacturers and one of the fastest production bikes in the world. Models such as the T120R were exported around the world, and by the time the original Bonneville ceased production in 1983, it had become a legend—the coolest sports motorcycle to come out of Great Britain.

IN 1956, A MOTORCYCLE powered by a Triumph engine broke the land speed record at the Bonneville Salt Flats, Utah, with Johnny Allen reaching a scorching 214 mph (345 km/h). The 650cc twin-carb engine, designed by Edward Turner, Triumph's acclaimed design chief, would provide the basis for Britain's most celebrated motorcycle, while the site of the achicvement would inspire its name: the Bonneville T120. First presented in 1958, the twin-carb T120 had strong acceleration and a top speed of around 115 mph (185 km/h). By the time the 1966 T120R model (shown) was released, the Bonnie was in huge demand in the UK and worldwide, particularly the US. During the 1960s, engine performance was sharpened and handling greatly improved. Into the '70s, the Bonneville held its own by rivaling Japanese products on roadholding, economy, and ease of maintenance. The old Triumph factory closed in 1983, but the marque was reborn with an all-new Bonneville in production since 2000.

Germanic roots
The Triumph name was first used to sell motorbikes in 1902. An apparently thoroughbred English company, Triumph was actually founded in the 1880s by two Germans.

FRONT VIEW   **REAR VIEW**

Rear mudguard in stainless steel

Rear suspension system is adjustable with Girling dampers

Dual seat with ample space for rider and pillion passenger

Chromed headlight accentuates sporty look

Fork protected by rubber gaiters

Front drum brake is 8 in (20 cm) in diameter

Engine and gearbox combined in one single unit

Ribbed tire with dimensions of 3.25 x 19 in (8 x 48 cm)

SPECIFICATIONS

Model	Triumph Bonneville T120R (1966)	**Power output**	47 hp at 6,700 rpm
Assembly	Meriden, England	**Transmission**	Four-speed
Production	Not known	**Suspension**	Telescopic front forks, swingarm rear
Construction	Tubular steel cradle frame	**Brakes**	Drums, front and rear
Engine	649cc, inline twin	**Maximum speed**	110 mph (177 km/h)

Original "Cool Britannia"

This US export version of the Bonneville had clean lines, a sleek fuel tank, and judicious use of chrome and polished stainless steel, all of which helped make the Bonneville T120R a style icon that reflected Britain's position at the center of the Swinging Sixties. Despite being basically a 1930s design, the engine had the gutsy performance needed to make the T120 the most sensational ride of its time.

THE BIKE

"Think of a superlative, double it… but no, don't even try. Words alone cannot describe the Bonneville T120," ran a gushing review in *The Motor Cycle* magazine in 1964. A fine handler by 1966, the T120R's frame and suspension were much improved over the original and just as handy for city jaunts as for reaching breathtaking speeds on the open road. A redesign for 1970 misfired, but after the "Bonnie" grew to 750cc it recovered to survive into the 1980s as a versatile sports tourer.

1. New badge design for 1966 **2.** Engine cut-out button **3.** Fuel filler cap **4.** Chrome headlight **5.** Rear brake light mechanism **6.** Girling rear shock **7.** Tachometer and speedometer **8.** Hinged seat release **9.** Front brake drum **10.** Decal guide on oil tank **11.** Ammeter **12.** Rod-operated rear brake **13.** Lights switch and ignition **14.** Air filter **15.** Kick-starter **16.** Rear lamps **17.** Exhaust with muffler

THE ENGINE

The Bonneville's twin-carburetor, overhead-valve powerplant was constantly refined during the model's lifetime. Featuring a cast-iron barrel, high-compression pistons, and dry-sump lubrication, the engine was adapted to a combined engine-gearbox unit construction in 1963, with better engine performance on the 1966 T120R.

18. Engine and gearbox are single unit 19. Rocker box oil feed 20. Finned exhaust clamps 21. Tachometer drive 22. Amal Monobloc carburetor with integral floatbowl

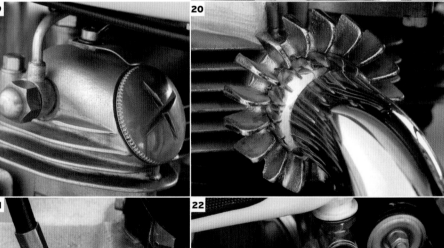

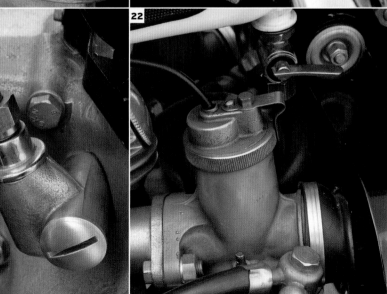

Youth Appeal

The light and lively end of the market saw the greatest change in the 1960s. The decade started with easy-to-handle but unsophisticated, mostly British bikes, and ended with the market awash with highly developed Japanese bikes with features like gearboxes with up to six gears and push-button starting. They outshone offerings from British and US marques, which failed to keep pace.

△ Honda C77 Dream 300 1961
Origin Japan
Engine 305cc, inline two
Top speed 88 mph (142 km/h)

First released in 1956 but redesigned for 1960, the Dream was a high-specification, well-equipped bike that looked rather expensive alongside more basic machines.

△ Honda CB92 Benly Super Sports 1961
Origin Japan
Engine 247cc, inline two
Top speed 80 mph (129 km/h)

The fastest 125 of its day, this model was a great standard-bearer for Japan's motorcycling industry. The little CB92's ruggedly made overhead-camshaft engine revved to more than 10,000 rpm.

△ FB Mondial 48 Sport 1960
Origin Italy
Engine 48cc, single-cylinder
Top speed 45 mph (72 km/h)

Mondial's racy 50cc model was aimed at enthusiastic young riders. This type of machine's popularity was reflected by the 1962 launch of a 50cc Grand Prix class.

△ Honda Dream 250 1961
Origin Japan
Engine 247cc, inline two
Top speed 80 mph (129 km/h)

Honda favored pressed-steel frames that used the power unit as a stressed member, leading link front forks, and styling that looked slightly odd to Western eyes. Noted for its quality engineering, this model sold well.

△ Harley-Davidson Sprint H 1962
Origin USA/Italy
Engine 246cc, single-cylinder
Top speed 76 mph (122 km/h)

Made in Italy by Aermacchi, the Sprint singles filled the gap in Harley's model line that was being exploited by Japanese imports. A 350cc bike was introduced for 1969.

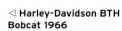

◁ Harley-Davidson BTH Bobcat 1966
Origin USA
Engine 175cc, single-cylinder
Top speed 60 mph (97 km/h)

The Bobcat was descended from the earlier Hummer two-stroke and this final version was unusually styled with an ABS molded fuel tank and tailpiece.

◁ **Ariel Arrow Super Sports 1963**

**◁ Ariel Arrow Super
Sports 1963**

Origin UK

Engine 249cc, inline two

Top speed 78 mph (126 km/h)

Sales resistance to their
all-enclosed "Leader" model
led Ariel to market the Arrow.
A fine handler, this bike was also
speedy in its "Golden Arrow"
Super Sport form.

△ **Greeves 32DC
Sports Twin 1961**

Origin UK

Engine 322cc, inline two

Top speed 70 mph (113 km/h)

The Villiers 3T two-stroke
engine powered the biggest
roadster made by Greeves,
a small factory with a great
reputation for trials and
motocross machinery.

△ **Ducati 250 Mach I 1964**

Origin Italy

Engine 249cc, single-cylinder

Top speed 100 mph (160 km/h)

A milestone in Ducati history, this was
the first roadgoing 250 to top 100 mph
(160 km/h), given the right gearing. In race
form, it gave Mike Rogers victory in the
1969 Isle of Man Production 250cc TT.

▷ **Bridgestone
Hurricane 1968**

Origin Japan

Engine 177cc, inline two

Top speed 70 mph (113 km/h)

A high-quality two-stroke with rotary
inlet valves and hard-plated cylinder
bores, the Hurricane is seen here in
the street scrambler guise.
After 1968 Bridgestone
only made tires.

△ **Suzuki X6 Scrambler 1968**

Origin Japan

Engine 247cc, inline twin

Top speed 90 mph (145 km/h)

Suzuki's X6 Hustler (or T20 Super
Six) of 1966 was the world's first
production six-speed motorcycle.
This voguish street scrambler
version has upswept exhausts.

Suzuki X6 Scrambler

Suzuki had already set pulses racing in late 1965 with the launch of the T20 Super Six—the machine that was to form the basis of the Scrambler. From their first appearance in 1952, Suzuki motorcycles were known for their dependable, solid build, rather than for blistering performance. The T20 and the stylish X6 Scrambler, available from 1967 to 1969, changed all that. Featuring technology straight from world-class-winning Grand Prix racers, these machines were a total sensation.

IN THE DAYS WHEN a five-speed gearbox was a rarity and something to shout about, the six-speeder featured on the T20 Super Six, and then on the Scrambler series, was almost beyond imagination. The 250cc Suzukis offered riders such a range of new experiences that they catapulted a reliable but previously rather unexciting firm into the consciousness of biking enthusiasts everywhere. With UK learners restricted to 250cc bikes, a sporty T20 Suzuki was at the top of the wish list of every bike-crazy 16-year-old.

The Scrambler version of the bike was aimed squarely at the US market. Europeans tended to equate performance with low handlebars and swept-back exhausts, but in the US high handlebars and upswept exhausts denoted power and the Scrambler's amended design reflected this preference. Its street scrambler styling had wide appeal among American teens, and also the power and drive to impress a wider audience because of its 30 hp engine—one hp more than the machine that spawned it.

FRONT VIEW

REAR VIEW

Making a name
Founder Michio Suzuki gave his name to the company. The stylized "S" graced the products from Hamamatsu in 1952 and continues to do so to this day.

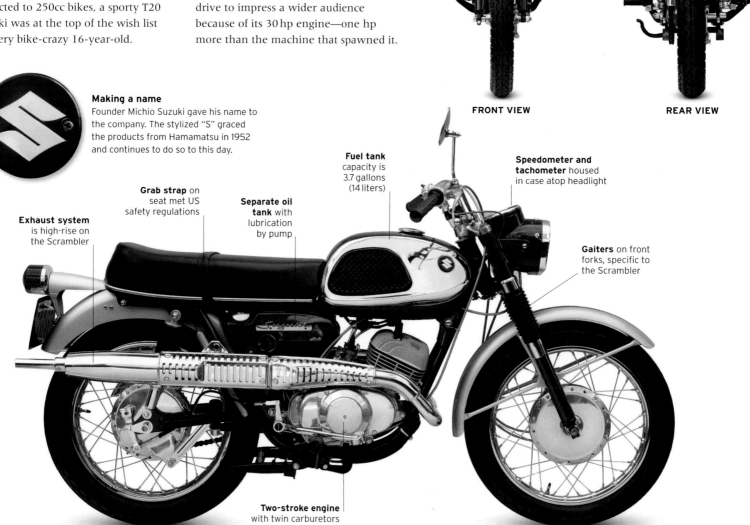

Fuel tank capacity is 3.7 gallons (14 liters)

Speedometer and tachometer housed in case atop headlight

Grab strap on seat met US safety regulations

Separate oil tank with lubrication by pump

Exhaust system is high-rise on the Scrambler

Gaiters on front forks, specific to the Scrambler

Two-stroke engine with twin carburetors

SPECIFICATIONS	
Model	X6 Scrambler (1968)
Assembly	Hamamatsu, Japan
Production	Not known
Construction	Twin-shock cradle frame
Engine	247cc, inline twin
Power output	29 hp at 7,500 rpm
Transmission	In-unit six-speed
Suspension	Telescopic front forks, twin-shock rear
Brakes	Drums, front and rear
Maximum speed	90 mph (145 km/h)

Japan on the rise
In many ways the Scrambler epitomizes the extraordinary progress Japanese companies were making in the 1960s. With a ridiculously high specification and performance for its time, it signaled that the Japanese were not just serious contenders, but were also on their way to domination of the motorcycle industry.

THE BIKE

The X6 Scrambler, or TC250 as it was known outside the US, used the more powerful engine from the Japanese market "super sports" T21. It came equipped with a raised exhaust, gaitered forks, and deep-treaded tires, making it appear suitable for light off-road use. In truth, these extra features were little more than a styling exercise and certainly not a serious tool for avid fans of the rough stuff. A so-called GT kit, which consisted of a different fuel tank and seat, installed by dealers on request, was also available.

1. Tank script **2.** Side panel script **3.** Steering damper knob **4.** Ignition key slot on headlight **5.** Combined instruments **6.** Horseshoe headlight **7.** Fork gaiter **8.** Oil tank cap **9.** Gearbox oil filler **10.** Fuel level indicator **11.** Front brake operation **12.** Kick-starter **13.** Rear sprocket **14.** Rear light **15.** Tire inflator **16.** Muffler outlet

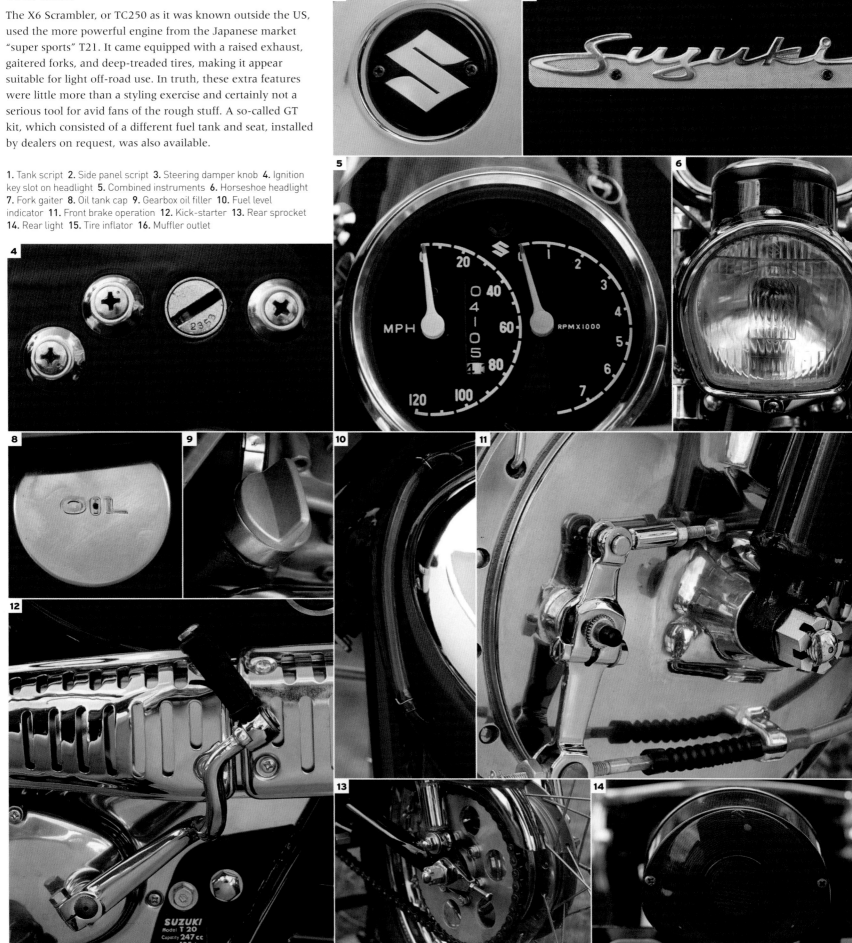

THE ENGINE

The Scrambler used the T20's twin-cylinder, two-stroke 250cc engine. At first glance, the engine appeared to be simply a development of its forerunner, the T10; however, all that remained from the earlier version were the horizontally split crankcases, the inclined cylinders (the heads and barrels remained separate), and the outer covers for the primary drive and generator. Of square dimensions (54 mm bore and stroke, which gave a capacity of 247 cc), the engine was estimated to make 29 hp at 7,500 rpm. These were outstanding figures for the time and meant that the Scrambler was able to comfortably outperform most machines twice its size—and some that were three times its capacity.

17. View of engine showing deep cylinder fins **18.** Upswept exhaust
19. Fuel tap **20.** Carburetor with cold-start lever

Scooters and Mopeds

In the 1960s scooters became lighter and more sophisticated, as riders—often women—sought machines that demanded less physical effort to lift, start, and ride. Increasingly, two-wheelers were used instead of cars for short trips, shopping, or just for fun, especially in countries and regions with a warm, dry climate. Mopeds were ideal for teenagers seeking freedom through mobility.

△ **Lambretta Li 125 1960**

Origin Italy

Engine 123cc, single-cylinder

Top speed 43 mph (69 km/h)

Stylish and an excellent buy, the Series 2 Li 125 and 150 had a faired-in headlight and larger carburetor to help maintain Lambretta's worldwide sales supremacy.

△ **Honda Juno M85 1962**

Origin Japan

Engine 169cc, flat-twin

Top speed 62 mph (100 km/h)

Made for only one year, the Juno was an innovative steel monocoque scooter with an exposed flat-twin engine and variable hydraulic mechanical transmission.

△ **Lambretta TV175 "Slimline" 1963**

Origin Italy

Engine 175cc, single-cylinder

Top speed 58 mph (93 km/h)

The first production two-wheeler with a disc brake, the TV was the top of Lambretta's range in the early 1960s with more modern, slimmer bodywork than their earlier scooters.

▽ **Mustang Thoroughbred 1962**

Origin USA

Engine 320cc, single-cylinder

Top speed 60 mph (97 km/h)

Built by a wartime aircraft manufacturer in California, the Mustang had a basic side-valve engine but, on this model, a swingarm rear suspension and four-speed transmission.

△ **Honda 50 Super Cub 1963**

Origin Japan

Engine 49cc, single-cylinder

Top speed 45 mph (72 km/h)

Still going strong, the sturdy Honda 50 step-through was well on its way to becoming the world's best-selling vehicle, with more than 60 million built.

◁ **Vespa VBB Sportique 1963**

Origin Italy

Engine 150cc, single-cylinder

Top speed 50 mph (80 km/h)

The VBB brought four gears to Vespa's smaller scooters for the first time to create one of the most usable classic scooters, with extremely durable running gear.

▷ **Vespa GS160 1963**

Origin Italy

Engine 159cc, single-cylinder

Top speed 62 mph (100 km/h)

The Vespa, with its pressed-steel unitary construction (no frame) was designed to get Italy mobile again after WWII. This Gran Sport (GS) was the luxury sporting model.

△ Triumph Tina 1964

Origin UK

Engine 99cc, single-cylinder

Top speed 45 mph (72 km/h)

BSA Triumph expected big sales for this belt-drive, automatic transmission scooter, promoted by British singer Cliff Richard, but its dated appearance meant sales were poor.

△ NSU Quickly S2/23 1964

Origin Germany

Engine 49cc, single-cylinder

Top speed 27 mph (43 km/h)

Built from 1953 to 1963, the NSU Quickly was a simple yet attractive moped with a distinctive pressed-steel frame and two gears (three on this updated model); over a million were sold.

△ Harley-Davidson AH Topper Scooter 1964

Origin USA

Engine 164cc, single-cylinder

Top speed 40 mph (64 km/h)

Harley's Topper had little in common with other scooters; the horizontal two-stroke engine drove through an advanced, continuously variable transmission.

◁ Raleigh RM5 Supermatic 1964

Origin UK

Engine 50cc, single-cylinder

Top speed 30 mph (48 km/h)

Cycle-maker Raleigh began selling mopeds in 1958 and had a range of 10 mopeds by the mid-1960s; the RM5 was a Motobécane built under license.

▷ Agrati Capri Scooter 1966

Origin Italy

Engine 78cc, single-cylinder

Top speed 45 mph (72 km/h)

The Agrati cycle group owned Garelli, which produced the engine for this attractive but very conventional scooter, sold with 50cc, 70cc, 80cc, or 98cc two-stroke engines.

▽ Vespa Allstate Cruisaire 1964

Origin Italy

Engine 123cc, single-cylinder

Top speed 47 mph (76 km/h)

The Sears catalog offered Vespas badged "Allstate," which sold in huge numbers in the US. These had a lower specification (for example, no front dampers) than the normal Vespas.

△ Clark Scamp 1968

Origin UK

Engine 50cc, single-cylinder

Top speed 30 mph (48 km/h)

A clever adaptation of a small-wheeled bicycle, this was made by a mast-maker on the Isle of Wight. Production was halted by a court case with the engine designer.

▽ Motobécane Mobylette 1968

Origin France

Engine 50cc, single-cylinder

Top speed 40 mph (64 km/h)

France's largest motorcycle-maker sold 14 million Mobylettes over 48 years, starting from 1948. "La Bleue" was a simple, reliable, motorized yet sophisticated model for the 1960s.

Count Domenico Agusta in 1949 with a rider on one of the marque's 125cc racers

Great Marques
The MV Agusta Story

The Italian MV Agusta company initially made its name as a manufacturer of innovative, low-capacity motorcycles in the years following World War II. After diversifying into larger models, the marque achieved legendary status in Grand Prix racing. Production ceased in the 1970s, but MV Agusta was resurrected in the 1990s.

MV AGUSTA'S ORIGINS date back to 1910, when Count Giovanni Agusta first set up his aircraft manufacturing company in the Lombardy region of northern Italy. The count's death in 1927 forced his wife, Giuseppina, and son, Domenico, to take up the reins during a decline in the aeronautical industry. Their decision to venture into motorcycle manufacture would lead to the formation of one of the world's most respected marques.

Development of the first model, a 98 cc two-stroke, was halted by the outbreak of war, but resumed in 1945 when Count Domenico Agusta set up Meccanica Verghera (MV) – named for the region of Lombardy where the bikes were made. His plan to market the debut bike as the Vespa 98 failed when rival Piaggio used the name first, so in the fall of 1945 it was unveiled as simply the 98. The next year MV Agusta entered the racing arena with almost instant success on the track and the first of many wins on the hallowed Monza circuit.

By the end of the decade, the 98 had been supplemented, and then replaced, by 125cc and

MV Agusta badge
(introduced late 1940s)

250cc models. In the 1950s MV Agusta achieved memorable racing success through the use of advanced components on bikes such as the 175 CSS. The result was increased demand for the marque's road models, with standout machines such as the 125 Motore Lundo— then considered one of the finest sports motorcycles on the market—boosting the company's growing reputation both at home and abroad.

The company ethos of applying creative solutions at every level was reflected in the

two-seater 83 model from 1956. The marque also showed a willingness to experiment with new technology, such as fuel injection and hydraulic gears on a series of prototypes. In 1959 this pioneering approach resulted in an advanced new lubrication system, which was later adopted on MV Agusta's whole range of bikes. By increasing engine reliability to a level never previously seen,

the company was able to offer impressive 100,000-km warranties on its powerplants.

The 1960s and early 1970s saw MV Agusta in its prime on the Grand Prix motorcycle circuit. Count Agusta's

Race legend
Among the many iconic riders for MV Agusta was John Surtees, who became world champion. The Englishman is pictured in 1956 breaking the lap record at Crystal Palace on a 250cc MV Agusta.

125 Turismo

600

Ipotesi Sport

910S Brutale

1945 The MV Agusta company is formed by Count Domenico Agusta.
1947 The Luxury 98cc and 250cc 4T models are presented at the Milan Salon.
1950 The 125 Motor Lungo model is unveiled, and goes on to become a class-leading sports bike.
1953 MV Agusta builds a new plant in Spain specifically for the assembly of export models; the 175 CSS model debuts.
1956 MV Agusta wins the 125cc, 250cc, and 500cc world championships.

1958 The marque's racing team wins 63 out of 76 races between now and 1960.
1966 The three-cylinder 500cc model is unveiled, ridden to Grand Prix victory for several years by Giacomo Agostini.
1967 The four-stroke, four-cylinder 600 bike debuts with front disc brakes.
1969 The 250B model is introduced.
1969 The 350B Sport machine is unveiled.
1971 Count Domenico Agusta dies.
1975 The 750 Sport America is unveiled, a powerful bike aimed at the US market.

1976 This is the last year that MV Agusta competes in Grand Prix racing. Giacomo Agostini takes the team's final 500cc win at the Nürburgring.
1980 A slump in the late 1970s means that by this time the production of motorcycles has ceased.
1986 The entire stock of MV Agusta motorcycles is bought by Roberto Iannucci for 1.5 billion lire.
1992 The Cagiva Group buys the MV Agusta trademark.

1997 The F4 is the first new model from the new MV Agusta company.
2008 The MV Agusta wins the Italian Superbike Championship.
2010 Having bought MV Agusta company two years previously, Harley-Davidson sells the company back to Claudio Castiglioni again.
2011 MV Agusta announces the release of the F4 RR Coscacorta superbike, featuring ultra-lightweight materials and 200+ hp performance.

Model swan song
The 125 Sport from 1975 was one of MV Agusta's final new models before the company went out of business at the end of the decade.

obsession with securing competition success led him to hire the world's finest engineers and riders. It paid off spectacularly; sporting a silver and red livery, the marque's bikes won the World Championship in the 500cc class for 17 consecutive years from 1958 to

strong by broadening its lineup. Competition triumphs continued into the 1970s, but MV Agusta now faced dark times, with competition from Japanese imports flooding the market,

Italy but also around the world. However, in 1992, after sinking into obscurity, the MV Agusta name was revived when the Italian Cagiva Group bought the company trademark. Cagiva's finest engineers were tasked with building a new model that would incorporate innovative features in the tradition of the original company.

Unveiled in 1997, the resulting 750cc F4 model immediately won over fans and journalists with its classic MV Agusta silver and red livery, plus futuristic technological components such as a removable transmission. Sporting a carbon frame and achieving astonishing performance figures of

close to 186 mph (300 km/h), it was a worthy machine to resurrect the iconic racing marque. Originally available in a limited edition of 300 Gold Series bikes, this was a model for wealthy motorcycle aficionados.

The F4 was received so positively that Cagiva went on to create the more affordable F45 variant. Over the next few years the company introduced an expanded lineup of sports bikes under the MV Agusta name, including the Brutale. In 2005 the Tamburini 1000 model was released in recognition of motorcycle designer Massimo Tamburini, and it was regarded by many critics as the finest sports bike in the world.

A series of changes in the ownership of MV Agusta through the 2000s have not prevented the marque's resurgence, and a return to competition has delighted fans who remember when MV Agusta's unbeatable Grand Prix bikes were the finest racing machines for a generation.

> "**MV Agusta** offered me the **chance** to ride some **beautiful machines**, some of the best I ever rode."

GIACOMO AGOSTINI, ITALIAN RIDER FOR MV AGUSTA FROM 1966 TO 1972

1974. The winning riders included legends such as John Surtees, Mike Hailwood, and Giacomo Agostini (who alone won seven titles in a row).

The wide range of road models offered by MV Agusta during the 1960s included several that benefited from racing technology; in particular, the four-cylinder 600, from which the blisteringly fast 750S America developed, as well as smaller offerings like the long-running 50cc Liberty. In a period when sales were generally in decline in the face of competition from cheaper cars, the marque skillfully found a way of remaining

and the death of Count Agusta in 1971. The result was a change in direction, with new owners EFIM phasing out the marque's racing program to cut costs. But even this was not enough to prevent the company from quickly falling into decline. By 1980 it was no longer producing models of any kind. The loss of such a prestigious marque was felt by motorcycle enthusiasts not just in

Powerful new machines
Unveiled in 1997, the 750cc F4 was the first new model from the rejuvenated MV Agusta marque. Initially released in limited edition, it was expanded to a full range into the 2000s.

Willing Workers

For some workers and businesses in the 1960s, motorcycles still represented the most practical and cost-effective means of transportation, either for getting to and from work or for police duties or transporting tools for the breakdown services. Machines ranged from simple commuter or learner bikes to heavy-duty, powerful-engined bikes that could haul sidecars.

▷ **James L25 Commodore 1960**

Origin UK

Engine 249cc, single-cylinder

Top speed 65 mph (105 km/h)

An attractive economy ride, the Commodore was unfortunately let down by the poor design of its two-stroke engine, made by AMC, the company that had owned James since 1951.

▽ **BSA M21 1960**

Origin UK

Engine 591cc, single-cylinder

Top speed 63 mph (101 km/h)

Developed from BSA's WWII military bike, the M21 with its big, lazy, side-valve engine was used by the UK's Automobile Association to haul a sidecar full of tools and spares.

△ **BSA Bantam D10 1967**

Origin UK

Engine 173cc, single-cylinder

Top speed 65 mph (105 km/h)

By the 1960s, Bantams sported a two-stroke 175cc engine and a four-speed gearbox. They remained a firm favorite with UK novices and commuters.

▷ **Allstate Compact 1961**

Origin Austria

Engine 60cc, single-cylinder

Top speed 44 mph (71 km/h)

"More sizzle than a schnitzel," ran the US advertising for the Allstate Compact, an Austrian Puch D60 sold under its own name by the US retail giant Sears from 1961 to 1963.

◁ **Norton Model 50 1963**

Origin UK

Engine 348cc, single-cylinder

Top speed 75 mph (120 km/h)

Introduced in 1956, the Model 50 was based on a prewar design, used Norton's "Featherbed" frame from 1959, but was a gentle, traditional British bike.

△ **Royal Enfield Bullet 1962**

Origin UK

Engine 499cc, single-cylinder

Top speed 90 mph (145 km/h)

Virtually unaltered since 1948, this 500cc version of the long-running Bullet slogger, in its final British form, boasted coil ignition and a big long-haul fuel tank.

▷ **Velocette Vogue 1964**

Origin UK

Engine 192cc, flat-two

Top speed 55 mph (89 km/h)

With a water-cooled engine and an all-enveloping fiberglass body, the Vogue was aimed at the scooter market, but was expensive and slow. Fewer than 400 were sold.

△ **Triumph 6TP "Saint" 1966**

Origin UK

Engine 649cc, inline two

Top speed 100 mph (160 km/h)

Triumph's machine, supplied to British police fleets for pursuit duties, was based on the 650cc Thunderbird tourer. Said to "Stop Anything In No Time," it became known as the "Saint."

◁ Honda CL90 Scrambler 1967

Origin Japan

Engine 90cc, single-cylinder

Top speed 59 mph (95 km/h)

A rugged little bike with a punchy, overhead-camshaft engine and full road equipment, the CL90 was a fashionable street scrambler, rather than a serious off-roader.

◁ Honda CD175 1967

Origin Japan

Engine 174cc, inline two

Top speed 78 mph (126 km/h)

Quieter and more comfortable than most of the competition, the "touring" CD175 offered an attractive combination of a lively, overhead-camshaft engine and effective silencing.

△ Suzuki 50 1969

Origin Japan

Engine 49cc, single-cylinder

Top speed 35 mph (56 km/h)

Suzuki's practical and comfortable baby motorcycle with a two-stroke 49cc engine, twin seat, and full mudguards introduced many young riders to motorcycling.

▷ MZ ES250/2 Trophy 1969

Origin East Germany

Engine 243cc, single-cylinder

Top speed 78 mph (126 km/h)

Simple, soundly built, and cheaper than any other 250 when new, the ES250/2 found a ready market among those not concerned with its looks.

▽ Harley-Davidson Servi-Car GE 1969

Origin USA

Engine 740cc, V-twin

Top speed 63 mph (101 km/h)

Made from 1932 to 1973, the three-wheeler utilitarian Servi-Car, with its side-valve engine and a reverse gear, had many uses, including police work.

Easy Rider, 1969
The customized choppers ridden by Peter Fonda and Dennis Hopper in the movie *Easy Rider* were based on Harley-Davidson Hydra-Glides. The sense of wanderlust inspired by this film made the chopper style extremely popular.

Tourers

When speed was not a priority, there were plenty of luxurious touring bikes available, with BMW's horizontally opposed, twin-cylinder machines preeminent for reliability, smooth running, and comfort. While British marques mostly offered dressed-up 1950s or even 1940s designs, Japanese motorcycles showed their hand in the touring market too—their reliability and low maintenance were a big plus for long-distance riders.

▽ Triumph Thunderbird 1960

Origin UK

Engine 649cc, inline twin

Top speed 98 mph (158 km/h)

The successful 1946 Thunderbird entered the 1960s with a new duplex tube frame and stylish rear skirt. It was now regarded as a touring, not performance, machine.

▽ Harley-Davidson FLH Duo-Glide 1960

Origin USA

Engine 1,213cc, V-twin

Top speed 100 mph (160 km/h)

Harley's big tourer finally received swingarm rear suspension in 1958, and a new name to advertise this: Duo-Glide. Many were equipped with touring accessories.

▽ Norton Dominator 99 De Luxe 1960

Origin UK

Engine 597cc, inline twin

Top speed 100 mph (160 km/h)

For 1960 Norton updated the Dominator range with narrower top frame tubes for improved comfort, and offered semi-enclosed bodywork on De Luxe models.

◁ Norton Navigator 1963

Origin UK

Engine 349cc, inline twin

Top speed 82 mph (132 km/h)

Norton's Jubilee grew up in 1960, with a completely revised and enlarged engine, heavier forks, and a bigger front brake; with minor changes it could reach 100 mph (160 km/h).

△ Allstate 250 "Twingle" 1965

Origin Austria/USA

Engine 248cc, single-cylinder

Top speed 69 mph (111 km/h)

The Puch SGS250, sold under license by Sears, was nicknamed the "Twingle" due to its unusual double-piston, two-stroke system. It was made up to 1970.

△ **BMW R60/2 1965**

Origin Germany

Engine 594cc, flat-twin

Top speed 80 mph (129 km/h)

Designed principally for sidecar hauling, over 20,000 R60s were built from 1956 to 1969. Smooth and sturdily built, they proved ideal long-distance touring machines.

◁ **Honda CB450 1965**

Origin Japan

Engine 444cc, inline twin

Top speed 110 mph (177 km/h)

With double overhead camshafts, torsion bar valve springs, and electric starting, this Honda showed the quality of engineering that would make Japanese bikes preeminent.

△ **BMW R75/5 1969**

Origin Germany

Engine 749cc, flat-twin

Top speed 110 mph (177 km/h)

BMW reinvented its R Series, adding 12-volt electrics, electric starting, telescopic forks, and better brakes to make a versatile touring bike, not just a sidecar hauler.

◁ **Kawasaki W1 1965**

Origin Japan

Engine 624cc, inline twin

Top speed 108 mph (174 km/h)

Developed from a 1950s BSA design that Kawasaki acquired with the Meguro company, the W1 was aimed at export markets, especially the US, but it was outdated.

▽ **Gilera 124 Speciale Strada 1966**

Origin Italy

Engine 124 cc, single-cylinder

Top speed 70 mph (113 km/h)

Gilera built small-engined motorcycles with big performance and its 124cc single was sold in the US by Sears, as well as in Europe. Piaggio bought Gilera in 1969.

△ **Moto Guzzi V7 Special 1969**

Origin Italy

Engine 757cc, V-twin

Top speed 115 mph (185 km/h)

Designed by Giulio Carcano to win a contest to be the new Italian police bike, the sturdy, shaft-drive V-twin would become Moto Guzzi's staple into the 2000s.

The first Suzuki Isle of Man TT team, in 1960

Great marques
The Suzuki story

Suzuki began production almost 50 years after other manufacturers, but quickly became one of the world's leading motorcycle makers. A consistent technological flair has kept it ahead of its competitors, and the marque's production models have benefited from the many notable competition successes in several racing disciplines.

NOW A GLOBAL CORPORATION producing everything from motorcycles to cars and outboard motors to ATVs, Suzuki had its origins in textiles. In 1909 Michio Suzuki set up the Suzuki Loom Works in the Japanese town of Hamamatsu. The Suzuki Loom Manufacturing Company, established in 1920, built first an apparatus for weaving cotton, and later, silk. Over the next few decades the venture became a major success.

After a break from production during World War II, the immediate postwar period saw the company suffer financially, which led to the decision to diversify. Seeing an opening in the market for cheap personal transportation in a country whose infrastructure had largely been destroyed, in 1947 Suzuki began testing out motors attached to bicycles.

In 1952 the 36cc Power Free became the debut offering from what was still Suzuki Loom Manufacturing. Featuring

Suzuki Logo
(introduced 1958)

an intuitive motor drive system, the two-stroke, air-cooled motorized bicycle attracted numerous plaudits, and the following year was joined by the larger-capacity Diamond Free. Demand for the new model rocketed after its class success in the Mount Fuji Hill Climb event, and the firm was soon manufacturing 6,000 units a month.

The company's name was changed to Suzuki Motor Company in 1954, but it would be a few years until models carried the Suzuki name. From 1954 the business introduced a series of genuine motorcycles—rather than bicycles with engines—using the name Colleda (meaning "This is it!") The first was the CO, a steel-framed four-stroke of 125cc. By the time an electric starter was introduced on the Colleda Twin at the end of the decade, the Suzuki "S" logo had been adopted and the marque was forging an identity as a two-stroke specialist.

Grand tourers
First presented in the early 1970s, Suzuki's GT range featured two-strokes from 125cc to 750cc, with one, two, and three cylinders.

Early in the 1960s Suzuki gained international recognition after winning the 50cc class at the 1961 Isle of Man TT races, and reigned as 50cc World Champions from 1962 until 1967. Meanwhile, an expansion in overseas operations led to the US Suzuki Corporation being set up in Los Angeles in 1963 to sell machines directly to the North American market. Among these was the X6 Hustler (T20 Super Six in Europe) from 1965, billed as the world's fastest 250cc motorcycle. Its innovative features included a tubular-steel cradle frame and six-speed transmission. Exceptionally popular around the world, it was joined three years later by the T500, which was the largest-capacity two-stroke bike on the market and capable of 112 mph (180 km/h) performance.

By the 1970s, export markets were at the fore of Suzuki's business, and the company's first overseas manufacturing plant had been built in Thailand. This was also a decade of notable racing

Factory gates
Rows of Suzuki models are lined up outside the company's headquarters in Hamamatsu City, Japan, in 1967. Today, the city is home to six plants.

TC250

GS750

RG500

Hayabusa GSX1300R

1909 Michio Suzuki founds the Suzuki Loom Works in Hamamatsu, Japan.	**1965** The T-20 model is unveiled as the world's fastest 250cc production bike.	**1976** The four-stroke GS series is introduced, first with the 250cc, 400cc, and 750cc.	**1999** The Hayabusa 1300, the world's fastest production bike, is launched; the total number of Suzuki motorcycle sales reaches 40 million.
1920 The Suzuki Loom Manufacturing Company is formed; this date is seen as the birth of the motor company.	**1966** The Suzuki company flag and official song are introduced.	**1980** GSX models are released, sporting a range of engines from 250cc to 750cc.	**2002** The Burgman 650 debuts as the largest-capacity scooter on the market.
1952 Suzuki enters the motorcycle market with the 36cc Power Free model.	**1967** The first Suzuki motorcycles to be made outside Japan are built at a plant in Thailand.	**1982** The Love model is unveiled, the first of several 50cc scooters in the 1980s.	**2006** The M109R model is released, with a 1,783cc engine that features the largest pistons in any production motorcycle or car.
1954 Formation of the Suzuki Motor Company.	**1971** The GT750 two-stroke model, featuring a novel three-cylinder engine, is introduced.	**1993** Suzuki makes a landmark deal to produce motorcycles in China; Kevin Schwantz wins the 500cc World Championship for Suzuki.	**2007** The B-King is unveiled as the marque's flagship "naked" (unfaired) bike.
1958 The "S" logo is used for the first time on Suzuki's motorcycles.	**1974** The RE-5 becomes the first Japanese motorcycle with a rotary engine.	**1996** The first Suzuki motorcycles are built in Vietnam.	
1962 Suzuki wins its first TT race and the inaugural 50cc World Championship.			

success as Suzuki took World Championship titles in top categories, including the 250cc Road title and the 125cc and 500cc Motocross titles. Arguably the greatest wins were in the 500cc category, in which British rider Barry Sheene became World Champion in 1976 and 1977.

New road models in the 1970s included the marque's first four-stroke, four-cylinder bikes in the GS series, which was launched in a range of capacities, including up to 1,000cc. Experimentation led Suzuki to develop a rotary-engined machine, the RE-5, in the mid-70s, though ultimately it was a commercial failure.

The 1980s and 90s were a period of Grand Prix glory for Suzuki as it won the 500cc World Championship once more. New machines were introduced, among them several scooters, class-leading motocross bikes, and the pioneering GSX Series, which included the top-spec 1,100cc Katana designed for overseas markets.

The company also struck deals with China, initially to export bikes and then to set up manufacturing plants in the country. This was another example of Suzuki's successful ongoing overseas expansion; by 1995, 20 million motorcycles had sold outside Japan.

In 1999 Suzuki introduced the Hayabusa 1300—a lean, aerodynamic sports bike for riders eager to push the limits; its top speed of just over 186 mph (300 km/h) made it the world's fastest road bike at the time.

Into the first decade of 2000, Suzuki further strengthened its position through tie-ins with General Motors and a deal with fellow Japanese motorcycle manufacturer Kawasaki.

"... I felt tremendous **pressure** as well as **pride**, in the unified **Suzuki spirit**... "

MITSUO ITO, ONLY JAPANESE RIDER TO WIN THE ISLE OF MAN TT

In the 2000s, novel products set new standards across various market sectors. The GSX-R1000 of 2001 combined fine handling, light weight, and great fuel-injected performance in a world-beating track bike, while the Burgman 650 redefined the scooter, with its massive 650cc engine and pioneering transmission system with one manual and two automatic modes.

With strong worldwide sales, Suzuki maintains its reputation for solid growth. With a futuristic fuel-cell scooter released in 2011, a raft of futuristic prototypes, and dedication to investing in alternative technologies, this famous marque with its forward-thinking ethos remains at the fore.

Superbike winners
Suzukis pictured in action during a superbike event in 2005, the year when the manufacturer won both the Riders' (with Troy Corser) and Constructors' Superbike World Championships.

Built for Speed

An explosion of advanced technology occurred in racing as the main Japanese contenders vied with each other in the World Championships. Honda, the four-stroke maker that had led the way in 1960, was under attack from Suzuki and Yamaha's ever more powerful two-strokes. Some European factories were in contention, however, while the US stuck with its own multidisciplinary championships.

▽ **Harley-Davidson KR 750 1961**

Origin USA

Engine 744cc, V-twin

Top speed 110 mph (177 km/h)

Despite an archaic side-valve engine, the KR was the one to beat on the US flat-track ovals. Tarmac versions with brakes like this could hit 150 mph (241km/h) with fairings installed.

▷ **Norton Manx Norton 30M 1962**

Origin UK

Engine 499cc, single-cylinder

Top speed 135 mph (217 km/h)

While no match for multi-cylinder machines, the Manx was still a strong grid presence in 1960s racing, the final, most refined edition being sold in 1962.

▽ **Honda RC163 1962**

Origin Japan

Engine 249cc, inline four

Top speed 136 mph (219 km/h)

With four cylinders, twin camshafts, and 16 tiny valves, the Honda won all nine 250cc Grands Prix in 1962. Jim Redman, winner of six, became champion.

◁ **Kreidler Renn-Florett 1963**

Origin Germany

Engine 50cc, single-cylinder

Top speed 100 mph (160 km/h)

Moped-maker Kreidler contested early 50cc World Championships with tiny 12-speed two-strokes developed to a high pitch. They won seven Grands Prix in 1962 and 1963.

DIY Winners

Even though well-funded, factory-run teams now dominated mainstream motorcycle racing, there was still scope for individuals to show their engineering prowess in sidecar road racing, record attempts, and drag racing. This produced some of the most dramatic-looking and wildly engineered machines of the decade, such as the supercharged Sprint winning Vincent "Methamon," drag racer "Mighty Mouse," and Tom Kirby's BSA sidecar.

▷ **Vincent Sprinter Methamon 1962**

Origin UK

Engine 1,148cc, V-twin

Top speed 150 mph (241km/h)

Maurice Brierley's supercharged sidecar unit set world records two-up in 1964 and averaged 100 mph (161 km/h) on the standing start km; its name meant "methanol-burning monster."

△ Yamaha RD05 1965

Origin Japan

Engine 249cc, V4

Top speed 135 mph (217 km/h)

Giving a phenomenal 200 hp per liter, Yamaha's water-cooled, twin crankshaft, disc-valve, two-stroke V4 engine took Phil Read to World Championship victory in 1968.

△ Harley-Davidson CRTT 1967

Origin USA

Engine 250cc, single-cylinder

Top speed 100 mph (161 km/h)

The Italian-designed single was a leading privateer machine in Europe's 250cc and 350cc classes. Part ownership of Aermacchi meant it was also raced in the US.

△ MZ RE125 1965

Origin East Germany

Engine 123cc, single-cylinder

Top speed 120 mph (193 km/h)

Despite small budgets, MZ had pioneered disc valves in the 1950s and remained competitive in the smaller classes through the 1960s.

△ Suzuki GP RT63 1963

Origin Japan

Engine 124cc, inline two

Top speed 115 mph (185 km/h)

Suzuki's early successes were in the 50cc and 125cc classes. The little RT63 twin took Hugh Anderson to a world title in 1963.

△ ESO Speedway DT-5 1966

Origin Czechoslovakia

Engine 497cc, single-cylinder

Top speed 90 mph (145 km/h)

Top choice for hectic methanol-fueled Speedway racing on cinder ovals in the 1960s. By 1966 Eso had been absorbed by the bigger Jawa company.

△ Suzuki TR500R 1969

Origin Japan

Engine 493cc, inline two

Top speed 147 mph (237 km/h)

Suzuki's first 500 had an air-cooled engine based on the T500 roadster. Its first victory was at Sears Point, CA, in 1969 with Art Baumann aboard.

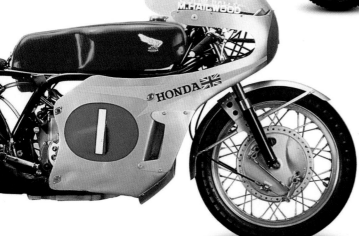

◁ Honda RC166 1966

Origin Japan

Engine 249cc, inline six

Top speed 150 mph (241 km/h)

Honda's deafening 18,000 rpm six-cylinder engines represented the ultimate in 1960s racing development. They took Mike Hailwood to two 250cc and one 350cc world titles.

▷ Vincent Mighty Mouse 1966

Origin UK

Engine 498cc, single-cylinder

Top speed 160 mph (257 km/h)

Drag-raced by builder Brian Chapman with a supercharged 500cc Vincent engine, "Mighty Mouse" ran the world's first 500cc sub-nine-second ¼-mile (400m) at Santa Pod, UK in 1977.

◁ Kirby BSA sidecar outfit 1968

Origin UK

Engine 750cc, inline twin

Top speed 150 mph (241 km/h)

Ridden by Terry Vinicombe and John Flaxman, this machine won the 1968 Isle of Man 750cc Sidecar TT. Sponsored by Tom Kirby, it was the last British outfit to win a TT for 18 years.

Rough Riders

As the popularity of rough road "trials" competition in the 1940s/50s waned, the 1960s spawned a new craze: scrambling. Bikes were ridden across virgin countryside; the rougher and more slippery it was, the better. Specially built scramble tracks were constructed to increase the challenge. In response, manufacturers developed compact machines with low gearing, high exhausts, and long-travel suspension.

△ **Greeves Hawkstone 1961**

Origin	UK
Engine	249cc, inline two
Top speed	70 mph (113 km/h)

Villiers single- or twin-engined scrambling bikes from the small British manufacturer Greeves had many wins, including Dave Bickers' 1960 and 1961 250cc Motocross World Championships.

△ **Husqvarna 250 1963**

Origin	Sweden
Engine	250cc, single-cylinder
Top speed	75 mph (120 km/h)

Better known for chainsaws, Husqvarna has made motorcycles since 1903. Their custom-built 250cc and 500cc competition bikes won many scramble titles in the 1960s.

△ **Rokon Trail-breaker 1963**

Origin	USA
Engine	134cc, single-cylinder
Top speed	20 mph (32 km/h)

The only all-wheel drive motorcycle to enter production—invented by Charlie Fehn of California in 1958—is the Rokon. It was designed for low-speed use on rough terrain.

△ **Honda 250 Scrambler 1964**

Origin	Japan
Engine	247cc, inline two
Top speed	75 mph (120 km/h)

Honda entered the scrambling market with this beautifully engineered 9,000 rpm parallel-twin-engined machine. It was based on the C72 Dream 250 road bike.

◁ **Velocette MSS Scrambler 1963**

Origin	UK
Engine	499cc, single-cylinder
Top speed	82 mph (132 km/h)

Big and heavy, despite its all-aluminum four-stroke engine, the MSS was a powerful and dependable scrambling machine but seldom a winner in competition.

△ **Bultaco Sherpa T 1964**

Origin	Spain
Engine	238cc, single-cylinder
Top speed	75 mph (120 km/h)

Bultaco worked with Irish Trials ace Sammy Miller to produce a light two-stroke bike that changed the face of trials overnight, giving Bultaco many wins from 1965.

◁ Dot Demon 1965

Origin UK

Engine 250cc, single-cylinder

Top speed 75 mph (121 km/h)

Dot of Manchester increasingly specialized in scramble/ motocross bikes during the 1950s and often won UK under-250cc classes with the Demon.

◁ Rickman Metisse MK3 Scrambler 1965

Origin UK

Engine Triumph 490cc, inline two

Top speed 85 mph (137 km/h)

Derek and Ron Rickman made scramble bikes from 1960, supplying them as kits for buyers to add their own engines. They proved to be very successful motocross machines.

▽ Triumph Bonneville TT Special 1966

Origin UK

Engine 649cc, inline two

Top speed 120 mph (193 km/h)

The TT Special was a limited production, ultra-light Bonneville racer, with a tuned engine, no mufflers, no lights, ultra-light mudguards, and a magneto ignition.

△ BSA Victor Enduro 1967

Origin UK

Engine 441cc, single-cylinder

Top speed 85 mph (137 km/h)

Jeff Smith's 1964–65 Scrambling World Championship winners inspired BSA to launch the competition Victor model, in race Grand Prix form and slightly detuned Enduro specification.

◁ Yamaha DT-1 1968

Origin Japan

Engine 246cc, single-cylinder

Top speed 80 mph (129 km/h)

Yamaha spotted an untapped market for a mass-production dirt road bike in the US. Much cheaper than custom-built scramble bikes, the DT-1 sold very well.

△ Yamaha YR2-C Grand Prix 1968

Origin Japan

Engine 348cc, inline two

Top speed 100 mph (160 km/h)

The YR1 of 1967 was Yamaha's first 350, closely followed by the 110 mph (177 km/h) YR2. This is the dual-purpose scrambler version, which offers a great on/off road compromise.

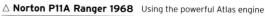

△ Norton P11A Ranger 1968

Origin UK

Engine 745cc, inline twin

Top speed 115 mph (185 km/h)

Using the powerful Atlas engine in a light Matchless frame, the P11 was built for the growing US sport of desert racing. This P11A is the road-legal model.

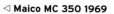

◁ Maico MC 350 1969

Origin Germany

Engine 352cc

Top speed 90 mph (145 km/h)

Established German motocross marque, Maico was typical of manufacturers who enlarged 250cc two-stroke engines to make light, yet powerful 500cc class contenders.

▷ AJS Stormer 1969

Origin UK

Engine 247cc, single-cylinder

Top speed 75 mph (120 km/h)

Norton Villiers Group bought AJS in 1967 and launched the Stormer scramble bike with the Villiers Starmaker engine. It was so successful it is still made today.

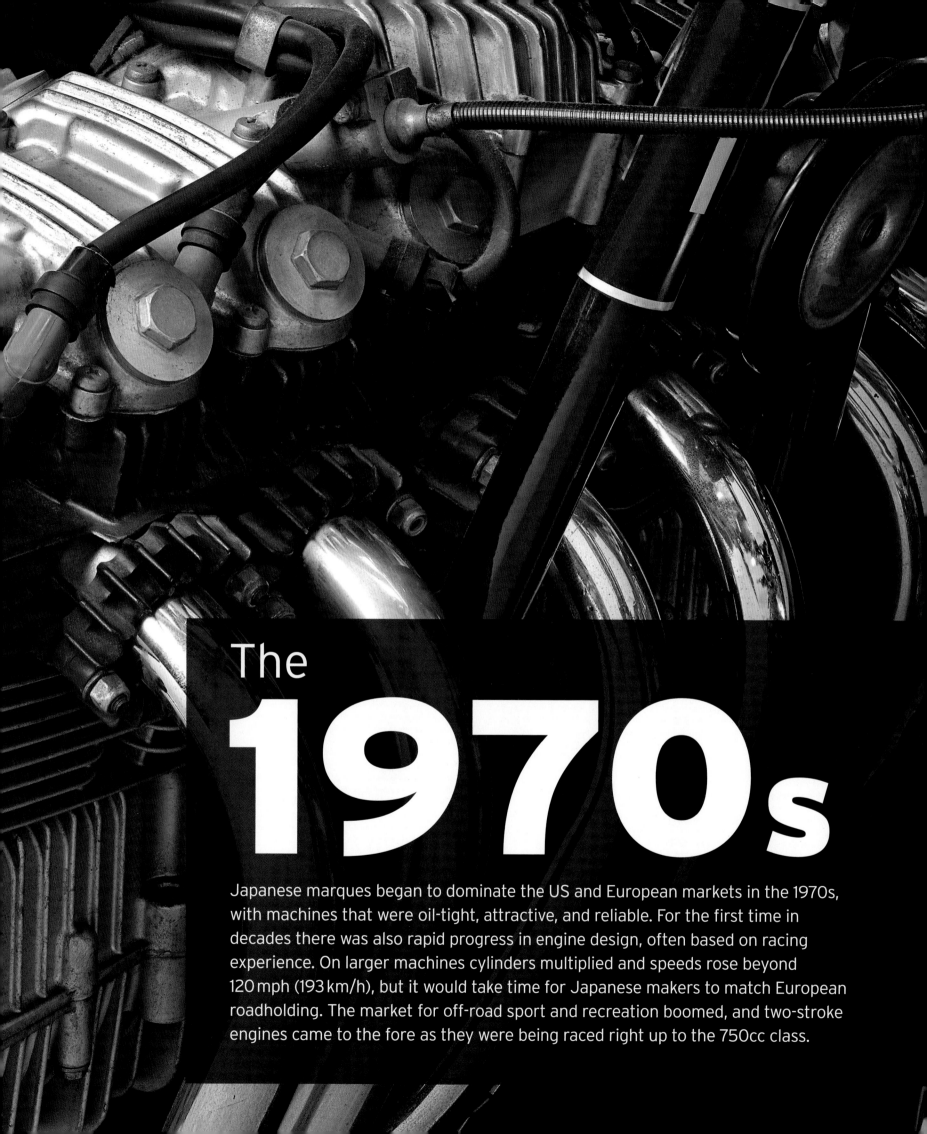

The
1970s

Japanese marques began to dominate the US and European markets in the 1970s, with machines that were oil-tight, attractive, and reliable. For the first time in decades there was also rapid progress in engine design, often based on racing experience. On larger machines cylinders multiplied and speeds rose beyond 120 mph (193 km/h), but it would take time for Japanese makers to match European roadholding. The market for off-road sport and recreation boomed, and two-stroke engines came to the fore as they were being raced right up to the 750cc class.

Superbikes

Led by Honda's launch of the 125 mph (201 km/h) four-cylinder CB750, a new generation of glamorous high-performance machines transformed the motorcycling scene in the 1970s. The term "superbike" was coined to describe these exciting new motorcycles that mostly came from Japan and Italy. Having set the pace for so long, the antiquated the British industry was being eclipsed.

△ **Honda CB750 1970**
Origin Japan
Engine 736cc, inline four
Top speed 125 mph (201 km/h)

This was the first superbike: Honda changed the face of sports bikes in 1969 with its overhead-camshaft four-cylinder engine, disc brake, and refined details.

△ **Honda GL1000 1975**
Origin Japan
Engine 999cc, flat-four
Top speed 125 mph (201 km/h)

Advanced automotive technology made the GL1000 a sophisticated, powerful, and heavy machine that became the definitive touring motorcycle.

△ **Laverda 750SF2 1972**
Origin Italy
Engine 744cc, ohc parallel-twin
Top speed 118 mph (190 km/h)

Laverda's first large-capacity bikes were sturdily built overhead-camshaft twins with inclined cylinders. The SF sport versions handled well and were successful in Endurance races.

△ **Kawasaki Z1 1973**
Origin Japan
Engine 903cc, inline four
Top speed 135 mph (217 km/h)

The double overhead-camshaft Z1 was immensely powerful, good-looking, and affordable. Handling was not first-rate but the engine was raced successfully.

◁ **Ducati 750 Sport 1973**
Origin Italy
Engine 747cc, ohc V-twin
Top speed 122 mph (196 km/h)

Based on Ducati's proven singles, this sleek bike was an elemental sporting mount built for speed, not comfort. It revived interest in V-twin engines.

△ MV Agusta Sport America 1975

Origin Italy

Engine 789cc, inline four

Top speed 120 mph (193 km/h)

MV's uprated shaft-drive 750S four had a bigger engine and twin disc brakes in the front. As its name implies, this machine was aimed directly at the US market.

△ MV Agusta 750S 1972

Origin Italy

Engine 743cc, dohc inline

Top speed 115 mph (185 km/h)

This famous Grand Prix marque based its four-cylinder road bikes on racer technology, but used shaft drive. The machines were expensive and consequently very rare.

◁ Kawasaki Mach IV 1975

Origin Japan

Engine 748cc, three-cylinder

Top speed 126 mph (203 km/h)

The Mach IV was the most powerful of Kawasaki's charismatic, high-performance two-strokes, which were killed off by increasingly stringent emissions controls.

△ Rickman Enfield Metisse 1974

Origin UK

Engine 736cc, ohv parallel-twin

Top speed 110 mph (177 km/h)

Using 750cc Royal Enfield engines in a chassis of their own construction, the Rickman brothers built a limited number of the Metisse bikes.

△ Moto Guzzi V7 Sport 1972

Origin Italy

Engine 748cc, ohv V-twin

Top speed 120 mph (193 km/h)

Guzzi's rugged V-twin engine and shaft drive were ideal for touring bikes, but they were also used successfully in sports machines like this V7 Sport.

△ Moto Guzzi Le Mans MkI 1976

Origin Italy

Engine 844cc, ohv V-twin

Top speed 132 mph (212 km/h)

Developed from the earlier V7 Sport, the capacity of the Le Mans was increased to 844cc and it was equipped with disc brakes with linked operation.

Honda CB750

The original superbike, the Honda CB750, was a landmark motorcycle, influencing the future of large-capacity bikes like no other model. Honda combined a powerful four-cylinder engine with features usually only available as extras, all for a competitive price. Launched in 1969, the CB750 heralded the arrival of Japanese manufacturers in the big-bike market, and initiated a seismic shift in the design, efficiency, and production of large-capacity bikes.

HONDA ALREADY had a reputation for manufacturing motorcycles on a grand scale, with its 1958 50cc Cub proving an instant worldwide hit. But by the late 1960s the Japanese marque had yet to produce a large-capacity model for export. Drawn to the big-bike market in the US, Honda set about developing a machine that could break into a sector traditionally dominated by US and British marques. The result—the CB750—was a total revelation. Never before had a standard road machine offered such a specification: an overhead-camshaft four-cylinder engine, five speeds, electric starting, and the first hydraulic disc front brake on a production motorcycle. Suddenly BSA, Triumph, and Harley-Davidson products looked outdated. Motorcycling was transformed. The big, fast Honda set new standards for power, reliability, and sophistication, and threw down the gauntlet to other Japanese manufacturers.

Rapid growth
Named after its founder, Soichiro Honda, the Honda Motor Company came into being in 1948. Early Honda logos were always accompanied by an illustration of wings—symbolic of the classical winged goddess of Victory. By 1963 the Honda name was internationally known.

FRONT VIEW

REAR VIEW

Fuel tank design is traditional yet stylish

Engine tachometer and speedometer angled for easy reading at high speed

Mudguards are chrome, which is also used on other detailing

Deep-padded seat can accommodate rider and passenger

Four carburetors supply fuel/air mixture to the engine

Exhaust system is four-into-four with megaphone mufflers

Stopping power
For big-bike owners used to relying on drum brakes for stopping power, the CB750's hydraulic front disc was revolutionary. It provided safe, judder-free deceleration from the bike's high top speeds, with the disc's performance unaffected by water or dirt. From 1975, the model received a disc brake at the rear as well.

SPECIFICATIONS	
Model	Honda CB750 (1970)
Assembly	Hamamatsu/Suzuka, Japan
Production	Not known
Construction	Tubular-steel cradle frame
Engine	736cc, inline four
Power output	67 hp at 8,500 rpm
Transmission	Five-speed
Suspension	Telescopic front forks, swingarm rear
Brakes	Disc front, drum rear
Maximum speed	Over 125 mph (201 km/h)

THE BIKE

"Speak to the wind. And listen to the answer. Freedom!"
Honda's marketing team promoted this new machine as a bike
that broke boundaries. The CB750, originally called the Dream
Four, boasted a dazzling array of refinements, while retaining
well-proven conventional features, including a cradle frame,
telescopic front forks, and twin-shock, swingarm rear
suspension. The CB750 was the bike that changed the face of
motorcycling, crushing the British competition along the way.

1. Tank script 2. Fork gaiters 3. Side reflector 4. Honda wing badge
on side panel 5. Handlebar switchgear 6. Front brake lever 7. Front
brake disc 8. Rear shock 9. 140 mph (225 km/h) speedometer
10. Passenger footrest 11. Kick-starter provides backup 12. Front
wheel hub cone 13. Exhaust outlets

THE ENGINE

The CB750 was powered by the world's first mass-produced transverse four-cylinder engine, developed using Honda's Grand Prix racing experience. The fuel/air mixture was supplied by four carburetors, and the overhead-cam, four-stroke, 736cc power plant was smooth and powerful, with an exciting tone from the exhaust.

14. Overhead-camshaft engine **15.** Choke lever on carburetor **16.** Alternator beneath circular cover **17.** Chromed exhaust pipes

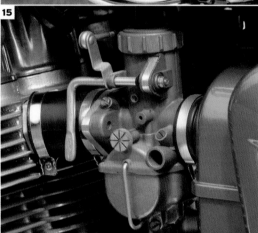

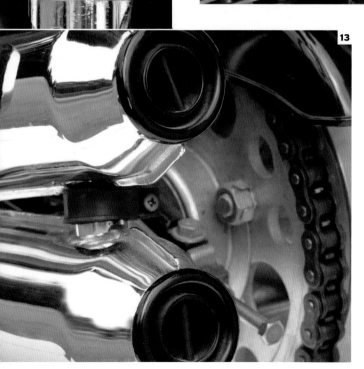

Superbikes (cont.)

The choice for buyers in the 1970s was mainly between the power and sophistication of the Japanese machines and simpler, but better handling, European bikes. The Italian manufacturers Ducati, Laverda, and Moto Guzzi achieved Japanese levels of performance with tuned versions of their basic models, while BMW used superior aerodynamics.

◁ **Ducati 860GTS 1977**

Origin Italy

Engine 864cc, ohc V-twin

Top speed 118 mph (190 km/h)

To create the 860GTS, Ducati enlarged the capacity of their V-twin engine and commissioned car designer Giorgetto Giugiaro to style the bike.

◁ **Yamaha XS750 1977**

Origin Japan

Engine 747cc, inline triple

Top speed 115 mph (185 km/h)

Yamaha sidestepped the superbike race with the XS750, a heavy, shaft-drive machine that was clearly more touring than sporting, yet not far behind in performance.

△ **BMW R100RS 1978**

Origin Germany

Engine 980cc, flat-twin

Top speed 123 mph (198 km/h)

This bike had a fairing developed in a wind tunnel, which meant big distances could be covered at high speed and in comfort despite the modest output of the engine.

▷ **Yamaha XS1100F 1979**

Origin Japan

Engine 1,101cc, inline four

Top speed 138 mph (222 km/h)

Yamaha went head-to-head with BMW for the luxury touring market, offering more power and sophistication but also more weight and mediocre handling.

△ **Honda CBX 1978**

Origin Japan

Engine 1,047cc, inline six

Top speed 136 mph (219 km/h)

Hondas had become boring in the 1970s, but this bike changed all that, with a stunning 24-valve, twin-cam, six-cylinder engine that made it the fastest road bike of its time.

◁ Ducati 900SD Darmah 1979

Origin	Italy
Engine	864cc, V-twin
Top speed	114 mph (183 km/h)

With good balance and its unusual 90-degree (V-twin), desmodromic-valve engine integral to a stiff and lightweight frame, the SD was very fast on twisty roads.

△ Kawasaki Z1000 Z1-R 1978

Origin	Japan
Engine	1,015cc, inline four
Top speed	136 mph (219 km/h)

Japan's first "custom" café racer, with 1970s sharp-edged styling, black-painted engine, and alloy wheels, was the most powerful Z yet, though sales were sluggish.

▷ Suzuki GS750 1978

Origin	Japan
Engine	748cc, inline four
Top speed	120 mph (193 km/h)

Suzuki abandoned two-strokes for four-strokes with this machine, building a superb twin-cam four that outclassed the opposition, yet remained a usable everyday commuter bike.

△ Kawasaki Z650 1979

Origin	Japan
Engine	652cc, inline four
Top speed	118 mph (190 km/h)

First launched in 1976, Kawasaki added extra chrome, alloy wheels, and pinstriping in 1979, hoping to increase sales—but buyers wanted 750 bikes.

△ Suzuki GT750 1978

Origin	Japan
Engine	738cc, inline triple
Top speed	123 mph (198 km/h)

The only water-cooled two-stroke ever to make mass production, the GT750 was a fast, comfortable machine, but it lacked handling finesse on the road.

△ Suzuki GS1000S 1979

Origin	Japan
Engine	987cc, inline four
Top speed	139 mph (224 km/h)

Built to commemorate Wes Cooley and Yoshimura's AMA Superbike title in 1978, this faired GS1000S was among the fastest of its day, but was civilized to ride.

◁ Laverda Jota 1000 1979

Origin	Italy
Engine	981cc, inline triple
Top speed	139 mph (224 km/h)

For a short time the Jota was the world's fastest production motorcycle. It was loud, raw, and uncompromising, which was an appealing prospect for many enthusiasts.

Middleweights

In the midrange motorcycle market, some buyers were still looking for reliable "get-me-home" transportation like the dependable Spanish Sanglas, while for others, speed and better handling mattered. European manufacturers refined earlier developments to build fast, but often somewhat crude and unreliable, labor-intensive machines, while the Japanese made perfectly engineered motorcycles: from Honda's smallest-yet 350 Four to Yamaha's twin-cam, four-valve 500 parallel-twin.

△ **Ducati 350 Desmo 1974**
Origin Italy
Engine 340cc, single-cylinder
Top speed 92 mph (148 km/h)

Fabio Taglioni devised a desmodromic system that opened and closed the valves without springs, to give these singles an exceptionally high performance.

▽ **Ducati 450 Desmo 1974**
Origin Italy
Engine 436cc, single-cylinder
Top speed 98 mph (158 km/h)

Its supremely powerful desmodromic-valve engine combined with superbly light nimble handling more than made up for the shoddy build quality of the 1970s' Ducatis.

△ **Ducati Silver Shotgun 1970**
Origin Italy
Engine 436cc, single-cylinder
Top speed 98 mph (158 km/h)

With its fiberglass café-racer body panels painted in silver metalflake, you could not miss this Ducati, nor the sound of its desmodromic engine revving at 7,000 rpm.

△ **MV Agusta 350S Elettronica 1972**
Origin Italy
Engine 349cc, inline twin
Top speed 103 mph (166 km/h)

This bike had excellent handling thanks to a lightweight frame that incorporated the engine as a structural member. The 1972 model was equipped with an early form of electronic ignition.

▽ **Triumph T100R Daytona 1972**
Origin UK
Engine 490cc, inline twin
Top speed 111 mph (179 km/h)

Named after Triumph's first victory at Daytona Raceway in 1966, this high-performance version of the Tiger 100 was built to beat the Japanese competition.

△ **Yamaha TX500 1972**
Origin Japan
Engine 498cc, inline twin
Top speed 110 mph (177 km/h)

This was the first road bike to combine double overhead camshafts and four valves per cylinder on a parallel-twin. It was docile and civilized to ride.

◁ **Sanglas 400E Electrico 1973**

Origin Spain

Engine 422cc, single-cylinder

Top speed 81 mph (130 km/h)

Sanglas built simple, low-revving, four-stroke singles in Barcelona from 1945 until absorbed by Yamaha in 1981. This electric-start model offered dependable transportation.

▽ **Honda CB350F 1973**

Origin Japan

Engine 347cc, inline four

Top speed 99 mph (159 km/h)

An overhead camshaft inline four of such small dimensions was unique at the time. This was a beautifully made, smooth, and quiet machine, though not especially fast.

△ **Benelli 500 Quattro 1975**

Origin Italy

Engine 498cc, inline four

Top speed 107 mph (172 km/h)

Under De Tomaso's control, Benelli's Honda-like engine was built by Moto Guzzi. With a disc front brake, good power output, and excellent economy, this was an attractive bike.

▽ **Suzuki GT550 1975**

Origin Japan

Engine 543cc, inline triple

Top speed 108 mph (174 km/h)

The 550 sat between a 380 and a 750 in Suzuki's two-stroke triples. This bike is modified with aftermarket bodywork and exhaust, as well as cast wheels.

△ **Suzuki T500 1975**

Origin Japan

Engine 492cc, inline twin

Top speed 106 mph (170 km/h)

This first two-stroke to win an AMA National race was also the world's largest two-stroke twin at the time, prone to vibration but worth it for the performance it offered.

Middleweights (cont.)

As the decade progressed, any decent 500cc bike was expected to top 100 mph (160 km/h), and the really sporty ones 10–15 mph (16–24 km/h) above that. Though at this stage they were not always getting every detail right, the Japanese marques took big chunks of the mid-range market with their sophisticated, clean, and stylish machines, and a new era began as Kawasaki started building motorcycles in the US.

◁ Honda CB400F 1975
Origin Japan
Engine 408cc, inline four
Top speed 98 mph (158 km/h)

Small but perfectly formed, the 400 Four was one of the bikes that helped Japanese makes to dominate the market. It had a delightful engine, great looks, and great performance.

△ Morini 3½ Sport 1975
Origin Italy
Engine 344cc, V-twin
Top speed 97 mph (156 km/h)

Using the "Heron head" design gave the Franco Lambertini–designed V-twin engine great power and flexibility, easily exploited in this lightweight, great-handling frame.

◁ Honda CB550 Four 1976
Origin Japan
Engine 544cc, inline four
Top speed 105 mph (169 km/h)

Considered one of the finest compromises between performance, economy, and handling quality at the time, the 550 Four was an extremely well-integrated design.

△ Honda CB500T 1976
Origin Japan
Engine 499cc, parallel-twin
Top speed 100 mph (160 km/h)

Quiet, with good handling, the CB500 suffered vibration that a few years earlier would have been acceptable, but not in 1975. This bike has been given a racer look.

△ Honda CX500 1978
Origin Japan
Engine 497cc, V-twin
Top speed 105 mph (169 km/h)

Honda appeared to try every engine configuration for its midrange bikes in the mid-1970s. The CX was the most innovative, with a water-cooled V-twin engine and shaft drive.

△ **Ducati 500 Sport Desmo 1977**

Origin Italy

Engine 497cc, inline twin

Top speed 106 mph (170 km/h)

Ducati's trademark desmodromic valves were hardly necessary on a road bike, but added cachet to this rapid, nimble, compact class-leading 500.

△ **Ducati 500SL Pantah 1977**

Origin Italy

Engine 497cc, V-twin

Top speed 117 mph (188 km/h)

The desmodromic-valve V-twin was a structural element in the Pantah's light but stiff trellis frame, which helped to give it superb handling to match its performance.

△ **Moto Guzzi V50 1977**

Origin Italy

Engine 490cc, V-twin

Top speed 105 mph (169 km/h)

Under De Tomaso's control, smaller versions of Guzzi's trademark transverse V-twin were introduced, with alloy wheels, good performance, and a shaft drive.

△ **MV Agusta 350S Ipotesi 1978**

Origin Italy

Engine 349cc, inline twin

Top speed 94 mph (151 km/h)

The MV 350 was restyled by Giorgio Guigiaro for 1975, with a new frame and modern features. The overhead-camshaft engine remained largely unchanged.

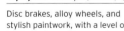

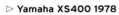

▷ **Yamaha XS400 1978**

Origin Japan

Engine 392cc, inline twin

Top speed 105 mph (169 km/h)

Disc brakes, alloy wheels, and stylish paintwork, with a level of equipment equal to many larger machines, made the four-stroke XS400 an attractive buy.

▷ **Kawasaki KZ400 1978**

Origin Japan

Engine 398cc, inline twin

Top speed 93 mph (150 km/h)

Kawasaki opened the first "foreign" motorcycle factory in the US to build bikes like this, designed to be an all-around better version of Honda's CB360.

A rider on Meguro-based W-series model

Great Marques
The Kawasaki story

There is often an unusually strong bond between a Kawasaki and its owner. Unlike other Japanese manufacturers, whose output may sometimes feel generic and interchangeable, Kawasaki has pursued a path of innovation and individuality that has created a loyalty between riders and its fearsomely muscular machines.

IN THE LAST FEW YEARS of the 19th century, Shozo Kawasaki established the Kawasaki Shipyard in Tokyo. Success in that sphere resulted in the company's branching out into locomotives and aircraft. In the difficult times after World War II, the motorcycle was seen as a cost-effective means of transportation in financially crippled Japan. At this time Kawasaki began to produce engines for other manufacturers, but by the end of the 1950s the company started full motorcycle production. An assembly plant was built in Akashi, while technical know-how was absorbed through a merger with Meguro, an established name in the field.

Kawasaki badge
(introduced 1968)

Initial efforts were competent, if uninspiring. The debut model wholly built by Kawasaki was 1961's 125cc, two-stroke B7. The first machine to carry a Kawasaki badge was the B8 of 1963, which was similarly efficient but unexciting. Models such as the long-running B1 of 1966 consolidated the company's reputation for fairly mundane machines rather than bikes that reinvented the motorcycling world.

That all started to change, especially in the US, with the 1967 A1, a twin-cylinder, 250cc bike that was also known as the Samurai. This machine showed that Kawasaki was capable of game-changing revolution as well as steady evolution, but the motorcycling world was not fully prepared for what would come in 1968. The H1 was a 500cc machine, with fearsome acceleration that reduced competitors to also-rans. Handling could be hard work, but motorcycle journalist Ian Falloon summed up the general fervor, calling it "the motorcycle that every adolescent, including myself, dreamed about."

If it was performance a rider was seeking, there was little need to look any further than Kawasaki's Z1 of 1972. This 900cc double-overhead camshaft beast was capable of 131 mph (211 km/h). More than 40 speed and endurance records fell before it at Daytona in 1973. The H1 and H2

were admired for their sheer aggression, but the four-cylinder Z1 was an all-around superior machine, with poise added to its undoubted power. Its nickname—"the King"—was no overstatement.

The decade that followed the arrival of the Z1 was a golden age for Kawasaki. On the road the KZ1000A and the KZ650 continued the success in 1976. Later there was

All-terrain marque
Kawasaki has a long tradition for producing some of the finest off-road bikes, a fact borne out by numerous motocross and endurance World Championships secured by the marque.

unprecedented world dominance for the racers. The aerodynamically supreme KR250 and KR350 made the respective world championships their own personal property in the late 1970s and early 1980s.

It is often said that getting to the top is one thing, but staying there is quite another. The six-cylinder Z1300 tourer confirmed Kawasaki's position in the field with power that even

Pioneering model
Unveiled in 1972, the 903cc Kawasaki Z1 had class-leading performance and, with its disc brakes, exceptional stopping power. It was one of the world's first "superbikes."

W1

Z1

ZX-12R

KX250F

1954 Meihatsu's 125V bike is powered by the new Kawasaki KB-5 engine.
1961 The first bike completely built as a Kawasaki machine—the B7—hits the market.
1963 The first full-fledged Kawasaki arrives in the form of the badged B8.
1967 The A1, also known as the Samurai, is introduced.
1968 Kawasaki debuts in the three-cylinder market with the H1, trumpeted as the world's fastest production machine.

1972 The four-cylinder Z1 throws wide open the market for power machines.
1976 The KZ650 is released.
1978 Kork Ballington wins both the 250cc and 350cc World Championships in this and the following year.
1980 Anton Mang wins the first of four titles over three years in the 250cc and 350cc categories.
1981 Jean Lafond and Raymond Roche win the World Endurance title; the company releases the AR 50.

1983 The GPZ900R becomes the world's best-selling two-wheeler.
1991 Alex Vieira starts a sequence of five World Endurance titles in six years for the marque.
1994 The ZZ-R1100, the world's fastest production bike, is released.
1994 The 900cc class, traditionally a strong category for the company, proves so again with the release of the ZX-9R.
1996 Production numbers of Kawasaki vehicles hit the 10 million mark.

1998 Sebastian Tortelli wins the 250cc World Motocross title to build on his 125cc triumph of two years earlier.
2000 Kawasaki solves the conundrum of reducing weight but increasing power with the ZX-12R "Ninja."
2008 The 1400GTR draws from the ZZ-R1400 of two years earlier as Kawasaki enters the tourer field once again.
2009 In the VN1700 Voyager, the Harley Davidson Electra Glide Ultra has a serious rival in the tourer class.

eclipsed many cars. Then, into the fiercely competitive markets of the mid-1980s, came the liquid-cooled GPZ900R. The GPZ Series was a reminder of Kawasaki's quality and breathtaking performance, and the 900R helped them maintain this profile for many years. The growing list of

"The engineering was **magnificent**, it was all **beautifully made**."
KORK BALLINGTON, 250/350CC WORLD CHAMPION, ON THE KR500

Kawasaki classics lengthened with the release of the ZZ-R1100 in 1990. Capable of 175 mph (282 km/h), it took the title of the fastest production model motorcycle in the world.

During the 1990s Kawasaki had impressive competition successes. From 1991 the marque took five

Endurance World Championships in six years. In the middle of that run, American Scott Russell edged out England's Carl Fogarty for the 1993 World Superbike championship. Years of endeavor in the mud-spattered arena of motocross were rewarded in 1995 as the brilliant Belgian Stefan Everts lifted the 250cc crown.

The ZX-7R of the mid-1990s was often underappreciated by critics, but its looks, handling, and speed were a big hit with the public. Taking charge of the top end of the market in 2000 was the flagship ZX-12R "Ninja," in

FRENCH CLASSIC
The Kawasaki team of Gregory Leblanc, Olivier Four, and Julien Da Costa celebrate winning the 2010 Le Mans 24 Hours event, part of the Endurance World Championship.

which a formidable power-to-weight ratio was designed for breaking records. With the Z1000 of 2003 and the ZZ-R1400 of 2006, there has been little let-up from Kawasaki. The latter bike can reach 60 mph (97 km/h) in 2.5 seconds. This makes it a more-than-honorable heir to the bikes of Kawasaki's power-packed past.

Kawasaki's "Green Meanies" competition bikes and mold-breaking road machines have often been in a class of their own. Although part of the giant Kawasaki Heavy Industries group, the marque is the smallest of Japan's Big Four motorcycle makers, after Honda, Suzuki, and Yamaha, but that hasn't prevented it from being a heavy-hitter at the top end of the market.

Standing Out

For the customer who could afford to stand out from the crowd in the 1970s, there was plenty of choice, including Wankel rotary-engined bikes from Germany, Japan, and the Netherlands. Some marques employed top industrial car stylists in an attempt to gain an advantage over their opponents; others looked to technology. Sales were not always strong, but survivors are regarded as cult classics today.

▷ Harley-Davidson FLH Custom 1970

Origin USA

Engine 1,208cc, V-twin

Top speed 90 mph (145 km/h)

Harley's restyled FL engine was nicknamed "Shovelhead." Custom makeovers, with elongated front forks, high handlebars, and aftermarket exhausts, were fashionable.

▽ Triumph X-75 Hurricane 1973

Origin UK

Engine 741cc, inline triple

Top speed 114 mph (183 km/h)

This bike was designed for the US market by custom builder Craig Vetter. Originally a BSA, the striking X-75 was sold with Triumph badging as the first factory-built custom.

△ Hercules/DKW W2000 1974

Origin Germany

Engine 294cc, Wankel 1-rotor

Top speed 90 mph (145 km/h)

The first motorcycle with a pistonless Wankel-rotary engine was sold as a Hercules in Germany and a DKW elsewhere; the strange air-cooled unit put buyers off.

▷ Suzuki RE-5 1974

Origin Japan

Engine 497cc, Wankel 1-rotor

Top speed 104 mph (167 km/h)

Japan's first rotary-engined bike was typically sophisticated but alien to most motorcyclists' eyes, being top-heavy, and thirsty for fuel. Suzuki dropped the idea after 1977.

◁ Triumph Bonneville T140D Special 1979

Origin UK

Engine 744cc, inline twin

Top speed 105 mph (169 km/h)

This attractive D variant of the T140 had cast-alloy wheels, a small tank, high handlebars, and a two-into-one exhaust. Aimed at the US market, the "D" stood for Daytona.

▽ **Harley-Davidson XLCR 1978**

Origin USA

Engine 998cc, V-twin

Top speed 115 mph (185 km/h)

Derived from the 1,000cc Sportster, the XL Cafe Racer was stylistically inspired by European sports bikes. However, it lacked their speed and handling and attracted few buyers.

◁ **BMW R90S 1975**

Origin Germany

Engine 898cc, flat-twin

Top speed 124 mph (200 km/h)

Normally somber BMW colors were abandoned when the company joined the superbike sales race with a big-engined sports tourer that was both fast and comfortable.

▷ **IZH Jupiter 3 1975**

Origin Russia

Engine 348cc, inline twin

Top speed 72 mph (115 km/h)

The Izhevsk-made Jupiter was expensive but dated, both mechanically and cosmetically. This example was sold in the UK under the Cossack brand.

△ **MV Agusta Ipotesi Sport**

Origin Italy

Engine 349cc, inline two

Top speed 106 mph (170 km/h)

Styled by preeminent car stylist Giorgetto Giugiaro, the Ipotesi (Hypothesis) was speedy with sharp handling and braking, but its overhead-valve engine vibrated.

△ **Benelli 750 Sei 1976**

Origin Italy

Engine 747cc, inline six

Top speed 126 mph (203 km/h)

After buying Benelli, Alejandro de Tomaso challenged Japan with a straight six. The engine design is similar to Honda's CB500, but with two more cylinders.

△ **Quasar 1977**

Origin UK

Engine 848cc, inline four

Top speed 110 mph (177 km/h)

Created by Malcolm Newell and Ken Leaman, the feet-forward, roofed Quasar used a Reliant car engine, and had a heater and windshield wipers. Just 21 were built.

△ **Van Veen OCR 1000 1978**

Origin Netherlands

Engine 996cc, Wankel 2-rotor

Top speed 125 mph (201 km/h)

Henk van Veen designed a motorcycle around the Comotor (NSU/Citroën) engine. It was larger and more powerful than other early Wankels. Just 38 were built.

Fun on Wheels

By the 1970s, small-capacity machines needed to be more than cheap, ride-to-work hacks, since used cars were inexpensive and widely available. Manufacturers began to look around for new markets and different ways to present bikes as a must-have purchase. Off-road minibikes for children were part of the answer; here was an opportunity to get the very young addicted to two wheels.

◁ **Honda CT70 1970**

Origin Japan

Engine 72cc, single-cylinder

Top speed 29 mph (47 km/h)

With its tiny, 10-in (25-cm) wheels and folding handlebars, the CT70 was not road legal in some countries, but this minibike with a pressed-steel frame was a lot of fun.

△ **Honda CB250 K4 1972**

Origin Japan

Engine 249cc, inline twin

Top speed 92 mph (148 km/h)

A reliable, economical workhorse, Honda's 250 was restyled in 1968, and was a perfect learner bike, as well as ideal everyday transportation throughout the 1970s.

▷ **Vespa Super 150 1970**

Origin Italy

Engine 145cc, single-cylinder

Top speed 56 mph (90 km/h)

Piaggio's smaller scooters (with 8-in/20-cm wheels) were given sharper styling for the mid-1960s, which carried them through to 1976; over half a million were sold.

△ **Lambretta GP/DL 150 1970**

Origin Italy

Engine 148cc, single-cylinder

Top speed 63 mph (101 km/h)

A sporty new design by Bertone (and a disc brake on 200s) took Lambretta into the 1970s. When British Leyland closed Lambretta in 1972, production moved to India.

△ **Lambretta J50 Special 1971**

Origin Italy

Engine 49cc, single-cylinder

Top speed 25 mph (40 km/h)

Introduced in 1964, the J50 was the baby Lambretta intended for women riders. It was stylish and lightweight, but low-powered; similar models were offered with 98cc or 122cc engines.

△ **Zündapp GS 125 1972**

Origin Germany

Engine 123cc, single-cylinder

Top speed 72 mph (116 km/h)

Zündapp built motorcycles from 1922 to 1984. The two-stroke GS 125 was a successful and attractive trail/enduro bike that was also speedy on the road.

▷ **CZ Sport 175 1972**

Origin Czechoslovakia

Engine 172cc, single-cylinder

Top speed 68 mph (109 km/h)

Czech bike-maker Jawa-CZ traded on its motocross-success record with these machines. However, they tended to be rather noisy and crude compared to Japanese competitors.

▷ **Indian MT5A 1973**

Origin USA

Engine 46cc, single-cylinder

Top speed 25 mph (40 km/h)

The historic Indian name went through several lives. In the 1970s it found itself on minibikes like this 50cc Italjet-derived "Trials" machine for children, with 10-in (25-cm) wheels.

△ **MZ ETS 250 Trophy Sport 1973**

Origin East Germany

Engine 249cc, single-cylinder

Top speed 82 mph (132 km/h)

East German MZ's immensely powerful, two-stroke engines earned it many race wins. Road bikes were usually heavy and durable, but the ETS was a lively sports machine.

△ **Yamaha RD200 1972**

Origin Japan

Engine 195cc, inline twin

Top speed 85 mph (137 km/h)

A performance leader in its class, this 200cc was the same size as a 125cc, and had electric starting. Its two-stroke engine had performance equal to that of a four-stroke 250cc.

△ **Yamaha SS50 1973**

Origin Japan

Engine 49cc, single-cylinder

Top speed 45 mph (72 km/h)

Yamaha equipped the SS50 with bicycle-style pedals that could be locked into position, in order to create a model for 16-year-olds who could only ride mopeds legally on the road.

△ **Italjet M5B 1973**

Origin Italy

Engine 48cc, single-cylinder

Top speed 25 mph (40 km/h)

Italjet built a range of mostly 50cc-engined bikes from 1959, including minibikes like this child's scrambler, for a rapidly expanding leisure market in the 1970s.

Fun on Wheels (cont.)

Sharp styling, bright colors, and increasing sophistication made small-engined bikes and lightweight scooters appealing, while highly tuned, two-stroke-engined sporty machines offered exciting performance, though they also raised pollution issues. Japanese manufacturers added disc brakes and alloy wheels to pep up their cheaper models, giving them the "big bike" look for a "fun" price.

△ MV Agusta Minibike 1973

Origin Italy

Engine 48cc, single-cylinder

Top speed 30 mph (48 km/h)

When Phil Read won the 500cc world title for MV Agusta, the factory commissioned a "racing" minibike for his son, and a limited run of replicas in MV Agusta colors.

△ Puch MS50 1973

Origin Austria

Engine 49cc, single-cylinder

Top speed 28 mph (45 km/h)

Puch made dependable, well-engineered mopeds from the 1950s with little change to their basic model from 1956. It has two gears and a twistgrip change.

▷ Vespa Rally 180 US Edition 1974

Origin Italy

Engine 180cc, single-cylinder

Top speed 65 mph (105 km/h)

The US version of the Rally 180 had many small additions, from different lights to the inclusion of a battery as standard. The 180 was the first rotary-valve Vespa.

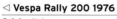

◁ Vespa Rally 200 1976

Origin Italy

Engine 198cc, single-cylinder

Top speed 70 mph (113 km/h)

With electric starting, 10 hp in a compact body with a large, comfortable dual seat, and performance to match its stripes, the Rally 200 was one of the most desirable Vespas.

▷ Vespa ET3 1977

Origin Italy

Engine 123cc, single-cylinder

Top speed 56 mph (90 km/h)

The final incarnation of Vespa's small-body Primavera model boasted an electronic ignition for improved reliability and a third transfer port, giving 7 hp instead of 5½ hp.

▷ **Harley-Davidson SS-250 1975**

Origin	US/Italy
Engine	243cc, single-cylinder
Top speed	85 mph (137 km/h)

Harley introduced a new range of lightweight two-stroke machines, built at their Italian subsidiary, in the 1970s. The bikes looked good but could not match Japanese reliability.

△ **Casal K196 Sport Moped 1977**

Origin	Portugal
Engine	49cc, single-cylinder
Top speed	38 mph (61 km/h)

Portuguese moped-maker Casal started in 1964, building Zundapps under license. This slightly sporty offering had a two-speed manual gearchange and back-pedal brake.

◁ **Yamaha XS250 1978**

Origin	Japan
Engine	248cc, inline two
Top speed	85 mph (137 km/h)

Yamaha introduced the good-looking XS range in 1977 with 250, 360, and 400cc overhead-camshaft engines and disc brakes. They were capable but not outstanding machines.

△ **Suzuki GT185 1979**

Origin	Japan
Engine	184cc, inline two
Top speed	82 mph (132 km/h)

This attractive and lively bike was aimed at young riders, though perhaps awkwardly positioned below its 200cc rivals. It featured an electric starter/generator and ram air cooling.

△ **Suzuki GT100 1975**

Origin	Japan
Engine	98cc, single-cylinder
Top speed	72 mph (115 km/h)

Introduced in the 1960s, this slim, elegant, and usually brightly colored rotary-valve, two-stroke bike weighed just 183 lb (83 kg), offering excellent performance.

△ **Cagiva SST350 1979**

Origin	Italy
Engine	342cc, single-cylinder
Top speed	90 mph (145 km/h)

With mopeds and two-stroke fun bikes like this, the Castiglioni brothers became Italy's largest bike-makers within a few years of buying the AMF-Harley factory in 1978.

Mint 400 motocross race, 1971
Also known as the Great American Desert Race, the Mint 400 is an annual endurance race through the Mojave Desert, Nevada. Motorcycles competed alongside cars until 1977, during a period of huge growth in the sport of motocross.

Chrome and Smoke

The great power-to-weight ratio of two-stroke engines was exploited to create a new generation of sports machines with sizzling performance. The Japanese factories were the leaders; they applied race technology and made their products more attractive with chrome plate and bright paintwork. No one cared too much about the exhaust smoke, but the heavy fuel consumption was a drawback.

▷ Suzuki T350 1971

Origin Japan

Engine 315cc, inline two

Top speed 91mph (146 km/h)

Suzuki's six-speed two-strokes offered great performance for price, with sales enhanced by racing. In Australia, a T350 beat much larger bikes in the 1972-73 Amaroo six-hour race.

◁ Suzuki T125 Stinger 1972

Origin Japan

Engine 124cc, inline two

Top speed 74mph (119 km/h)

Advertised as a "road racer you can ride on the street," the Stinger had a high-revving parallel-twin two-stroke, and its styling mixed race and scramble elements.

▷ Suzuki T500 1975

Origin Japan

Engine 492cc, inline two

Top speed 106mph (171km/h)

The 1968 T500, called both "Cobra" and "Titan," was Suzuki's first large-capacity model. Making rival 500s obsolete, from 1976 it evolved into the GT500 tourer.

◁ Suzuki GT380 1976

Origin Japan

Engine 371cc, inline three

Top speed 105mph (169 km/h)

Featuring Ram Air cooling, Suzuki's 380cc and 550cc triples were torquey and smooth. This GT380 is modified with aftermarket wheels, seat, and exhaust system.

◁ Suzuki GT250 1979

Origin Japan

Engine 247cc, inline two

Top speed 100mph (160 km/h)

Descended from the earlier 1960s X6 and later GT250, the 100 mph (161 km/h) X7 was an agile sport bike, ideal for the Café Racer customizing seen on this example.

△ Yamaha CS5 1972

Origin Japan

Engine 195cc, inline two

Top speed 84mph (135 km/h)

Offering terrific performance and good handling for their small dimensions, the little 200cc two-stroke Yamahas made many friends in the late 1960s and early 1970s.

◁ **Kawasaki H1 1973**

Origin Japan

Engine 499cc, inline three

Top speed 115 mph (185 km/h)

This two-stroke road stormer produced a formidable 60 hp and covered $^1/_4$ mile (400 m) in 12.4 sec. It was a hit in the US, but dangerous for inexperienced riders.

◁ **Yamaha RD400 1978**

Origin Japan

Engine 399cc, inline two

Top speed 109 mph (175 km/h)

The RD400 evolved from the racerlike RD350, offering more refinement and cleaner running without losing any of its tremendous performance; it was listed until 1981.

△ **Kawasaki G3SSD 90 1974**

Origin Japan

Engine 89cc, single-cylinder

Top speed 65 mph (105 km/h)

Well equipped and beautifully built, the 90cc SS Series ran from 1969 to 1974, with a rotary-valve, two-stroke engine featuring oil injection, and a five-speed gearbox.

△ **Kawasaki KH400 1978**

Origin Japan

Engine 400cc, inline three

Top speed 103 mph (166 km/h)

Kawasaki's air-cooled two-stroke triples were a great success due to their performance and competitive pricing. The civilized 400 stayed in production up to 1980.

▽ **Bultaco Metralla GT 1975**

Origin Spain

Engine 244cc, single-cylinder

Top speed 90 mph (145 km/h)

Light and lively with 24 hp from its two-stroke engine, the Metralla was a road bike from a factory that had a strong racing, trials, and motocross pedigree.

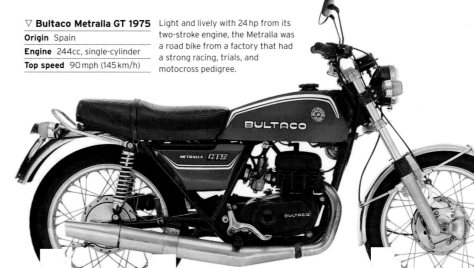

△ **Yamaha RD350 1975**

Origin Japan

Engine 347cc, inline two

Top speed 106 mph (170 km/h)

Yamaha's rapid 350cc two-stroke was upgraded for 1973 with reed valves, a six-speed gearbox, and a front disc brake, resulting in rave reviews for its race-bred feel.

Off the Highway

Trail riding was the boom leisure occupation in the US and elsewhere in the 1970s, and manufacturers catered to the massive new market by selling trail bikes: street-legal machines with genuine off-road capability. Some riders wanted to take rough-riding skills to a new level in competitive events, so the choice of machinery for motocross, enduros, and observed trials also grew.

◁ **Kawasaki Trail Boss 1970**

Origin Japan

Engine 99cc, single-cylinder

Top speed 67 mph (108 km/h)

Switchable high/low ratios giving a 10-speed gearbox, and an aluminum cylinder like its bigger sisters, made this a very desirable little trail bike in the 1970s.

◁ **Honda CT50 Trail Cub 1970**

Origin Japan

Engine 49cc, single-cylinder

Top speed 27 mph (43 km/h)

From 1964 Honda built a series of four-stroke bikes with high/low ratio gearing for casual off-road use. It was sold as "Trail Cub" in North America and "Hunter Cub" elsewhere.

△ **Honda XR75 1971**

Origin Japan

Engine 72cc, single-cylinder

Top speed 45 mph (72 km/h)

Primarily for children or used as a pit bike, the four-stroke XR75 minibike was not usually road-legal but was an effective race winner in children's motocross series.

▷ **Hodaka Super Rat 1971**

Origin Japan

Engine 98cc, single-cylinder

Top speed 54 mph (87 km/h)

Joint US-Japanese company Pabatco, owned by Shell Oil, built trail bikes for the US market. The Super Rat was its first competition bike and was very successful.

△ **Suzuki TS125 1971**

Origin Japan

Engine 123cc, single-cylinder

Top speed 68 mph (109 km/h)

With a small two-stroke engine but plenty of punch, the TS125 was also sold in a more serious off-roading guise as the TS 125R Duster.

◁ **Hodaka SS 1973**

Origin Japan/USA

Engine 98cc, single-cylinder

Top speed 55 mph (89 km/h)

Synthetic oil and minibike guru John Steen took Ace 100 Hodakas, stripped them, and turned them into race winners, with Ceriani forks, Rickman bars, and more.

▽ **Husqvarna Enduro 504 WR 1973**

Origin Sweden

Engine 504cc, inline two

Top speed 100 mph (161 km/h)

The 500cc twin-engine was made by grafting two 250s together. Gunnar Nilsson won the European FIM Cup with one enlarged to 504cc to qualify for the 500-750 class.

▷ **Husqvarna 390 WR 1979**

Origin Sweden

Engine 384cc, single-cylinder

Top speed 85 mph (137 km/h)

This fast and rugged two-stroke machine was designed for enduro riding with tremendous torque, six speeds, long-travel suspension, and equipped with lights.

▷ **CZ 175 Enduro DT 1974**

Origin Czech Republic

Engine 172cc, single-cylinder

Top speed 62 mph (100 km/h)

In standard form the Enduro was a crude, heavy, old-fashioned machine that was widely criticized. However, in lightened DT form it was very effective off-road.

◁ **CZ 250 Motocross 1974**

Origin Czech Republic

Engine 246cc, single-cylinder

Top speed 65 mph (105 km/h)

CZs were at the forefront of motocross from the late 1960s and, despite strong opposition from the Japanese, Jaroslav Falta dominated the 250cc World Championship.

△ **Yamaha YZ250 1974**

Origin Japan

Engine 249cc, single-cylinder

Top speed 80 mph (129 km/h)

This hugely successful motocross racer pioneered monoshock suspension. The two-stroke engine gave the boldest riders very strong midrange and top-end power.

△ **Yamaha XT500 1975**

Origin Japan

Engine 499cc, single-cylinder

Top speed 82 mph (132 km/h)

Yamaha's first big, four-stroke single "Thumper" was very well received. It won the grueling Paris-Dakar Rally in 1979 and 1980.

▷ **Montesa Cota 172 1977**

Origin Spain

Engine 158cc, single-cylinder

Top speed 65 mph (105 km/h)

The Cota was a top trials contender in 250 form, while this smaller-engined but similarly agile 158cc version was more suited to extreme trail riding.

△ **Bultaco Alpina 1975**

Origin Spain

Engine 244cc, single-cylinder

Top speed 65 mph (105 km/h)

Bultaco won the World Trials Championship for its first five years from 1975, and adapted its winning model into the Alpina to make it suitable for trail riding or enduros.

Jack Marshall on his 1908 TT-winning Triumph

DU·1299

The Triumph Story

The celebrated Triumph marque has come to represent classic motorcycle engineering, boasting a raft of stylish models like Speed Twin, Bonneville, and Thunderbird—names that evoke an era when British bikes reigned supreme. After a brief pause in the 1980s, the rejuvenated company resumed production of distinctive motorcycles that continue to stand out for their looks and powerful engines.

THE QUINTESSENTIALLY BRITISH company Triumph Motorcycles actually owes its existence to the entrepreneurial spirit of two Germans who arrived in England in the late 19th century. In 1895 Siegfried Bettmann began selling bicycles under the Triumph name. He was soon joined in business by an engineer named Mauritz Schulte, and, like other entrepreneurs of the era, they quickly saw the potential of adding engines to bicycle frames. After finding suitable premises in Coventry, in 1902 Bettmann and Schulte presented their first powered Triumph bike, which was driven by a 2¼-hp Minerva engine.

Triumph soon developed its own powerplant. In 1905 the 3-hp model quickly earned a reputation as a reliable single-cylinder machine, and over the next decade was developed into more powerful versions. Some

"Swooping R" logo (introduced mid-30s)

of these would be modified into competition bikes, and Triumph made its mark early in the racing arena. In 1908 Jack Marshall took first place in the single-cylinder class of the Isle of Man TT races. The win provided the impetus for domestic growth, with around 3,000 motorcycles produced in 1909. By the onset of World War I in 1914, Triumph was sufficiently well regarded to be called on to supply military-use motorcycles to the British government. The principal machine on order was the Type H, with around 30,000 examples of this sturdy 499cc single produced for the war effort.

Early in the 1920s, Triumph commissioned engine maestro Harry Ricardo to develop a new powerplant. The result was the 499cc unit that featured four valves in the cylinder head. Installed on the Model R, it increased the bike's performance to such a level that it set several speed records. Later in the decade, the company branched out into car production, but new motorcycles like Triumph's first twin-cylinder model in 1933 showed that two-wheeled transportation was still very much the core of the business.

Nevertheless, the general economic downturn hit the company hard, and in 1936 Triumph's motorcycle division was taken over by Jack Sangster, who had previously turned around the Ariel motorcycle company.

The new owner installed ex-Ariel employee Edward Turner as design chief. This would prove a pivotal move, as the engineering genius immediately revamped the range, introducing the Tiger models with their attractive designs, good performance, and competitive price.

Turner's greatest contribution came in 1937 with the landmark Triumph T100 Speed Twin, arguably the most

1934 Triumph TT race team
Triumph's riders line up for the 1934 Isle of Man TT. From left to right: Tommy Spann, Jock West, and Ernie Thomas.

> **"**Ain't **no finer thrill**/You **ain't lived** until/You climb aboard a **Triumph Bonneville."**
>
> STEVE GIBBONS BAND, "TRIUMPH BONNEVILLE," 2007

influential British motorcycle of the 20th century. The engineer's ability to fit two cylinders into the space usually occupied by one proved to be so revolutionary that it shaped twin-cylinder motorcycle design for the next few decades. Here was a 500cc parallel twin that was lighter, faster, and better-looking than any previous machine of this capacity and configuration.

Having developed this seminal twin-cylinder engine, Triumph briefly turned its attentions to making side-valve models for the military in World War II. Early in the war, in 1940, German bombs destroyed the

Triumph factory in Coventry. But two years later a new plant had been built in nearby Meriden.

Postwar production concentrated on twin-cylinder machines, beginning a prosperous era when Triumph made the most sought-after bikes in the world. Turner enlarged his 500cc engine to 650cc, creating the 1950 Thunderbird and a line of derivatives expressly aimed at American riders who found the 500cc engine too small. The new model's image gained added prestige when Marlon Brando rode a Thunderbird in the cult 1953 biker movie *The Wild One*. Though Triumph had been sold to BSA in

Perfect tourer
Triumph was eager to promote its models as being the best of British, and a perfect way of exploring the countryside.

Type R Fast Roadster

Speed Twin

T120 Bonneville

Daytona 955i

1902 Triumph releases its first motorized model, a 2¼-hp bicycle utilizing a Belgian-made Minerva engine.
1908 Jack Marshall wins the Isle of Man Tourist Trophy single-cylinder race on a Triumph.
1921 The Model R with a Harry Ricardo-designed engine hits 75 mph (120 km/h).
1924 The 494cc Model P is the first of Triumph's mass-produced models.
1936 Jack Sangster buys Triumph. The Tiger 70, 80, and 90 singles are introduced.

1937 The Speed Twin model with radical twin-cylinder design is superior to all rival 500ccs, providing a blueprint for postwar British motorcycle makers.
1942 After the Coventry plant is bombed, Triumph is able to move to a new factory in Meriden.
1951 BSA buys Triumph, although the marque is run independently.
1953 The T110 Tiger model is released.
1954 The 650cc Tiger 110 joins the range.
1956 A Triumph-engined vehicle sets a new

land-speed record at the Bonneville Salt Flats in Utah.
1958 Twin-carburetor T120 Bonneville is unveiled, to become Britain's best-known motorcycle.
1963 *The Great Escape* features Steve McQueen on a Triumph twin.
1969 Launch of the 750cc Trident, with a three-cylinder engine.
1973 Norton-Villiers-Triumph is formed.
1979 The T140 Bonneville is unveiled, the last Triumph exported to the US in quantity.

1983 Triumph closes its Meriden plant.
1990 The reborn Triumph Motorcycle Company unveils six new models with capacities of 750cc to 1,200cc.
1994 The Speed Triple is unveiled.
1995 T595 Daytona is released with three cylinders and fuel injection.
2002 The Hinckley plant is devastated by fire but rebuilt six months later.
2004 The Rocket III model features a 2,293cc powerplant, the largest production motorcycle engine to date.

1951 it remained an independently run marque, and as well as large machines the company rolled out smaller models like the 149cc Terrier and 199cc Tiger Cub. In 1956 the marque received worldwide publicity when it was involved in setting a new land-speed record. On the Bonneville Salt Flats in Utah, Johnny Allen reached more than 214 mph (345 km/h) in a streamlined vehicle powered by a 649cc Triumph engine. This led to the release of

Screen idols
Steve McQueen made his iconic attempt to leap to freedom over the barbed wire border fence on a Triumph TR6 in the 1963 movie *The Great Escape.*

the T120 Bonneville in 1958. This speedy 650cc twin became Britain's most famous motorcycle. During the 1960s, output rose to 50,000 bikes a year, most for export.

The decade also saw ever-larger Japanese machines entering the market, a threat that was partly countered by

Triumph's 125 three-cylinder Trident in 1969. Nevertheless, Triumph's BSA owners were in financial difficulty. After they incurred substantial losses, a new company was formed in 1973 featuring three British manufacturers: Norton-Villiers-Triumph (NVT). A 750cc Bonneville had been launched, but when NVT attempted to close down Meriden, a large proportion of the workforce occupied and blockaded the factory. Production stopped until a government-backed workers' cooperative resumed manufacture of the 750cc twins in 1975.

When the cash-strapped co-op folded in 1983, home builder John Bloor bought the Triumph name and set up an entirely new operation. Triumph Motorcycles Ltd.

True Brit
A world-class British company, Triumph has five manufacturing plants: two in Leicestershire, UK, and three in Thailand.

unveiled its first new offerings in 1990, impressing fans with models featuring evocative names such as Trident, Daytona, and Trophy. In the following years a series of new models confirmed that Triumph was back as a world-class manufacturer. In the 2000s a long-awaited modern version of the Bonneville arrived. It was no longer the ultimate speedster, but a versatile rider-friendly machine. The modern twin and its variants have been a huge sales success.

More than half a century ago motorcyclists were drawn to Triumph machines' clean lines, superb handling, and impressive speeds. Now a younger generation appreciates these qualities in the Triumph motorbikes of today.

Racers

On the racetracks, the 1970s saw technology leap to the fore. Manufacturers employed exotic alloys and experimented with monocoque construction in stainless steel, while seeking more power from ever-higher-revving engines using multiple valves and camshafts, fuel injection, and forced induction. The Japanese dominated grand prix, but European and US marques battled on and still cleaned up in more obscure competitions.

◁ **Triumph F750 1971**

Origin UK

Engine 741cc, inline twin

Top speed 140 mph (225 km/h)

A combined Triumph/BSA factory team dominated US and European 750cc racing with three-cylinder machines in 1971. This Triumph was raced by 1970 US champion Gene Romero.

△ **Norton F750 1973**

Origin UK

Engine 746cc, inline two

Top speed 155 mph (259 km/h)

With a stainless steel monocoque chassis, the aerodynamic Norton handled superbly, compensating for a lack of power. Peter Williams rode it to a 1973 Formula 750 TT victory.

△ **Ducati 750SS 1972**

Origin Italy

Engine 748cc, V-twin

Top speed 140 mph (225 km/h)

Finishing both first and second in Italy's Imola 200 international race in 1972 was a breakthrough for Ducati's early, high-revving V-twin with desmodromic-valve gear.

△ **Harley-Davidson XRTT 1972**

Origin USA

Engine 750cc, V-twin

Top speed 145 mph (233 km/h)

The faired road-racing version of the factory XR750 was also used in flat-track trim. This machine, with a Fontana front brake, was ridden by legendary US racer Carl Rayborn.

◁ **Harley-Davidson RR250 1976**

Origin USA

Engine 250cc, inline twin

Top speed 110 mph (177 km/h)

Developed and built at the Aermacchi factory, water-cooled twins defeated Yamaha in 250cc and 350cc races, taking the Italian Walter Villa to four world titles.

Drag Racers

Born in the US, motorcycle drag racing spread to Europe in the 1960s. During the 1970s, top contenders used doubled-up engines to get maximum power for ¼-mile (400-m) sprints from a standing start. Nithromethane fuel, massive rear tires, quick-shift transmissions, and superchargers were added to elongated frames. Maintaining control on the drag strip took consummate skill and incredible bravery.

▽ **Norton Hogslayer Dragster 1975**

Origin UK/USA

Engine 2 x 880cc, inline two

Top speed 180 mph (290 km/h)

Tom Christenson dominated American dragstrips in the 1970s on this twin-engined machine, christened "Hogslayer" for its ability to beat Harley-Davidsons.

▷ Jawa Briggo Speedway 1975

Origin Czech Republic

Engine 599cc, single-cylinder

Top speed 110 mph (177 km/h)

Top riders Neil Street and Barry Briggs revolutionized speedway in the 1970s with four-valve conversions for Jawa engines. The Briggo was sold by New Zealander Briggs.

△ Honda RCB1000 1976

Origin Japan

Engine 941cc, inline four

Top speed 175 mph (282 km/h)

In 1976 Honda dominated European and World Endurance racing with this bike derived from the CB750 but with double overhead camshafts and many innovations.

△ Suzuki RG500 1978

Origin Japan

Engine 498cc, square-four

Top speed 175 mph (282 km/h)

Suzuki adopted the unusual square-four layout with a separate crankshaft for each cylinder. Barry Sheene won world championships on factory versions of the RG500 in 1976 and 1977.

◁ Yamaha YZR 500 OW48 1979

Origin Japan

Engine 500cc, inline four

Top speed 175 mph (282 km/h)

Yamaha developed the YZR 500, which went on to win many Grands Prix from 1973 onward. By 1980 the OW48 had an all-new aluminum frame, helping Kenny Roberts win his third World title.

◁ Yamaha TZ250 1977

Origin Japan

Engine 247cc, inline two

Top speed 130 mph (209 km/h)

Yamaha experimented with water-cooled heads for the 250cc and 350cc Grand Prix in 1972 and installed them in the TZ in 1973. The TZ was updated annually until 1986.

▷ Kawasaki KR250 1979

Origin Japan

Engine 250cc, inline two

Top speed 150 mph (241 km/h)

This two-stroke tandem-twin Grand Prix racer was very successful, winning World Championships for Kork Ballington in 1978 and 1979, and for Anton Mang in 1981.

◁ Kawasaki 2400cc Dragster 1977

Origin UK/Japan

Engine 2 x 850cc, inline two

Top Speed 220 mph (354 km/h)

Bob Webster bolted two Kawasaki 850cc engines together and added a supercharger, hitting 150 mph (241 km/h) at the climax of a 7.75 sec 1/4 mile (400 m) sprint at Santa Pod in Northampton.

△ Weslake Hobbit Dragster 1978

Origin UK

Engine 2 x 850cc, inline two

Top speed 210 mph (338 km/h)

John Hobbs built the fearsome Hobbit with two Weslake engines and two Shorrocks superchargers. Steadily improved from 1975 to 1979, it could run an 8.2 sec 1/4 mile (400 m).

Classic Style

In the early 1970s the contrast between Japanese and British motorcycle manufacturers became abundantly clear. While their machines looked superficially similar and were built along well-established lines, a closer look revealed superior levels of sophistication in Japanese engines, mechanical components, and the equipment supplied: the fate of the British industry was clear.

▽ **Harley-Davidson FX Super Glide 1971**

Origin USA

Engine 1,213cc, V-twin

Top speed 108 mph (174 km/h)

By combining the FL frame with the XL Sportster front forks, Harley created the Super Glide as a "production custom"; it sold better later, with less radical rear-end styling.

△ **BSA A65 Thunderbolt 1971**

Origin UK

Engine 654cc, inline twin

Top speed 104 mph (167 km/h)

The single-carburetor Thunderbolt was not a bad bike, despite a tall seat height due to its frame design, which incorporated the oil tank in the top tube.

▽ **Honda CB350 K4 1973**

Origin Japan

Engine 326cc, inline twin

Top speed 110 mph (177 km/h)

The overhead cam, parallel-twin CB350 became the best-selling motorcycle in American history with over 300,000 sold between 1968 and 1973. Six gears featured on the K4 Super Sport.

◁ **BSA B25SS Gold Star 1975**

Origin UK

Engine 247cc, single-cylinder

Top speed 80 mph (129 km/h)

BSA was struggling against Japanese rivals when it built this model. It was let down by the antiquated engine—BSA motorcycles were soon to become history.

▷ **Jawa 350 Type 634 1974**

Origin Czech Republic

Engine 343cc, inline twin

Top speed 80 mph (129 km/h)

Built from the late 1940s right into the 21st century, the parallel-twin, two-stroke-engined Jawa was sold in huge numbers throughout the world.

▷ Norton Commando Interstate MkIII 850 ES 1975

Origin UK

Engine 829cc, inline twin

Top speed 120 mph (193 km/h)

Battling with Japanese entries in the superbike market, Norton enlarged the Commando's parallel-twin, strengthened the running gear, and added electric starting.

△ Benelli Tornado S 1975

Origin Italy

Engine 643cc, inline twin

Top speed 105 mph (169 km/h)

A family business making motorcycles since 1911, Benelli targeted the US and UK markets with this traditional but fast parallel-twin. De Tomaso bought Benelli in 1973.

◁ Triumph Trident T160V 1975

Origin UK

Engine 750cc, inline three

Top speed 115 mph (185 km/h)

Sloping the engine forward to fit in a larger airbox and adding a rear disc brake and electric starting kept the aging BSA/Trident on the market for its final year or two.

▽ BMW R60/6 1976

Origin Germany

Engine 599cc, flat-twin

Top speed 99 mph (159 km/h)

The /6 Series BMW twins, launched in 1973, added front disc brakes and a five-speed gearbox to the R60/5's virtues of shaft drive and great balance.

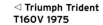

△ Triumph Bonneville T140J Jubilee 1977

Origin UK

Engine 744cc, inline twin

Top speed 111 mph (179 km/h)

To mark the Queen's Silver Jubilee in 1977, Triumph made 1,000 each of both US and UK spec bikes and 400 Commonwealth special editions, with fancy paint, decals, and extra chrome.

◁ Yamaha XS650B 1976

Origin Japan

Engine 653cc, inline twin

Top speed 113 mph (182 km/h)

Modeled on the BSA 650 and launched in 1969, Yamaha's big parallel-twin outlasted the BSA thanks to its leak-free build, electric starting, and twin disc brakes.

△ Triumph Bonneville T140E 1979

Origin UK

Engine 744cc, inline twin

Top speed 118 mph (190 km/h)

Triumph enlarged the 650 Bonneville in 1973, and added front, and later rear, disc brakes. The T140E had electronic ignition and modifications to pass emissions laws.

▷ Yamaha SR500 1979

Origin Japan

Engine 499cc, single-cylinder

Top speed 93 mph (150 km/h)

Well engineered with a leak-free, overhead-camshaft engine, the simple, agile, and relatively light SR500 retained kick-starting and a drum rear brake.

The
1980s

Technology marched on, spurred by intense competition between the Big Four: Honda, Kawasaki, Suzuki, and Yamaha. Sometimes it reached overkill, exemplified by a brief infatuation with turbocharging, but it also produced sound, new machines, from tiny commuters to big and fast superbikes. Harley-Davidson, America's only maker of any size, emerged from lean years with new vigor, and Europeans like Aprilia, BMW, and Ducati were also moving forward. At the same time, a growing interest in classic machinery of the past was beginning to influence design.

Road Sport

During the 1980s, manufacturers' ranges became more diverse, with sports bikes taking their inspiration from racing machines. Higher power outputs and the need for more compact engines meant that water-cooling of sports engines became almost universal, and chassis design evolved too. Rear suspension using a single shock absorber, mounted ahead of the rear wheel, became standard.

▷ **Kawasaki GPZ 550 1981**

Origin Japan

Engine 553cc, inline four

Top speed 119 mph (192 km/h)

Five-spoke alloys and a black engine and exhaust marked out the 61 hp GPZ. It was Kawasaki's leading midrange bike with a Uni-Trak air-assisted rear suspension.

◁ **Yamaha RD250LC 1981**

Origin Japan

Engine 247cc, inline twin

Top speed 98 mph (158 km/h)

A racer for learner riders, the LC's 100 mph (160 km/h) capability stemmed from the power of its reed-valve, water-cooled, two-stroke twin, equivalent to over 140 hp per liter.

▷ **Yamaha RD350LC YPVS 1983**

Origin Japan

Engine 347cc, inline twin

Top speed 117 mph (188 km/h)

Launched in 1981, the liquid-cooled, two-stroke RD350 is legendary for its unique blend of fast and furious fun at an affordable price. The YPVS system introduced in 1983 further improved performance.

△ **Kawasaki Z1100 1984**

Origin Japan

Engine 1,089cc, inline four

Top speed 137 mph (220 km/h)

Kawasaki needed only two valves per cylinder to extract 108 bhp— the highest four-cylinder output of the time—from its 1100, giving it tremendous acceleration.

▽ **Yamaha RZ500 1984**

Origin Japan

Engine 499cc, V-four

Top speed 148 mph (238 km/h)

With a water-cooled, reed-valve, two-stroke engine the Grand Prix-inspired 500 was sold with either a steel or alloy chassis, depending on the market. Either way, it was light, powerful, and stunning.

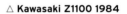

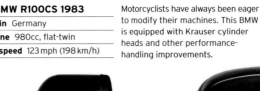

▷ BMW R100CS 1983

Origin Germany

Engine 980cc, flat-twin

Top speed 123 mph (198 km/h)

Motorcyclists have always been eager to modify their machines. This BMW is equipped with Krauser cylinder heads and other performance-handling improvements.

△ Kawasaki Ninja GPZ900 1984

Origin Japan

Engine 908cc, inline four

Top speed 154 mph (248 km/h)

Kawasaki was late in developing water cooling and four valves per cylinder for its sports machines. Their new 900 was compact, sophisticated, powerful, and well-balanced.

▽ Honda VF400F 1983

Origin Japan

Engine 399cc, V-four

Top speed 112 mph (180 km/h)

An innovative machine with a 16-valve, V-four engine in a naked-bike style with bikini-type fairing, this bike featured inboard disc brakes and an anti-dive, air-assisted suspension.

◁ Moto Guzzi Le Mans 1000 1983

Origin Italy

Engine 949cc, V-twin

Top speed 137 mph (220 km/h)

Moto Guzzi's top sports bike started as an 850 in 1977. One of the original café racers, it had low seating, linked brakes, high gearing, and a lovely, balanced feel.

△ Honda MBX50 1984

Origin Japan

Engine 59cc, single-cylinder

Top speed 42 mph (68 km/h)

Honda targeted the European youth market with the stylish, six-speed, disc-braked MBX50, its water-cooled two-stroke surprisingly nippy when unrestricted.

△ Honda VF500F2 1984

Origin Japan

Engine 498cc, V-four

Top speed 132 mph (212 km/h)

Small, beautifully built, and with performance that put most other 500s to shame, the water-cooled twin-cam, 16-valve VF500 had much to justify its high price tag.

▷ Ducati 1000 MHR 1985

Origin Italy

Engine 973cc, V-twin

Top speed 127 mph (204 km/h)

The MHR (Mike Hailwood Replica) had a 90 hp enlargement of the 900SS V-twin and commemorated Hailwood's 1978 comeback victory at the Isle of Man TT.

Honda RC30

One of the all-time great Japanese sports models, the Honda RC30 was a race replica with a difference: on this bike, private, unsponsored riders could take part in competition—and win. Created for the Superbike World Championship, it helped Honda win the Constructor's Title for three years running from 1988 to 1990. The RC30's record-breaking feats at the Isle of Man TT races earned the bike a cult status that was further heightened by limited production.

RELEASED IN JAPAN in 1987, Honda's RC30 was bred for the racetrack. The new model—also known as the VFR750R—had an excellent pedigree, based as it was on the RVF750, which had dominated prestigious endurance events such as the Le Mans 24 Hours and the Bol d'Or since 1985. Featuring a 748cc water-cooled V-four engine, the RC30 may not have been exceptionally powerful for a bike of its size, but its race components were used so effectively that the machine outstripped its rivals. Honda's competition expertise

was unparalleled and the success of their strategy became apparent when rider Fred Merkel took the Superbike World Champion title in 1988 and 1989 on the RC30, plus four Isle of Man TT race wins in the same years. In the first few years of production, the bike spread into other markets, to be warmly received by race teams, privateer riders, and sports bike fans. The bike's last year of production was 1990, by which time Honda had assembled fewer than 5,000 examples of this very special piece of machinery.

FRONT VIEW

REAR VIEW

Winning start
The Honda badge was first seen on racing circuits in 1953, when the marque entered a number of bikes in the Nagoya Grand Prix in Japan, taking the Manufacturer's Team Prize.

Single seat for racing

Windshield made from sheer plastic for low distortion

Front fork is multi-adjustable

Front brake discs are 310mm in diameter and 6mm thick

One-sided swingarm for rapid wheel changes

Low center of gravity aids handling

Racing chassis
Light, rigid, and strong, the RC30's frame was cleverly tailored to reinforce stress points, while weight was removed from areas on the structure that took less strain. The bike was clothed in a lightweight full fairing, constructed from ultra-thin, fiberglass-reinforced plastic.

SPECIFICATIONS	
Model	Honda VFR750R RC30 (1988)
Assembly	Hamamatsu, Japan
Production	4,780
Construction	Triple-box, tubular-steel frame
Engine	748cc, V-four
Power output	122 hp
Transmission	Six-speed
Suspension	Telescopic forks front, monoshock rear
Brakes	Dual-discs front, single-disc rear
Maximum speed	152 mph (245 km/h)

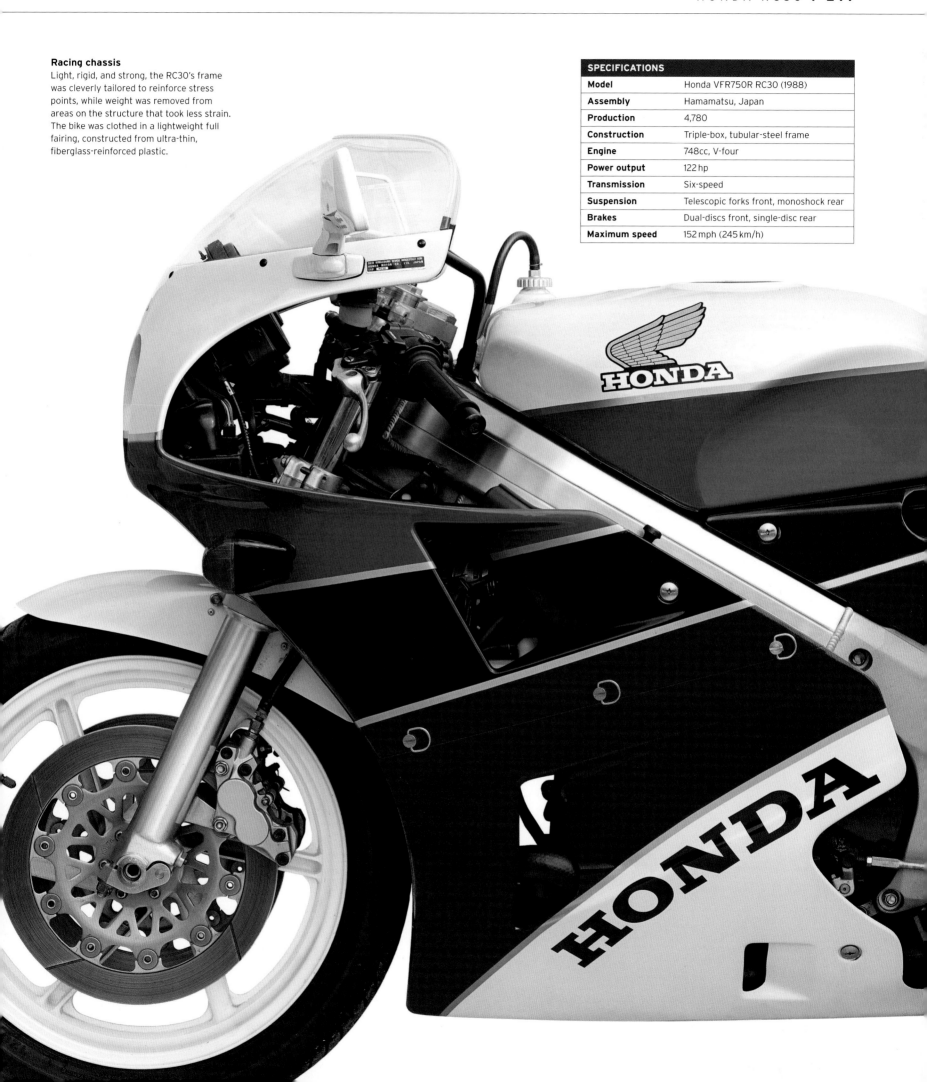

THE BIKE

The RC30 was designed to be ridden hard. Its single-sided PRO-arm swingarm worked alongside the resilient chassis to give the bike a tautness that inspired confidence when cornering at high speed, while the close-ratio, six-speed gearbox offered precision shifting. Fully adjustable suspension and four-piston front brake calipers were further evidence of the model's racing character. By simultaneously designing a stable bike and one with supreme ride quality, Honda had united track and road in a single sensational package.

1. Maker's badge on fairing **2.** Model code on panel behind seat **3.** Twin headlights **4.** Light switch on handlebar **5.** Cockpit **6.** Fuel quick-filler **7.** Fuel tank breather **8.** Choke control **9.** Right footrest **10.** Radiator fan **11.** Front wheel, designed for rapid wheel change **12.** Quick-change sprocket **13.** Muffler **14.** Rear light

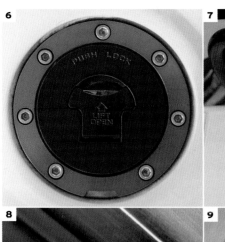

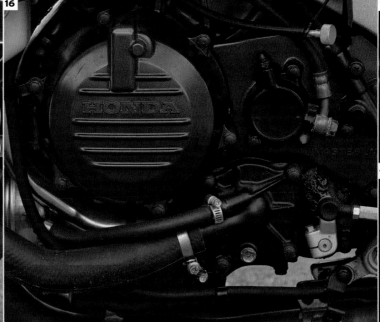

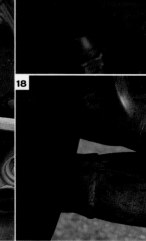

ENGINE

High-tech components featured prominently in the RC30's 16-valve, 90 degree, V-four engine. The unit's two-ring pistons were connected to the crankshaft by ultra-light, super-strong titanium connecting rods, contributing to the model's impressively low weight of 408 lb (185 kg). Four 38 mm carburetors supplied mixture to the power plant, while the engine was cooled by fan-assisted, lightweight aluminum radiators. Its reliable engine full of torque made the RC30 a favored mount for endurance racing. At the Isle of Man TT races, Steve Hislop was the first rider to lap the fearsome Mountain Course at more than 120 mph (193 km/h) on an RC30 in 1989.

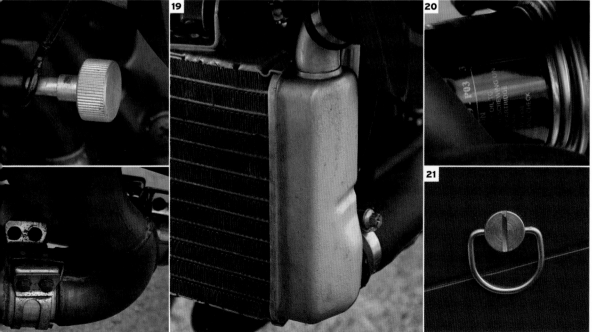

15. Right side of crankcase **16.** Alternator and water pump housings **17.** Idle setting knob **18.** Four-into-one exhaust **19.** Lower radiator **20.** Oil filter **21.** Fairing fastener

Road Sport (cont.)

While ultimate speed freaks still opted for big engines, manufacturers showed that they could offer just as much usable performance from a 750 or a smaller engine, provided the aerodynamics and engine were optimized. Midrange engines were lighter too, making the bikes easier to handle at low speeds and, more importantly, nimbler and much more manageable on twisty, bumpy roads.

▷ Suzuki GSX-750 ES 1986

Origin Japan

Engine 747cc, inline four

Top speed 135 mph (217 km/h)

Suzuki rejuvenated its 750 with a box-section frame, full-floating rear suspension, anti-dive, and street-racer styling. Though not the fastest in its class, it was great to ride.

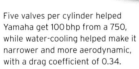

▽ Honda VFR 700F Interceptor 1987

Origin Japan

Engine 699cc, V-four

Top speed 130 mph (209 km/h)

Devised to beat US import tariffs, this was a short-stroke derivation of the 1983 VF750, the sports bike with racing DNA, from its triple-disc brakes to its water-cooled V-four.

△ Yamaha FZ750 1985

Origin Japan

Engine 749cc, inline four

Top speed 145 mph (233 km/h)

Five valves per cylinder helped Yamaha get 100 bhp from a 750, while water-cooling helped make it narrower and more aerodynamic, with a drag coefficient of 0.34.

◁ Buell RR1000 1986

Origin USA

Engine 998cc, V-twin

Top speed 140 mph (225 km/h)

The first new US motorcycle-maker for 60+ years, Erik Buell set out to beat Japanese superbikes with a tuned Harley engine in a light frame with an aerodynamic body.

▽ Harley-Davidson XLH883 Sportster 1987

Origin USA

Engine 883cc, V-twin

Top speed 100 mph (160 km/h)

Harley's entry-level four-speed cruiser of the mid-1980s was slow, loud, vibrated heavily, and had a tiny tank with a 100-mile (160-km) range; but buyers lined up for it.

△ Ducati 851 1989

Origin Italy

Engine 851cc, V-twin

Top speed 150 mph (241 km/h)

The new-generation Ducati had a 90-degree V-twin engine, but with water cooling, fuel injection, and four valves per cylinder. It was a brutally fast road bike and successful racer.

△ **Suzuki GSX-R400 1989**

Origin Japan

Engine 398cc, inline four

Top speed 115 mph (185 km/h)

The first lightweight race replica with an aluminum cradle frame and twin-cam, 16-valve, water-cooled, inline four, the GSX-R400 was restyled in 1988.

▷ **Gilera Saturno Bialbero 500 1989**

Origin Italy

Engine 492cc, single-cylinder

Top speed 110 mph (177 km/h)

This compact Café Racer, using the highest-quality components to recreate the 1939 Saturno in a modern context, was a light, lively, and stunning-looking bike.

△ **Honda CBR1000F 1988**

Origin Japan

Engine 998cc, inline four

Top speed 155 mph (249 km/h)

Good build quality and a comfortable riding position were not enough to endear this bike to road testers, who found it deceptively fast but bland—yet it sold for 10 years.

△ **Honda VFR750R RC30 1988**

Origin Japan

Engine 748cc, V-four

Top speed 152 mph (245 km/h)

This top-quality machine blends the lightweight, quick steering and fantastic handling of a race bike with excellent ride quality, reliability, and stability.

△ **Honda CBR600F 1989**

Origin Japan

Engine 598cc, inline four

Top speed 145 mph (233 km/h)

Introduced in 1987, the CBR's stunning performance made it a class leader. A redesign in 1989 gave it 10 percent more power and upgrades kept it competitive.

Power Play

As the world became more prosperous in the 1980s, manufacturers played with new technology on their ultimate road bikes, since buyers would now pay extra for something really special. Turbocharging was tried (see below); Kawasaki offered a transverse straight-six engine and also introduced digital fuel injection; while Suzuki had a roadgoing two-stroke GP racer. Alternatively, specialists offered frame kits so people could build their own bikes.

◁ **Yamaha XS1100 LG Midnight Special 1980**

Origin Japan

Engine 1,101cc, inline four

Top speed 126 mph (203 km/h)

Yamaha went to extreme lengths with the black and gold finish, even down to black chrome exhausts with unified braking, to prove this bike was not just about looks.

▽ **Honda CB1100R 1983**

Origin Japan

Engine 1,062cc, inline four

Top speed 142 mph (229 km/h)

This was a high-quality sporting machine that was competitive in production racing, but it also made an excellent sports tourer. It was comfortable, fast, and handled well.

▷ **Kawasaki GPZ 1100 1983**

Origin Japan

Engine 1,089cc, inline four

Top speed 137 mph (220 km/h)

The GPZ 1100 was upgraded in 1982 with a digital fuel injection and bikini fairing. Kawasaki's fastest bike of the day could be a handful but rewarded the experienced rider.

▷ **Kawasaki Z1300 1984**

Origin Japan

Engine 1,286cc, inline six

Top speed 139 mph (224 km/h)

This huge machine was launched as a flagship model but missed the mark. Performance was no better than Kawasaki's 1,000cc fours, but excess weight meant that it did not handle as well.

▽ **Moto Martin CBX 1260 Special 1985**

Origin France

Engine 1,260cc, inline six

Top speed 150 mph (241 km/h)

Built in France, the Moto Martin café racer frame could house the customer's choice of engine and components; this is a Honda CBX, which has been modified for extra power.

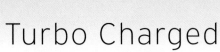

△ **Harley-Davidson XR1000 1984**

Origin USA

Engine 998cc, V-twin

Top speed 115 mph (185 km/h)

Harley's racing boss Dick O'Brien built the first road XR out of his dirt track race-winning bikes in 60 days. More sportster than racer, it was light, strong, and fun.

Turbo Charged

Turbocharging was the latest craze for cars in 1980 and supercharging was normal for drag bikes, so it was no surprise when the Japanese "big four" announced turbocharged bikes in 1982 to 1983. Mid-range acceleration, when the turbo was most efficient, was very quick, but off boost performance was sluggish and that inflexibility just did not suit motorcycles.

△ **Suzuki XN85 Turbo 1983**

Origin Japan

Engine 673cc, inline four

Top speed 128 mph (206 km/h)

Suzuki's turbo ran at low pressure, giving minimal power increase. The 16-in (41-cm) front wheel was supposed to improve handling—but that was a gimmick as well.

△ **Honda CX650 Turbo 1983**

Origin Japan

Engine 674cc, V-twin turbocharged

Top speed 125 mph (201 km/h)

Despite the difficulty of turbocharging a V-twin, Honda launched a CX500 turbo with integrated bodywork in 1981, but soon increased capacity to 650.

△ **Yamaha V-Max 1985**

Origin Japan

Engine 1,198cc, V4

Top speed 146 mph (235 km/h)

Built like a drag bike with 135 bhp and its fuel tank under the seat, this was the fastest-accelerating production bike, capable of a sub-10-second quarter-mile (0.40 km).

△ **Laverda SFC 1000 1986**

Origin Italy

Engine 981cc, inline triple

Top speed 143 mph (230 km/h)

Refined and tamed for the 1980s, Laverda's ultimate air-cooled triple was still plenty fast, but was seen more as a sports tourer than a superbike.

△ **Suzuki RG500 1986**

Origin Japan

Engine 498cc, square-four

Top speed 147 mph (237 km/h)

Suzuki won the 1976, 1977, 1981, and 1982 World Championships with two-stroke RG500s. In 1984 it was finally released as a road bike: light, peaky, and blisteringly fast.

◁ **Kawasaki ZX750 Turbo 1983**

Origin Japan

Engine 738cc, inline four turbo

Top speed 146 mph (235 km/h)

Last of the big four to produce a turbo bike, Kawasaki built the best, minimizing turbo lag to give huge acceleration well ahead of conventionally aspirated superbikes.

△ **Yamaha XJ650 Seca Turbo 1984**

Origin Japan

Engine 653cc, inline four

Top speed 126 mph (203 km/h)

The second turbo bike on the market after Honda's, the Seca had terrific acceleration on boost, but turbo lag hampered rapid road progress and it only lasted two years.

Test riders pictured with the 125cc YA-1

Great Marques
The Yamaha Story

Having built a reputation for high performance and quality engineering with lightweight two-strokes, Yamaha diversified to offer a large range of bikes from scooters to cruisers. Always forward-looking and technically adventurous, the company maintains a high sporting profile in both track racing and off-road competition.

THE TUNING FORKS in the Yamaha logo are a reminder of the company's background in musical instruments. Torakusu Yamaha founded Nippon Gakki to make reed organs in 1887, and his company grew to be one of the world's largest instrument makers.

In 1955 Nippon Gakki president Genichi Kawakami set up the Yamaha Motor Company. Its first bike, based on a 1930s German DKW design, was the YA1, which had a 125cc single-cylinder two-stroke engine. This was swiftly followed by a 250cc twin, influenced by the German Adler. Coded YD1, this sturdy machine sold well in Japan's crowded motorcycle market and set the pattern for a long line of two-stroke twins.

Yamaha soon became a leading contender in Japanese motorbike racing and made a foray into US

Yamaha badge
(introduced 1964)

racing in 1958, contesting the Catalina Grand Prix with a 250cc twin. Official US distribution was set up in 1960 to supply the 250cc YD2 twin and the more exciting YDS1 sports variant. But it was the YDS2 of 1962 that alerted the motorcycling world to the scintillating performance of Yamaha's twin-cylinder bikes.

An international campaign, begun in 1961, reinforced the marque's racing credentials. Within two years, US rider Don Vesco won the 250cc US Grand Prix and the factory rider Fumio Ito took victory in the Belgian Grand Prix. In 1964 Yamaha ended Honda's supremacy in the 250cc world championships, when British rider Phil Read took the first of two consecutive titles.

To gain more power while also ensuring reliability, Yamaha engineers turned to four-cylinder, water-cooled engines. Britain's Bill Ivy won the 125cc crown in 1967, while Phil Read collected both the 250cc and 125cc titles in 1968. In the same year Bill Ivy became the first 125cc rider to lap the Isle of Man TT circuit at 100mph (161km/h) on his Yamaha V-four with two crankshafts.

High output

The Yamaha Motor Company started out building 200 bikes a month and became a world leader within 10 years.

Weekend getaway
This 1972 poster advertising Yamaha's 125cc and 175cc Enduros surely would have appealed to the sense of adventure and freedom of young people of the time.

From the mid-1960s Yamaha built less exotic track machines aimed at independent "privateer" racers. The original 250cc TD air-cooled twin was followed by the 350cc TR twin and, from 1973, the lightning-fast 250cc and 350cc TZs.

After new rules restricted the number of cylinders and gear ratios in Grand Prix racing, Yamaha won four 250cc and three 350cc world championships in the 1970s. It became the first two-stroke factory to top the 500cc class when Italian Giacomo Agostini took the premier title on a two-stroke inline four in 1975. Kenny Roberts, who trained on dirt tracks, became the first American asphalt world champion with his 500cc title

YAMAHA The great machines for '72.

twin-cylinder engine, directly challenged British imports from 1970.

Yamaha forged ahead with innovation. Monoshock rear suspension devised for motocross transferred to road machines in the

> ## "The most **Western-thinking** of the Japanese makers and always **forward-looking.**"
> KENNY ROBERTS, YAMAHA WORLD CHAMPION 1978-1980

in 1978 and gave Yamaha two more titles in the following seasons.

Meanwhile, the company's ever-widening array of bikes had gained a foothold in world markets. The 250cc DT1 Enduro of 1968 established Yamaha as a top marque on America's booming off-road scene, while the XS-1 (later the XS650), with a vertical

late 1970s, and racing spinoffs of the 1980s included the Yamaha Power Valve System, which improved two-stroke engines, and the Deltabox aluminum frame. Cataloged machines ranged from 50cc step-throughs to 1,100cc four-strokes and 1,200cc V-twins with maintenance-free shaft drives. The high-performance road

DT-1

TX500

RD350

YSZ-R1

1955 The Yamaha Motor Company is formed; it launches the 125cc YA1.
1957 Yamaha's first twin-cylinder bike, the 250cc YD1, is released.
1958 Cooper Motors begins to sell Yamaha motorbikes in the US.
1960 The Yamaha International Corporation is founded as the US base; European distribution begins in the Netherlands.
1963 Yamaha's first production racer, the 250cc TD1, is released; Fumio Ito wins the 250cc Belgian Grand Prix.

1964 Phil Read wins Yamaha's first 250cc world championship.
1967 Bill Ivy wins Yamaha's first 125cc world championship.
1970 Yamaha's first four-stroke, the 650cc XS-1, is launched.
1977 The 130 mph (209 km/h) shaft-driven XS1100 is introduced.
1978 Kenny Roberts wins Yamaha's first 500cc world championship.
1980 Yamaha releases the water-cooled two-stroke RD250 LC.

1984 The FZ750 debuts Yamaha's five-valve Genesis engine.
1985 Yamaha's V-Max cruiser begins its 20-year production run.
1987 The EXUP power valve system is introduced.
1992 Wayne Rainey wins his third 500cc world championship in a row.
1994 Yamaha cruisers start to be sold under the Star brand in the US.
1998 The powerful 1000cc YZF-R1 sports bike is released.

2000 Riding a Yamaha YZF-R1, David Jefferies is the first rider to lap the Isle of Man TT road circuit at 125 mph (201 km/h).
2004 Valentino Rossi wins the MotoGP world championship on a YZR-M1.
2007 The YZF-R1 production bike is updated with MotoGP technology.
2009 The new 1,700cc VMAX is launched; Ben Spies wins the World Superbike series on a YZF-R1.
2010 Jorge Lorenzo wins the MotoGP series on a Yamaha YZR-M1.

theme persisted with 250cc, 350cc, and 500cc water-cooled two-strokes, while off-road options ran from versatile trail and enduro models to ferocious YZ motocross racers. Yamaha's 500cc world championship of 1977 was the first of many motocross titles, and the company won the Dakar Rally nine times between 1979 and 1998.

Two exciting high-performance four-strokes appeared in the mid-1980s. The 1,200cc V-Max cruiser rapidly achieved cult status with the devastatingly strong acceleration of its water-cooled V-four engine. The FZ750 super sport launched Yamaha's Genesis four-cylinder engine. It also sired the FZR line, notably the FZR1000, with an engine featuring Yamaha's pioneering Exhaust Ultimate Power Valve (EXUP) system.

Relentless two-stroke engine and chassis development led to Eddie Lawson's victory in four world championships between 1984 and 1989, and Wayne Rainey's three wins in the early 1990s using

MotoGP champion
Spanish star Jorge Lorenzo won the 2010 MotoGP championship on a YZR-M1. Lorenzo follows Valentino Rossi, who was champion four times on a Yamaha.

YZR500 V-four engines. The 900cc four-stroke YZR-M1, built for the MotoGP formula introduced in 2002, came through in 2004 and 2005 with titles for ex-Honda champion Valentino Rossi.

Race-bred technology fed through to showroom machines, notably the 1,000cc YZF-R1, launched to acclaim in 1998 with an extremely compact 1,000cc five-valve engine in a well-balanced chassis. The R1 later gained fuel injection, an uprated Deltabox frame, and, from 2007, an improved four-valves-per-cylinder engine. The latest R1 benefits from M1 racer development with a cross-plane crankshaft layout for better power delivery.

Just as sophisticated in their own way are Yamaha's cruisers, which have been sold under the Star brand in the US since the mid-1990s. V-twin engine sizes go up to a massive 1,854cc and Star's ultimate muscle machine is the current 1,679cc VMAX.

Retro technology
Yamaha's air-cooled pushrod V-twin engine has been used in heavy cruisers since 1999. However, a version of this engine is also used in the Yamaha MT-01 muscle bike.

Design Diversity

A hundred years of motorcycle development had led to a degree of conventionality of design for popular motorcycles, but that did not stop manufacturers in the 1980s from looking for alternative engineering solutions or new niche markets. While some continued to build bikes that had been designed 50 years earlier, others experimented with rotary engines, tilting three-wheelers, and extreme streamlining.

▷ **Yamaha XV920 1981**

Origin Japan

Engine 920cc, V-twin

Top speed 115 mph (185 km/h)

This bike was built for the US market and intended to offer a wide spread of power for sporty touring. A larger-capacity 980cc model was sold in European markets as the TR1.

△ **Suzuki Katana 1000 1982**

Origin Japan

Engine 998cc, inline four

Top speed 137 mph (220 km/h)

Suzuki Germany commissioned Target Design to conceive a bike for the German market. This 1,000cc version of that 1100 was built for one year only for race homologation.

▽ **Hesketh V1000 1982**

Origin UK

Engine 992cc, V-twin

Top speed 119 mph (192 km/h)

First shown in 1980 but not built until 1982, Lord Hesketh's indulgent V-twin motorcycle was a status symbol on par with his successful Formula 1 team.

△ **Triumph TSX 750 1982**

Origin UK

Engine 748cc, inline twin

Top speed 119 mph (192 km/h)

US designer Wayne Moulton was commissioned by the Triumph workers' cooperative to design a bike for the US market based on the Bonneville; the cooperative failed in 1983.

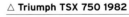

▷ **Triumph Thunderbird TR65 1982**

Origin UK

Engine 649cc, inline twin

Top speed 110 mph (177 km/h)

Built by the workers' cooperative, this was a cheaper, economy-oriented version of the 750 Bonneville with a shorter stroke, drum rear brake, and points ignition.

△ Greer Streamliner 1983

Origin USA

Engine 185cc, single-cylinder

Top speed 90 mph (145 km/h)

Jerry Greer and Chuck Guy built this aerodynamic machine with a Yamaha engine for a 3,000-mile (4,828-km) trans-US run, California to New York on 15 gallons (57 liters) at 196.5 mpg (83.53 km/l).

△ Honda Stream 1982

Origin Japan

Engine 49cc, single-cylinder

Top speed 30 mph (48 km/h)

Honda licensed the design of George Wallis, first sold as the Ariel 3, to build this tilting three-wheeler with a two-stroke engine and continuously variable transmission.

◁ Honda CB250RS 1982

Origin Japan

Engine 249cc, single-cylinder

Top speed 85 mph (137 km/h)

Honda looked to earlier British singles with this popular twin-exhaust machine, though it had four valves, vibration damping, and, from 1982, electric starting.

▷ Honda XBR500 1988

Origin Japan

Engine 498cc, single-cylinder

Top speed 108 mph (174 km/h)

Honda wanted to hark back to the traditional British "sports single" using a radial, four-valve arrangement similar to a 1930s Rudge. It was a fun bike, and not too fast.

△ KMZ Dnepr MT11 1985

Origin Russia

Engine 649cc, flat-twin

Top speed 80 mph (129 km/h)

Based on the 1930s BMW R71, the Kiev-built Dnepr was steadily, if slowly, refined with a swingarm rear suspension, overhead valves, and 12-volt electrics.

◁ Honda Hawk 650 1989

Origin Japan

Engine 398cc, V-twin

Top speed 94 mph (151 km/h)

Introduced in Japan as the Bros, this bike was later sold more widely as the NT400. Ideal for new riders, it was a classy, aluminum-framed machine with all-around ability.

△ Norton Classic Rotary 1988

Origin UK

Engine 588cc, twin-rotor Wankel

Top speed 126 mph (203 km/h)

Norton unveiled its rotary in 1975, but could not afford to build it. However, 300 bikes were built for the British police from 1982 and 100 of these special consumer versions were sold in 1988.

△ Honda Pacific Coast 1989

Origin Japan

Engine 800cc, V-twin

Top speed 120 mph (193 km/h)

Looking like a super-scooter, the innovative Pacific Coast boasted a water-cooled engine capable of over 100,000 miles (160,934 km), shaft drive, a large trunk, and an all-enveloping body.

Mile Eaters

The 1980s brought an economic boom, early retirement for many, and with it the leisure time and funds to buy the ultimate, luxurious cruising motorcycles and set off across countries and continents to enjoy them. While some chose to follow their dream on an expanding range of Harley-Davidsons, others went for slightly sportier rides, or pure luxury from Honda's Goldwing.

◁ **Moto Guzzi California II 1980**

Origin Italy

Engine 949cc, V-twin

Top speed 119 mph (192 km/h)

Introduced as an 850 in 1972, Moto Guzzi's big V-twin was mounted transversely. Being Italian, it handled with brio while remaining a great cruising machine.

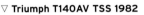

△ **Honda GL1100 Goldwing Aspencade 1982**

Origin Japan

Engine 1,085cc, flat-four

Top speed 103 mph (166 km/h)

A cockpit-controlled air suspension, stereo radio, and vanity mirror were standard features on the super-luxury Aspencade, which was still faster than an FL Harley.

▽ **Triumph T140AV TSS 1982**

Origin UK

Engine 744cc, inline twin

Top speed 118 mph (190 km/h)

This was the last of the Meriden-built Triumphs, before the British marque was overwhelmed by Japanese opposition. It had eight valves, an electric starter, and anti-vibration measures.

◁ **Honda VF500C Magna 1983**

Origin Japan

Engine 498cc, V-four

Top speed 112 mph (180 km/h)

The compact and powerful Honda V-four engine was used in cruisers as well as sports bikes. The Magna was a sales success in many markets around the world.

△ **Honda VF1000F Interceptor 1985**

Origin Japan

Engine 998cc, V-four

Top speed 145 mph (233 km/h)

Impressively fast and sophisticated, with only 6 bhp less than the exotic (and much more expensive) race-derived 1000R, the Interceptor was a superb all-arounder.

◁ **Honda GL1500 Goldwing 1988**

Origin Japan

Engine 1,520cc, flat-six

Top speed 108 mph (174 km/h)

Honda blew the big touring opposition out of the water with its monster flat-six, a super-smooth engine with lots of power. Its reverse gear was electronically powered.

◁ **BMW K100 1983**

Origin	Germany
Engine	987cc, inline four
Top speed	137 mph (220 km/h)

After experimenting with a lying-down Peugeot car engine, BMW built its own longitudinally mounted four, with a low center of gravity and shaft drive, perfect for touring.

△ **BMW K75 1985**

Origin	Germany
Engine	740cc, inline four
Top speed	122 mph (196 km/h)

After building its longitudinal four, BMW lopped off one cylinder to make a triple, which proved even smoother. It was BMW's cheapest bike in the 1980s.

▽ **Harley-Davidson FLT Tour Glide 1989**

Origin	USA
Engine	1,337cc, V-twin
Top speed	93 mph (150 km/h)

The Tour Glide, with frame-mounted fairing and rubber-insulated engine, was the world's heaviest production roadster; it was difficult at low speeds.

△ **Harley-Davidson FLHT Electra Glide Classic 1984**

Origin	USA
Engine	1,337cc, V-twin
Top speed	100 mph (160 km/h)

Getting ever bigger and more expensive, the FLHT was super-luxurious on a long ride, but a real handful on twisty, hilly roads and heavy in every way, especially on fuel.

▽ **Harley-Davidson FXR Super Glide 1989**

Origin	USA
Engine	1,337cc, V-twin
Top speed	110 mph (177 km/h)

Harley's factory custom model was quicker and more economical than its huge touring sisters, with a lighter-gauge frame and its engine rubber-mounted to reduce vibration.

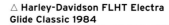

△ **Honda VT1100C Shadow 1989**

Origin	Japan
Engine	1,089cc, V-twin
Top speed	107 mph (172 km/h)

For little over half the price of a big touring Harley, Honda offered its own large cruising V-twin, but water-cooled with multiple valves and plugs for flexibility and speed.

Ice speedway
The sport of ice speedway has a category in which competitors ride bikes with studded tires. These produce huge amounts of traction, which requires special gearboxes. Four-stroke Jawa motorbikes have dominated the sport.

Dirt Diggers

Motorcycles evolved to stay competitive in the various disciplines of off-road sport. The changes in motocross machines over the course of the decade were obvious, as they went from air to water cooling, from drum to disc brakes, and from twin-shock to single-shock rear-suspension systems. By comparison, bikes used for speedway, or American dirt-track racing, saw little change from the beginning of the decade to the end.

△ **Harley-Davidson XR-750 1980**
Origin USA
Engine 748cc, V-twin
Top speed 115 mph (185 km/h)

This dirt tracker became the most successful bike in American Motorcyclist Association racing history; Harley's racing department built 200 each year.

▽ **Honda CR250R Elsinore 1980**
Origin Japan
Engine 248cc, single-cylinder
Top speed 65 mph (105 km/h)

Honda's Elsinore motocross bikes were successful and the new, more powerful engine made this model even better, but it needed improved suspension to remain competitive.

△ **GM Speedway 1980**
Origin Italy
Engine 500cc, single-cylinder
Top speed 90 mph (145 km/h)

In the late 1970s former Italian champion Giuseppe Marzotto designed his own GM Speedway engines with four overhead-valves, running on methanol fuel.

▽ **Godden GR500 1980**
Origin UK
Engine 500cc, single-cylinder
Top speed 90 mph (145 km/h)

Speedway star Don Godden began making his own frames in the 1970s and developed his own four-valve, overhead-cam engine for the world title-winning GR500.

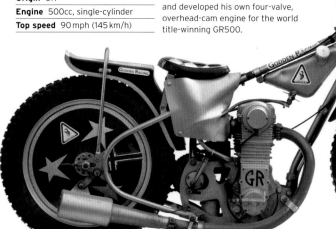

△ **Honda CR125 1988**
Origin Japan
Engine 124cc, single-cylinder
Top speed 60 mph (97 km/h)

Part of Honda's range since 1973, the CR125 was always at the forefront of motocross competition thanks to its powerful reed-valve, two-stroke engine.

▷ **Maico Mega 490 1981**

Origin Germany

Engine 488cc, single-cylinder

Top speed 90 mph (145 km/h)

The Maisch brothers started building motorcycles in 1926 and after the war became famous for bikes like this one. It was not competitive at Grand Prix level, but was popular with amateurs.

◁ **Moto Morini 500 Camel 1981**

Origin Italy

Engine 478cc, V-twin

Top speed 105 mph (169 km/h)

Built for the growing trail-bike market, using an engine from Morini's road bike, early versions of the Camel, like this one, were surprisingly capable off-road.

▷ **Suzuki PE250X Enduro 1981**

Origin Japan

Engine 246cc, single-cylinder

Top speed 70 mph (113 km/h)

Suzuki's reed-valve, two-stroke PE model was launched in 1977, with electronic ignition and wide-ratio gearing for enduro events. Weighing just 240 lb (109 kg), it put out 38.5 hp.

◁ **Armstrong MT500 1985**

Origin UK

Engine 481cc, single-cylinder

Top speed 80 mph (129 km/h)

British Army motorcycles, with Austrian Rotax engines, were made by the Armstrong company. The design was subsequently made by Harley-Davidson, using a 350cc engine.

▷ **MZ GE 250 ISDT Replica 1985**

Origin Germany

Engine 243cc, single-cylinder

Top speed 75 mph (120 km/h)

MZ's two-stroke engines were powerful. Around 200 bikes of this "kleine serie" were made from 1984 to 1987 as replicas of the factory 1982 International Six Days Trial bikes.

△ **Montesa Cota 304 1987**

Origin Spain

Engine 238cc, single-cylinder

Top speed 75 mph (120 km/h)

Honda bought out Montesa in 1985; the 304 had its first production disc brake and monoshock rear suspension, enabling Montesa to maintain its competitive edge.

Racers

Although 1980s Grand Prix racing was dominated by thoroughbred two-stroke machines, the emergence of the Superbike class provided a showcase for production-based motorcycles. While Grand Prix continued to be dominated by the Japanese manufacturers, the Superbike class encouraged Italian manufacturer Ducati to bring out its booming, desmodromic valve V-twin to devastating effect; with added electronic fuel-injection, it kept on winning.

◁ **Yamaha YZR500 OW46 1980**

Origin Japan

Engine 499cc, V-four

Top speed 170 mph (274 km/h)

Yamaha's 500 two-stroke Grand Prix bike switched to a V-four engine layout in 1982, adopting crankcase reed valves in 1984, when Eddie Lawson won the Riders Championship.

△ **Yamaha TZ250H 1981**

Origin Japan

Engine 249cc, inline twin

Top speed 130 mph (209 km/h)

The TZ production race bikes were hugely successful and constantly evolved. Exhaust power valves were added for 1981, giving variable port timing for increased power.

△ **Suzuki RG500 1982**

Origin Japan

Engine 495cc, square-four

Top speed 170 mph (274 km/h)

This water-cooled, disc-valved, "stepped" square-four two-stroke won Franco Uncini the 500cc World Championship in 1982, his first year as a Suzuki team rider.

◁ **Weslake Speedway 1981**

Origin UK

Engine 499cc, single-cylinder

Top speed 75 mph (120 km/h)

The four-valve Weslake Speedway engine, in a traditionally skeletal chassis, achieved preeminence in the 1970s. Bruce Penhall rode this bike at the 1981 World Championship.

▷ **Kawasaki ZX750 GPz 1983**

Origin Japan

Engine 738cc, inline four

Top speed 186 mph (300 km/h)

To everyone's surprise, Wayne Rainey won the 1983 US AMA Superbike Championship on this machine, beating the theoretically superior Honda V-fours.

△ **Kawasaki KR500 1983**

Origin Japan

Engine 499cc, square-four

Top speed 155 mph (249 km/h)

Debuted in 1980, the two-stroke KR was highly innovative with a monocoque frame and anti-dive forks, but it failed to achieve Grand Prix success.

◁ **MBA 125 1984**

Origin Italy

Engine 125cc, inline twin

Top speed 125 mph (201 km/h)

Successful disc-valve, two-stroke racers were built by Morbidelli in the 1970s and won the 125 Grand Prix 36 times. Consumer versions of this model were sold by MBA.

△ **Honda R500R 1984**

Origin Japan

Engine 499cc, V-triple

Top speed 170 mph (274 km/h)

Freddie Spencer won the 1983 500cc World Championship on a three-cylinder two-stroke NS500, while the consumer version (the RS500) achieved national success.

▷ **Honda RVF750 1986**

Origin Japan

Engine 749cc, V-four

Top speed 174 mph (280 km/h)

Ultra-light materials such as titanium connecting rods helped Honda keep the RVF's weight down to just 370 lb (168 kg) without fuel. This is Joey Dunlop's F1 TT winning bike.

▽ **Honda VF750F Interceptor 1983**

Origin Japan

Engine 748cc, V-four

Top speed 155 mph (249 km/h)

This bike raced in the US Superbike Championship in 1983. Honda did not win the title that year, but it was successful the following year with a similar machine.

△ **Honda NSR500 1989**

Origin Japan

Engine 499cc, V-four

Top speed 165 mph (266 km/h)

Debuted in 1984, the NSR won 10 World Championships before the Grand Prix rules changed to favor four-strokes in 2002. This is Eddie Lawson's 1989 championship winner.

▽ **Ducati 851 Superbike 1989**

Origin Italy

Engine 851cc, V-twin

Top speed 195 mph (314 km/h)

Ducati became the dominant force in World Superbike racing with its desmodromic eight-valve engine, fuel-injected V-twins. This is the road version on which the racers were based.

The 1990s

Aside from Asia and Southern Europe, the use of two-wheelers for essential transport continued to decline, but the industry as a whole offered an evermore diverse range of products. There was a move away from fully enclosed sports machines towards retro styling, with engines proudly displayed. The on/off-road category matured, with more products suited to the rigors of inter-continental adventure. The US-oriented, cruiser class expanded, although Harley-Davidson still dominated. A successful revival of the Triumph marque put Britain back in the frame.

Mike Hailwood leading the 1959 TT race on a 125cc Ducati

Great Marques
The Ducati Story

Once a maker of tiny clip-on bicycle engines, Ducati has become a leading force in modern motorcycle technology and design. Success has come from continual involvement in racing development, an enduring passion for creative engineering, and a Latin panache that gives Ducati's bikes their distinctive character.

DUCATI'S HISTORY dates back to 1926, when Antonio Ducati and his three sons started a business making radio components in Bologna, northern Italy. Although the company diversified into cameras, shavers, and other consumer products, after World War II it turned its attention to motorcycles when they, produced a clip-on bicycle engine for Siata, a car tuning and accessories company in Turin. The 48cc four-stroke Cucciolo ("Puppy") unit provided basic transportation in war-torn Italy and was phenomenally successful. By 1952, when more than 200,000 of their machines were in use, Ducati had started to make their own motorcycles and scooters with small engines—the transportation favored by most of the nation's motorcycle manufacturers.

Ducati badge
(introduced 2008)

It was the arrival of Fabio Taglioni as technical chief in 1954 that put Ducati on the road to glory. A brilliant engineer, he designed a 100cc single, with an overhead camshaft, that set a pattern for future Ducati models. Potent and sturdy, it excelled in Italy's long-distance road races and was soon enlarged to 125cc. A double-overhead-camshaft version developed for international racing was further refined by Taglioni's Desmodromic system. This used cams to close the valves as well as to open them, preventing power loss at high revs. Ducati's first "Desmo" engine won on its race debut in the 1956 125cc Swedish Grand Prix and narrowly missed clinching the 1958 125cc world championship.

Single-cylinder road bikes were launched onto world markets. Early Ducatis often had crude electrical equipment, a poor finish, and few concessions to comfort, but sports riders were seduced by their snappy performance and sound handling. Taglioni's singles grew in stages, arriving at their 450cc maximum by the end of the 1960s, when Desmo engines were offered on premium models.

Ducati entered the superbike arena in the 1970s with a 750cc model. When building the engine, Taglioni

Speed sells
Its racing success with streamlined 125cc Desmodromic singles was exploited by Ducati when publicizing its products during the mid-1950s.

Mike Hailwood and Ducati
The young racing star sits on a 125cc single at the 1960 Isle of Man TT. Hailwood would take his 13th TT victory on a Ducati twin.

placed two of the proven single cylinders at a 90-degree V angle, creating a slim format often referred to as an L-twin. Its reputation was assured when factory Desmo versions took first and second place in the 1972 Imola 200 race.

Road twin-cylinders were offered in Touring, Sport, and Super Sport versions, at first with 750cc engines and then 900cc (actually 864cc) units. The larger engine further enhanced Ducati's prestige when popular Ducati veteran Mike Hailwood won the 1978 Formula 1 TT.

In the 1980s, control of the company passed to Cagiva, a younger motorcycle maker. Fears that the Ducati brand would disappear were proved to be unfounded when ex-Bimota designer Massimo Tamburini came on board and revitalized the marque. His most

radical early work was the all-enclosed Paso 750 of 1986, which, although not a big seller, set the style for sports motorcycles.

As ever, it was racing success that maintained Ducati's reputation. The new generation of water-cooled, four-valve Desmoquattro engines dominated twin-cylinder racing, and in 1988 the road-legal 851 Strada,

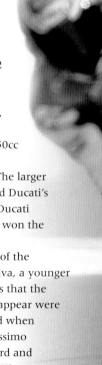

Cucciolo

350 Desmo

916

Desmosedici GP8

1926 The Ducati Patented Wireless company is founded in Bologna.
1946 Production of the Cucciolo T1 bicycle engine begins.
1950 The 65 cc Touring and Sport Ducatis with rear suspension are introduced.
1953 98 cc ohv Touring and Sport models are released.
1955 The launch of Taglioni-designed Gran Sport 100.
1956 The first Desmo engine wins the Swedish Grand Prix.

1965 The 250cc Mach 1 roadster is released.
1969 The first Desmo road machine, the 250cc Mk3D, debuts.
1970 The Street Scrambler versions of singles are a sales success.
1971 The first road V-twin, the overhead-cam GT750, goes on sale.
1972 Paul Smart and Bruno Spaggiari finish first and second on Desmo 750s in the Imola 200 race.
1979 Pantah 500 is Ducati's first production machine with belt-driven cams.

1981 Ducati rider Tony Rutter wins the first of four consecutive TT Formula 2 championships.
1985 The Cagiva group acquires Ducati from the Italian government.
1988 The four-valve 851 Strada gives road riders race technology.
1990 Ducati wins the first of its 16 world superbike championships.
1993 First of the best-selling unfaired Monster twins, the M900.
1994 The 916 sports is released to acclaim.

1998 US-based Texas Pacific Group becomes the majority stakeholder in Ducati.
2003 Ducati enters the MotoGP championship with a V-four engine.
2005 The company is bought by the Italian group Investindustrial Holdings.
2007 Ducati rider Casey Stoner wins the MotoGP World Championship.
2008 The limited-edition 170-hp road version of the Desmosedici four sells out.
2011 The 1,198cc Diavel marks a new departure in high-performance models.

with fuel injection, was introduced as a possible World Superbike Championship contender. Twin-cylinder 1,000cc machines could race against four-cylinder 750cc models in this competition, and Ducati's agile bikes were extremely competitive. Frenchman Raymond Roche became the 1990 World Superbike Champion, which helped popularize the twins and their booming exhausts. A vogue for single-cylinder racing prompted the 1993 Supermono, a high-tech 550cc racer with svelte styling by Pierre Terblanche. Then came another masterpiece, the 916, designed by Tamburini with the latest 114 hp Desmoquattro engine. Aggressive yet undeniably beautiful, the 916's looks influenced the designs of other leading manufacturers. However, not everyone wanted a semi-racer, which is why the unfaired and rider-friendly M900 Monster accounted for half of Ducati's bike sales in the 1990s.

Throughout the decade Ducati dominated the

Ducati engine
The 90-degree V-twin engine configuration has been employed for four decades, with toothed belts adopted for camshaft drive in the late 1970s.

superbike class, with Carl Fogarty taking four world titles, Doug Polen, two, and Troy Corser, one. The marque joined the MotoGP world series from 2003 with the 990cc four-cylinder, 16-valve Desmosedici. Essentially a doubled-up L-twin with pairs of cylinders firing together, the 215 mph (346 km/h) bike took its first victory in 2005. After it was adapted to the revised 800cc MotoGP formula, Australian Casey Stoner won Ducati's first MotoGP championship in 2007. In 2011 the marque signed Italy's multiple world champion Valentino

engine layout and, despite the near-universal adoption of aluminum frames, the tubular steel "trellis" chassis construction remained.

> ## "**Simplicity** has been the **basic principle** of all my designs."
> FABIO TAGLIONI, DUCATI'S TECHNICAL DIRECTOR 1954–1989

Rossi as the team's number one, and the development rider of a 1,000cc Desmosedici for 2012.

Off the track, both Honda and Suzuki unveiled new 1,000cc, 90-degree V-twin sport bikes in the late 1990s. However, Ducati stuck to its basic

Ducati in MotoGP
Casey Stoner, on the 800cc Desmosedici V-four, leads Honda's Andreas Dovizioso in the 2010 Japanese round of the MotoGP World Championship on the Twin Ring Motegi circuit.

In 2003 the marque widened its range by releasing a sport tourer, the Multistrada. The Testastretta ("narrow head") 1,098cc was debuted in 2007 and subsequently grew to 1,198cc, while the Diavel of 2011, with shattering performance and menacing appearance, defied easy labeling.

From a position of near-extinction in the 1980s, Ducati has grown into a world brand so strong that it now sells a variety of prestige merchandise, from watches to men's fragrances. Nonetheless, it continues to be best known for its stylish range of bikes.

Sports Bikes

Progress meant that speeds of at least 150 mph (241 km/h) could be expected from any serious superbike contender in the 1990s. Aerodynamics were more important than ever to ensure that a bike could slice through the air without being blown around by crosswinds. Some countries limited learners to 125cc bikes, prompting a light-hearted (but strong-selling) rash of mini-superbike and cruiser lookalikes.

▷ Yamaha TZR250 1990

Origin Japan

Engine 249cc, inline twin

Top speed 112 mph (180 km/h)

Yamaha's two-stroke, Grand Prix-inspired road bike went through a series of incarnations from 1985 to 1995, but was never as quick as the equivalent Suzuki.

▷ Yamaha FZR1000 1992

Origin Japan

Engine 1,002cc, inline four

Top speed 167 mph (269 km/h)

A new, more compact Deltabox frame, 20-valve cylinder head, and brilliant Exup motor-driven exhaust restrictor made the FZR more flexible, nimble, and fast than ever.

◁ Norton F1 Sport 1991

Origin UK

Engine 588cc, twin-rotor Wankel

Top speed 145 mph (233 km/h)

Smooth, flexible, and with a distinctive howl from its Wankel rotary engine, the F1 was a roadgoing version of Norton's 1989 National Championship race winner.

△ Honda CBR900RR 1992

Origin Japan

Engine 893cc, inline four

Top speed 163 mph (262 km/h)

Civilized yet phenomenally fast, the 900 was smaller and nimbler than other superbikes, enabling it to combine everyday practicality with superb handling.

△ Honda NR750 1992

Origin Japan

Engine 748cc, V-four

Top speed 160 mph (257 km/h)

Five times more expensive than Honda's top sports bike, the stunning and techno-mad NR750 boasted oval cylinders with eight valves each and was a dream to ride.

◁ Honda CBR600 F2 1993

Origin Japan

Engine 598cc, inline four

Top speed 152 mph (245 km/h)

The fastest middleweight in 1987, the 600 received a new chassis and engine in 1991, giving it 100 bhp. This new model was lighter, stiffer, and beautifully balanced.

▷ Honda VFR400 NC30 1994

Origin Japan

Engine 399cc, V-four

Top speed 125 mph (201 km/h)

Small, firmly sprung, and eager to rev, the VFR400 was launched in 1987 but enjoyed a long life thanks to 1990s EU rules restricting newly licensed riders to 400cc for two years.

△ Honda RVF750 RC45 1994

Origin Japan

Engine 749cc, V-four

Top speed 161 mph (259 km/h)

Built to meet new World Superbike rules, with fuel injection and 119 bhp in road form, the very fast 750cc RC45 took a while to come good on the racetrack.

◁ **Suzuki RGV 250 1990**

Origin	Japan
Engine	249cc, V-twin
Top speed	125 mph (201 km/h)

When introduced in the late 1980s, this was akin to a Grand Prix bike on the road—sensational to ride and very fast if revved—with characteristic two-stroke aroma.

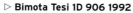

△ **Suzuki GSX-R 1100 1994**

Origin	Japan
Engine	1,074cc, inline four
Top speed	169 mph (272 km/h)

At its 1986 launch, the GSX-R was the quintessential sports bike—but over the years it put on weight, until a radical slim-down in 1994 sharpened it up again.

▷ **Bimota Tesi 1D 906 1992**

Origin	Italy
Engine	904cc, V-twin
Top speed	155 mph (249 km/h)

The first production motorcycle with hub-center steering, this bike used a bored and fuel-injected Ducati engine. It was hugely expensive but beautifully built, in small numbers.

▽ **Ducati 888 SPS 1992**

Origin	Italy
Engine	888cc, V-twin
Top speed	162 mph (260 km/h)

The nearest Ducati came to putting a racing bike on the road was this stunning machine, with carbon-fiber mufflers and fuel tank, and searing acceleration.

△ **Cagiva Mito 125 Evoluziono 1994**

Origin	Italy
Engine	126cc, single-cylinder
Top speed	107 mph (172 km/h)

Looking like a big Ducati, this was a racer for the road, with a stiff aluminum twin-spar frame and the equivalent of 240 hp per liter from a reed-valve 125 two-stroke.

◁ **Buell S2 Thunderbolt 1994**

Origin	USA
Engine	1,203cc, V-twin
Top speed	145 mph (233 km/h)

In 1993 Harley needed a sports bike and Buell needed investment, so Harley bought in. This was the result: a lighter, more powerful, and much faster bike than the Sportster.

Sports Bikes (cont.)

There was no standard specification for the sports bike of the 1990s: V-twins and inline fours (all with overhead camshafts) were the most common choices, but Triumph's return with its great-sounding inline triples showed that different could be good. Buyers began to turn away from out-and-out racers in favor of well-rounded machines that placed comfort and handling first.

◁ Moto Guzzi Daytona 1000 1994

Origin Italy

Engine 992cc, V-twin

Top speed 143 mph (230 km/h)

A race replica with belt-driven cams and fuel injection, the Daytona was more flexible and comfortable than some rivals, but nothing like as nimble in handling.

◁ Ducati 916 1995

Origin Italy

Engine 916cc, V-twin

Top speed 160 mph (257 km/h)

Considered the finest street bike of its day, the 916 was beautifully engineered, with a chrome-molybdenum spaceframe and top-quality Showa suspension.

△ Ducati 748 1995

Origin Italy

Engine 748cc, V-twin

Top speed 150 mph (241 km/h)

A smaller capacity version of the beautiful 916, the engine was crisper and more free-revving than its bigger sibling, which gave the bike its unique character.

◁ Bimota Mantra 1996

Origin Italy

Engine 904cc, V-twin

Top speed 125 mph (201 km/h)

Ducati-powered with a stiff trellis frame, the wacky-looking and extremely expensive Mantra was an impressively agile and straightforward machine to ride.

◁ Triumph T595 Daytona 1997

Origin UK

Engine 955cc, inline triple

Top speed 160 mph (257 km/h)

An extremely rapid, sweet-handling superbike but not quite as fast as some others, the Daytona won favor with a great-sounding engine. However, it had reliability issues at first.

▷ Suzuki TL1000S 1997

Origin Japan

Engine 996cc, V-twin

Top speed 165 mph (266 km/h)

The fuel-injected TL1000S had an impressive 125 hp, but its reputation was marred by questionable handling when ridden hard, partly due to the unique design of the rear damper.

◁ **Kawasaki ZZ-R1100 1994**

Origin Japan

Engine 1,052cc, inline four

Top speed 172 mph (277 km/h)

The fastest production motorcycle for five years, the ZZ-R1100 proved a great all-arounder, remarkably easy to ride despite its immensely powerful engine.

▽ **Kawasaki ZX-7R 1995**

Origin Japan

Engine 748cc, inline four

Top speed 165 mph (266 km/h)

Though heavy and unable to match its rivals on track, the ZX7R was a great road bike with predictable handling, great brakes, and (surprisingly for a Japanese bike) its own character.

△ **Kawasaki ZX-9R 1999**

Origin Japan

Engine 899cc, inline four

Top speed 175 mph (282 km/h)

Launched in 1994, the ZX-9R had a new, lighter frame and engine in 1998. Though not the best sports bike, it had a great engine and was a durable sports tourer.

▽ **Yamaha YZF600R 1998**

Origin Japan

Engine 599cc, inline four

Top speed 145 mph (233 km/h)

Although a reliable sports tourer with ample performance, the 600 was not intended as a match for superbikes; instead, it offered softer suspension and good durability.

△ **Yamaha YZF-R1 1998**

Origin Japan

Engine 998cc, inline four

Top speed 171 mph (275 km/h)

With an ultra-short wheelbase, 150 bhp, and weighing just 423 lb (192 kg), this was a sensational superbike, yet so powerful it could be a real handful to ride.

△ **MV Agusta F4 750S 1999**

Origin Italy

Engine 749cc, inline four

Top speed 175 mph (282 km/h)

This beautifully styled F4S, with single-sided swingarm and underseat exhausts, heralded the return of the famous MV marque. The engine was developed with the help of Ferrari.

Ducati 916

The Ducati 916 shook the motorcycle world to its foundations on its release in 1994. In one stroke, the Italian manufacturer redefined the superbike, creating the most desirable and influential sports machine in the world. The model featured a class-leading frame, high-tech components, and the most advanced twin-cylinder engine ever seen. The 916 and its later 996 variant won six World Superbike Championships in eight years. The ultimate pinup machine of the 1990s, the 916 was the bike that turned enthusiasts into fanatics.

THE FIRST MOTORCYCLES to carry the Ducati name were produced in 1950, although the marque had its origins in an electronics company founded in the mid-1920s by the Ducati family in Bologna, Italy. Over the years the brand became synonymous with motorcycle speed and power. When the decision was made to develop a new Ducati sports-racing bike in the early 1990s, the task was assigned to the Centro Ricerche Cagiva. Created by the studio's celebrated chief, Massimo

Tamburini, the 916 catapulted Ducati into the limelight with its winning mix of futuristic technology, superlative performance, and most importantly— for riders tired of the homogenous nature of Japanese sports bikes— distinctive styling. Lauded as the finest motorcycle for a generation, the 916 was produced for just five years before its larger-engined 996 sibling took over in 1999. A groundbreaking model, it raised the bar so high on virtually every specification that it took many years for rival manufacturers to equal it.

FRONT VIEW

REAR VIEW

Mufflers positioned under seat

Firm seat with a raised red passenger portion behind it

Fuel tank holds 4.5 gal (17 liters)

Tiny windshield deflects air over rider's head

Headlights set within the fairing

Twin 320mm brake discs

Tire measures 17 in (43 cm) at front and rear

Tubular-steel frame fabricated in chromoly steel

Adjustable head
One of the 916's numerous cutting-edge features was its adjustable steering head. An industry first on a production bike, it allowed varying degrees of rake (angle on the front fork) to be selected, so that riders could fine-tune their riding positions.

SPECIFICATIONS			
Model	Ducati 916 (1995)	**Power output**	114 hp at 9,000 rpm
Assembly	Bologna, Italy	**Transmission**	Six-speed
Production	17,870	**Suspension**	Adjustable forks, front and rear
Construction	Tubular-steel trellis frame	**Brakes**	Dual-disc front, single-disc rear
Engine	916cc V-twin, liquid-cooled	**Maximum speed**	160 mph (257 km/h)

THE BIKE

The 916 was such a successful marriage of style and substance that it was one of the bikes selected for inclusion in the Guggenheim Museum's "The Art of the Motorcycle" exhibition, which ran from the late 1990s. Heralded as the finest-handling motorcycle on the market, a hydraulic steering damper, an exceptional braking system, and race-tuned, adjustable suspension all contributed to making this a sports-racer par excellence. Just as important was the design of the bike's tubular frame, single-sided swingarm, and relatively small wheelbase, all of which gave the rider complete control of the machine.

1. Script on fairing **2.** Stylish headlights **3.** Front turn signal
4. Aircraft-type fuel cap **5.** Speedometer reads to 180 mph (290 km/h)
6. Handlebar switchgear and lights **7.** Hydraulic clutch operation
8. Steering damper **9.** Adjustable front suspension **10.** Gauze air vents
11. Cooling air apertures **12.** Lightweight tubular frame construction
13. Rear suspension unit **14.** Quick-release rear wheel **15.** Final drive
sprocket **16.** High-level exhausts

THE ENGINE

If the 916's innovative design provided the beauty, the bike's L-twin engine supplied the serious brawn, with the compact Desmodromic eight-valve power plant fitting snugly in the frame. The massive 114 bhp was impressive, but that this was achieved at 9,000 revolutions per minute was a phenomenal feat.

17. Left-side fairing removed to show engine unit **18.** Quick-release fairing fasteners **19.** Cooling fan motor **20.** Concave radiator **21.** Oil cooler

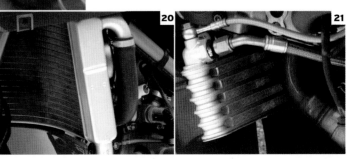

Street Style

Looks had always been important in the motorcycle market, but never more so than in the 1990s. Manufacturers worldwide tried every option, some choosing unashamed retro styling while others cribbed their designs from auto racing. Still more went for clean, enveloping, aerodynamic styling that looked suitably "space age." Classic British marque Triumph came back with a remarkably good range of modern bikes.

◁ **Triumph Trident 900 1990**

Origin UK

Engine 885cc, inline triple

Top speed 133 mph (214 km/h)

John Bloor brought Triumph back to life in 1990 with an impressive range of three- and four-cylinder bikes, of which the Tridents were affordable and outstanding all-arounders.

△ **Kawasaki 750 Zephyr 1990**

Origin Japan

Engine 738cc, inline four

Top speed 126 mph (203 km/h)

Blending 1970s styling with modern detail such as three-spoke alloy wheels, good brakes and suspension, and a competitive price, brought Kawasaki another winner in the 750 Zephyr.

△ **Triumph Trident 750 1991**

Origin UK

Engine 749cc, inline three

Top speed 134 mph (216 km/h)

With easily enough power to be fun and a relatively upright driving position ideal for city riding, the water-cooled 750 was a welcome addition to the Triumph range.

▽ **Triumph Speed Triple 1994**

Origin UK

Engine 885cc, inline triple

Top speed 135 mph (217 km/h)

Inspired by the 1950s Café Racers, the Speed Triple was the lightest and lowest of the new Triumphs, with great balance and response; it sold well.

△ **Honda Dream 50 1996**

Origin Japan

Engine 49cc, single-cylinder

Top speed 50 mph (80 km/h)

Conceived to commemorate Honda's early racing success in tiny capacity classes, the retro-racing-styled Dream 50 was powered by a double overhead-cam four-stroke.

▷ **Gilera Nord West 600 1991**

Origin Italy

Engine 556cc, single-cylinder

Top speed 106 mph (170 km/h)

Super Motard styling and a big thumping single-cylinder engine added character to the Nord West, a fine urban and back-road machine with good, nimble handling.

△ **Enfield India Bullet 350 1992**

Origin India

Engine 346cc, single-cylinder

Top speed 68 mph (109 km/h)

The Bullet has been built in India since 1955, and with minimal upgrades. It still has the same period charm of the original British-built machines.

△ BMW K1 1992

Origin Germany

Engine 987cc, inline four

Top speed 150 mph (241 km/h)

A lower drag coefficient than any contemporary, with really striking bodywork, helped the K1 break BMW's image of staid-but-solid bikes and make full use of its 100 hp.

△ Morbidelli V8 1994

Origin Italy

Engine 847cc, V8

Top speed 150 mph (241 km/h)

Giancarlo Morbidelli built his own racing bikes from 1969, selling them from 1976. This astounding V8 was beautifully made but hugely expensive; just four were built.

△ Ducati M900 Monster 1994

Origin Italy

Engine 904cc, V-twin

Top speed 129 mph (208 km/h)

An all-new machine with great street credibility, fun handling, and a hard ride, the Monster became a big seller and smaller-capacity versions were also produced.

△ Yamaha XJ400 Diversion 1994

Origin Japan

Engine 399cc, inline four

Top speed 100 mph (160 km/h)

With 53 hp, a six-speed gearbox, and all-disc brakes, the XJ400 offered excellent road performance without any pretensions to superbike looks or drama.

▽ Harley-Davidson FXSTB Night Train 1997

Origin USA

Engine 1,449cc, V-twin

Top speed 112 mph (180 km/h)

The black-and-chrome Night Train was all image, taking over from Harley's Bad Boy with an aggressive stance and a laid-back riding position; twin cams came in 1999.

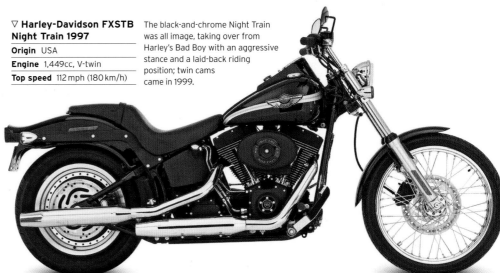

Cruisers

This was the decade when motorcyclists worldwide recognized the appeal of Harley's big American V-twin cruisers. Harley exploited it with ever more variations for style-conscious buyers who wanted a different Harley that would stand out from the crowd. Other manufacturers responded by undercutting Harley with similar machines for half the price, or trying to outdo it with even larger V-twins.

△ **Honda EML GL1500 Trike 1994**

Origin	Japan/Netherlands
Engine	1,520cc, flat-six
Top speed	95 mph (153 km/h)

By the 1990s the Goldwing had grown so big and powerful that specialists like EML began converting them to trikes for more stability, luxury, and towing ability.

◁ **Boss Hoss V8 1994**

Origin	USA
Engine	5,735cc, V-eight
Top speed	160 mph (257 km/h)

Monte Warne's mighty cruisers from Tennessee had General Motors V-eight power with one-speed manual transmission. The early ones were unrefined, but they got better.

△ **Moto Guzzi California EV 1997**

Origin	Italy
Engine	1,064cc, V-twin
Top speed	117 mph (188 km/h)

Originally an 850, the California evolved in 1994 and gained sequential fuel injection in 1997 which, with great handling for a cruiser, prolonged its appeal.

◁ **Kawasaki Vulcan VN1500 1995**

Origin	Japan
Engine	1,470cc, V-twin
Top speed	115 mph (185 km/h)

Kawasaki went big, launching the largest production V-twin of its time in 1998. Reliable and immensely torquey, it proved successful and was in production for 16 years.

▷ **Yamaha XVZ 1300 Royal Star Venture 1997**

Origin	Japan
Engine	1,294cc, V-four
Top speed	115 mph (185 km/h)

Very low, with limited ground clearance and soggy suspension, the XVZ was more for posing on than for pressing on. However, it was very well equipped and finished.

◁ **Yamaha XVS 1100 Dragstar 1999**

Origin	Japan
Engine	1,063cc, V-twin
Top speed	110 mph (177 km/h)

As cruisers grew, Yamaha's shaft-drive 1100 moved from being a big cruiser to a middleweight, still appealing for its reliability and manageable weight, even if it was a little outdated.

▷ Honda VT750 Shadow 1998

Origin Japan

Engine 745cc, V-twin

Top speed 105 mph (169 km/h)

Honda's smooth, water-cooled, middleweight cruiser filled a niche for those who could not afford or did not want to "go whole Hog," and was the best in its class.

△ Honda F6C Valkyrie 1996

Origin Japan

Engine 1,520cc, flat-six

Top speed 115 mph (185 km/h)

Honda's stripped-down Goldwing made an interesting cruiser alternative: beautifully made and supremely reliable, it was too quiet and smooth for some tastes.

△ Harley-Davidson Super Glide 1999

Origin USA

Engine 1,450cc, V-twin

Top speed 108 mph (174 km/h)

Harley's entry-level big twin was a basic, old-school, steel-framed machine with a big, thudding, thumper of an engine: the classic Harley feel for a reasonable price.

△ Harley-Davidson Wide Glide 1999

Origin USA

Engine 1,450cc, V-twin

Top speed 109 mph (175 km/h)

The ultimate "Easy Rider" chopper from Harley with wide-splayed, raked-out forks and low, relaxed seating was a reliable, well-built, and understressed cruiser.

◁ Harley-Davidson FLSTF Fat Boy 1999

Origin USA

Engine 1,450cc, V-twin

Top speed 105 mph (169 km/h)

Immortalized in the movie *Terminator 2*, the Fat Boy was king of the boulevard and one of the most popular Harleys of the 1990s. Originally 1,338cc, it grew in 1999.

Tour and Adventure

Super-size trail bikes catered to adventurous riders ready to explore every part of the globe, while road-touring machines offered ever-higher levels of comfort and convenience. The Honda Goldwing even had a reverse gear to help with parking. There was also a wide choice of more general-purpose machines with storming performance as well as long-distance travel capability.

◁ **Yamaha TDM850 1991**

Origin Japan

Engine 849cc, inline twin

Top speed 130 mph (209 km/h)

The novel and ergonomic TDM street/trail bike hybrid made a fine Alpine pass-stormer but was limited off-road. It blazed an exciting comeback trail for the parallel-twin.

◁ **Triumph Trophy 900 1991**

Origin UK

Engine 885cc, inline triple

Top speed 140 mph (225 km/h)

Helping Triumph become established on world markets, the versatile Trophy had a smooth and sweet-sounding three-cylinder engine with character, and durable cycle parts.

△ **Triumph Sprint 900 1993**

Origin UK

Engine 885cc, inline triple

Top speed 135 mph (217 km/h)

The tall yet comfortable half-faired triple with a torquey engine was a capable all-arounder. It heralded a successful line of Sprint models to come from Triumph.

△ **Triumph Adventurer 900 1996**

Origin UK

Engine 885cc, inline triple

Top speed 120 mph (193 km/h)

This cruiser-style bike, which features the powerful engine of Triumph's much-admired Thunderbird, was aimed at the US market. It missed the mark and was soon withdrawn.

▷ **BMW R1100GS 1994**

Origin Germany

Engine 1,085cc, flat-twin

Top speed 122 mph (196 km/h)

The definitive adventure vehicle with a long-range fuel tank, generous ground clearance, and enclosed shaft drive. It features BMW's Paralever front suspension.

◁ Yamaha Seca II 1998

Origin Japan

Engine 599cc, inline four

Top speed 117 mph (188 km/h)

Known as the Diversion in Europe, the Seca II all-arounder was derived from Yamaha's earlier XJ600 and combined a docile and dependable air-cooled engine in a tubular frame with pliant suspension.

◁ Suzuki RF900R 1994

Origin Japan

Engine 937cc, inline four

Top speed 162 mph (260 km/h)

Considered a terrific package of performance and handling for its budget price, this bike received less attention than more edgy and glamorous sports bikes.

△ Harley-Davidson FLHR Road King 1997

Origin USA

Engine 1,340cc, V-twin

Top speed 100 mph (160 km/h)

A luxury long-distance tourer in the Electra-Glide tradition, this bike has built-in panniers, twin-shock rear suspension, a high screen, and a lazy fuel-injected twin-cam V-twin.

◁ Honda XRV750 Africa Twin 1990

Origin Japan

Engine 742cc, V-twin

Top speed 110 mph (177 km/h)

Honda based the XRV750 on the multiple winner of the Paris-Dakar Rally. The tractable V-twin engine led the super trail bike field. This model is in rally trim.

△ Honda XL1000V Varadero 1999

Origin Japan

Engine 996cc, V-twin

Top speed 126 mph (203 km/h)

Powered by a version of the Firestorm V-twin engine tuned for strong torque, the Varadero was designed for long-distance travel in comfort—solo or two-up.

◁ Honda Goldwing GL1500 SE 1999

Origin Japan

Engine 1,520cc, flat-six

Top speed 112 mph (180 km/h)

Powered by a bigger flat-six engine from 1988, this iconic luxury tourer offered a reverse gear, a stereo, air conditioning, and armchair comfort for the passenger.

Taxi to market, 1992
By the 1990s, affordable motorcycles had become an essential mode of transportation for millions of people. Here, one scooter tows a cart laden with people to market in the Kompong Thom region of Cambodia.

After
2000

Electronics brought extraordinary sophistication to 21st-century motorcycles. Driven by the need to reduce emissions, electronically controlled fuel injection became universal. Anti-lock brakes were followed by traction control to prevent rear-wheel slip, plus push-button selection of engine characteristics for different conditions, or even according to mood. Suspension improvements continued to proliferate, sometimes offering a mind-boggling permutation of settings. By the second decade, "clean" motorcycle technology was making great strides.

Hypersport

The superbike market was stronger than ever in the new millennium, with manufacturers worldwide battling for a share of the market as well as for results on the racetrack. Design changes in the hypersport sector were driven by the need to win in production-based Superbike and Supersports racing, as much as the need to improve bikes for road use.

▷ **Honda RC51 SP1 2001**

Origin Japan

Engine 996cc, V-twin

Top speed 170 mph (274 km/h)

Built to beat Ducati in World Superbikes, the SP1 featured a brand new oversquare, four-cam V-twin in a radical twin-spar aluminum frame; it won in 2000.

△ **Honda CBR600RR 2003**

Origin Japan

Engine 599cc, inline four

Top speed 163 mph (262 km/h)

This new model for 2003 featured two-stage fuel injection, rear suspension used in Honda's Grand Prix bikes, and underseat exhaust.

△ **BMW K1200S 2006**

Origin Germany

Engine 1,157cc, inline four

Top speed 175 mph (282 km/h)

The K Series BMWs featured a radically new design, an all-new water-cooled, four-stroke engine with a claimed 167 bhp, and an electronically controlled suspension.

▷ **Honda CBR1000RR Fireblade 2012**

Origin Japan

Engine 998cc, inline four

Top speed 176 mph (283 km/h)

The original 1992 Fireblade defined the Hypersport class. As well as having detail upgrades, this model carries stickers to celebrate its 20th anniversary.

◁ **Triumph Daytona 955i 2006**

Origin UK

Engine 955cc, inline triple

Top speed 153 mph (246 km/h)

Triumph's revised twin-cam, twelve-valve 955i proved less popular than earlier models and was considered more touring than sporting, despite its impressive specification.

▽ **Triumph Daytona 650 2006**

Origin UK

Engine 646cc, inline four

Top speed 155 mph (249 km/h)

Triumph made its superb Daytona 600 sports bike more usable for 2005 by increasing the stroke, which made the engine more flexible, as well as boosting power.

▷ **Triumph Daytona 675 2006**

Origin UK

Engine 675cc, inline three

Top speed 155 mph (249 km/h)

Triumph boosted its middleweight superbike to the head of the pack with a new three-cylinder engine and razor-sharp handling owing to its ultra-light new chassis.

▷ Kawasaki ZX-12R 2000

Origin	Japan
Engine	1,199cc, inline four
Top speed	189 mph (304 km/h)

Kawasaki set out to reclaim the "world's fastest production bike" title, and succeeded, thanks to an aluminum monocoque, a compact 180 bhp engine, and a slippery body.

◁ Kawasaki Ninja 250R 2008

Origin	Japan
Engine	249cc, inline twin
Top speed	96 mph (154 km/h)

Kawasaki's midrange sports bike received a major update in 2008, resulting in a more flexible engine and improved suspension with larger wheels and brakes.

◁ Ducati 1098S 2007

Origin	Italy
Engine	1,099cc, V-twin
Top speed	180 mph (290 km/h)

"Pure, unadulterated sports bike heaven," said the reviews: this Ducati had the most powerful V-twin engine yet, in a beautifully built, superbly tuned chassis.

△ Suzuki GSX-R750 2004

Origin	Japan
Engine	749cc, inline four
Top speed	178 mph (286 km/h)

With its new, more compact engine (up to 147 hp in 2004 as in this model), a new twin-spar frame, lighter wheels, and a more aerodynamic body, Suzuki offered the fastest 750 by far.

▷ Suzuki GSX-R600 2009

Origin	Japan
Engine	599cc, inline four
Top speed	160 mph (257 km/h)

Suzuki's aggressive new look for the late 2000s was combined with the ultimate race-bred technology to make a light, nimble, and very powerful 600.

△ Triumph Speed Triple 1050 2008

Origin	UK
Engine	1,050cc, inline three
Top speed	155 mph (249 km/h)

With its looks updated in 2008, as here, the 1050 was based on a 1997 design but was enormous fun, with a flexible engine that sounded great.

▷ Suzuki GSX-R1000 2010

Origin	Japan
Engine	999cc, inline four
Top speed	180 mph (290 km/h)

Suzuki started a clean sheet for the decade, with a new, light, compact engine, twin-spar frame, suspension, brakes, and aerodynamics—all racetrack-proven.

Hypersport (cont.)

Less weight and more power are continual demands of the hypersport market. Advances in material technology made during the 2000s meant that the machines could become lighter, while sophisticated electronics were increasingly used to control brakes, suspension, and traction for improved rider safety. Meanwhile, European marques such as Triumph, BMW, and Ducati in particular, found a new lease on life in a market that wanted charisma as well as technical excellence.

△ Yamaha YZF-R6 2005

Origin Japan

Engine 599cc, inline four

Top speed 160 mph (257 km/h)

Upgraded almost every year from its introduction, the R6 was a serious supersport bike offering close to superbike performance in a lighter, nimbler package.

◁ Yamaha YZF-R1 2010

Origin Japan

Engine 998cc, inline four

Top speed 174 mph (280 km/h)

A revolutionary crossplane crankshaft, an uneven firing order for ultimate torque, and smooth power delivery helped the R1 become the best-handling superbike of its day.

▷ Yamaha YZF-R125 2011

Origin Japan

Engine 125cc, single-cylinder

Top speed 82 mph (132 km/h)

Yamaha's entry-level sports bike has a sophisticated, water-cooled engine and offers all the styling cues of its superbike sisters to appeal to young riders.

△ Kawasaki ZX-10R 2011

Origin Japan

Engine 998cc, inline four

Top speed 184 mph (296 km/h)

Kawasaki effectively refreshed its ZX10 to produce a class-leading superbike, with a great blend of handling and braking plus the best power-to-weight ratio.

◁ Kawasaki Ninja ZX-6R 2011

Origin Japan

Engine 599cc, inline four

Top speed 162 mph (260 km/h)

Commended for its razor-sharp handling and huge performance for a middleweight superbike, the beautifully engineered ZX-6R led its class.

◁ Kawasaki ZZR1400 2011

Origin Japan

Engine 1,352cc, inline four

Top speed 187 mph (301 km/h)

The fastest, most powerful motorcycle money could buy, but speed-limited for safety, it could be a practical touring bike or commuter as well as a drag race winner.

▷ KTM RC8R 2011

Origin Austria

Engine 1,195cc, V-twin

Top speed 170 mph (274 km/h)

KTM's first superbike appeared in late 2007 and by 2011 packed a massive 175 bhp punch that was great on the racetrack but could be a handful on the road.

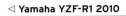

◁ **BMW S1000RR 2011**

Origin Germany

Engine 999cc, inline four

Top speed 186 mph (300 km/h)

Conceived for the 2009 World Superbike Championship (where its best was fifth position; it took third in 2010), this devastatingly fast road bike has antilock brakes and traction control.

△ **BMW K1300S 2011**

Origin Germany

Engine 1,293cc, inline four

Top speed 170 mph (274 km/h)

For the K1300S, BMW boosted the K1200S to 175 bhp and increased torque with an extra 136cc. This wonderfully civilized sporting machine delivers 0–62 mph (0–100 km/h) in 2.9 seconds.

△ **Aprilia RSV Mille R 2011**

Origin Italy

Engine 998cc, V-twin

Top speed 173 mph (278 km/h)

Introduced in late 1999 with a Rotax engine from Austria, the RSV-R shot to the top of the superbike pack, offering good comfort levels as well as superb performance.

◁ **Aprilia RSV4 2011**

Origin Italy

Engine 999.6cc, V-four

Top speed 180 mph (290 km/h)

Developed to win the World Superbike Championship, the narrow-angle V4 put out 180 bhp with electronic engine management and a fully adjustable suspension.

Aprilia RSV4

Aprilia made a spectacular contribution to the superbike arena with the RSV4, unveiled in 2008. The fast and compact, four-cylinder machine won the 2010 Superbike World Championship, changing the landscape of a series previously dominated by rival Italian factory Ducati. With Aprilia's most powerful engine to date and ultra-aerodynamic design, the RSV4 was undoubtedly one of the finest sports bikes of its time.

AFTER WINNING ACCLAIM for its world-championship-winning 125cc and 250cc machinery, Aprilia raised its game to contest the 2000 World Superbike series with a 1,000cc V-twin, developed in conjunction with the Austrian engine manufacturer Rotax. Aprilia then went on to unveil the RSV4 in 2008. The first four-cylinder machine to be produced by the company, it was designed with superbike racing in mind, an ambition realized when former Italian Grand Prix star Max Biaggi clinched the World Championship on an RSV4 in 2010.

Styled by Aprilia's head of design, Miguel Galluzzi, the bike's sleek lines were teamed with a wealth of technology. The RSV4 Factory road version featured sensors and gyrometers that were capable of detecting the dynamic conditions throughout the entire machine, adapting and adjusting the management of the engine appropriately. The host of forward-thinking features included traction control for monitoring rear-wheel slippage; wheelie control; ride-by-wire throttle control; and a quick-shift assister for swift, smooth adjustment of the six-speed gearbox.

FRONT VIEW

REAR VIEW

Rear shock absorber with remote nitrogen canister is multi-adjustable

Fuel tank has capacity of 3¾ gallon (17 l), with ⁹⁄₁₀ gallon (4 l) in reserve

Steering headlock is adjustable to alter geometry

Turn signals integrated into rear-view mirrors

Front forks with titanium-nitride coated tubes

Dual disc front brakes are 320 mm stainless steel

Titanium racing exhaust is a four-into-two-into-one arrangement

Frame constructed from aluminum

Aerodynamic lines
From its mini windshield to its angular fairing and compact size, the RSV4 was designed with windbreaking aerodynamics at the fore. The aggressive-looking triple headlight arrangement was a typical Aprilia design feature.

SPECIFICATIONS			
Model	Aprilia RSV4 (2011)	Power output	180 hp at 12,500 rpm
Assembly	Noale, Italy	Transmission	Six-speed
Production	Not known	Suspension	Upside-down front forks; swingarm rear
Construction	Aluminum dual-beam chassis	Brakes	Dual discs front, single disc rear
Engine	999.6cc, V-four	Maximum speed	180 mph (290 km/h)

THE BIKE

To secure the company's first Superbike World Championship, Aprilia incorporated several key elements on its RSV4, one of which was its cutting-edge frame: extensive work was done in formulating a suitable design, after which the prototype was fine-tuned in a wind tunnel. The final chassis, based on a rigid aluminum frame, was exceptionally light while offering great control. RSV4 owners also enjoyed a multi-adjustable front and rear suspension by racing-equipment specialist Öhlins, powerful disc brakes by Brembo, and a Sachs steering damper.

1. Tank script **2.** Model name on side panel **3.** Engine setting selector switch, turn signal switch, and horn **4.** Powerful triple headlights **5.** Front turn signal **6.** Tachometer calibrated to 15,000 rpm **7.** Sculpted fuel tank **8.** Twin 320 mm front discs **9.** Rider's footrest **10.** Passenger foot peg **11.** Rear shock absorber **12.** Rear drive sprocket **13.** Rear lamp **14.** Clutch operating lever **15.** Rear turn signal **16.** Exhaust outlet

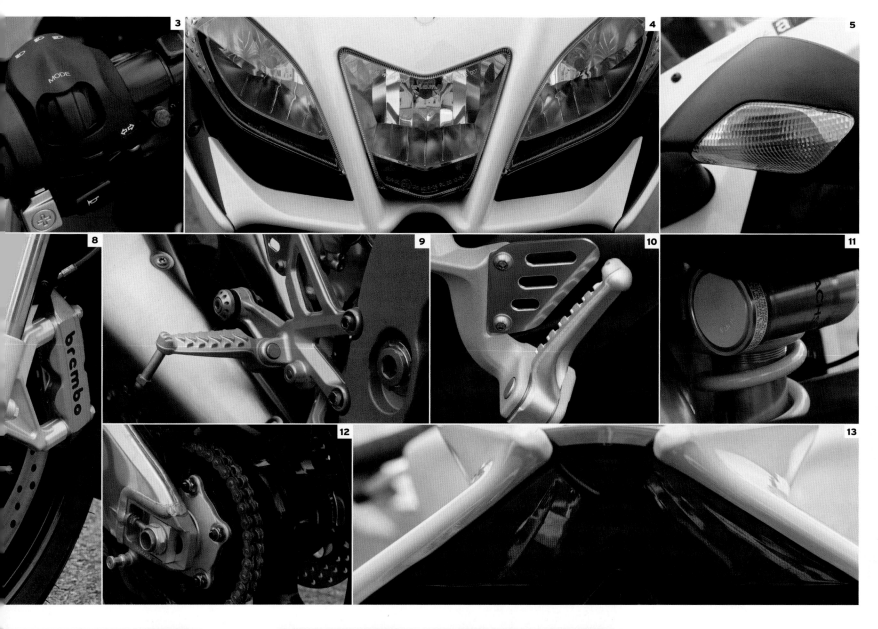

ENGINE

The 65-degree V-four power plant on the RSV4 was a technological marvel, capable of delivering more than 200 hp. Aprilia's engineers found that the four-cylinder configuration was the best format for a compact and well-balanced machine. Four valves and two fuel injectors per cylinder were combined with the most advanced engine management electronics of the day to obtain colossal and yet controllable power. The ride-by-wire system gave the rider a choice of three engine settings—track, sport, or road—at the touch of a switch on the handlebar.

17. Clutch housing 18. Water pump
19. Alternator cover 20. Gearchange linkage

Street Muscle

In the early part of the decade, bright was best, and radical styling and paint jobs abounded as manufacturers battled for a share of the stylish city riders' market. Then, suddenly, black was back in fashion in a bizarre reincarnation of the early years of motorcycling when every bike was black. Motorsports still had a powerful influence, but now more enduro than racetrack.

▷ **Yamaha FZ1 2002**

Origin Japan

Engine 998cc, inline four

Top speed 160 mph (257 km/h)

Despite a 143 bhp punch at high revs, the FZ1 remained a usable, everyday bike with a forgiving nature, making it possibly the ultimate all-arounder of its day.

△ **Buell X1 Lightning 2003**

Origin USA

Engine 1,203cc, V-twin

Top speed 140 mph (225 km/h)

Motorbike fan Erik Buell worked for Harley before starting his own company, which Harley bought in 1998. This model has a tuned Harley engine in a modern sport chassis.

▽ **MV Agusta 910S Brutale 2007**

Origin Italy

Engine 910cc, inline four

Top speed 157 mph (253 km/h)

With 136 bhp from its twin-cam engine, this bike was best kept for fun on dry, sunny days and smooth roads; in the wet or on bumps it could be a real handful.

◁ **Yamaha MT01 2005**

Origin Japan

Engine 1,670cc, V-twin

Top speed 131 mph (211 km/h)

With an immense V-twin almost out-Harleying Harley, the MT01 looked and sounded hugely impressive, but lacked the performance to match its looks.

▽ **Yamaha XJR1300 2011**

Origin Japan

Engine 1,251cc, inline four

Top speed 139 mph (224 km/h)

This fine cruising machine was introduced in 1998, and upgraded with fuel injection in 2007. Its traditional looks and an air-cooled engine betray its long production life.

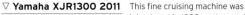

◁ **Triumph Street Triple R 2009**

Origin UK

Engine 675cc, inline triple

Top speed 141 mph (227 km/h)

Triumph showed it could trump the opposition with this middleweight stormer, equipped with a fully adjustable suspension, top brakes, and a great-sounding engine.

△ **Norton Commando 961 Sport 2010**

Origin UK

Engine 961cc, inline twin

Top speed 125 mph (201 km/h)

For a revival of the once-great Norton name, a parallel-twin engine and retro styling were inevitable. Although 79 hp was not much in 2010, this bike sold on nostalgia alone.

◁ **Harley-Davidson Sportster XR1200X 2010**

Origin USA

Engine 1,202cc, V-twin

Top speed 125 mph (201 km/h)

This bike was more sporty than earlier models thanks to multi-adjustable suspension, but way behind rivals in performance and specification. Still, Harley buyers did not seem to care.

△ **Harley-Davidson Sportster XL883N Iron 2011**

Origin USA

Engine 883cc, V-twin

Top speed 105 mph (169 km/h)

All matt black and menace, the H-D Sportster Iron carries echoes of Harley's dirt-track racers of the past, though the electronic ignition is evidence of modernity.

◁ **BMW R1200R Classic 2011**

Origin Germany

Engine 1,170cc, flat-twin

Top speed 136 mph (219 km/h)

Reverting to wire-spoke wheels, a chromed exhaust, and polished cam covers for the sake of nostalgia, in an ultra-modern chassis, the Classic is a curious mix.

▷ **KTM 990 Super Duke 2011**

Origin Austria

Engine 999cc, V-twin

Top speed 151 mph (243 km/h)

Frenetic and hugely exciting to ride, the 120 hp Super Duke combines stunning acceleration with exceptionally agile handling. Strictly solo, it is for fun, not touring.

▽ **Honda CB1000R 2012**

Origin Japan

Engine 998cc, inline four

Top speed 150 mph (241 km/h)

High quality, powerful, and a good buy, the CB1000R carries enough style and technology to turn heads, without making riding a scary or uncomfortable experience.

△ **Honda CB1300 2012**

Origin Japan

Engine 1,284cc, inline four

Top speed 136 mph (219 km/h)

Designed for seamless power right through the rev range, with a peak of 114 bhp, the twin-cam CB1300 is a consummate road machine, tractable but rapid.

Far and Fast

The choice of machinery for riders seeking a powerful yet flexible motorcycle without the handling difficulties or the discomfort of a race replica had never been greater. Enthusiasts could opt for full-touring capability with strong performance, as exemplified by Honda's ST1100, or the muscularity tempered by good street manners of Yamaha's XJR 1300, with plenty of other options between the two extremes.

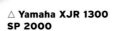

△ **Yamaha XJR 1300 SP 2000**

Origin Japan

Engine 1,251cc, inline four

Top speed 139 mph (224 km/h)

The hard-hauling air-cooled "naked" four that first appeared in the 1990s proved its staying power in a changing market by remaining in production with some chassis updates.

△ **Aprilia RST Futura 2001**

Origin Italy

Engine 998cc, V-twin

Top speed 150 mph (241 km/h)

This versatile, faired, sports tourer, with its ultra-modern look, is powered by a detuned version of Aprilia's one-liter engine. Its strong chassis features pliant suspension.

▽ **Honda ST1100 2000**

Origin Japan

Engine 1,084cc, V-four

Top speed 134 mph (216 km/h)

This bike was powered by an engine built in a Honda car plant and equipped to carry two people comfortably over long distances. It was supplanted by the ST1300 model in 2002.

△ **Aprilia SL1000 Falco 2001**

Origin Italy

Engine 998cc, V-twin

Top speed 156 mph (251 km/h)

Aprilia launched its race-winning RSV Mille in 1998, followed by this sport-touring variant. A fairly high seat is compensated by a great blend of comfort and performance.

△ **Honda CBR1100XX Super Blackbird 2002**

Origin Japan

Engine 1,137cc, inline four

Top speed 188 mph (303 km/h)

Sensational on its original 1996 launch for its 185 mph (298 km/h) top speed, the big CBR1100 four also proved comfortable and practical for touring or everyday riding.

△ **Honda XL650V Transalp 2007**

Origin Japan

Engine 647cc, V-twin

Top speed 105 mph (169 km/h)

With Honda's super-dependable, three-valve, V-twin engine, the latest incarnation of the venerable Transalp model (launched in the 1980s) was still useful as a commuter or gentle tourer.

△ Triumph Sprint RS 2001

Origin UK

Engine 955cc, inline triple

Top speed 154 mph (248 km/h)

Though not a big seller, the Sprint RS was a competent sports tourer with a great-sounding engine. It was boosted from 108 to 118 bhp in 2002 and built up to 2004.

▽ Suzuki V-Strom 1000 2003

Origin Japan

Engine 996cc, V-twin

Top speed 130 mph (209 km/h)

This bike is a derivative of Suzuki's thundering TL1000 sports machine. It is a useful blend of strong performance and rider comfort, but is ready to explore less well-beaten tracks.

△ Benelli Tornado Tre 900LE 2002

Origin Italy

Engine 898cc, inline triple

Top speed 169 mph (272 km/h)

Reborn in the mid-1990s, Benelli built this state-of-the-art, super-light sports bike for the new millennium, based on its racers. It has an all-carbon-fiber tank and fairings.

△ Suzuki GSX1250 2007

Origin Japan

Engine 1,255cc, inline four

Top speed 145 mph (233 km/h)

Descended from the first do-it-all Bandits of the 1990s, with a more torquey, water-cooled engine and stronger frame, the GSF1250 kept the real-life riding posture.

△ KTM 950 Adventure 2005

Origin Austria

Engine 942cc, V-twin

Top speed 140 mph (225 km/h)

Developed in grueling Dakar rallies, the trail-style Adventure combines go-anywhere ruggedness with the grunty power of its V-twin engine and eye-catching cosmetics.

◁ BMW R 1200 RT 2005

Origin Germany

Engine 1,170cc, flat-twin

Top speed 131 mph (211 km/h)

BMW designed the RT to be the ultimate long-range tourer, with fairings set up to minimize turbulence around the rider. The model also had an electrically adjustable windshield.

△ Kawasaki Z1000 2006

Origin Japan

Engine 953cc, inline four

Top speed 148 mph (238 km/h)

Not for the faint-hearted, this razor-sharp muscle bike with a revved 1970's Kawasaki model name uses its feisty engine as a stressed-frame member.

Far and Fast (cont.)

Extraordinary developments in electronic controls—for suspension, traction, brakes, and engine—brought great advances in performance and handling. These were matched by increased safety margins that had become essential as top speeds of all types of bikes from Enduro to Cruiser headed well over 100 mph (160 km/h). Ultimate machines like Suzuki's Hayabusa had switches to reduce the power—a vital safety measure in poor weather conditions.

◁ Yamaha FZ1 2009

Origin Japan

Engine 998cc, inline four

Top speed 160 mph (257 km/h)

Seen as one of the best premium sporty, all-around motorcycles of the late 2000s, the FZ1 had a great engine in a nicely compliant chassis at a competitive price.

△ Moto Guzzi Griso 1100 8V 2006

Origin Italy

Engine 1,064cc, V-twin

Top speed 127 mph (204 km/h)

Striking style and quality build brought Moto Guzzi back to the front of the pack with this fine, shaft-driven roadster, equipped with top-level suspension and brakes.

△ Yamaha XT1200Z Super Ténéré 2010

Origin Japan

Engine 1,199cc, inline twin

Top speed 130 mph (209 km/h)

Ténéré models had once dominated desert rally events but had been overtaken in the marketplace by BMW. This well-equipped but expensive model was Yamaha's response.

◁ Victory Cross Country 2010

Origin USA

Engine 1,731cc, V-twin

Top speed 115 mph (185 km/h)

Polaris Industries started its new all-American motorcycle brand in 1998, rapidly expanding in the late 2000s. This classic cruiser with a huge V-twin was a good buy.

△ Yamaha FJR1300A 2011

Origin Japan

Engine 1,298cc, inline four

Top speed 154 mph (248 km/h)

This is a well-equipped tourer with shaft drive, custom luggage, and an adjustable screen and riding position. There is also an automatic gearbox option.

▽ Harley-Davidson FLHR Road King 2010

Origin USA

Engine 1,584cc, V-twin

Top speed 110 mph (177 km/h)

Hugely expensive but built to last and hold its value, the Road King steadily increased in engine size from its 1993 launch, yet remained easy to handle.

△ Suzuki Hayabusa GSXR 1300 2010

Origin Japan

Engine 1,340cc, inline four

Top speed 186 mph (300 km/h)

At 194 hp the Hayabusa had the most powerful production-bike engine of its day, which translated to the road most effectively; a switch gave reduced power options.

▽ **KTM 990 Adventure 2011**

Origin Austria

Engine 999cc, V-twin

Top speed 130 mph (209 km/h)

This well-developed adventure trail bike offers serious off-road potential if knobby tires are used, yet performs well on-road, with sports-bike acceleration.

△ **KTM 990 SMT 2011**

Origin Austria

Engine 999cc, V-twin

Top speed 140 mph (225 km/h)

KTM injected a big dose of fun with this SuperMoto Touring variant on its adventure bike, tuning it more for road use, and exploiting the wide power band of the big V-twin.

▽ **Triumph Tiger 800XC 2010**

Origin UK

Engine 799cc, inline triple

Top speed 130 mph (209 km/h)

An all-out adventure bike with a jewel of an engine, the XC has decent off-road ability with the right tires. It is also a capable long-distance tourer on-road.

◁ **BMW K1200GT 2011**

Origin Germany

Engine 1,157cc, inline four

Top speed 165 mph (266 km/h)

BMW introduced an advanced inline four and a new twin-spar aluminum frame for the 2006 K1200GT, a superbly equipped and comfortable sports tourer.

◁ **BMW F800ST 2009**

Origin Germany

Engine 798cc, inline twin

Top speed 141 mph (227 km/h)

It was a surprise to see a parallel-twin (developed with Rotax) in a BMW, but this sports tourer makes an impressively well-equipped all-arounder with a toothed belt.

▷ **BMW R1200GS Adventure 2011**

Origin Germany

Engine 1,170cc, flat-twin

Top speed 130 mph (209 km/h)

The biggest monster trail bike yet, the Adventure was designed more for on- than off-road but was surprisingly capable at both, thanks to sophisticated suspension with electronic control.

△ **BMW K1600GT 2011**

Origin Germany

Engine 1,649cc, inline six

Top speed 140 mph (225 km/h)

The water-cooled transverse six is the smoothest bike engine ever, yet exceptionally light and compact. Complex electronics make this a highly sophisticated machine.

BMW K1600GT

Touring doesn't get any grander than on BMW's K1600GT model, unveiled to widespread critical acclaim in 2011. Even for a marque renowned for its fine long-distance bikes, its specification level left rivals trailing in its panniered wake. At its heart was a mighty six-cylinder engine which, teamed with a wealth of sophisticated accoutrements providing every possible comfort for rider and passenger, created a ground-breaking 21st-century sporting Grand Tourer.

THE K1600GT's stunning debut came in the nick of time for BMW. In spite of its reputation for building some of the world's finest touring bikes, the marque was facing stiff competition from its Japanese rivals. The K1300GT had gone some way to reestablishing the company's market-leading position in 2009, but the mighty K1600GT enabled the manufacturer to fully flex its engineering muscles once more. This was most clearly expressed through the model's ultra-smooth 160bhp inline six engine. Also present was a raft of features that made a K1600GT rider the most pampered motorcyclist on the road. Standard equipment, such as heated seats and grips, and a color monitor for the onboard computer, could be supplemented by extras—including traction control and an electronic suspension system. Combining power, comfort, and safety in one beautifully designed package, the model—UK magazine *Motor Cycle News*' 2011 Tourer of the Year—took open-road touring to a new level of luxury.

FRONT VIEW

REAR VIEW

Bavarian roots
The blue and white quartered circle in the BMW logo is thought to represent a moving aircraft propeller against the sky. While this reflects the company's background in aircraft engines, the colors are also those featured in the flag of Bavaria, where BMW is based.

Windshield can be electronically adjusted

Luggage space in color-matched pannier cases

Heated seat for rider and pillion passenger

Fuel tank holds 6.3 gal (24 liters)

Headlight with pioneering adaptive system

Fairing designed to provide maximum weather protection for rider

Vermilion red metallic is one of two color schemes offered

Suspension is electronically adjusted to suit ride conditions

Six-speed gearbox and final drive shaft

SPECIFICATIONS			
Model	BMW K1600GT (2011)	**Power output**	160 hp at 7,500 rpm
Assembly	Berlin, Germany	**Transmission**	Six-speed
Production	Not known	**Suspension**	Duolever front, paralever rear
Construction	Aluminum bridge frame	**Brakes**	Dual-disc front, single-disc rear
Engine	1,649cc, inline six	**Maximum speed**	140 mph (225 km/h)

Lighting the way

The adaptive headlight system was a world first on a production motorcycle. Electronic controls monitored and adjusted the headlight beam so that it remained at exactly the same level, even when the bike leaned through corners.

THE BIKE

With an unladen weight of 703 lb (319 kg), the K1600GT may have seemed a heavy bike, but it handled superbly, largely due to its compact engine design, traction control (if specified), and the use of lightweight materials such as aluminum, magnesium, and molded plastics. The optional ESA II (Electronic Suspension Adjustment) system gave the rider even more control, with three settings—Standard, Comfort, and Sport—providing distinctive suspension setups. Stopping power was provided by super-efficient 320 mm disc brakes and an ABS system. Controlled from a unit on the handlebars, an electronic engine management system offered a choice of three settings—Road, Rain, and Dynamic—to suit the riding conditions and the rider's mood.

1. "GT" denotes Grand Touring **2.** "6" for six-cylinder **3.** Ergonomic controls **4.** Self-adjusting headlights **5.** Dashboard with functions display **6.** Radio with push-button controls **7.** Fuel filler cap **8.** Cooling radiators **9.** Water pump **10.** Twin-disc front brakes **11.** Rear brakes with BMW antilock braking system **12.** Luggage rack **13.** Gearchange pedal **14.** Front turn signal **15.** Aluminum wheels **16.** LED rear lights **17.** Muffler outlets

THE ENGINE

BMW trumpeted that its new model had "the most compact six-cylinder inline engine ever built." It was undeniably impressive. Engineered to enable rapid acceleration even at low revs—70 percent of the maximum torque was available from just 1,500 rpm—the transverse-mounted 1,649cc unit featured twin overhead camshafts and four valves per cylinder.

18. High-quality engine castings **19.** Camshaft drive casing **20.** Shaft final drive **21.** Inclined cylinders

Cruising

Despite the new millennium's fixation on "green," some of the least economical motorcycles ever were produced—even though lighter frames and exotic materials reduced the weight of the engines and the hardware required to transmit their massive torque safely to the road. Harley set the standard, but the Japanese worked hard to steal their thunder; then Triumph introduced the world's biggest production engine, at 2,294cc.

▷ **Suzuki VL1500C Intruder 2000**

Origin Japan

Engine 1,462cc, V-twin

Top speed 110 mph (177 km/h)

Long, low, and wide, the VL1500 felt ponderous, underpowered, and cheaply finished, with marginal braking. Though well priced, it struggled to match its competitors.

◁ **Suzuki M1800R Intruder 2007**

Origin Japan

Engine 1,783cc, V-twin

Top speed 120 mph (193 km/h)

With the market for cruisers booming, Suzuki launched the Intruder. It was low and wide and especially long, which resulted in ponderous handling. It also had shaft drive.

△ **Moto Guzzi California EV 2001**

Origin Italy

Engine 1,064cc, V-twin

Top speed 115 mph (185 km/h)

The big Guzzi was given a general upgrade in 2001, notably the more thickly padded seat, with a whole range of special editions for the individualistic cruiser buyers.

△ **Harley-Davidson FLHX Street Glide 2010**

Origin USA

Engine 1,584cc, V-twin

Top speed 110 mph (177 km/h)

Low and ultra-cool, the Street Glide offers practical long-distance touring with unbeatable style, and a twin-cam, sequential port, fuel-injected engine.

△ **Harley-Davidson CVO Softail Convertible 2010**

Origin USA

Engine 1,803cc, V-twin

Top speed 115 mph (185 km/h)

Customizing Harleys became such big business that Harley opened a Custom Vehicles Operation division to build exclusive limited edition machines like this one.

△ **Harley-Davidson VRSCA V-Rod 2003**

Origin USA

Engine 1,130cc, V-twin

Top speed 135 mph (217 km/h)

With a fuel-injected, twin-cam, eight-valve, race-derived, water-cooled engine, a water-formed frame, and alloy disc wheels, the V-Rod was a Harley for the new millennium.

▽ **Harley-Davidson VRSCDX Night Rod Special 2010**

Origin USA

Engine 1,250cc, V-twin

Top speed 135 mph (217 km/h)

Ultra-low, with its seat just 25 1/8 in (64 cm) above ground, and ultra-dark, the Night Rod Special was like a caricature of the most "evil" of custom Harleys; yet it was a production model.

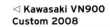

△ **Kawasaki VN1500 Mean Streak 2002**

Origin Japan

Engine 1,470cc, V-twin

Top speed 120 mph (193 km/h)

Kawasaki dressed up its 1996 VN1500 as a low-riding "production-custom" cruiser with a 27 1/2 in (70 cm) high seat and fuel injection for this big water-cooled V-twin.

◁ **Kawasaki VN900 Custom 2008**

Origin Japan

Engine 903cc, V-twin

Top speed 115 mph (185 km/h)

A comfortable, good-looking, and understressed production custom at a very competitive price, the VN900 owed much of its looks to the 21-in (53-cm) cast-alloy front wheel.

△ **Yamaha XVS650 Drag Star 2003**

Origin Japan

Engine 649cc, V-twin

Top speed 96 mph (154 km/h)

Great value for money, comfortable, easy-to-use, and nice-looking, the Drag Star was well finished and understressed, but its performance and braking were poor.

▷ **Yamaha XV1900 Stratoliner Midnight 2010**

Origin Japan

Engine 1,854cc, V-twin

Top speed 120 mph (193 km/h)

Massively torquey, the XV1900 accelerated effortlessly in any gear. Despite its size, it was lighter than many rivals and easier to handle thanks to an aluminum frame.

▽ **Triumph Thunderbird 1600 2010**

Origin UK

Engine 1,597cc, inline twin

Top speed 115 mph (185 km/h)

The world's biggest parallel-twin had balancer shafts to smooth out its ride. Though not very fast, it handled better than most rivals and was beautifully built.

◁ **Triumph Rocket III Roadster 2011**

Origin UK

Engine 2,294cc, inline triple

Top speed 136 mph (219 km/h)

Introduced in 2004 with power increased in 2009, the incredible Rocket III with its carlike, inline engine—the biggest production motorcycle engine ever—makes a good customized model.

▷ **Honda Goldwing GL1800 2012**

Origin Japan

Engine 1,832cc, flat-six

Top speed 120 mph (193 km/h)

With a high-tech aluminum frame, the Goldwing is not quite as heavy as it looks. Laden with luxury, it returns only 38 mpg (16 km/l) and is the ultimate cruising machine.

City Rides

The scooter returned with a vengeance in the new millennium. Legislation in Europe and elsewhere permitting 16-year-olds to ride bikes under 50cc and requiring learner motorcyclists to ride nothing larger than 125cc, then nothing larger than 250cc for two years, boosted the market for smaller-engined machines. This led to the appearance of some charming superbike and cruiser lookalikes with diminutive engines.

▷ **BMW C1 200 2001**

Origin Germany

Engine 176cc, single-cylinder

Top speed 75 mph (120 km/h)

Seat belts and an aluminum safety cage that kept the rider dry were radical and welcome for motorcycling, but the high cost relative to looks and performance meant few sales.

▷ **Suzuki RV125 2005**

Origin Japan

Engine 124cc, single-cylinder

Top speed 60 mph (97 km/h)

This six-speed, dual-purpose road/trail bike is ideally suited to sandy environments, where its chunky rear tire gives excellent grip without sinking into the sand.

▷ **Suzuki Burgman 650 Executive 2007**

Origin Japan

Engine 638cc, inline twin

Top speed 110 mph (177 km/h)

This was really a mid-size motorcycle dressed up as a luxury, long-wheelbase scooter for executive commuting. It is easy to ride, yet is also impressively fast.

△ **Honda PCX 125 2010**

Origin Japan

Engine 124cc, single-cylinder

Top speed 70 mph (113 km/h)

This is the first two-wheeler to have a fuel-saving idle-stop device (already widely used on cars). A practical city commuter, it is novice-friendly with good performance.

▷ **Generic Race 2 125 2010**

Origin Austria/China

Engine 124cc, single-cylinder

Top speed 56 mph (90 km/h)

Offered with 125cc or 50cc engines, the stylish Race 2 scooter has youth appeal and a competitive price but lacks performance with under 10 hp to play with.

◁ **Generic Epico 2011**

Origin Austria/China

Engine 49cc, single-cylinder

Top speed 35 mph (56 km/h)

An affordable scooter with electric starting and continuously variable transmission (CVT), the Epico is built in China for its Austrian parent company, which has been making scooters since 2004.

▷ **Generic Roc 2011**

Origin Austria/China

Engine 49cc, single-cylinder

Top speed 37 mph (60 km/h)

All 50cc bikes are limited to 30 mph (48 km/h) in Europe, but this stylish two-stroke with continuously variable transmission (CVT) is capable of more when derestricted.

◁ **Kymco Agility 125 2011**

Origin Taiwan

Engine 124cc, single-cylinder

Top speed 65 mph (105 km/h)

Built to carry two people in reasonable comfort, the Agility is Kymco's sporting model, offering good handling and performance for its type at the expense of a harder ride.

◁ **Kymco Like 125 2011**

Origin Taiwan

Engine 124cc, single-cylinder

Top speed 62 mph (100 km/h)

Kymco has built bikes since 1970, and is expanding. This luxurious "retro chic" scooter claims Italian styling, disc brakes, good performance, and 100 mpg (42.51 km/l).

▷ **Kymko Agility 50 2011**

Origin Taiwan

Engine 49cc, single-cylinder

Top speed 35 mph (56 km/h)

An entry-level scooter with a competitive price, this four-stroke 50 is well-equipped for a passenger. Its seat converts to a backrest when riding solo.

◁ **PGO PMX Naked 2011**

Origin Taiwan

Engine 49cc, single-cylinder

Top speed 37 mph (60 km/h)

Aiming to be the coolest 50cc scooter for 16-year-olds, the Naked has a "wave" front brake disc, mock carbon-fiber mudguards, "moto-x handlebars," and a yellow rear spring.

▷ **PGO Ligero 50 2011**

Origin Taiwan

Engine 49cc, single-cylinder

Top speed 37 mph (60 km/h)

Motor Power Industry of Taiwan started in 1964 and later made these Piaggio scooters under license. This inexpensive machine had continuously variable transmission (CVT) and helmet storage.

▽ **Hyosung GT125R 2011**

Origin South Korea

Engine 124cc, V-twin

Top speed 70 mph (113 km/h)

Hyosung's pretend superbike for learners is another clever niche machine, squeezing all of 15 bhp out of its little V-twin, and providing big-bike looks.

△ **Hyosung Aquila GV125 2011**

Origin South Korea

Engine 124cc, V-twin

Top speed 68 mph (109 km/h)

Looking so much bigger-engined than it really is, this bike, aimed at the learner market, is a rather charming miniature cruiser, complete with V-twin engine.

City Rides (cont.)

Suddenly it was cool to be "green" and riding a 50cc or 125cc bike with racy scooter styling and a highly efficient fuel-injected, four-stroke engine capable of well over 100 mpg (42 km/l) of unleaded fuel. The new decade saw a surge in sales worldwide from hitherto unknown makes from India and East Asia competing with existing Japanese marques.

◁ Yamaha T-Max 2010
Origin Japan
Engine 499cc, inline twin
Top speed 100 mph (160 km/h)

Sturdily built and fun to ride, Yamaha did a better job of making a large scooter than most, but it was heavy and expensive compared to a conventional motorbike.

△ Yamaha Neos 4 2011
Origin Japan
Engine 49cc, single-cylinder
Top speed 35 mph (56 km/h)

Yamaha's four-stroke scooter with 12-in (30-cm) alloy wheels, front disc brake, and LCD instruments was light, clean, quiet, and reliable, with room for a passenger and a spare helmet.

△ Yamaha Jog RR 2011
Origin Japan
Engine 49cc, single-cylinder
Top speed 40 mph (64 km/h)

With a lively, two-stroke engine capable of 45–50 mph (72–80 km/h) with a little tuning, plus 12-in (30-cm) wheels and a front disc brake, the Jog RR became popular teenage transportation.

▽ Yamaha YBR125 2011
Origin Japan
Engine 124cc, single-cylinder
Top speed 70 mph (113 km/h)

Light, with forgiving handling and a reliable fuel-injected, four-stroke engine, the YBR125 was a great buy and an ideal choice for learner motorcyclists.

◁ Yamaha Zuma 125 2011
Origin Japan
Engine 124cc, single-cylinder
Top speed 65 mph (105 km/h)

The Zuma sported big wheels with chunky treads for potholed, bumpy roads. Its rugged styling was targeted at male buyers, though it was quite small for taller riders.

▽ Yamaha X-Max 250 Sport 2011
Origin Japan
Engine 250cc, single-cylinder
Top speed 70 mph (113 km/h)

Introduced in 2004 and updated as a "Sport" for 2011, this is a 21bhp four-stroke with constant velocity transmission (CVT), easy handling, and storage for two helmets under the seat.

△ Yamaha Aerox R 2011

Origin Japan

Engine 49cc, single-cylinder

Top speed 40 mph (64 km/h)

Light and nimble with a water-cooled two-stroke and bigger wheels than most, the Aerox R was expensive but better built than its opposition.

▷ Yamaha Vity 125 2011

Origin Japan

Engine 124cc, single-cylinder

Top speed 60 mph (97 km/h)

Yamaha's basic, bargain-basement scooter offered helmet storage under the seat and was well-built, but lacked performance and refinement.

△ Piaggio Yourban 300ie LT 2011

Origin Italy

Engine 278cc, single-cylinder

Top speed 75 mph (120 km/h)

Evading some countries' motorcycle license rules by being classed as a tricycle, this nippy, best-selling machine also offers much better braking and cornering in the wet.

◁ Moto-Roma SK125 2011

Origin China

Engine 124cc, single-cylinder

Top speed 70 mph (113 km/h)

An exceptional-value bike for learners, this sporty, dual-purpose road/trail machine boasted a four-stroke engine with an electric start, five-speed gearbox, and a hydraulic front brake.

▷ LML Star 4 2011

Origin India

Engine 124cc, single-cylinder

Top speed 60 mph (97 km/h)

Lohia Machinery Ltd made scooters with Piaggio from 1984 and in the 2000s could still offer the classic, all-metal, Vespa-based Star four-stroke in 125, 150, or 200cc.

▽ Vespa LX50 2011

Origin Italy

Engine 49cc, single-cylinder

Top speed 35 mph (56 km/h)

Piaggio's entry-level Vespa has a two-stroke engine (a four-stroke was also offered, but was slower). It looks great, but is neither cheap nor lively compared to rivals.

The instigator of Aprilia motorcycle production, Ivano Beggio (left), with designer Philippe Starck and the Moto 6.5 he styled

Great Marques
The Aprilia Story

A comparative latecomer to the Italian motorcycle industry, Aprilia applied enthusiasm and fresh thinking to achieve remarkable growth. While prominent in racing and other sports, the marque has always offered a variety of practical and stylish products alongside its more exotic machinery.

IN THE YEARS AFTER World War II, Alberto Beggio opened a factory, turning out bicycles for the locals in and around the small town of Noale, just outside Venice. But by 1968, with postwar gloom a fading memory and Alberto's son Ivano now at the helm, the Aprilia bicycle factory was poised to take off in a new direction. Spotting an expanding youth market, Ivano decided to enter the motorcycle trade with a clutch of small 50cc models. One of these—the little Scarabeo motocross bike of 1970—would establish Aprilia as key manufacturer of specialized competition hardware.

Ivano Beggio
Former president

By the end of the 1970s, Aprilia rider Ivan Alborghetti had won the 125cc and 250cc Italian motocross championships and also achieved commendable results at World Championship level, helping publicize the marque outside Italy.

In 1982 a highly competent road machine was launched: the ST125, which featured mono-shock rear suspension and a water-cooled engine made by Hiro in Japan. The ensuing years saw factory output rise dramatically, placing Aprilia among the top contenders in Italy.

Meanwhile, racetrack success enhanced Aprilia's sporting prestige. Using rotary-valve two-stroke engines, supplied by the Austrian Rotax company, Aprilia developed Grand Prix racers that made a strong showing. The company also staked out a place in the world of observed trials with the Climber, powered by a water-cooled 280cc engine. Its credentials were confirmed when Finnish rider Tommi Ahvala won the 1992 Trial World Championship.

During the 1990s, Aprilia was a top performer in 125cc and 250cc Grand Prix racing. The company's track campaign against the might of big Japanese marques was overseen by Dutch engineer Jan Witteveen. In 1992, Aprilia team member Alessandro Gramigni broke Honda's domination of the 125cc class; then, from 1994 to 1997, Max Biaggi had a run of three consecutive 250cc titles. Valentino Rossi won the 125cc championship for the company in 1997, and the 250cc title two years later.

Circuit prowess was exploited by the release of the RS125 two-stroke road machine, a long-standing favorite with speed-hungry young

Rugged Enduro model
The Aprilia ETX 6.35 of 1988 was designed for on- and off-road riding, with a 350cc single-cylinder four-stroke engine.

Falco

Pegaso 650

RSV4 Racer

RSV Mille

1968 Ivano Beggio takes over his father Alberto Beggio's bicycle factory and starts manufacturing motorcycles.
1970 The Scarabeo 50cc motocross bike is launched.
1976 Ivan Alborghetti becomes the Italian champion.
1977 Alborghetti wins the 125cc and 250cc Italian motocross championships on Aprilia motorbikes.
1982 The ST125 road machine is launched with a Hiro engine.

1987 Aprilia has its first Grand Prix win, in the 125cc class, by Loris Reggiani.
1989 The largest-engined model to date, the 560cc Tuareg Wind, is launched.
1992 Aprilia takes two World Championships: Alessandro Gramigni in the 125cc Grand Prix, and Tommi Ahvala in the Trials.
1993 The Scarabeo four-stroke scooter begins a long production life.
1994 Max Biaggi wins the 250cc World Championship on a RS250 for three years running.

1998 Aprilia launches a series of RSV Mille 1,000cc V-twins built around a Rotax engine.
1999 Valentino Rossi wins Aprilia's fourth 250cc World Championship.
2000 Laverda and Moto Guzzi are acquired by Aprilia.
2002 Aprilia takes two Grand Prix World Championships: Marco Melandri on a 250cc and Arnaud Vincent on a 125cc prototype RS3 Cube MotoGP machine.
2004 Piaggio Group takes control of Aprilia.

2006 Aprilia takes a second double win: a 250cc title for Jorge Lorenzo, and 125cc crown for Gábor Talmácsi.
2007 Lorenzo takes a second 250cc title.
2008 The high-tech 850cc Mana with auto-clutch is released.
2009 The 1,000cc four-cylinder RSV4 becomes a top-of-the-line model.
2010 Aprilia's 276th win in the 125cc Czech GP makes it the Italian marque with the most wins in the Grand Prix. Max Biaggi becomes World Superbike champion.

riders. The RS250 also debuted, featuring a fiery Suzuki RGV250-based engine and superb handling.

Rather than focusing entirely on racing and super sporting products, the company survived by pursuing

Rough rider
Chilean rider Francisco Lopez Contardo, a stage winner in the 2011 Dakar Rally, on his Aprilia. Formerly held in North Africa, the tough Enduro is now run in South America.

an ambitious program of design and development to create a range of street machines. One was the Pegaso, a much-admired trail-style single with a 650cc Rotax engine, that is still in production today. The Moto 6.5, radically shaped by Philippe Starck for style-conscious urban riders, found fewer admirers. The Scarabeo name was also revived for a stylish large-wheeled scooter launched in 1993, which would be continually updated, up to the present day. Mopeds were a constant feature of Aprilia's catalog.

Entry to the superbike arena came in 1998 with the arrival of a long-planned V-twin, the 1,000cc Aprilia

With their RSV Mille–based machine, Aprilia went on to strongly contest the World Superbike series from 1999 to 2003.

Aprilia's Moto Grand Prix contender for 2002 was typically novel: the experimental RS3 Cube had a 990cc three-cylinder engine with pneumatic valves and ride-by-wire throttle operation. Powerful but difficult to control, it was shelved after three seasons, although Aprilia did have the consolation of storming the 250cc Moto Grand Prix class with the marque's eighth and ninth World Championships in 2006 and 2007, respectively.

transmission. Aprilia also brought a fresh concept to off-roading with the MXV Motocross, RXV Enduro, and SXV Supermoto models, powered by V-twin engines of 450cc and 550cc.

Max Biaggi returned to the Aprilia fold in 2009, when the marque returned to Superbike racing with a formidable new contender, the RSV4, with a 65-degree V4 engine of 1,000cc, the maximum size allowed for fours since the 2003 rule update. Biaggi grabbed the marque's first World Superbike title in 2010.

A road-legal version of the racer, called the RSV4 Factory, supplanted the RSV twin as flagship of the range. With shattering performance and the finest handling, it bristled with smart technology, including self-adjusting traction control to suit different tires.

Although it is now part of a conglomerate, Aprilia retains a strong brand identity, reflecting decades of adventurous engineering, sophisticated design, and sporting ambition.

"Passion, determination, technological research, and a capacity for innovation..."

IVANO BEGGIO, FORMER OWNER, ON APRILIA'S DEFINING QUALITIES

RSV Mille, built around a 60-degree Rotax power unit. Lighter than other super-sporting V-twins, the Mille featured a throttle-linked slipper clutch for enhanced controllability when cornering. A series of variants on the 1,000cc twin series followed, including the higher-specification Mille R, the more street-friendly Falco, the Futura sports tourer, and the unfaired Tuono.

In 2000 the company took over two revered older Italian brands, Laverda and Moto Guzzi, which indicated just how rapidly Aprilia had grown.

Aprilia had become Europe's second biggest manufacturer of two-wheelers when, in 2004, it was acquired by the Piaggio Group.

In 2007, the marque unveiled the Aprilia Shiver, a versatile high-performer with a 750cc V-twin engine made in-house. This was soon followed in 2008 by the more novel Mana, an 850cc twin with automatic

The RSV Mille Engine
Made by Rotax in Austria, this 998cc 60-degree V-twin unit was first used on the 1998 RSV Mille, Aprilia's first model with an engine larger than 650cc.

Practical Fun

Although it is usually the ultra-high-performance machines that grab the headlines, many motorcyclists look for something more realistic and less demanding for everyday use or recreation. By the 2000s, buyers could choose from a huge variety of machinery and performance levels for budget transportation, commuting, leisurely country rides, or making a style statement on city streets.

▷ **Suzuki SV650S 2000**

Origin	Japan
Engine	645cc, V-twin
Top speed	123 mph (198 km/h)

Introduced in 1999, Suzuki's easily manageable and versatile, middleweight V-twin gained a big following. It was available with a fairing in S form, or without at lower cost.

▷ **IMZ-Ural Tourist 2007**

Origin	Russia
Engine	749cc, flat-twin
Top speed	65 mph (105 km/h)

IMZ developed this machine directly from a Russian, BMW-derived, WWII outfit. No-frills transportation, ideal for rough roads, the Tourist's flat-twin engine has moderate power.

◁ **Royal Enfield 350 Bullet Machismo 2006**

Origin	India
Engine	346cc, single-cylinder
Top speed	69 mph (111 km/h)

Still based on the original UK-designed Bullet, built in India from 1954, this comes with an all-alloy, lean-burn engine to comply with modern emission regulations.

◁ **BMW F800R 2009**

Origin	Germany
Engine	798cc, inline twin
Top speed	138 mph (222 km/h)

An all-arounder that copes with city riding or sport touring, the F800R boasts a zesty, 800cc parallel-twin engine and a chassis with taut handling.

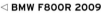
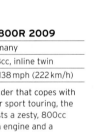

◁ **Aprilia Pegaso 650 Trail 2009**

Origin	Italy
Engine	659cc, single-cylinder
Top speed	101 mph (163 km/h)

The stylish and versatile Pegaso trail bike also proved to be highly street friendly. From 2008, it was equipped with a Yamaha engine, in place of the previous Rotax type.

△ **Hero Honda Passion Pro 2010**

Origin	India
Engine	97.2cc, single-cylinder
Top speed	53 mph (85 km/h)

Honda's India division is the country's biggest bike-maker, producing millions of simple, small-engined machines, like this one, with racy paintwork.

▷ **Honda Falcon NX4 2009**

Origin	Brazil
Engine	397cc, single-cylinder
Top speed	80 mph (129 km/h)

Built by Honda of Brazil, this sturdy road/trail bike sold throughout South and Central America and in Portugal. It was produced for 10 years virtually unaltered.

▷ Can-Am Spyder Trike 2011

Origin Canada

Engine 998cc, V-twin

Top speed 110 mph (177 km/h)

From snowmobile-maker BRP, this trike has steered front wheels, a rear wheel belt-driven by a Rotax engine, and a five-speed gearbox with a semiautomatic option.

△ Suzuki Bandit 650 2011

Origin Japan

Engine 656cc, inline four

Top speed 130 mph (209 km/h)

Suzuki's Bandit models have been popular since the early 1990s. The half-faired Bandit 650 makes a perfect runabout, also favored by city couriers.

◁ KTM Duke 125 2011

Origin Austria

Engine 125cc, single-cylinder

Top speed 78 mph (126 km/h)

The small, entry-level version of KTM's Duke Supermoto single has a punchy engine, coupled with responsive handling, mean looks, and fuel injection to give 15 bhp.

▷ Yamaha WR 125X 2011

Origin Japan

Engine 125cc, single-cylinder

Top speed 73 mph (117 km/h)

A durable, small-engined 125cc Supermoto, this bike comes as well equipped as bigger machines. Although aimed at young novice riders, the build is very high.

△ Yamaha XJ6 Diversion F ABS 2011

Origin Japan

Engine 599cc, inline four

Top speed 125 mph (201 km/h)

Full fairings and anti-lock brakes turn this fun all-arounder into an ideal commuter bike, especially over longer distances and in all weathers.

△ Yamaha FZ8 2011

Origin Japan

Engine 779cc, inline four

Top speed 134 mph (216 km/h)

At the serious end of practicality, the FZ8 combines colossal, open-road performance, hard braking, and nimble handling with unclothed, rugged looks.

▽ Triumph America 2012

Origin UK

Engine 865cc, inline twin

Top speed 110 mph (177 km/h)

Mixing a cruiser-style twin with a low seat and a Bonneville-based engine with a 270-degree firing interval gave this bike the leisurely feel of a V-twin.

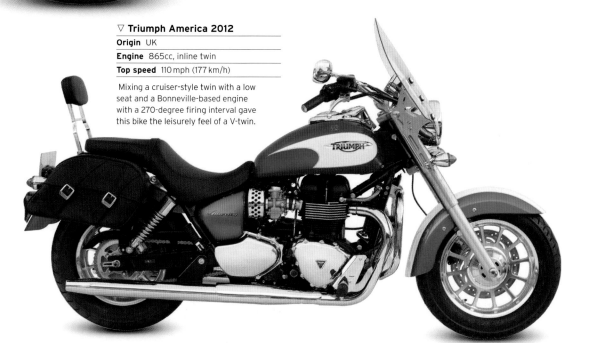

△ Triumph Bonneville 2011

Origin UK

Engine 790cc, inline twin

Top speed 112 mph (180 km/h)

Triumph's old-model name sat on this easy-to-live-with, retro-style twin, later issued with a 865cc engine. A strong seller, it was offered in several variants.

Off-road

The off-road motorcycle spans a range of types, from the trail/street-style bike that rarely leaves a paved road surface, to motocross mounts with huge amounts of suspension travel that are ridden high in the air with astonishing skill, even by youngsters. After decades on top in motocross, the two-stroke engine is being eclipsed by a new generation of four-stroke "thumpers."

▷ **Yamaha VZ250F 2007**

Origin Japan

Engine 250cc, single-cylinder

Top speed 75 mph (120 km/h)

Like other makers, Yamaha began switching from two-stroke to four-stroke engines, mainly to comply with US anti-pollution measures. This new line was a success.

△ **BMW F650GS 2009**

Origin Germany

Engine 798cc, inline twin

Top speed 120 mph (193 km/h)

Confusingly coded 650, this is a trail variant of BMW's 800cc twin. This machine is equally suited to the road or the woods and hills.

△ **Yamaha Super Ténéré 2010**

Origin Japan

Engine 659cc, single-cylinder

Top speed 99 mph (159 km/h)

Named after a region of the Sahara Desert, this ultimate adventure tourer was closely based on the bike that Stephane Peterhansel rode to victory seven times in the Paris-Dakar.

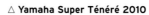

△ **Yamaha XT660X 2011**

Origin Japan

Engine 659cc, single-cylinder

Top speed 105 mph (169 km/h)

Following Supermoto style, with an off-road profile and on-road wheels and tires, the snappy XT single is aimed at urban street riders with attitude.

△ **BMW G650GS 2011**

Origin Germany

Engine 652cc, single-cylinder

Top speed 105 mph (169 km/h)

BMW's entry-level adventure bike was a good buy. It was easy to ride, with a low seat height, but still great off-road. The single-cylinder engine is now built in China.

▷ **Suzuki DR650R 2011**

Origin Japan

Engine 198cc, single-cylinder

Top speed 73 mph (117 km/h)

Fully road-equipped but very capable off-road, the small DR650R was a continuation of Suzuki's 1998 DR 200 SE, with a gutsy four-stroke single producing over 20 hp.

△ **Suzuki RM-Z 450 2011**

Origin Japan

Engine 449cc, single-cylinder

Top speed 85 mph (137 km/h)

This motocross bike with an aluminum frame and a water-cooled, four-stroke engine was launched in 2004 and revised with electronic fuel injection and a lighter frame in 2008.

△ Kawasaki KX250F 2011

Origin Japan

Engine 249cc, single-cylinder

Top speed 85 mph (137 km/h)

The world's first dual-injection motocrosser and a proven race winner, the KX250F is a factory race machine unsuitable for road use but hugely impressive off-road.

△ KTM 65 SX 2011

Origin Austria

Engine 65cc, single-cylinder

Top speed 50 mph (80 km/h)

Aimed at young motocrossers from eight to 12 years old, this well-built, six-speed, water-cooled, two-stroke minibike is a serious competitor.

△ Husaberg TE250 2011

Origin Austria

Engine 249cc, single-cylinder

Top speed 95 mph (153 km/h)

KTM bucked the trend of its traditionally four-stroke Husaberg marque with this two-stroke enduro machine, featuring alternative engine power modes, selected at the flick of a switch.

△ KTM 50 SX 2011

Origin Austria

Engine 49cc, single-cylinder

Top speed 42 mph (68 km/h)

KTM's smallest motocross machine was a winner for six- to nine-year-olds, with a long-travel suspension, all-disc brakes, chain guard, and the best power in its class.

△ KTM 85 SX 2012

Origin Austria

Engine 85cc, single-cylinder

Top speed 65 mph (105 km/h)

German teenager Henry Jacobi won the 2010 Junior World Championship on the 85 SX, a flyer for younger riders. This bike weighs just 143 lb (65 kg).

△ KTM 350 SX-F 2012

Origin Austria

Engine 350cc, single-cylinder

Top speed 88 mph (142 km/h)

KTM's compact, light, and powerful 350 gives the best of both worlds: with the nimbleness of a 250 and the power of a 450, it is beautifully made and looks set for success.

Racers

Early in the 2000s the premier 500cc Grand Prix class was phased out and replaced by the MotoGP formula, which favored four-strokes more closely related to production models than the two-strokes that had reigned for decades. Superbike racing, which had always been for roadster-based machinery, continued to be ultra-competitive. The second decade of the 2000s has also seen a sudden upsurge of electric bike racing.

◁ Ducati 999F06 2006

Origin Italy

Engine 999cc, V-twin

Top speed 195 mph (314 km/h)

This 999 V-twin was Ducati's Superbike contender from 2002, boosted by engine and chassis redesigns. Gregorio Lavilla defended his 2005 British Superbikes title on this type.

△ Ducati 996S 2000

Origin Italy

Engine 996cc, V-twin

Top speed 190 mph (306 km/h)

A successor to the World Superbike series-winning 916, the 996 had two fuel injectors per cylinder. This one was raced by Neil Hodgson, later 2003 champion.

▷ Ducati Desmosedici GP8 2008

Origin Italy

Engine 800cc, V-four

Top speed 213 mph (343 km/h)

Ducati's four-cylinder MotoGP entry was first raced in 2002, and by 2008 the 800cc version raced by Casey Stoner had a top speed approaching 220 mph (354 km/h).

△ Harley-Davidson VR1000 2001

Origin USA

Engine 1,000cc, V-twin

Top speed 182 mph (293 km/h)

Harley-Davidson's final year in Superbike racing marked the end of a 16-year effort that was just too slow, too little, and too late, with only occasional flashes of competitiveness.

△ Yamaha YZR-M1 MotoGP 2005

Origin Japan

Engine 990cc, inline four

Top speed 210 mph (338 km/h)

Ex-Honda Champion Valentino Rossi worked with Yamaha to transform the unsuccessful 2003 YZR-M1 into a dominant winner in 2004 and 2005.

▷ Yamaha YZF R1 Superbike Racer 2010

Origin Japan

Engine 998cc, inline four

Top speed 200 mph (320 km/h)

This standard showroom R1 can readily be turned into a competitive national-level Superbike or Isle of Man TT racer using a Yamaha engine and chassis racing parts.

▷ Honda RC212V 2007

Origin Japan

Engine 800cc, V-four

Top speed 210 mph (338 km/h)

After racing the V-four Superbikes, Honda switched to the Fireblade inline four. This machine saw major success in the Isle of Man TT, with 13 race wins from 2006 to 2011.

△ Honda CBR1000RR 2009

Origin Japan

Engine 999cc, inline four

Top speed 200 mph (320 km/h)

Honda's World Superbike contender never quite equaled Ducati or Suzuki in the late 2000s, but Jonathan Rea managed wins in San Marino and Germany in 2009.

△ MotoCzysz E1pc 2009

Origin USA

Engine 200 hp, triple electric motors

Top speed 150 mph (241 km/h)

Leading the way in electric bike racing, the whispering MotoCzysz with its massive battery pack dominated the 2009 Isle of Man TT Zero event.

△ Mission One PLE 2009

Origin USA

Engine 100 Kw, 3-phase AC electric

Top speed 165 mph (266 km/h)

Pioneering maker Mission began electric bike racing in 2009 with this strikingly styled machine that was timed at 150 mph (241 km/h). An improved Mission R machine followed.

△ BMW HP2 2010

Origin Germany

Engine 1,170cc, flat-twin

Top speed 150 mph (241 km/h)

As well as racing four-cylinder machines, BMW has enjoyed track success with this flat-twin that features double overhead-camshaft cylinder heads.

▷ Aprilia RSV4 Racer 2010

Origin Italy

Engine 998cc, V-four

Top speed 204 mph (328 km/h)

Aprilia designed its first four-cylinder to contest the World Superbike Championship. Max Biaggi took one win amid nine podiums in 2009 and then the title in 2010.

Freestyle motocross, 2000
Big Air is a crowd-pleasing, freestyle motocross
discipline in which riders perform gravity-defying
stunts high in the air. The bikes used in motocross
are particularly light and maneuverable and
have highly developed suspension systems.

The
ENGINE

Motorcyclists have always been fascinated by engines, and manufactuers have made them in countless different forms over the decades—for functional reasons or simply to dazzle with technology. Some designers have been convinced that out-of-the-mainstream ideas, such as the Wankel rotary engine, are the answer. But the practical realities of production engineering, the constraints of construction regulations, and sometimes customer conservatism have seen configurations of the conventional gasoline engine prevail. On the following pages, the main engine types are explained, and examples from over a century of engineering are examined.

How an Engine Works

Since the first motorcycles appeared in the late 19th century, the vast majority of them have been propelled by internal combustion engines that run on a mixture of gasoline and air. Descended from steam-driven engines of earlier times, gasoline engines rely on the same basic principle of converting energy into motion, by using a piston sliding in a bore and connected to an eccentric shaft. When the fuel mixture is ignited, it drives the piston down the bore and turns the shaft, in the same way that pedaling a bicycle rotates the chainwheel. To make such an arrangement work effectively, methods have to be found of inducing the right fuel/air mix, providing precisely timed ignition sparks, efficiently expelling spent gases, and keeping all the moving parts running freely and adequately lubricated. Although myriad solutions have been found over the years, the engines traditionally used to power motorcycles can be divided into two main types: the four-stroke and the two-stroke.

FOUR-STROKE ENGINES

These engines are the most common type used in modern motorcycles. Four-stroke engines generate power through a series of events—called the four-stroke cycle—that occurs in each of the engine's cylinders dozens of times a minute. The four stages, or "strokes," are: intake, compression, combustion, and exhaust. It is the combustion stroke that generates power, and in each cylinder it occurs just once for every two crankshaft turns. In a multi-cylinder engine, the spark plugs fire in sequence, so there is always a power stroke in at least one cylinder. Four-stroke engines are generally cleaner, more reliable, and more fuel-efficient than two-strokes.

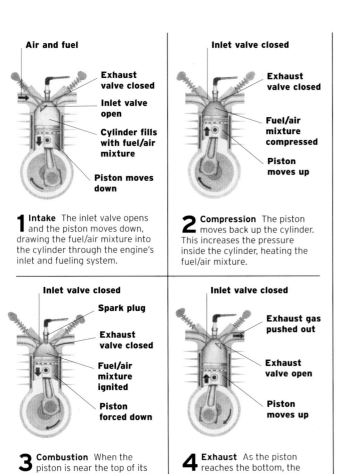

Air and fuel

- Exhaust valve closed
- Inlet valve open
- Cylinder fills with fuel/air mixture
- Piston moves down

1 **Intake** The inlet valve opens and the piston moves down, drawing the fuel/air mixture into the cylinder through the engine's inlet and fueling system.

Inlet valve closed

- Exhaust valve closed
- Fuel/air mixture compressed
- Piston moves up

2 **Compression** The piston moves back up the cylinder. This increases the pressure inside the cylinder, heating the fuel/air mixture.

Inlet valve closed

- Spark plug
- Exhaust valve closed
- Fuel/air mixture ignited
- Piston forced down

3 **Combustion** When the piston is near the top of its stroke, a spark plug fires. The burning gas expands, forcing the piston down the cylinder again.

Inlet valve closed

- Exhaust gas pushed out
- Exhaust valve open
- Piston moves up

4 **Exhaust** As the piston reaches the bottom, the exhaust valve opens. As it rises again, the piston forces waste gases out of the exhaust.

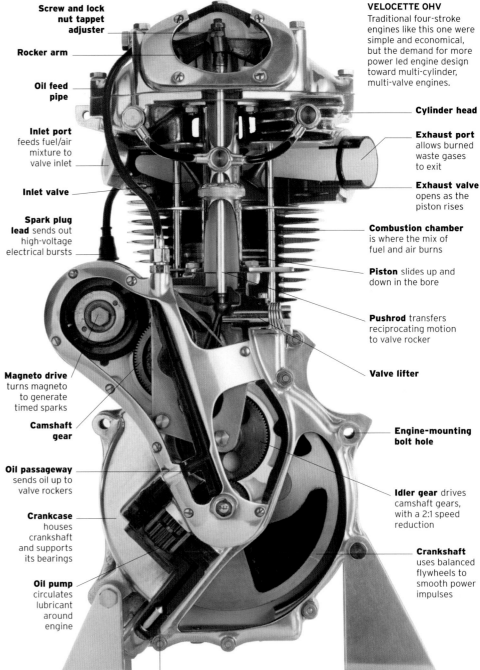

Screw and lock nut tappet adjuster

Rocker arm

Oil feed pipe

Inlet port feeds fuel/air mixture to valve inlet

Inlet valve

Spark plug lead sends out high-voltage electrical bursts

Magneto drive turns magneto to generate timed sparks

Camshaft gear

Oil passageway sends oil up to valve rockers

Crankcase houses crankshaft and supports its bearings

Oil pump circulates lubricant around engine

Non-return valve

VELOCETTE OHV
Traditional four-stroke engines like this one were simple and economical, but the demand for more power led engine design toward multi-cylinder, multi-valve engines.

Cylinder head

Exhaust port allows burned waste gases to exit

Exhaust valve opens as the piston rises

Combustion chamber is where the mix of fuel and air burns

Piston slides up and down in the bore

Pushrod transfers reciprocating motion to valve rocker

Valve lifter

Engine-mounting bolt hole

Idler gear drives camshaft gears, with a 2:1 speed reduction

Crankshaft uses balanced flywheels to smooth power impulses

FOUR-STROKE ENGINE COMPONENTS

CAMSHAFT
The flow of fuel and gases in a four-stroke engine is controlled by a camshaft opening the inlet and exhaust valves. The valves open once every two engine revolutions, so the camshaft rotates at half the engine's speed.

Bearing surfaces

Raised lobes push open the valves as the camshaft turns

Lubrication holes

Drive sprocket mounting

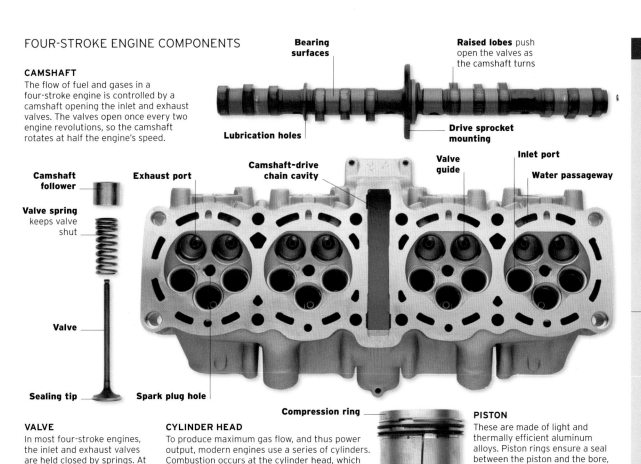

Camshaft follower

Valve spring keeps valve shut

Exhaust port

Camshaft-drive chain cavity

Valve guide

Inlet port

Water passageway

Valve

Sealing tip

Spark plug hole

VALVE
In most four-stroke engines, the inlet and exhaust valves are held closed by springs. At an engine speed of 10,000 rpm the valves will open and close 5,000 times every minute.

CYLINDER HEAD
To produce maximum gas flow, and thus power output, modern engines use a series of cylinders. Combustion occurs at the cylinder head, which contains the valves and the spark plugs. This makes it the hottest part of the engine, and most modern engines are liquid-cooled.

Compression ring

PISTON
These are made of light and thermally efficient aluminum alloys. Piston rings ensure a seal between the piston and the bore, preventing pressure and oil loss.

Piston skirt

OTHER ENGINES

ROTARY ENGINES
The advantages of the Wankel rotary engine include high power output, few moving parts, and minimal vibration. A three-sided rotor turns inside a chamber, allowing the four combustion processes to occur at the same time. The drawback is that lubrication is achieved only when oil burns with the fuel/air mix, producing high emissions.

ROTARY ENGINE

ELECTRIC POWER
Since the turn of the 21st century, concern over emissions from gasoline engines and the availability of hydrocarbon fuels has accelerated the development of electric bikes. Manufacturers offer a variety of products—and not just commuter bikes. There are electric motocross machines, plus racers that can exceed 150 mph (241 km/h).

TWO-STROKE ENGINES

Although two-stroke engines perform much the same cycle of events as four-stroke engines—intake, compression, combustion, and exhaust—this occurs during just two strokes of the piston. This means that the engine produces a power stroke for every revolution, rather than every other revolution, making its potential power output relatively high. Two-stroke engines are simpler in design than four-strokes and can be much smaller than four-stroke engines of similar power. However, as two-stroke engines are lubricated by oil mixed with the fuel, their exhaust fumes are much dirtier. This is why the two-stroke motorcycle engine has become less common in recent years.

LAMBRETTA LD 150
Simple and light, two-stroke engines, such as this compact 148cc, air-cooled, single-cylinder Lambretta power unit, were widely used to drive scooters.

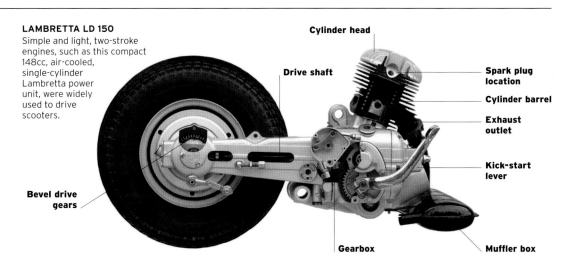

Cylinder head

Drive shaft

Spark plug location

Cylinder barrel

Exhaust outlet

Kick-start lever

Bevel drive gears

Gearbox

Muffler box

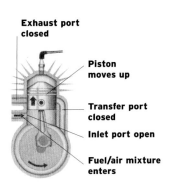

Exhaust port closed

Piston moves up

Transfer port closed

Inlet port open

Fuel/air mixture enters

1 Intake The fuel/air mixture is sucked through the open inlet port and into the crankcase by the upward movement of the piston.

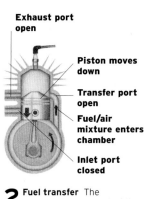

Exhaust port open

Piston moves down

Transfer port open

Fuel/air mixture enters chamber

Inlet port closed

2 Fuel transfer The downward movement of the piston forces the fuel/air mixture into the combustion chamber through the open transfer port.

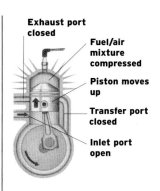

Exhaust port closed

Fuel/air mixture compressed

Piston moves up

Transfer port closed

Inlet port open

3 Compression The rising piston compresses the fuel/air mixture in the combustion chamber. Fresh fuel/air mixture enters the crankcase.

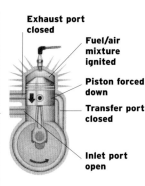

Exhaust port closed

Fuel/air mixture ignited

Piston forced down

Transfer port closed

Inlet port open

4 Combustion The spark plug ignites the fuel/air mixture in the combustion chamber, causing an explosion that forces the piston down.

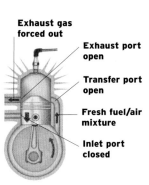

Exhaust gas forced out

Exhaust port open

Transfer port open

Fresh fuel/air mixture

Inlet port closed

5 Exhaust More fuel/air mixture, forced upward by the piston, enters the chamber and expels the exhaust gas, and the whole process repeats.

Engine Types

In designing motorcycle engines, engineers have had to meet particular requirements. Power units with their ancillary parts such as generators and radiators cannot be too bulky or heavy if the vehicle is to be manageable. They should perform reliably and appropriately for their intended use, whether that is high-speed riding, off-roading, or economy transportation; be smooth in operation; and, where power units are not enclosed, be pleasing to the eye. Added to all that, the design must be economically viable for the manufacturer to produce.

Brand identity is a factor as well: some makers like to make one type of engine their own, notable examples being BMW's flat-twins, Triumph's inline triples, and Harley-Davidson's V-twins. Others like

Honda have actively explored many technical avenues, some of them proving more fruitful than others.

Fashion has played a part, too. In the 1920s, sports riders clamored for single-cylinder engines with long piston strokes, while in the 1940s and 1950s the parallel-twin reigned. The 1970s saw the rise of the transverse four and a simultaneous resurgence of the nearly forgotten V-twin in Europe, while that had been the definitive American configuration for decades. In the 1980s, both the V-four and race-bred two-stroke twins were in vogue.

The history of motorcycles has thrown up a panoply of engine configurations, from small, simple two-strokes to large and complex multi-cylinder four-strokes.

RUDGE ULSTER SINGLE CYLINDER

Dates produced	1936 to 1939
Engine capacity	499cc
Maximum power output	28hp at 5,750rpm

Slim and relatively simple, the single has always been favored for economy road bikes and off-road competition machines, and was once commonly used in racing. Many enjoyed the punchy feel of high-performance four-stroke singles like the Rudge, but at larger capacities the thudding vibration could be annoying.

See Speed Club, pp.76-77

TRIUMPH HURRICANE INLINE TRIPLE

Dates produced	1973
Engine capacity	741cc
Maximum power output	58hp at 7,250rpm

Previously tried by both Scott and Moto Guzzi, the inline triple was established by the 1970s as an effective high-performance engine by Laverda, MV Agusta, and Triumph. Slimmer than a four, this engine suffers less from vibration than an inline twin and has a raw feel that endears it to sport riders.

See Standing Out, pp.194-95

HONDA GL1000 FLAT FOUR

Dates produced	1975 to 1980
Engine capacity	999cc
Maximum power output	80hp at 9,000rpm

Previously used by Zundapp and others, the flat-four configuration was chosen by Honda for its successful GL1000, launched in 1975. With excellent balance for carlike comfort, it placed weight usefully low in the chassis, was quiet thanks to water-cooling, and was ideal for use with shaft final drive.

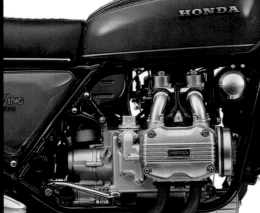

See Superbikes, pp.180-81

HONDA VF500 C30 MAGNA V-FOUR

Dates produced	1982 to 1985
Engine capacity	498cc
Configuration	70hp

Although V-Fours appeared in the 1930s, it was Honda that made the most of the layout in road and race machines. The engine's virtues include compactness relative to power output, the rigidity of a short crankshaft, and an inherent balance for smooth power delivery. Water cooling prevented overheating of the rear cylinders.

See Mile Eaters, pp.228-29

HARLEY-DAVIDSON PAN HEAD V-TWIN

Dates produced	1948 to 1960
Engine capacity	74 cu in (1,208cc)
Maximum power output	60 hp at 5,400 rpm

A layout used since the earliest days of motorcycles, when more than one cylinder was desirable to give power for racing or sidecar pulling. It fits neatly into a motorcycle frame and delivers torque in a pleasing, effortless fashion, with a syncopated exhaust beat. The V-twin engine's strongest exponent since 1909 has been Harley-Davidson.

See Roadburners, pp.150–51

TRIUMPH BONNEVILLE PARALLEL-TWIN

Dates produced	1959 to 1975
Engine capacity	649cc
Maximum power output	46 hp at 6,500 rpm

A popular configuration for sports and touring machines from the 1940s to the 1960s and still widely seen today. Crankshafts with 360-, 180-, and 270-degree firing intervals are used, giving different characteristics and exhaust notes. Larger 360-degree engines without a balancer mechanism, like this Triumph type, are prone to vibration.

See Sports Twins, pp.126–27

BMW R75/5 FLAT TWIN

Dates produced	1969 to 1973
Engine capacity	745cc
Maximum power output	50 hp at 6,200 rpm

Used from the early 1900s and favored by BMW since 1923, the flat-twin is often called a boxer engine, because of the way its pistons move back and forth relative to each other. The result is a near-perfect balance and smooth running, although transversely placed cylinders can ground in corners.

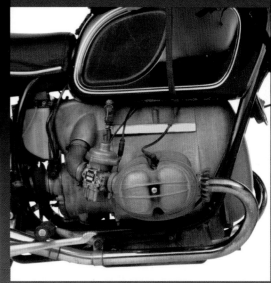

See Tourers, pp.170–71

HONDA F6C VALKYRIE FLAT SIX

Dates produced	1997 to 2003
Engine capacity	1,520cc
Maximum power output	98 hp at 6,000 rpm

To upgrade their successful GL1000, Honda introduced a water-cooled flat-six engine in the late 1980s. A similarly complex but silky-smooth and hushed power unit was also used in their Valkyrie high-performance cruiser in the 1990s. In both cases, the extreme bulk of the engine was not an issue.

See Cruisers, pp.250–51

YAMAHA FZ1 INLINE FOUR

Dates produced	2002 to 2005
Engine capacity	998cc
Maximum power output	142 hp at 10,000 rpm

Usually set transversely, this type of four-cylinder engine can generate high levels of power without vibration, is well exposed for air-cooling, and is relatively simple to produce. Seen in Italian racers of the 1950s, the transverse four was adopted by Honda and since the 1970s it has been much used by the big Japanese makers.

See Street Muscle, pp.266–67

BMW K1600GT INLINE SIX

Dates produced	from 2010
Engine capacity	1,649cc
Maximum power output	160 hp at 7,500 rpm

Even smoother than a four, an inline six can reach high rpm and generate colossal power. Honda adopted the six for 1960s Grand Prix racing, making very compact 250cc and 297cc versions. In the 2000s, BMW developed its 1,600cc six, which is remarkably narrow thanks to modern materials and manufacturing processes.

See Far and Fast, pp.270–71

Air-cooled Single

The single-cylinder, air-cooled power unit used in early Harley-Davidson machines is a typical four-stroke design of its time, also favored by other manufacturers. Its spray carburetor induction, magneto ignition, and cam-operated poppet valve were features that would be seen on motorcycle engines for decades to come. Though not powerful, this 494cc unit, installed in the 1912 Model X8A, was rugged and dependable.

F-HEADS

Single cylinder, air-cooled engines were suitably compact and light for installation on the rudimentary frames of early motorcycles. The combination of an automatic atmospheric inlet valve on the cylinder head with a mechanically operated exhaust valve was widely used on early, low-revving, four-stroke engines. On Harley-Davidsons, this configuration came to be known as the F-head, and was seen on both singles and V-twins. The last F-head twins were 1929 models. As engine speeds increased, the automatic valve could not keep up, and inlet valves had to be mechanically operated.

ENGINE SPECIFICATIONS	
Dates produced	1911 to 1912
Cylinders	One
Configuration	Inclined
Engine capacity	30 cu in (494cc)
Power output	4.3 hp
Type	Conventional four-stroke air-cooled gasoline engine
Head	Automatic inlet valve over mechanical exhaust valve
Cooling	Air
Fuel system	Schebler carburetor
Bore and stroke	3.3 in x 3.5 in (84 mm x 89 mm)
Compression ratio	not stated

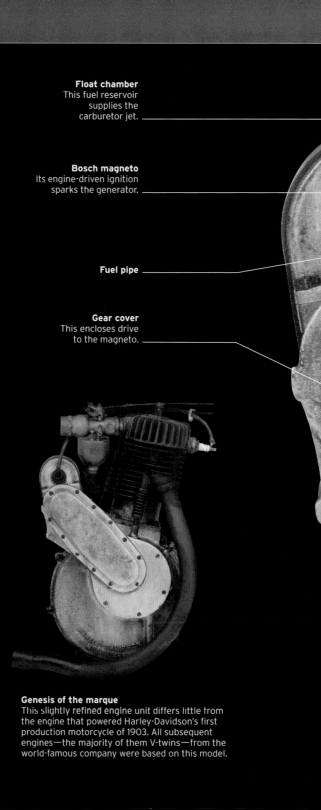

Float chamber
This fuel reservoir supplies the carburetor jet.

Bosch magneto
Its engine-driven ignition sparks the generator.

Fuel pipe

Gear cover
This encloses drive to the magneto.

Genesis of the marque
This slightly refined engine unit differs little from the engine that powered Harley-Davidson's first production motorcycle of 1903. All subsequent engines—the majority of them V-twins—from the world-famous company were based on this model.

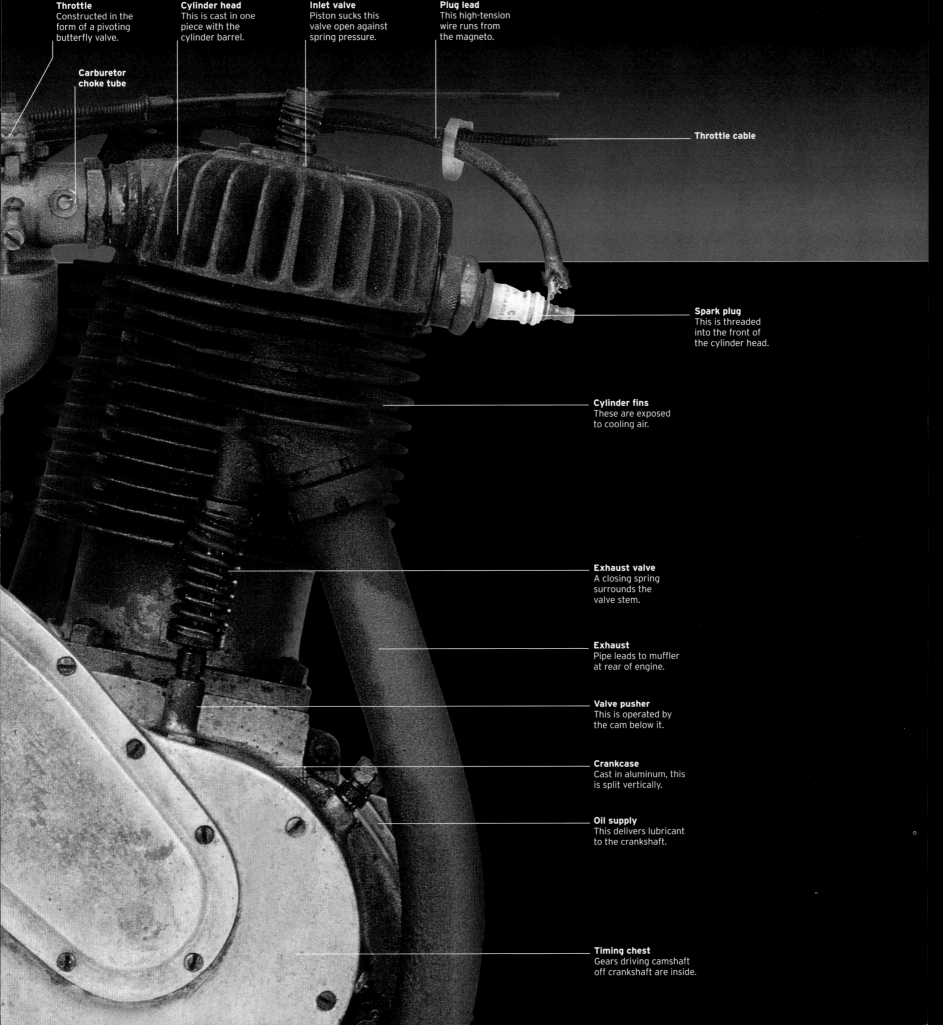

Throttle
Constructed in the form of a pivoting butterfly valve.

Carburetor choke tube

Cylinder head
This is cast in one piece with the cylinder barrel.

Inlet valve
Piston sucks this valve open against spring pressure.

Plug lead
This high-tension wire runs from the magneto.

Throttle cable

Spark plug
This is threaded into the front of the cylinder head.

Cylinder fins
These are exposed to cooling air.

Exhaust valve
A closing spring surrounds the valve stem.

Exhaust
Pipe leads to muffler at rear of engine.

Valve pusher
This is operated by the cam below it.

Crankcase
Cast in aluminum, this is split vertically.

Oil supply
This delivers lubricant to the crankshaft.

Timing chest
Gears driving camshaft off crankshaft are inside.

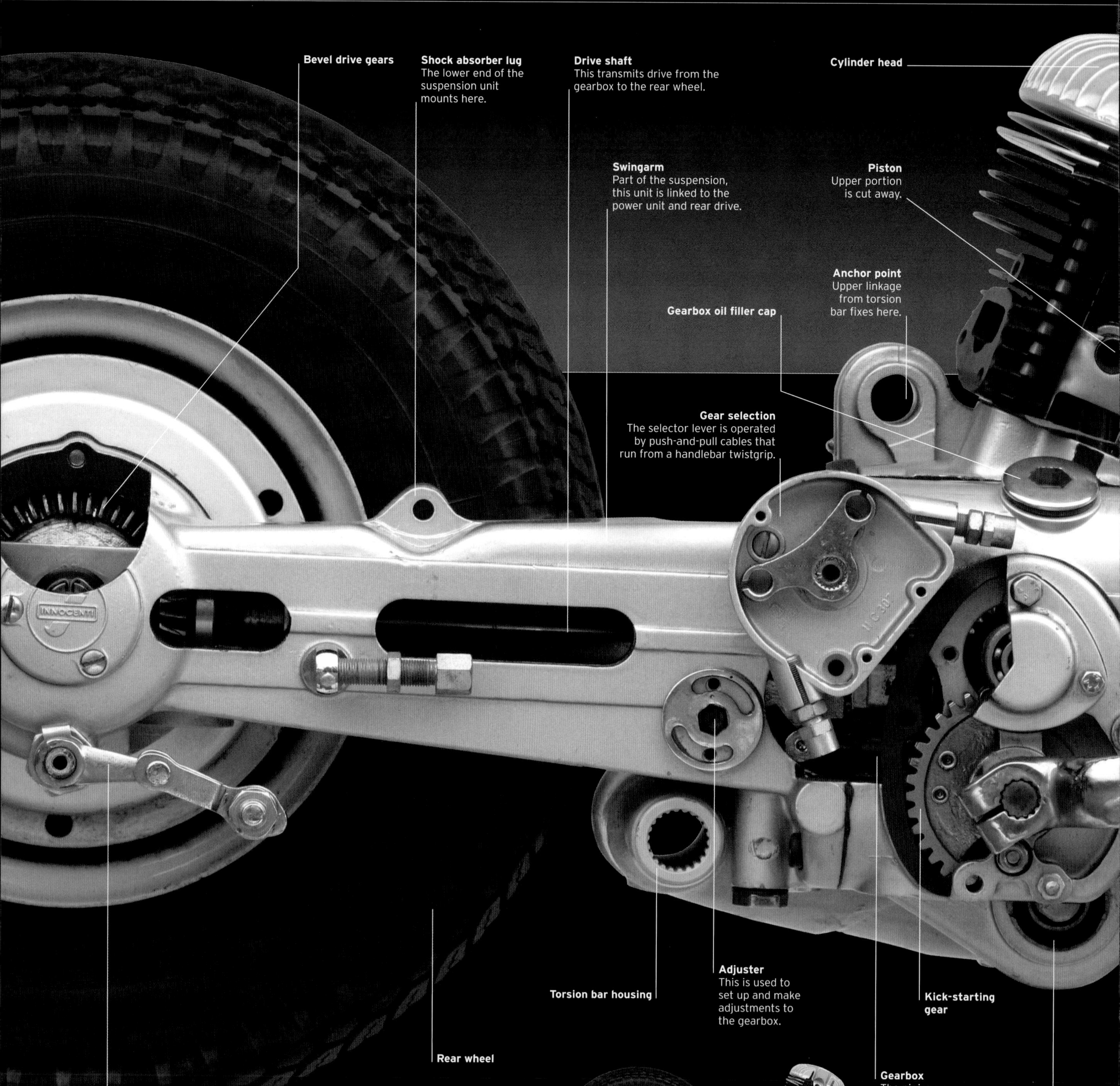

Bevel drive gears

Shock absorber lug
The lower end of the suspension unit mounts here.

Drive shaft
This transmits drive from the gearbox to the rear wheel.

Cylinder head

Swingarm
Part of the suspension, this unit is linked to the power unit and rear drive.

Piston
Upper portion is cut away.

Anchor point
Upper linkage from torsion bar fixes here.

Gearbox oil filler cap

Gear selection
The selector lever is operated by push-and-pull cables that run from a handlebar twistgrip.

Adjuster
This is used to set up and make adjustments to the gearbox.

Torsion bar housing

Kick-starting gear

Rear wheel

Gearbox
The pinions are arranged on two shafts.

Engine pivot point
Movement is damped by a rubber bushing.

Swinger
The engine and drive unit also act as the swingarm for the rear suspension, reducing weight and saving space. When the rear wheel goes over a bump, the whole unit pivots in the frame, its movement damped by a torsion bar and linkage levers, with an additional damper unit acting on the arm of the drive enclosure.

Brake operating arm

Lambretta LD 150
Air-cooled Two-stroke

Innocenti, manufacturer of the early Lambretta scooters, chose the light weight and simplicity of a two-stroke engine to propel its innovative vehicles, along with a compact, clean, maintenance-free, shaft-driven transmission. Pivoting the entire power unit, as well as having the drive housing double as a suspension arm, is typical of the ingenuity applied to Italian scooter design in the 1950s.

Spark plug location

Cylinder barrel
Ducting cools the cylinder with air from a crankshaft-mounted fan on the other side of the unit.

Exhaust ring
This secures the exhaust to the cylinder head.

Clutch adjuster
Turning a locknut releases the cap, to give access to the adjuster.

Exhaust
A downpipe leads from the exhaust port into the muffler.

Kick-start lever

Muffler box
Made from pressed steel, this has an outlet to the rear.

CLEAN MACHINE

Conventional for a 1950s two-stroke, the engine uses a single intake port to supply mixture to the crankcase below the piston. Two passages in the cylinder walls then transfer it to the combustion chamber, with the single exhaust port facing forward. The transversely disposed crankshaft carries the ignition and lighting generator on the left side, and transmits power to the clutch and gearbox on the right via bevel gears that take the drive through 90 degrees. Scooter design in the 1950s prioritized a clean machine that was easy to use and maintain over performance.

ENGINE SPECIFICATIONS	
Dates produced	1954 to 1956
Cylinders	Single
Configuration	Inclined
Engine capacity	148cc
Power output	6hp @ 4,750rpm
Type	Piston port two-stroke
Head	Valveless
Cooling	Air, with fan
Fuel System	Dell' Orto carburetor
Bore and Stroke	2.24 in x 2.28 in (57 mm x 58 mm)
Compression Ratio	6.5:1

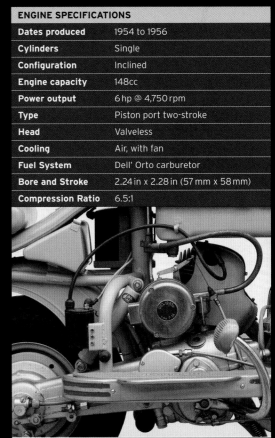

BSA A10 Golden Flash
Air-cooled Twin

Following the success of Triumph's 1938 500cc vertical twin, every other major British manufacturer adopted a similar engine format in the period just after World War II. The giant BSA company's sturdy and versatile 650cc Golden Flash unit remained in production throughout the 1950s.

SIDE BY SIDE

At the heart of the BSA twin is a crankshaft with its two big-end journals in line. The pistons rise and fall together, but one is on the compression stroke, while the other is on the exhaust stroke. Power delivery is smoother than a single, but an inherent lack of balance results in some vibration at higher rpm. The valves are activated by pushrods, from a single gear-driven camshaft in the crankcase behind the cylinders. The dry-sump lubrication system has a pump driven off the crankshaft that provides oil at high pressure to plain big-end and timing side main bearings, with an additional feed to the valve gear.

ENGINE SPECIFICATIONS	
Dates produced	1950 to 1962
Cylinders	Vertical
Configuration	360-degree twin
Engine capacity	646cc
Power output	35 hp @ 5,500 rpm
Type	ohv four-stroke
Head	Valves actuated by pushrods and rockers; two valves per cylinder
Cooling	Air
Fuel system	Amal Monobloc carburetor
Bore and stroke	2.73 in x 3.3 in (70 mm x 84 mm)
Compression ratio	6.5:1

Exhaust valve
This slides into a cast-iron guide.

Cylinder head
Made as a single iron casting.

Flange nuts
These attach the cylinder to the crankcase.

Lucas dynamo
This generates the charge for the battery.

Connecting rod

Engine mainshaft
A sprocket fits on here for drive takeoff.

Crankcase
Engine-mounting bolts pass through the holes around the edges.

Flywheel
This is bolted to the middle of the crankshaft.

Vertical joint
The crankcase is in two halves, with a vertical joint running down the center. A roller main bearing supports the crankshaft on the drive takeoff side.

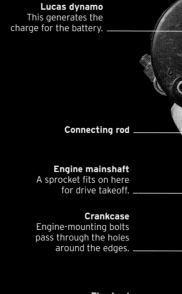

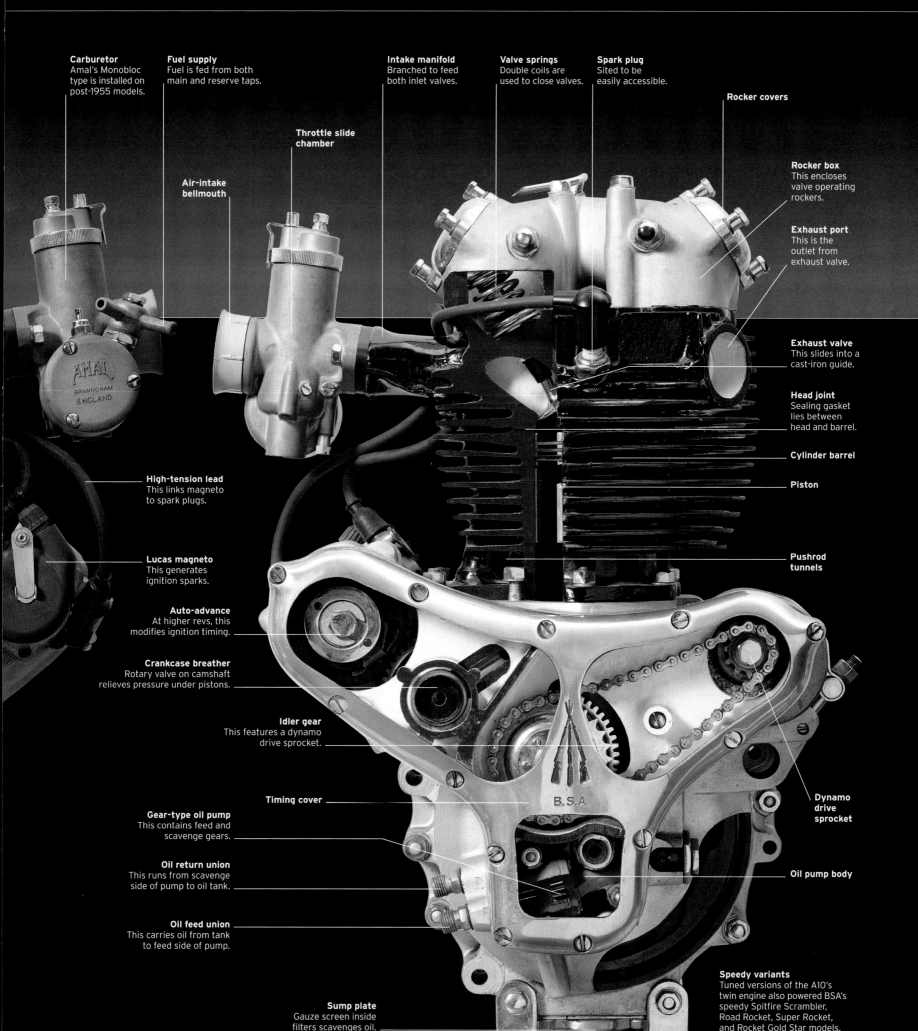

Carburetor
Amal's Monobloc type is installed on post-1955 models.

Fuel supply
Fuel is fed from both main and reserve taps.

Intake manifold
Branched to feed both inlet valves.

Valve springs
Double coils are used to close valves.

Spark plug
Sited to be easily accessible.

Rocker covers

Throttle slide chamber

Air-intake bellmouth

Rocker box
This encloses valve operating rockers.

Exhaust port
This is the outlet from exhaust valve.

Exhaust valve
This slides into a cast-iron guide.

Head joint
Sealing gasket lies between head and barrel.

Cylinder barrel

Piston

High-tension lead
This links magneto to spark plugs.

Lucas magneto
This generates ignition sparks.

Auto-advance
At higher revs, this modifies ignition timing.

Crankcase breather
Rotary valve on camshaft relieves pressure under pistons.

Idler gear
This features a dynamo drive sprocket.

Timing cover

Gear-type oil pump
This contains feed and scavenge gears.

Oil return union
This runs from scavenge side of pump to oil tank.

Oil feed union
This carries oil from tank to feed side of pump.

Pushrod tunnels

Dynamo drive sprocket

Oil pump body

Sump plate
Gauze screen inside filters scavenges oil.

Speedy variants
Tuned versions of the A10's twin engine also powered BSA's speedy Spitfire Scrambler, Road Rocket, Super Rocket, and Rocket Gold Star models.

Vincent Rapide
V-twin

The 1,000cc V-twin engine made by the small Vincent HRD factory in Stevenage, England, powered the world's fastest production motorcycles. Unlike any other power unit of the 1950s, this engine was the creation of company proprietor Philip Vincent, a design idealist, in collaboration with brilliant Australian engineer Phil Irving.

OFFSET CYLINDERS

Unveiled in 1947 to gain export sales for postwar "austerity Britain," the Rapide twin engine had an antecedent in Vincent's 1938 1,000cc twin. However, intensive work during World War II resulted in a more powerful, sophisticated, and neat-looking unit. The classic "V" configuration of the cylinders, at 55 degrees in this instance, was chosen to minimize the engine's height and width as well as give a relatively vibration-free power delivery. The connecting rods' big-end bearings are placed side-by-side on a single crankpin, so the rear cylinder's bore is offset to the right of the front one.

ENGINE SPECIFICATIONS	
Dates produced	1947-55
Cylinders	50-degree V-twin ohv four-stroke
Configuration	"V"
Engine capacity	998cc
Power output	45 bhp (34 Kw) @ 5,300 rpm
Type	Conventional four-stroke, air-cooled gasoline engine
Head	ohv actuated by pushrods and rocker arms; two valves per cylinder
Cooling	Air
Fuel system	Type 276 Amal carburetors
Bore and stroke	84 mm x 90 mm
Compression ratio	7:1

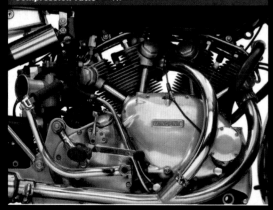

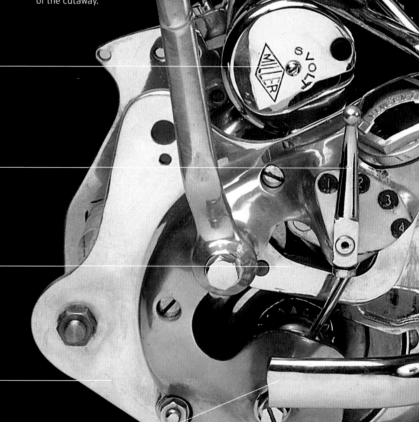

Deep-skirted aluminum piston
This has three sealing rings.

Inlet valve
Valve has an austenitic cast iron seat.

Oil pipe
Oil is fed to the rockers via this pipe.

Valve springs
Placing the springs above the valve operating rockers keeps them cool.

Compact and strong
Many internal details are revealed on this partially cut-away display engine (red areas). It can be seen that the whole unit, with its built-in four-speed gearbox, is very compact for a 1,000cc engine. It is also a strong enough structure to support Vincent's "frameless" chassis.

Pivots for the valve rockers
These locate in tunnels within the cylinder head casting.

Cutaway of cylinder

Gear shift lever
This is shown raised through 90 degrees to give a clear view of the cutaway.

Six-volt dynamo
Driven off the primary chain to charge the battery, a voltage regulator sits on top of the dynamo.

Gear ratio indicator

Selector mechanism
This is part of the four-speed gearbox.

Rear engine plates
These solid plates provide pivot point for cantilevered rear suspension.

Section of kick-start lever

Exhaust valve
This seats on an aluminum bronze insert.

Valve clearance adjusters
These are situated on the outer arms of the valve rockers.

Pushrod
Short pushrods activate the rockers engaged midway along valve stems.

Exhaust pipe

Inspection cap
This provides easy access to the valve clearance adjuster.

Cylinder head

Anchor point
The engine is bolted to the combined oil tank and bike's upper frame member here.

Bakelite spark plug cap

Valve spring top cover

Aluminum cylinder barrel
This has an iron bore liner.

High tension leads
These extend from the magneto to the spark plugs.

Exhaust collar

Pushrod tube

Inlet and exhaust cams
These are together on the camshafts, set high to reduce the pushrod length.

Metering jet
A small opening controls the flow of oil to the camshafts and cam followers.

Outrigger plate
This supports the camshaft and cam follower spindles within the timing chest.

Auto-advance mechanism on magneto driving gear

Large idler gear
This drives the camshafts at half crankshaft speed.

Oil pump
This is driven off the mainshaft by worm gears.

Mainshaft pinion
This provides drive for the camshafts and ignition magneto.

Oil pressure relief valve
This is situated at the crankshaft feed point.

Oil pipes
Supply lubricant to engine and return it to the oil tank after it circulates.

VINCENT

Inline Four

Since the 1970s, the inline four-cylinder configuration, set across the frame, has been widely adopted for motorcycles. In conjunction with overhead camshafts, the format can generate high rpm and power output while its frequent power impulses result in smooth running. Over the years, other developments, such as electronically controlled fuel injection and water-cooling, have boosted power from ever more compact units.

TECHNICAL WIZARDRY

Based on a cross-plane crankshaft with 90-degree firing intervals developed to give linear power delivery on Yamaha's M1 MotoGP racer, the R1 unit also features highly advanced fueling technology controlled by numerous sensors. A fly-by-wire system provides instant throttle response and electrically powered movement of the air intake funnels ensure that maximum torque is generated at any given engine speed. An upper set of funnels that make the intake tracts longer at low rpm move upward to effectively make the tract shorter at high rpm.

ENGINE SPECIFICATIONS	
Dates produced	From 2009
Cylinders	four
Configuration	inline
Engine capacity	998cc
Power output	152 hp @ 12,600 rpm
Type	four-stroke, gasoline engine
Head	double overhead camshafts, four valves per cylinder
Cooling	Water
Fuel system	electronically controlled injectors
Bore and stroke	78 mm x 52.2 mm
Compression ratio	12.7:1

YAMAHA

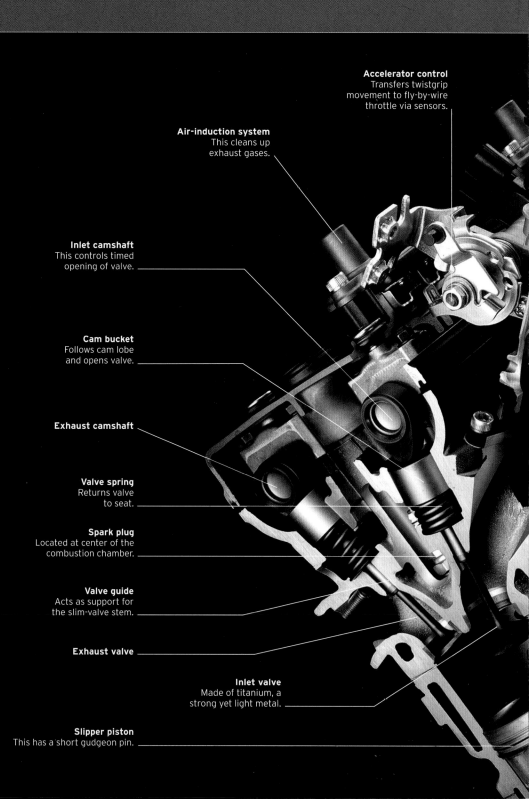

Accelerator control
Transfers twistgrip movement to fly-by-wire throttle via sensors.

Air-induction system
This cleans up exhaust gases.

Inlet camshaft
This controls timed opening of valve.

Cam bucket
Follows cam lobe and opens valve.

Exhaust camshaft

Valve spring
Returns valve to seat.

Spark plug
Located at center of the combustion chamber.

Valve guide
Acts as support for the slim-valve stem.

Exhaust valve

Inlet valve
Made of titanium, a strong yet light metal.

Slipper piston
This has a short gudgeon pin.

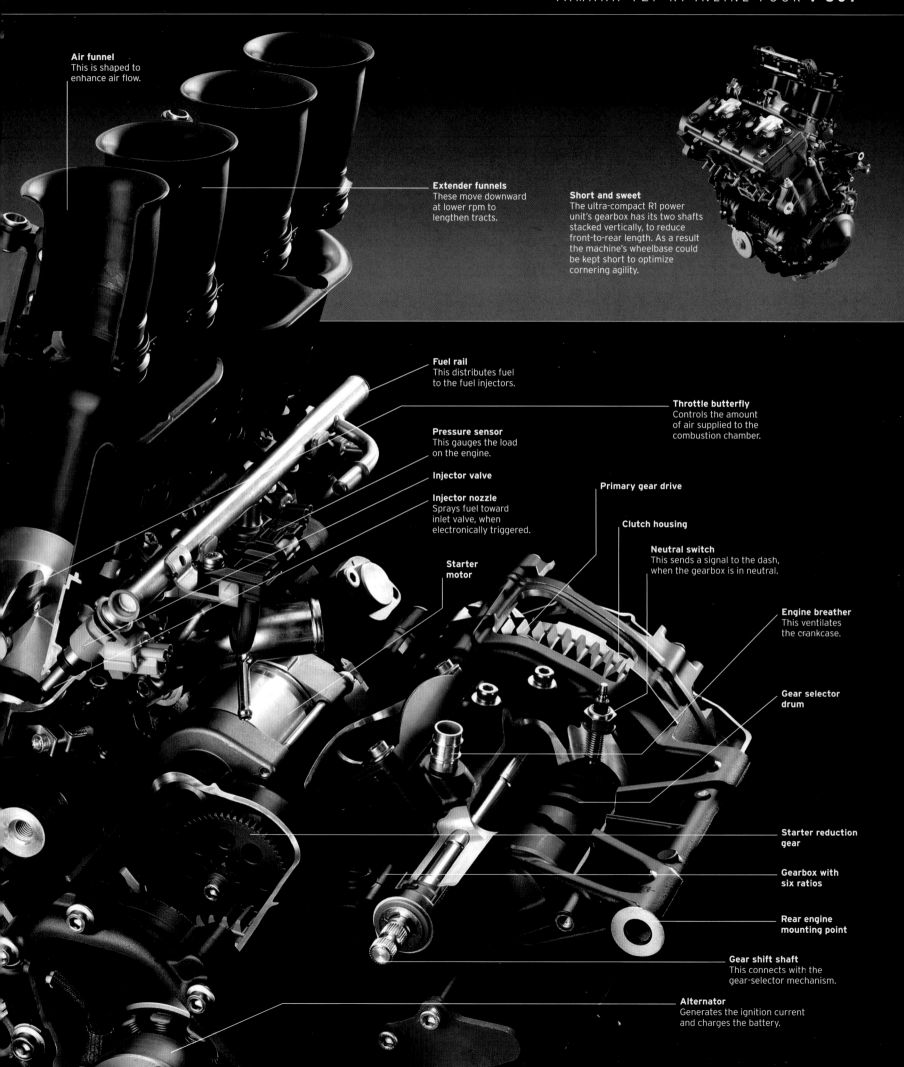

Air funnel
This is shaped to enhance air flow.

Extender funnels
These move downward at lower rpm to lengthen tracts.

Short and sweet
The ultra-compact R1 power unit's gearbox has its two shafts stacked vertically, to reduce front-to-rear length. As a result the machine's wheelbase could be kept short to optimize cornering agility.

Fuel rail
This distributes fuel to the fuel injectors.

Throttle butterfly
Controls the amount of air supplied to the combustion chamber.

Pressure sensor
This gauges the load on the engine.

Injector valve

Primary gear drive

Injector nozzle
Sprays fuel toward inlet valve, when electronically triggered.

Clutch housing

Neutral switch
This sends a signal to the dash, when the gearbox is in neutral.

Starter motor

Engine breather
This ventilates the crankcase.

Gear selector drum

Starter reduction gear

Gearbox with six ratios

Rear engine mounting point

Gear shift shaft
This connects with the gear-selector mechanism.

Alternator
Generates the ignition current and charges the battery.

Glossary

ABS (Antilock Braking System)
A braking system that stops the wheels from locking during braking, so the bike can be steered away from danger in an emergency.

Air-cooled
Engine cooled by air passing around the cylinders and the lubricating oil.

Air filter
A felt or paper component that cleans air of particles before it enters the engine.

Air-ride suspension
Suspension system that uses gas or pumped air as the shock-absorbing medium to help keep the machine level on rough roads.

Alternator
Electrical generator that uses magnetism to convert mechanical energy into alternating-current electrical energy to power electrical circuits on the bike. *See* dynamo.

Anodizing
Oxide-coating technique that increases corrosion and wear resistance. So called because the treated part serves as the anode of an electrical circuit in this electrolytic process.

Anti-dive
Reduction of the compressing of the front suspension under braking forces. It is often enhanced with favorable suspension design.

Anti-surge baffle
A plate that stops liquids from shifting position inside a reservoir, particularly an oil sump, as a result of the motorcycle's braking, turning, or accelerating.

Ape hangers
Handlebars so high that the rider's hands are above his or her shoulders. Popular with US-style choppers.

Atmospheric inlet valve
Inlet valve that is opened by the vacuum in the cylinder created by the falling piston. Used on very early machines.

Automatic transmission
A clutchless transmission that automatically selects the appropriate gear for the rider.

Backing it in
The practice of changing down the gearbox, and using the brakes to unsettle the rear end of a machine on the approach to corners, to reduce braking distances and get on the power earlier. Used by Supermoto racers.

Bearing
A device that provides a support between the fixed and moving parts of a machine, or between rotating parts, such as the connecting rod to crankshaft.

Bell mouth
Air-intake trumpet attached to carburetor.

Bhp (brake horsepower)
Gross bhp is a measurement of the power output of a standalone engine. Net bhp is an engine's output after the attachment of ancillary equipment, such as the alternator. Bhp is measured by applying a special brake to the crankshaft.

Big-end bearing
The larger, lower bearing of the connecting rod that links the pistons to the crankshaft.

Blown (engine)
A general term for an engine that has its power boosted by a turbocharger or by a supercharger.

Bore
A measurement of the diameter of an engine cylinder.

Braided brake lines
Hydraulic brake hoses covered in braided steel mesh, which protects them from debris, and which also contains the expansion of the hose when hydraulic pressure is applied.

Brooklands
The world's first specially built race circuit, near Weybridge, Surrey, UK. It was in use from 1909 to 1939.

Butterfly valve
A disc that pivots along its diameter within a duct, forming a valve that can be opened and closed to regulate the flow of air into an engine component, such as a carburetor.

Café racer
Motorcycles built and modified to resemble racing machines from the 1950s and 1960s, with polished alloy tanks and megaphone exhausts. Reputedly, their owners used to race them between cafés in London and Brighton—hence the name.

Camshaft
Shaft with eccentrically shaped rotors that convert rotational into linear movement to operate valves in a four-stroke engine. They can be mounted low in the engine casings (cam in block), singly above the cylinder head (single overhead cam), or doubly (double overhead cam).

Capacity
Displacement or swept volume of an engine, measured in cubic centimeters or cubic inches.

Carburetor
A device that mixes fuel and air into a combustible vapor and delivers it to the engine.

Catalytic converter
A device added to the exhaust of engines that run on unleaded gasoline. It uses a chemical catalyst to stimulate reactions that convert poisonous exhaust gases, such as carbon monoxide, oxides of nitrogen, and various hydrocarbons, into harmless ones.

Center stand
Stand attached to the frame that holds the motorcycle vertically upright when parked. *See* side stand.

Choke
A carburetor valve that temporarily restricts air flow, so that the fuel/air mixture is fuel-rich and therefore easier to ignite when the engine is cold.

Chopper
Highly modified motorcycle, often with extended front forks, a hard tail, and high-rise handlebars, popular in the US.

Clincher rims
Type of wheel rim used with some early inflatable tires.

Clip-on engine
An engine that attaches to a conventional bicycle frame.

Clip-ons
Low-mounted handlebars that usually attach directly to the fork legs.

Clutch
A device that disconnects the engine from the transmission so that a different gear can be selected. Early machines had only optional clutches, as early types were unreliable and prone to slipping.

Coil ignition
Near-universal ignition system to fire the spark plugs, using a transformer with twin windings.

Combination
Motorcycle with a sidecar, or chair, also known as an outfit.

Combustion chamber
The space at the top of an engine's cylinder, into which the fuel/air mixture is compressed by the piston when at its high point, and where the spark plug is located to initiate combustion.

Compression ratio
The ratio between the volume of one cylinder and the combustion chamber, when the piston is at the bottom of its stroke, and the volume of the combustion chamber alone, when the piston is at the top of its stroke.

Compression ring
See piston ring.

Compressor
A device that increases the pressure of a gas, by compressing it to reduce its volume. Compressors are used in turbochargers and superchargers to increase the performance of the engine.

Connecting rod
A mechanism that connects an engine's piston to the crankshaft.

Contact breaker
Switch on low-tension side of the ignition circuit that controls the timing of the spark in the high-tension circuit.

Counter steering
The technique of applying steering torque in the opposite direction to that required. The forces generated when doing this will lean the machine over in the direction required, which in turn generates camber and turning forces to propel it in the desired direction.

Country of origin
The country in which a motorcycle is manufactured.

Cradle frame
A motorcycle frame that cradles the bottom of the engine.

Crankcase
The lower part of the cylinder block that houses the crankshaft.

Crank pulley
The main pulley at the end of an engine's crankshaft. It drives ancillary devices, such as the alternator and the water pump.

Crankshaft
The main engine shaft that converts the reciprocating (up and down) motion of the pistons into the rotary motion needed to turn the wheels.

Crash bungs
Sacrificial nylon bobbins that bolt to the fairing of the motorcycle to protect it in the event of a crash.

Cubic centimeters (cc)
The standard volumetric measurement of cylinder capacity—and therefore of engine size.

Cubic inches (cu in)
A volumetric measurement of cylinder capacity—and therefore of engine size—for engines manufactured in the US, such as those produced by Harley-Davidson.

Customize
Modifying a production machine to suit an individual's requirements.

Cylinder
Usually a cylindrical bore, within which an engine's pistons move up and down.

Cylinder block
The body, of usually cast metal, into which cylinders are bored to carry the pistons in an internal combustion engine, and to which the cylinder head or heads attach.

Cylinder head
The upper part of an engine, attached to the top of the cylinder block. It contains the spark plugs that ignite the fuel in the cylinders and usually the valves.

Dakar Rally
An annual, off-road race, formally known as the Paris–Dakar Rally, with separate prizes for motorcycles, cars, and trucks. From 1979 to 2007, it ran from Paris, France to Dakar, Senegal. Canceled in 2008, owing to political events, it has been held in South America since 2009.

Daytona International Speedway
A motorsports race track in Daytona Beach, Florida, opened in 1959. The AMA Pro Superbike Championships are held here.

Desmodromic valve gear
An engine valve that is closed mechanically by a leverage system, rather than by a spring. It gives more exact control of valve motion, but is costly to manufacture and so tends to be reserved for racing engines. Most often seen on Ducatis.

Diamond frame
Early type of motorcycle frame with a profile resembling a diamond, where the engine serves as part of the structure.

DIN figures
A measure of an engine's power output. It is defined by Germany's Deutsches Institut für Normung.

Direct injection
See fuel injection.

Dirt track
Racing on loose-surface tracks, popular in North America.

Disc brakes
A braking system in which each wheel hub contains a disc that rotates with the wheel, and is gripped by brake pads to slow the machine.

Distributor
A device that switches and distributes a high-tension current between spark plugs. Sometimes it is also used to control the ignition timing.

Double overhead camshaft (dohc)
See camshaft.

Downdraft carburetor
A carburetor in which fuel is fed into a downward current of air.

Drag coefficient
A number that provides a measure of how aerodynamic a bike is. "Drag" is the resistance caused by air as an object passes through it.

Drag racing
A motor sport in which motorbikes (and cars) compete to see which can cover a set distance fastest in a straight line from a standing start.

Drivebelt
A belt that drives various devices that are in or attached to the engine, including the alternator. It is sometimes used as a primary drive to the rear wheel.

Driveshaft
A revolving shaft that takes power from the engine to the wheels.

Drivetrain
The group of mechanical assemblies—engine, transmission, driveshafts, and differentials—that generate and harness power. Sometimes "drivetrain" is used to refer to just the engine and the transmission.

Drum brake
A braking system, largely supplanted by disc brakes, in which braking shoes are pressed against the inner surface of a drum that is attached to the bike's wheel.

Dry-sump engine
An engine without a conventional sump or oil pump, where oil is stored in a tank elsewhere, pumped to the bearings, and then scavenged from the bottom of the engine back to the oil tank.

Dual-circuit brakes
A braking system that has two independent hydraulic circuits, to retain braking capability if one circuit fails.

Duolever suspension
Also known as Hossack/Fior suspension, this system uses a rigid wheel carrier mounted on wishbone-shaped arms and trailing links to give what the designer, Norman Hossack, describes as the effect of "steered upright". It completely removes the action of the suspension from the steering forces. Used on BMW models.

Duplex cradle frame
A cradle frame with twin front downtubes.

Dynamo
Direct-current generator, largely superseded by the use of alternators.

Earles forks
Type of leading-link fork where the pivot point is behind the wheel, so that the front of the machine can rise under braking. Designed by Ernest Earles, it was used by BMW.

Enduro
Off-road competition against the clock, usually over long distances.

Engine cycle
An indication of the operating cycle of the engine, usually two- or four-stroke.

Exhaust manifold
Tubular pipes that carry waste gases from the cylinders to the exhaust pipe.

Exhaust port
A passageway in the cylinder head, leading from the exhaust valve(s) to the exhaust manifold.

Exhaust valve
Valve that permits exhaust gases to leave the combustion chamber, and enter the exhaust.

Factory custom
A modified machine, sold as new from the factory.

Fairing
Aerodynamic bodywork for a motorcycle, designed to improve top speed or rider comfort.

Featherbed frame
Patented, twin-loop, welded frame, designed by the McCandless brothers for Norton, with vertically sprung swingarm suspension and a heavily braced headstock.

Final drive
The drive to the driven wheel, usually via a chain, shaft, or toothed belt.

Flathead
Type of 1950s Harley-Davidson V-twin engine. Other Harley-Davidson engines have names such as "Knucklehead," "Panhead," "Ironhead," and "Shovelhead."

Flat-twin engine
An engine with two cylinders mounted on opposite sides of the crankshaft, at 180 degrees relative to each other. Engines with this horizontally opposed cylinder configuration are sometimes (wrongly) called "boxers," because pistons in opposing pairs of cylinders move toward and away from each other alternately, as if trading punches. True "boxers" are where two pistons share a common bore, and move toward each other at the same time.

Flywheel
Heavy disc attached to the crankshaft that smooths firing impulses and power surges of the engine.

Foot pegs
The pivoting footrests for the rider and pillion passenger.

Forecar
Early three-wheeled vehicle with two front wheels on a motorcycle frame. Passengers sat above the front axle.

Four-stroke engine
Predominant type of motorcycle engine. There are four stages in the power cycle, which occupies two crankshaft rotations: intake, compression, combustion, and exhaust. Each of these is governed by the upward or downward movements, or "strokes," of the piston.

Fuel injection
A fuel-supply system, universal to new motorcycles, that dispenses with the need for a carburetor. Fuel is pumped from the gas tank and sprayed by injectors straight into the engine's inlet ports, where it mixes with air before being burned in the cylinder. In diesel and direct-injection gasoline engines, fuel is injected straight into the cylinder, rather than into the inlet port. Fuel injection gives a better combination of engine economy, power, and flexibility.

Garden gate
Popular name for the plunger-sprung frames used on Norton machines from the late 1930s.

Gas turbine
A jet-type, rotary engine that draws its energy from the continuous burning of a flow of fuel/air mixture, which drives a turbine. It has been used experimentally, but is too slow-reacting to directly replace the reciprocating engine.

Gear ratio
The ratio of the turning speed of a driving and driven gear, or the cumulative ratios of a series of gears.

Girder fork
A type of early front fork with rigid beams that is attached to the steering head by parallel links, which allow steering movement.

Hang on the cable
Motorcycle racer's term for riding as fast as your talent allows.

Head
See cylinder head.

Headstock
Front uppermost tube on a motorcycle frame, which contains a series of bearings, and attaches the front steering spindle to the main frame.

Heat shield
Rigid or flexible layers of heat-resistant material that protect a machine's components or bodywork from excessive engine—or exhaust-generated heat.

Helical gear
A gear with a spiral, or semi-spiral, meshing face.

High side
Type of motorcycle accident where the rear wheel breaks away but then regains traction, while the machine is leaning, causing it to violently flip over, so that the rider falls off on the opposite (high) side.

Hog
A nickname for a Harley-Davidson.

Homologation
A rigorous testing program that new motorcycles must undergo to ensure that they meet construction and usage-and-type approval rules in a particular country; only then can they be legally ridden on the road.

Horsepower (hp)
Horsepower originally gave a measure of the energy output of steam engines in terms of the equivalent amount of pulling power provided by a draft horse.

Hub-center steering
Steering system that uses a forward-facing swingarm and the front wheel pivoting around its center point with a fixed axle. It separates braking, steering, and suspension functions.

Hugger
A mudguard that closely follows the rear tire profile, in order to reduce the spray of dirt off the rear tire onto the rest of the machine.

Hybrid
A form of propulsion technology that combines the use of both electric and gasoline, or (rarely) diesel power. Electric power slashes emissions in urban riding as the braking energy is recycled as electricity, while the fossil-fuel power unit provides enough sustained power for highway cruising, and recharges the battery.

Hydraulic damper
A damper is the correct name for a shock absorber, which dissipates the energy of a the suspension movement and converts it hydraulically, via internal oil, into quickly dissipated heat.

Hydroplaning
Highly dangerous situation in which the tires rise off the road surface and start to run on the surface of standing water, giving almost no grip and reducing the potential to brake. Speed and tire-tread depth, rather than just water depth, are often more important causes of hydroplaning.

Idle-speed positioner
A device that optimizes the rate at which the engine runs at idle, when the throttle is closed, to maximize fuel efficiency.

Ignition timing
The timing of the spark plug firing, relative to the crankshaft and piston position.

Induction system
The apparatus through which air passes as it enters the engine.

Inlet-over-exhaust
Early engine-valve layout, where the exhaust valve was mounted to one side of the engine, and the mechanically operated inlet valve was above the exhaust.

Inlet port
The route within a cylinder head through which the fuel/air mixture passes to the inlet valve.

Inlet trumpet
A trumpet-shaped, engine air intake that exploits the effects of wave motion to force more air into the cylinders. *See* bell-mouth.

Inlet valve
A valve that allows the passage of air and fuel vapor from inlet into the engine.

Inline engine
Engine layout in which the cylinders are mounted in a row, in line with the wheels of the machine.

Intercooler
A radiator that cools the compressed air from a turbocharger or supercharger, before it enters the engine. This increases power and enhances reliability.

ISDT
International Six-Day Trial, a famous off-road event regarded as a tough test of both man and machine. Won by Steve McQueen in 1964.

Isolastic
Patented name for engine/swingarm rubber mountings, used by Norton on early Commando models.

JAP
British engine-maker, founded in 1903 by John A. Prestwich.

Keystone frame
American term for diamond frame, where the engine serves as part of the structure.

Kick-start
A sprung crank that is attached to the transmission, which allows the rider to start the machine with his foot.

Leading link
Early design of front suspension, with the axle mounted at the front of two short, sprung links that pivot at the base of solid forks.

Leading-link fork
Suspension system that suspends the wheel on a link with a pivot point at the rear of the wheel axle. Used by early motorcycles.

Leaf spring
A spring comprising strips of high-yield-strength, "spring" steel, clamped together, with one end fixed and the other attached to the sprung component.

Liquid cooling
Engine cooling with specific water jackets in the engine block and radiators.

Loop frame
Early frame design, in which the down-tube curves under the engine to become a seat post.

LPG
Liquified petroleum gas, a fuel that can be used in largely unmodified gasoline engines, and gives reduced noxious emissions.

MAG
Swiss engine-maker Motosacoche Accacias Geneva; also made entire machines.

Magneto
Engine-driven electrical generator that uses permanent magnets to create a high-tension spark, without the need for an external battery. Largely superseded by coil ignition.

Maxi scooter
Large-engined and commodious scooters.

Megaphone
Outwardly tapered, high-performance (and noisy) exhaust muffler.

Monkey bike
Small motorcycle with tiny wheels, usually powered by an engine of less than 50cc, sometimes with a folding frame. Name first used by Honda for its 1961 Z100 machine.

Monobloc
An engine design in which the cylinders are cast together as a single unit. This improves the mechanical rigidity of the engine, and the reliability of the sealing.

Monocoque
Frame made up as one unit from sheet material, used, for example, in Vespa scooters.

Monoshock
Rear suspension configuration, using a single, rear shock absorber/spring.

Monza circuit
Race track, opened in 1922, in Monza, northern Italy. Major biking events here include the Italian Motorcycle Grand Prix and Superbike World Championship (SBK).

Moped
A motorcycle of less than 50cc displacement, often with pedal assistance.

Motocross
Off-road racing over a circuit, also known as scrambling, or Moto-X.

Moto-GP
Grand Prix motorcycle racing.

Muffler
A chamber placed along the route of the exhaust pipe, and designed to reduce exhaust noise.

Muscle bikes
Naked machines with large, powerful engines and superlative low-speed performance.

Naked machine
One without any adornment, or fairings, except an instrument binnacle.

Open-cradle frame
Frame without tubes running under the engine, which acts as a stressed member.

Overhead camshaft
Camshaft(s) mounted above the cylinder head.

Overhead valve
Valves situated above the combustion chamber, operated by pushrods that are actuated by a camshaft situated below the cylinder head.

Over-square
An engine with a greater cylinder bore than piston stroke.

Paralever suspension
BMW's version of a parallel link for its shaft-drive machines, where a trailing arm runs parallel to the shaft drive, reducing the tendency for the rear end of the machine to rise up under acceleration—also used by Moto Guzzi.

Parallel-twin
Twin-cylinder engine with cylinders mounted vertically and parallel with each other.

Pillion passenger
Rear passenger on motorcycle.

Piston
Component that moves up and down inside the engine cylinder and which, on the combustion stroke, transfers force from the expanding gas to the crankshaft via a connecting rod.

Piston ring
Open-ended ring that fits into a groove in the outer surface of an engine's piston, sealing the combustion chamber. Piston rings also cool the piston by transferring heat to the cylinder wall, and regulate oil consumption.

Planetary gearset
US term for an epicyclic gearbox, in which small pinions revolve around a central "sun" gear and mesh with an outer ring gear.

Plunger suspension
Early rear suspension design, where the rear axle movement is controlled by twin vertical springs.

Port timing
In two-stroke engines, the critical moment, when the ports are covered and uncovered by the piston.

Power sliding
Practice of opening the throttle early on the exit of the corner and spinning the rear wheel faster than the speed of travel. This technique is used in racing to exploit the characteristics of the racing tires, and exit corners faster.

Pre-unit
An engine and gearbox that are not housed in the same casting. Often used for early motorcycles.

Primary drive
Drive system that transfers power from the engine to the clutch and gearbox.

Privateers
Racers without manufacturer backing.

Propshaft
A contraction of propeller shaft; a shaft that conveys engine torque from the rear of the transmission to the rear wheel.

Pushrod
Rod used to transmit linear motion, most often found in the valve gear to transmit movement from camshaft to rocker arm.

Pushrod engine
An engine in which the valves are not operated directly via the camshaft, but via intermediate rods. This allows the valves and camshaft to be widely separated.

Race replica
Road-going sports bike, dressed up to look like a racing machine.

Radiator
Heat-exchanger, used to cool liquids by presenting a large surface to a flow of air.

Ratting
The practice of stripping back a production machine to meet the minimum legal requirements, and painting it matt black.

Rear set
Racing-style footrests, added to the rear of the machine to allow the rider to adopt a racing crouch.

Reciprocating engine
Also known as a piston engine. Converts the up and down (or "reciprocating") motion of pistons to the rotary motion needed by the wheels.

Redline
The maximum speed at which an engine is designed to operate without incurring damage. It is usually indicated by a red line on the tachometer dial.

Reed valve
Automatic one-way valve, used in two-stroke engines, which allows the fuel/air mixture to flow from the carburetor into the crankcase.

Regenerative braking
A system found in electric and hybrid machines in which electric traction motors are operated as generators during braking, providing braking force while generating current to recharge the battery pack.

Rev
Short for revolutions per minute, a measure of engine speed.

Rigid frame
Motorcycle frame without rear suspension.

Rising rate
Suspension that becomes harder to compress the further it is compressed.

Road racing
Racing on public road circuits. Popular in Ireland and the Isle of Man.

Rocker arm
A pivoted lever, one end of which is raised and lowered by the camshaft, either directly or via a pushrod, while the other end acts on the stem of the engine valve.

Rotary engine
An engine that works on the Wankel principle, in which a shallow, lozenge-shaped piston revolves eccentrically in a chamber, making a combustion chamber where it touches the sides of the crankcase, with inlet and exhaust ports in the chamber wall.

Running gear
The wheels, suspension, steering, and drivetrain of a motorcycle.

Saddle tank
An early-type fuel tank placed over the top tube of the machine's frame.

Santa Pod Raceway
Europe's premier drag-racing venue, opened in Northamptonshire, UK in 1966. It hosts over 50 events a year, including the British National Drag Racing Championships.

Scavenge oil pump
In a dry-sump engine, this additional pump evacuates oil that collects at the bottom of the engine, sending it to a separate oil tank.

Scooter
Small, cheap, and economical machine with step-through frame.

Scrambler
A street bike, modified to travel on rough or wet surfaces and off-road. Nonessential parts are stripped off to reduce weight, and

features such as high-mounted exhaust pipes, widened and strengthened handlebars, and all-terrain tires are added.

Seizure
The locking up of moving parts, caused by lack of lubrication and/or overheating. Often affects highly stressed, two-stroke machines.

Semi-elliptic spring
See leaf spring.

Servo
Any system that assists a mechanism to apply great force than originally applied.

Servo-assisted braking
A braking system that uses a stored vacuum (or "vacuum servo") to magnify the force the driver applies to the brake pedal.

Side stand
Long-cranked stand that swings out from under the frame and supports the motorcycle when it is leaned over.

Side throttle
A type of throttle featuring a perforated plate that slides across the air inlet to allow more or less air to enter the engine.

Side-valve engine
A form of engine design in which the valves are placed at the side of the cylinder, rather than within the cylinder head. In an L-head engine, the inlet and exhaust valves are placed together on one side of he cylinder; on a T-head engine they are located on opposite sides.

Simplex frame
Usually applied to frames with a single downtube.

Single-cylinder engine
A basic engine with just one cylinder. Simple, compact, and economical, it was widely used in early motorcycles, and still appears in some mopeds, motor scooters, and scramblers.

Six-pot
"Pot" is a slang term for a cylinder; a "six-pot" engine is a unit with six cylinders.

Sleeve-valve engine
An engine that has a metal sleeve placed between the piston and cylinder wall. The sleeve oscillates with the motion of the piston, and has holes that align with the cylinder's inlet and exhaust ports, facilitating the entry and exit of gases.

Solenoid switch
An electronically controlled switch, more properly known as a relay, which allows a low-current electric circuit to control a high-current one.

Spark plug
An electrical device, screwed into the engine cylinder head of a gasoline engine, which ignites the fuel in the cylinder.

Speedway
Racing on short, cinder-covered tracks on highly specialized machines.

Sports tourer
Motorcycle designed for long-distance touring, with luggage, comfort, and some weather protection, but also with a high-performance engine and good handling.

Springer forks
Variation on girder forks.

Stanchion
A fork tube, used to link the front wheel to the bike's frame.

Steering damper
A damper mounted between the frame and the steering fork to add resistance and stability to the steering.

Step-through frame
Frame layout with large gap between the seat and the steering headstock to ease mounting the machine; also known as an open frame.

Stroke
Measurement of the distance traveled by the piston in the bore.

Sump
An oil reservoir at the bottom of an engine.

Supercharger
Mechanically powered device to force intake air into the combustion chamber. When driven by exhaust gas, it is known as a turbocharger.

Supermoto
Motorcycle racing on a circuit comprising both off-road and asphalt surfaces, using off-road motorcycles that have been converted with road-racing wheels and tires.

Suspension
A system that cushions the machine's structure (and rider) from motion of the wheels, as they traverse uneven roads.

Swingarm
Suspension arm pivoted at one end, with the other supporting the wheel.

Synchromesh gearbox
A gearbox in which gear wheels are in constant mesh.

Tank bag
Soft bag attached to the fuel tank of the machine, which tilts up to facilitate refueling.

Tank slapper
Violent vibration felt at the handlebars of the machine. At its worst the handlebars will shake across the full travel of the steering, almost hitting the fuel tank on each side. It is caused by instability in suspension geometry or tires, or by extreme speeds over rough surfaces.

Telelever forks
Fork design that includes an additional swingarm, which mounts to the frame to support the spring. This increases trail and castor or rake during braking. It is also known as Saxon-Motodd forks—as used by BMW.

Telescopic forks
Front suspension system with twin fork legs on either side of the wheel, with internal springs and dampers, which telescope together to allow suspension movement.

Throttle
A device that controls the amount of air flowing into the engine.

Ton up
Traveling at more than 100 mph (160 km/h). Popular but illegal pastime in the 1950s and 1960s, hence "Ton-Up Boys."

Top box
Hard luggage mounted on a rack behind the pillion passenger.

Torque
The tendency of a force to cause an object to rotate. In an engine, the torque is expressed as the force applied multiplied by the distance from the rotation center in pounds/feet, or newtons/meters.

Torsion-bar
A suspension part that acts as a spring when twisted by the wheel's movements.

Total loss
Concerning ignition or lubrication systems, in which electricity or oil is used without being generated or recirculated. Total-loss ignition uses a battery that eventually becomes exhausted; total-loss lubrication either burns the oil or leaves it on the road.

Tourer
Motorcycle designed for long-distance cruising, with commodious, comfortable seating and facilities for luggage.

Trail
The distance on the ground from the steering axis to the center of the tire's contact patch. Determines the weight and responsiveness of the steering.

Trail bike
Dual-purpose machine for use on- and off-road, but mainly on-road.

Trailing link
Front suspension similar to leading link, with reversed layout so the links pivot forward of the axle. Used by Indian and early BMWs.

Transmission
All the components of a bike's drivetrain, though often used for the gearbox alone.

Transverse engine
Across-the-frame mounting for engine.

Trials bike
Highly specialized competition machine for use in off-road motorcycle competition.

Tricycle
Three-wheeled motorcycle with no sidecar. Tends to have one wheel at the front, with motorcycle front end and a car (typically a VW Beetle) rear end, but some (such as a Triking or Morgan) have two wheels at the front, with one driven wheel at the rear.

TT races
Tourist Trophy races on the Isle of Man, held in the last week of May and first week of June. The first time-trial on the circuit was in 1907, and the 37¾-mile (60.75-km) Snaefell Mountain Course section is the oldest existing motor-racing circuit.

Tuned
A term to describe an engine that has been modified for extra performance.

Twin-cam
See camshaft.

Two-stroke engine
An engine with pistons that move up once and down once (performing two strokes) in the combustion cycle.

Unblown
A term used to describe an engine without a supercharger or turbocharger; correctly described as "naturally aspirated."

Undersquare
Engine where the piston stroke is greater than the bore.

Unitary construction
See monocoque.

Upside-down forks
Telescopic forks with the lower section, onto which the wheel is mounted, telescoping into the fixed upper tube; also known as inverted forks.

Upswept exhaust
An exhaust pipe with a turned-up or raised end. It is often used on trail bikes and scramblers, to stop mud and other debris from getting into the engine.

Vacuum advance
A mechanism that enables the distributor to adjust spark timing according to the engine load.

Valvetrain
The parts of the engine that control the operation of the valves.

V-twin engine
Engine configuration with cylinders opposed in a V shape.

Water-cooling
A system that uses circulating water to cool engine components. It is the most common cooling system used in modern engines, in order to comply with noise and exhaust-emission limits.

Wet-liner
A cylinder liner that is in direct contact with the engine's liquid coolant.

Wheelbase
The exact distance between the axles of the front and rear wheels.

Whitewall tires
Tires featuring a decorative ring of white rubber on their sidewalls. It was a popular styling, particularly in the US.

Wishbone suspension
An independent suspension system that uses two wishbone-shaped arms to link each wheel hub to the chassis.

Works racer
Factory-prepared, racing machine.

World Superbike Racing
Circuit racing on production-based, four-stroke machines that feature extensive, but carefully controlled, modifications.

Yoke
A hollow tube at the front of the motorcycle frame that is the pivot point of the steering column.

Index

All general page references are given in italics. References to main entries are in bold.

Acknowledgments

Dorling Kindersley would like to thank Editor-in-Chief Mick Duckworth for his unstinting support throughout the making of this book.

Editor-in-Chief Mick Duckworth is a journalist and author who has been writing about bikes and related subjects for more than 25 years, specializing mainly in the history of motorcycles. He began his career on the staff of *Classic Bike* magazine, and has been a full-time freelance writer since 1994, publishing regularly in several countries. His books include *Triumph* and *BSA Triples*, and *TT100: the official history of the TT races*. Mick grew up on the Isle of Man, the home of TT road racing. Now based in Nottingham, England, he tends a modest collection of machines, including one that he built entirely from parts, and is happy to ride in all weathers.

Mick Duckworth would like to thank the following people for their help: Dragonfly Motorcycles, Martin Crookes at Crookes Suzuki, The Vintage Motor Cycle Club Library, Nigel Cartwright, Simon Hartland at the National Motorcycle Museum.

The publishers would like to thank the following people for their help with making the book: Stephen Crozier at Butterfly Creative Solutions for color retouching; Victoria Foster, Kirsty Tizzard, and Kaitlin Calancy for design assistance; Cecile Landau for editorial help; Joanna Chisholm for proofreading; Helen Peters for the index.

DK India would like to thank: Sakshi Saluja and Malavika Talukder for arranging the India photo shoot; Antara Moitra and Archana Ramachandran for editorial assistance; Shruti Singh Soharia and Chhaya Sajwan for design assistance.

Reproduction by
Media Development & Printing, UK, Tag: Response, UK, Colourscan, Singapore, Bright Arts, Hong Kong, Scanhouse, Malaysia

The publisher would also like to thank the following companies, organisations, museums and individuals for their generosity in allowing Dorling Kindersley access to their motorcycles and engines for photography:
Dave Roach at the National Motorcycle Museum for moving all the bikes for photography; Geoff Selvidge for access to the Uttoxeter Classic Bike Show.

Beaulieu National Motor Museum, Brockenhurst, Hampshire, UK
www.beaulieu.co.uk

BMW, North Oxford Garage, Oxford, UK
www.oxfordbmwbikes.co.uk

Deutsches Zweiradmuseum und NSU-Museum, Neckarslum, Germany
www.zweirad-museum.de

Haynes International Motor Museum, Yeovil, Somerset, UK
www.haynesmotormuseum.com

National Motorcycle Museum, Birmingham, Bickenhill, Solihull, West Midlands, UK
www.nationalmotorcyclemuseum.co.uk

Harley-Davidson India, Gurgaon, Haryana, India
www.harley-davidson.in

Hughenden M40, Thame, Berkshire, UK
www.hughendenm40.co.uk

Motorcycle Hertitage Museum Westerville ohio, USA,
www.motorcyclemuseum.org

Mott motorcycles Ltd, Basingstoke, Hampshire, UK
www.mottmotorcycles.co.uk

Norfolk Motorcycle Museum, North Walsham, Norfolk, UK
www.mc-museum.freeserve.co.uk
Oxford Classic Honda, Oxford, UK
www.classichondamotorcycles.co.uk

Palmers motorcycles, Hemel Hempstead, Hertfordshire, UK
www.palmersmotorcycles.co.uk

Scootopia, Weston-Super-Mare, North Somerset, UK
www.casalambrettauk.com

The Lambretta Museum, Weston-Super-Mare, North Somerset, UK
www.lambrettamuseum.co.uk

The Vintage Motor Cycle Club – Banbury Run and Festival of 1,000 Bikes
www.vmcc.net

Trevor Pope Motorcycles, Gosport, Hampshire, UK
www.motodirect.co.uk

Village Motorcycles, Stowmarket, Suffolk, UK
www.villagemotorcycles.co.uk

Vintage Japanese Motorcycle Club (VJMC) – Uttoxeter Classic Bike Show
www.vjmc.com

The publisher would like to thank the following for their kind permission to reproduce their photographs:

(Key: a-above; b-below/bottom; c-center; f-far; l-left; r-right; t-top)

12-13 Corbis: Hulton-Deutsch Collection (c). **12 Alamy Images:** Vintage Images (tl). **The Bridgeman Art Library:** Hagley Museum & Library (bl). **Indian Motorcycle:** (cla). **13 Corbis:** Bettmann (c). **18-19 Getty Images:** Archive Holdings Inc (c). **22 Advertising Archives:** (bl). **Alamy Images:** Jeff Morgan 01 (cl); Trinity Mirror / Mirrorpix (tl). **22-23 Getty Images:** Popperfoto. **23 Corbis:** Jagadeesh NV/epa (c). **26 Jan Lundin:** (tl). **32 Don Morley:** (br). **Don Morley:** (ca). **34 Stilltime.net:** (tl). **42 Mary Evans Picture Library:** (tl). **48 CycleTownUSA.com:** jaykaylowrider (tl). **52 Alamy Images:** Motoring Picture Library (tl). **Getty Images:** (c).

53 Mary Evans Picture Library: (cl). **Don Morley:** (br). **58 Roland Brown:** (c, tl). **58-59 Roland Brown:** (c). **59 Roland Brown:** (cl, br). **62-63 Getty Images:** Roger Viollet (c). **67 Don Morley:** (crb). **72 Mick Duckworth:** (tl). **78 Don Morley:** (tc, cr). **80-81 Advertising Archives:** (c). **86 Alamy Images:** Kaplonski (cl). **Mary Evans Picture Library:** Interfoto (bl). **Target Press:** (tl). **86-87 TopFoto.co.uk:** National Motor Museum / HIP (c). **87 Rex Features: Sipa Press:** (cr). **89 Don Morley:** (crb). **95 akg-images:** Interfoto (crb). **Don Morley:** (cra). **96-97 Getty Images:** Fox Photos (c). **99 Don Morley:** (tl). **www.classic-motorbikes.com:** (cb). **100 Corbis:** Bettmann (tl). **108 Advertising Archives:** (bl). **Getty Images:** (cl). **Corbis:** Bettmann (tl). **108-109 The Kobal Collection:** A.I.P. (c). **109 Harley-Davidson Motor Company:** Harley-Davidson Europe (br). **111 Honda (UK):** (cr). **Don Morley:** (tr). **114 Getty Images:** (tl). **120 Lambretta Museum:** Richard Lunt (bc). **120-121 Lambretta Museum:** Richard Lunt (br). **Don Morley:** (c). **122 Getty Images:** **127 Don Morley:** (bl). **130-131 Corbis:** Albert Gea / Reuters (c). **130 Alamy Images:** imagebroker (cl). **Honda (UK):** (tl, bl). **131 Honda (UK):** (tr). **Science Photo Library:** Paul Fletcher (cr). **134 Honda (UK):** (br). **Don Morley:** (cra). **136-137 Getty Images:** Popperfoto (c). **136 Archivio Piaggio "Antonella Bechi Piaggio":** (bl). **Corbis:** Dave Lees (cl). **Getty Images:** Time & Life Pictures (tl). **137 The Kobal Collection:** Curbishley-Baird (c). **Don Morley:** (br). **140 Roland Brown:** (br). **141 Mirco Decet:** (cla). **142-143 Getty Images:** Popperfoto (c). **145 Mick Duckworth:** (cl). **Don Morley:** (tr). **147 Roland Brown:** (tr). **Honda (UK):** (cr, br). **Don Morley:** (tl, bl, ca). **152 Corbis:** Bettmann (tl). **158 Advertising Archives:** (tl). **162 Honda (UK):** (tl). **164 Getty Images:** (c). **MV Agusta:** (tl). **SuperStock:** Danilo Donadoni (cl). **165 Russ Murray:** (cl). **MV Agusta:** (br). **168-169 The Kobal Collection:** Columbia (c). **170-171 Honda (UK):** (c). **171 Roland Brown:** (br). **172 Roland Brown:** (cr). **Suzuki Motor Corporation:** (tl, bl). **172-173 Corbis:** William Manning (c). **174-175 Honda (UK):** (cb). **175 Courtesy of Yamaha Motor:** (tl). **Don Morley:** (cl). **181 Roland Brown:** (tr, bl, br). **182 Roland Brown:** (tl). **186 Andrew Morland:** (cra, tc). **188 Roland Brown:** (bl). **Don Morley:** (cl). **189 Roland Brown:** (bl). **Don Morley:** (tl). **190 Honda (UK):** (tl). **191 Roland Brown:** (cl). **Courtesy of Yamaha Motor:** (cb). **192-193 Corbis:** Frank Hoppen/Transtock (c). **192 Roland Brown:** (tl). **Target Press:** (bl). **193 Getty Images:** AFP (cr). **194 Don Morley:** (br). **196 Honda (UK):** (tc). **Lambretta Museum:** Richard Lunt (cl, cr). **201-202 Getty Images:** Time & Life Pictures (c). **206 Advertising Archives:** (bl). **Alamy Images:** Tim Gainey (cl). **Motoring Picture Library/National Motor Museum:** (tl, cr). **206-207 The Kobal Collection:**

Mirisch/United Artists (c). **207 Triumph Motorcycles Ltd:** Jason Critchell (cr). **209 Mick Duckworth:** (clb). **Honda (UK):** (cr). **Don Morley:** (cra). **214 Roland Brown:** (tr, cra). **215 Don Morley:** (cra, tr). **216 Roland Brown:** (tl). **220 Don Morley:** (tl, tr). **221 Don Morley:** (cra). **222 Don Morley:** (bc). **223 Don Morley:** (tr). **224 Advertising Archives:** (cr). **Alamy Images:** Andrew Walters (cl). **Roland Brown:** (tl). **Getty Images:** Keystone (bl). **225 Courtesy of Yamaha Motor:** (bl). **Getty Images:** AFP (cr). **227 Roland Brown:** (br). **228 Roland Brown:** (tl, tr, br). **Honda (UK):** (bl). **229 Roland Brown:** (bl). **Don Morley:** (tr, tl). **230-231 Getty Images:** Stockbyte (c). **233 Don Morley:** (br). **234 Roland Brown:** (tl, bl). **Courtesy of Yamaha Motor:** Yamaha Classic Race Team (tr). **Don Morley:** (cl). **235 Art Tech Picture Agency:** (br). **Don Morley:** (bl). **238 Ducati:** (bl). **Getty Images:** SSPL (cr). **Don Morley:** (tl). **238-239 Getty Images:** AFP (c). **239 © Phil Aynsley Photography:** (cl, tl). **240 Courtesy of Yamaha Motor:** (tr). **241 Art Tech Picture Agency:** (tl). **242 Roland Brown:** (bc). **Mirco Decet:** (cra). **243 Don Morley:** (br). **244 Roland Brown:** (tl). **248 Roland Brown:** (tc, cla). **249 Don Morley:** (br). **250-251 Don Morley:** (tc). **250 Roland Brown:** (tl, cr). **Honda (UK):** (bl, bc). **Don Morley:** (cl). **252-253 Art Tech Picture Agency:** (ca). **252 Courtesy of Yamaha Motor:** (tr). **Andrew Morland:** (tl). **Triumph Motorcycles Ltd:** (c, cl). **254-255 Corbis:** Tim Page (c). **258 Honda (UK):** (cl). **262 Roland Brown:** (tl). **266 Courtesy of Yamaha Motor:** (cla). **267 Honda (UK):** (bl, br). **268 Roland Brown:** (tl). **269 Roland Brown:** (tr). **270 Roland Brown:** (cl, cla). **272 Alamy Images:** Kaplonski (cl). **BMW AG:** (tl). **276 Art Tech Picture Agency:** (tr). **277 Honda (UK):** (br). **278 Honda (UK):** (cl). **282 Corbis:** Giuliano Bevilacqua / Sygma (cl). **Roland Brown:** (tl). **Target Press:** (bl). **282-283 Getty Images:** AFP. **283 Roland Brown:** (br, tc/Aprilia RSV4). **286 Courtesy of Yamaha Motor:** (tc). **288 Roland Brown:** (cr, bl). **289 BMW AG:** (crb). **Roland Brown:** (cla, cr, cra). **Honda (UK):** (tl, tr). **290-291 Corbis:** Stephane Mantey (c). **295 Mazda Motors UK Ltd:** (tr). **297 Don Morley:** (bl). **304 Alamy Images:** Rob Masters (bl). **306-307 Courtesy of Yamaha Motor:** (c). **307 Courtesy of Yamaha Motor:** (tr).

All other images © Dorling Kindersley
For further information see:
www.dkimages.com

The publishers would like to thank the following for their kind permission to photograph their motorbikes:

1 Phil Crosby: FN Four. **11 Micheal Penn:** Ormonde. **10 Phil Crosby:** Gaillardet Gaillardette, Singer 200. **17 John Fisher:** Rex 3 HP. **Phil Crosby:** Rex 500 SV. **Rick Haidon:** Lincoln Elk 3 HP. **20 Alec Hudson:** Triumph 2¼ Junior "Baby". **David McMahon:** Rudge

3½HP. **Nigel Hussey:** Triumph 3½HP Roadster. **Phil Crosby:** Humber 3½HP Touring, Rover 500 TT. **21 Alan Hummerstone:** Sun 2½HP. **Ian Anderson:** TD Cross TDC 3½HP. **Micheal Penn:** Sunbeam Single. **Rodney Hann:** Ariel 3½HP Roadster. **23 Rajnish Kashyap:** Royal Enfield 350 Bullet Machismo. **24 Phil Crosby:** Minerva 4½HP V-twin, FN Four. **25 Tony Donnithorne:** Zenith 8/10HP Gradua. **34 Phil Crosby:** Scott Two-speed TT racer. **40 Micheal Penn:** Triumph Model W. **41 Jeff Bishop:** Terrot FT. **Phil Crosby:** BSA Model B. **46 Clive Gant:** BSA Model A. **Don Hunt:** James Model 12. **Pascal Rabier:** Husqvarna T180. **Richard Duffin:** Burney V-twin. **47 Phil Crosby:** Harley-Davidson Model JD. **53 Bill Lennox:** Norton 3½HP. **Phil Crosby:** Norton 500T, Norton Dominator 88. **Wayne Tolson:** Norton F1 Sport. **54 George Harmer and Steven Harmer:** Blackburne 4HP. **Tim Walker:** Duzmo Sports. **57 Ireneusz Tomyslak:** Harley-Davidson Model B. **Steve Willis:** Ariel Model E. **Derek Wickes:** Dot J343. **Ian Kerr:** Norton 16H. **Roger Kimbell:** Sunbeam Model 9. **59 Cenwyn Ap Tomos:** Moto Guzzi Daytona 1000. **60 George Harmer and Steven Harmer:** Clyno 2¼HP, Sun Vitesse. **Micheal Penn:** Hawker Model C. **61 Alan Jennings:** BSA S28. **Phil Crosby:** Henley Blackburne Tourer. **Terry Green:** Triumph Model P. **64 George Harmer and Steven Harmer:** OK Bradshaw, Smart Celle du Salon. **66 Simon Whitaker:** Scott Harry Langman Works TT. **70 Phil Crosby:** Ariel SG. **71 Phil Crosby:** BMW R66. **76 Carl Chippendale:** Norton ES2 Model 18. **Sean Kelly:** Sunbeam Model 90. **77 Phil Crosby:** Brough Superior SS80. **82 David Beckett:** Stylson Blackburne. **John Fairclough:** Cotton Blackburne. **85 George Harmer and Steven Harmer:** Coventry Eagle 250. **Micheal Penn:** OK-Supreme 350. **Trevor Brookes:** Benelli 4TN. **87 Phil Davies:** BMW K1200S, BMW G650GS. **88 Geoffrey Hobbs:** Peugeot P108. **Jim Beckett:** BSA C11. **Martin Carter:** BSA H31 Sloper. **Paul Richmond:** Velocette GTP. **89 George Harmer and Steven Harmer:** Royal Enfield Bullet 250. **Phil Crosby:** Panther 250 Red Panther. **90 Micheal Penn:** Velocette KTT. **94 Phil Crosby:** Velocette MAC-MDD, Triumph 3TW, Triumph 3HW. **95 Phil Crosby:** Norton Big Four, Matchless G3LS, Norton 16H. **105 Phil Crosby:** Norton 500T, Royal Enfield J2. **106 Phil Crosby:** Norton International. **107 Phil Crosby:** Sunbeam S8. **108 Phil Crosby:** Harley Davidson Model JD. **111 George Harmer and Steven Harmer:** VéloSoleX. **113 Phil Crosby:** Triumph Grand prix, AJS 7R, Excelsior JAP

Speedway. **120 George Harmer and Steven Harmer:** Peugeot S157. **121 George Harmer and Steven Harmer:** Lambretta LI 150. **122 Stuart Lanning:** Lambretta LD 150. **126 George Manning:** Triumph T100. **127 Phil Crosby:** Norton Dominator 88. **129 Micheal Penn:** Triumph Tiger Cub. **131 Michael Delaney:** Honda Goldwing GL1500 SE. **134 George Harmer and Steven Harmer:** BSA Winged Wheel. **Jeremy Sykes:** Cyclemaster. **135 Maurice Drew:** Motom Super Sport. **George Harmer and Steven Harmer:** New Hudson Autocycle. **138 George Harmer and Steven Harmer:** James Comet, Excelsior Skutabyk, Express Radex 200. **140 Micheal Penn:** Vincent Comet. **Phil Crosby:** BSA Gold Star. **141 Jonathan E Osborne:** Velocette Mac. **144 Phil Crosby and Peter Mather:** Matchless G3L Trials. **145 Micheal Penn:** Triumph Tiger Cub Scrambler. **156 John Morris:** FB Mondial 48 Sport. **157 Donald Heath:** Greeves 32DC Sports Twin. **162 Micheal Penn:** Lambretta TV175 "Slimline". **Phil Crosby:** Lambretta LI 125. **163 George Harmer and Steven Harmer:** Triumph Tina, Raleigh RM5 Supermatic, Agrati Capri Scooter, Clark Scamp, Motobécane Mobylette. **Paul Tebbit:** NSU Quickly S2/23. **165 Ken Small:** M V Agusta. **Phil Bannister:** MV Agusta Ipotesi Sport. **166 Micheal Penn:** BSA M21, BSA Bantam D10. **167 Andy Baldwin:** Suzuki M15. **Dave Jupp:** Honda CD175. **170 Michael Gower:** Norton Navigator. **Micheal Penn:** Harley-Davidson FLH Duo-Glide. **Rick Lees:** Norton Dominator 99 De Luxe. **173 Adam Atherton:** Suzuki RG500. **Alfred Adebare:** Suzuki Hayabusa GSX 1300R. **Paul Storey:** Suzuki GS750. **174 Brian Chapman and Chris Illman:** Vincent Sprinter Methamon. **175 Brian Chapman and Chris Illman:** Vincent Mighty Mouse. **177 Phil Crosby and Peter Mather:** AJS Stormer. **186 Anthony Tomalin:** Yamaha XS1100F. **Kevin Hall:** Honda CBX 1000. **Michael Price:** Yamaha XS750. **187 Keith Waring:** Kawasaki Z650C. **Lawrence Aughton:** Suzuki GS1000S. **Neil Comstive:** Kawasaki Z1000 Z1R D1. **Paul Storey:** Suzuki GS750. **188 Phil Crosby:** Ducati Silver Shotgun, Yamaha TX500, Ducati 450 Desmo, **189 Phil Crosby:** Benelli 500 Quatro, Suzuki GT550. **190 Phil Crosby:** Honda CB500T, Honda CB550 Four, Honda CX500. **191 Phil Crosby:** MV Agusta 350S Ipotesi. **193 Alistair Marshall:** Kawasaki Z1. **George Manning:** Kawasaki ZX-12R. **194 Carl M Booth:** IZH Jupiter 3. **Phil Bannister:** MV Agusta Ipotesi Sport. **196 Charlie Garratt:** Honda

CB250 K4. **Micheal Penn:** CZ sport 175. **197 Charlie Owens:** Yamaha SS50. **199 Phil Crosby** Suzuki A100, Casal K196 Sport Moped, Yamaha XS250, Suzuki GT185. **202 Dave Jupp:** Suzuki T125 Stinger. **George Manning:** Suzuki T350 Rebel. **Paul Block:** Suzuki GT380. **Peter Hodson:** Suzuki T500. **Wayne Allen:** Suzuki GT250 X7. **203 Mark Taylor:** Yamaha RD400, Kawasaki KH400. **204 Charlie Garratt:** Suzuki TS125. **205 Doug Hill:** Yamaha XT500. **207 George Manning:** Triumph Daytona 955i. **209 Brian Chapman:** Weslake Hobbit Dragster. **Micheal Penn:** Jawa Briggo Speedway. **210 Charlie Garratt:** Honda CB350 K4, BSA B25SS Gold Star. **Ron Perkins:** BSA A65 Thunderbolt. **211 Chris Child:** Benelli Tornado S. **Tom Rogers:** Yamaha SR500. **Tony Thomas:** Yamaha XS650B. **214 Charlie Garratt:** Yamaha RD350LC YPVS. **215 Charlie Garratt:** Honda VF400F, Honda VF500F2. **Steve Mawson:** Honda MBX50. **221 Clive Minshell:** Yamaha XS1100 LG Midnight Special. **223 Adam Atherton:** Suzuki RG500. **George Manning:** Kawasaki ZX750E Turbo. **225 Charlie Garratt:** Yamaha RD350. **227 Barry Whitehead:** Honda Bros Product 2. **Carl M Booth:** KMZ Dnepr MT11. **John Mather:** Honda XBR500. **Mike Ridley:** Honda CB250RS. **228 Charlie Garratt:** Honda VF500C Magna. **232 Micheal Penn:** GM Speedway, Godden GR500. **234 Les Judkins:** MBA 125. **240 Ian Welford:** Honda VFR400 NC30. **Wayne Tolson:** Norton F1 Sport. **241 Andy Woolley:** Ducati 888 SPS. **242 Cenwyn Ap Tomos:** Moto Guzzi Daytona 1000. **Mark Hatfield:** Bimota Mantra. **243 George Manning:** Kawasaki ZZ-R1100. **Neil Trutwein:** Kawasaki ZX9R. **Nigel Cocks:** Yamaha YZF600R Thundercat. **248 Dave Jupp:** Honda CB50V Dream. **Martyn Roberts:** Triumph Trident 750. **250 Alan Peters:** Honda Goldwing EML Trike. **251 Harley-Davidson:** Harley-Davidson Softail FLSTF Fat Boy. **Justin Watson:** Honda VT 750CT Shadow. **253 Michael Delaney:** Honda Goldwing GL1500 SE. **Rolf Zanders:** Honda XL1000V Varadero. **258 Duncan Whinney:** Triumph Daytona 650. **George Manning:** Triumph Daytona 675, Triumph Daytona 955i. **Phil Davies** BMW K1200S. **Rob Young:** Honda VTR 1000 SP1. **259 George Manning:** Kawasaki ZX-12R, Kawasaki EX250/Ninja 250R, Triumph Speed Triple. **Rob Johnson:** Suzuki G5XR-R 750. **261 Phil Davies:**

BMW S1000RR, BMW K1300S. **266 David Driman:** Triumph Street Triple R. **David Farnley:** Yamaha XJR 1300. **George Manning:** Yamaha FZS 1000 Fazer. **John Pitts:** Norton Commando 961 Sport. **Ken Small:** MV Agusta 910S Brutale. **267 Harley-Davidson:** Harley-Davidson Sportster XR1200X, Harley-Davidson Sportster XL883N Iron. **268 G Mann:** Aprilia SL1000 Falco. **Satya Tandon:** Honda CBR 1100X Super Blackbird. **269 David Hall:** KTM 950 Adventure. **Eric Hayes:** Triumph Sprint RS. **George Manning:** BMW R1200RT. **Lloyd Benton and Damien Benton:** Benelli Tornado Tre 900LE. **Mark Band:** Kawazaki Z1000. **270 Alfred Adebare:** Suzuki GSX 1300R Hayabusa. **Michael D.Watson:** Harley-Davidson FLHR Road King. **271 George Manning:** Triumph Tiger 800XC. **Phil Davies:** BMW R1200GS Adventure, BMW K1600GT, BMW R1200GS Adventure. **276 Alan Purvis:** Harley CVO Softail Convertible. **David Jones:** Moto Guzzi California EV. **Harley-Davidson:** Harley-Davidson Touring FLHX Street Glide, Harley-Davidson VRSCDX Night Rod Special. **Wayne MacGowan:** Suzuki M1800R. **277 George Manning:** Kawasaki VN900 Custom, Triumph Rocket III Roadstar. **Ian Bull:** Triumph Thunderbird 1600. **Roy Dear:** Kawazaki VN1500 Mean Streak. **278 Micheal Penn:** BMW C1200. **Stuart Berenyi:** Suzuki VanVan. **283 G Mann:** Aprilia Falco. **284 George Manning:** Honda Falcon NX4. **Micheal Penn:** IMZ-Ural Tourist. **Nicci Hickman:** Suzuki SV65OS. **Pankaj Kumar Jha:** Hero Honda Passion Pro. **Phil Davies:** BMW F800R. **Rajnish Kashyap:** Royal Enfield 350 Bullet Machismo. **285 George Manning:** Can-am Spyder Trike, Triumph Bonneville, Triumph America. **286 Neil Mort:** Yamaha XT660Z Tenere. **Phil Crosby:** BMW F650GS, Yamaha XT660X, BMW G650GS, Suzuki 450z RMX. **Phil Davies:** BMW F650GS, BMW G650GS. **287 Phil Crosby:** Husaberg TE250, KTM 85 SX, Kawasaki KX250F, KTM 65 SX, KTM 350 SX-F. **299 George Manning:** Yamaha FSZ 1000 In-line Four Fazer. **Phil Davies:** BMW K1600GT In-line Six.

Chapter opener images
Before 1920: Norton 5HP V-twin1906
1920s: Martinsyde 680 combination 1921
1930s: BSA Empire Star 1936
1940s: Harley-Davidson WLC 1942
1950s: Lambretta LD 150 1957
1960s: Norton Dominator 650SS 1962
1970s: Benelli 750 Sei 1976
1980s: Suzuki RG500 1986
1990s: Honda CBR1000RR Fireblade 1999
After 2000: Yamaha YZF R1 2011
The Engine: Harley-Davidson FLSTF Fat Boy Engine 2011